ANTHROPOLOGY

ANTHROPOLOGY

An Introduction

Michael Alan Park
Central Connecticut State University

HARPER & ROW, PUBLISHERS, New York
Cambridge, Philadelphia, San Francisco,
London, Mexico City, São Paulo, Singapore, Sydney

Photo credits: Pp. 3, 5, 9, Mary Jane Hogan; p. 12, Kenneth Feder; p. 13, David Kideckel; p. 17, © Eugene Gordon, 1985; p. 23, © Tuttle, Photo Researchers; pp. 24, 26, American Museum of Natural History; p. 29, American Airlines, Photo Researchers; pp. 30, 39, 44, 49, American Museum of Natural History; p. 71, AP/Wide World; pp. 81, 83, © Ambler, National Audubon Society, Photo Researchers; p. 84, Sekulic, Anthro Photo; p. 85, © Ambler, National Audubon Society, Photo Researchers; p. 86, DeVore, Anthro Photo; p. 89, Alinari, Art Resource; p. 93, Photo by Chris Barker, copyright © Marshall Cavendish Ltd.; p. 107, Acebes, Photo Researchers; p. 113, San Diego Zoo; p. 121, Cooke, Photo Researchers; p. 124, © 1976, Wolff, Photo Researchers; p. 127, © Goldman, Rapho/Photo Researchers; p. 131, Edward Schullery; p. 136, Moore, Anthro Photo; p. 138, McHugh, Photo Researchers; p. 146, © Kimura, 1964, Photo Researchers; p. 148, Granger; p. 155, © Stuart Cohen; p. 162, Condon, Anthro Photo; p. 163, Halpern, Anthro Photo; p. 165, Shostak, Anthro Photo; p. 170, Robert S. Peabody Foundation, Phillips Academy, Andover, MA; p. 173, Halperin, Monkmeyer; p. 175, © Eugene Gordon; p. 177, Schinasi, Monkmeyer; p. 185, © Harcourt, Anthro Photo; p. 188, DeVore, Anthro Photo; p. 209, Kenneth Feder; p. 213, Michael A. Park; p. 216, Society of Antiquaries of London; pp. 222, 223, Kenneth Feder; pp. 230, 231, Michael A. Park; p. 235 (top), American Museum of Natural History; p. 235 (bottom), Mazonowicz, Anthro Photo; p. 254, Michael A. Park; p. 255, D. Fouts; p. 257, Dr. Ronald H. Cohn/The Gorilla Foundation; p. 265, Etter, Anthro Photo; p. 270, Zdenek Burian; p. 274, Shostal, Anthro Photo; p. 280, Granger; p. 281, AP/Wide World; p. 291, Irving Knopf; p. 321, United Nations; p. 323, Franken, Stock, Boston; p. 336 (top left), Michael A. Park; p. 336 (top right), Rodger, Magnum; p. 336 (bottom), © Eugene Gordon, 1985; p. 340, American Museum of Natural History; p. 349, AP/Wide World; p. 352, Muller, Woodfin Camp; p. 358, Mary Jane Hogan; p. 360, Irving Kopf; p. 362, Shostak, Anthro Photo; p. 367, AP/Wide World

Sponsoring Editor: Alan McClare
Project Editor: Holly D. Gordon
Cover Design: Diane Lufrano
Cover Illustration/Photo: S. Lindblad, DPI
Text Art: Reproduction Drawings, Ltd.
Photo Research: Mira Schachne
Production: Jeanie Berke
Compositor: Ruttle, Shaw & Wetherill, Inc.
Printer and Binder: R. R. Donnelley & Sons Company

ANTHROPOLOGY: An Introduction

Library of Congress Cataloging-in-Publication Data

Park, Michael Alan.
Anthropology: an introduction.

Bibliography: p.
Includes index.
1. Anthropology. I. Title.
GN25.P29 1986 306 85-16447
ISBN 0-06-045014-2

89 9 8 7 6 5 4 3 2

To Helen and Buford Park, who subscribed to *National Geographic* in 1952, and to Mary Jane and Shannon, who make home a special place.

CONTENTS

PREFACE

This book seeks to convey the excitement of today's anthropology. It grew out of an attempt to rethink my introductory course and is intended for use in college freshman introductory anthropology courses. It would be equally applicable to any such course in a two-year or four-year institution. It is written with a one-semester course in mind, but it could be used for a two-semester introduction, with the addition of some supplementary readings.

Most introductory courses, including mine, have presented anthropology as a collection of three or four subfields—physical anthropology, archaeology, linguistics, and cultural anthropology—related because they all deal with human beings, but not really interwoven in a holistic way. But anthropologists long ago saw that the cultural present, the cultural past, the biological present, and the biological past are inseparable and must be considered as such to understand the human species. Arranging a text or course with this in mind reveals a wealth of interrelationships among all aspects of human biology and behavior—and it is these relationships that anthropology seeks to explain.

To realize this sort of arrangement, this book focuses on the subject being studied rather than the discipline of anthropology. It treats humans as biological organisms, using categories from ethology, which is the biological study of behavioral adaptation. Acknowledging the primary role of culture in the adaptive behavior of the species, it treats culture as the ethologist would treat the behavior of any organism. In addition, by working from the subject to the discipline, the nature, theory, and methodology of anthropology gradually unfold as the identity, evolution, and adaptations of our species are studied.

An additional feature of this book is its emphasis on anthropology as a science; that is, as a discipline that uses the scientific method in all of its endeavors. All major ideas and conclusions are presented as the result of questions about our species that have been subjected to the logic and examination of the scientific method.

This book is written for students. I have tried to convey my material in a clear, accurate, and enjoyable form. I have written to get students to feel that I was talking to them personally. I have not shied away from colloquialisms, personal anecdotes, humor, and conversational tone. I hope I have successfully found the right mix between informality and the more formal style in which the main ideas of anthropology must be presented.

ACKNOWLEDGMENTS

The number of debts one incurs during an endeavor such as this is always surprising. I will try to mention all those who directly contributed to this book; I trust those I leave out will be forgiving.

I wish to thank the Anthropology Department at Indiana University; special thanks to Robert Meier, Paul Jamison, and the late Georg Neumann. Central Connecticut State University provided the sabbatical leave during which I organized this book and wrote much of the first draft. The CCSU Foundation and the Office of the Dean of Arts and Sciences provided a grant for additional research.

I am indebted to our departmental secretaries, Lorraine Jurgilewicz and the late Ann Ruddock, and to my colleagues in anthropology, Kenneth Feder, David Kideckel, Jack Lucas, and Frederic Warner. Special thanks to Feder for his valuable comments on Chapter 9.

Thanks to Marsha Park for her line drawings; to Mary Jane Hogan for the Hutterite photographs; to Ken Feder, David Kideckel, Edward Schullery, and Irving Knopf for their photographic contributions; to Aharon Moshe ben Dov Aryah Halevi for his information on Biblical matters; to Jack Zaleski and family, of Devils Lake, North Dakota, for providing a base of operations during my most recent research on the Hutterites; to the Hutterites of the four colonies I visited for their hospitality and friendly cooperation; and to all my students who through the years have been my inspiration and my best critics.

Special thanks to Professors Franklin Ng, California State University-Fresno; Susan Sutton, Indiana University-Purdue; Robert Bee, University of Connecticut-Storrs; and Robert W. Robinson, Antelope Valley College, who reviewed the manuscript in various stages and whose many suggestions I appreciate. Of course, I remain solely responsible for any errors. Thanks also to the people of Harper & Row, especially my hard-working sponsoring editor, Alan McClare. They have been understanding, helpful, and just demanding enough to keep me on my toes and on schedule.

Michael Alan Park

FOSSIL SITES
• Australopithecus and Homo habilis
○ Homo erectus
▲ Neanderthal
ARCHAEOLOGICAL SITES
① Torralba and Ambrona
② Terra Amata
③ Fayum
④ Choukoutein
⑤ Lascaux
⑥ Masada
⑦ Maiden Castle
⑧ Martin's Hundred

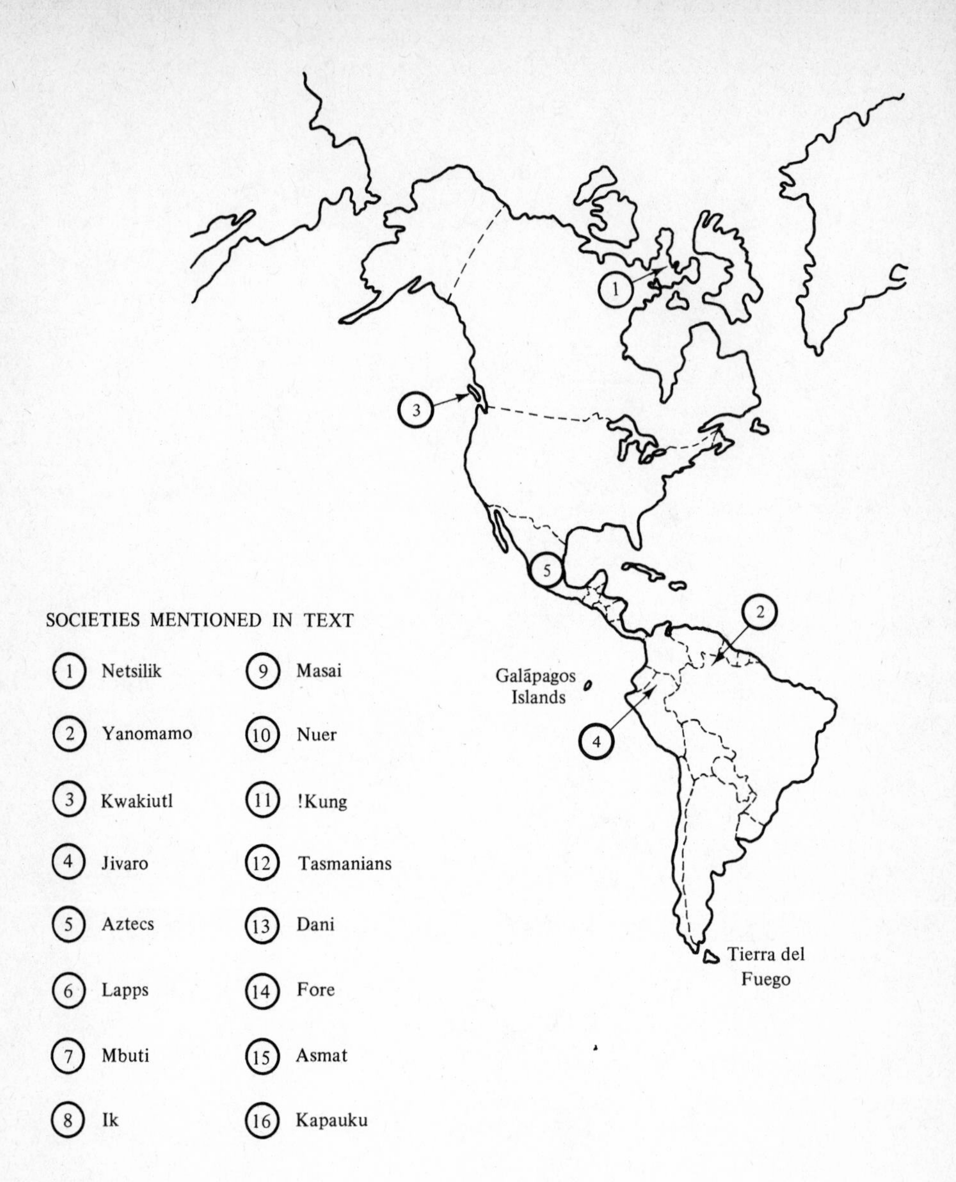
SOCIETIES MENTIONED IN TEXT
1 Netsilik
2 Yanomamo
3 Kwakiutl
4 Jivaro
5 Aztecs
6 Lapps
7 Mbuti
8 Ik
9 Masai
10 Nuer
11 !Kung
12 Tasmanians
13 Dani
14 Fore
15 Asmat
16 Kapauku
Galāpagos Islands
Tierra del Fuego

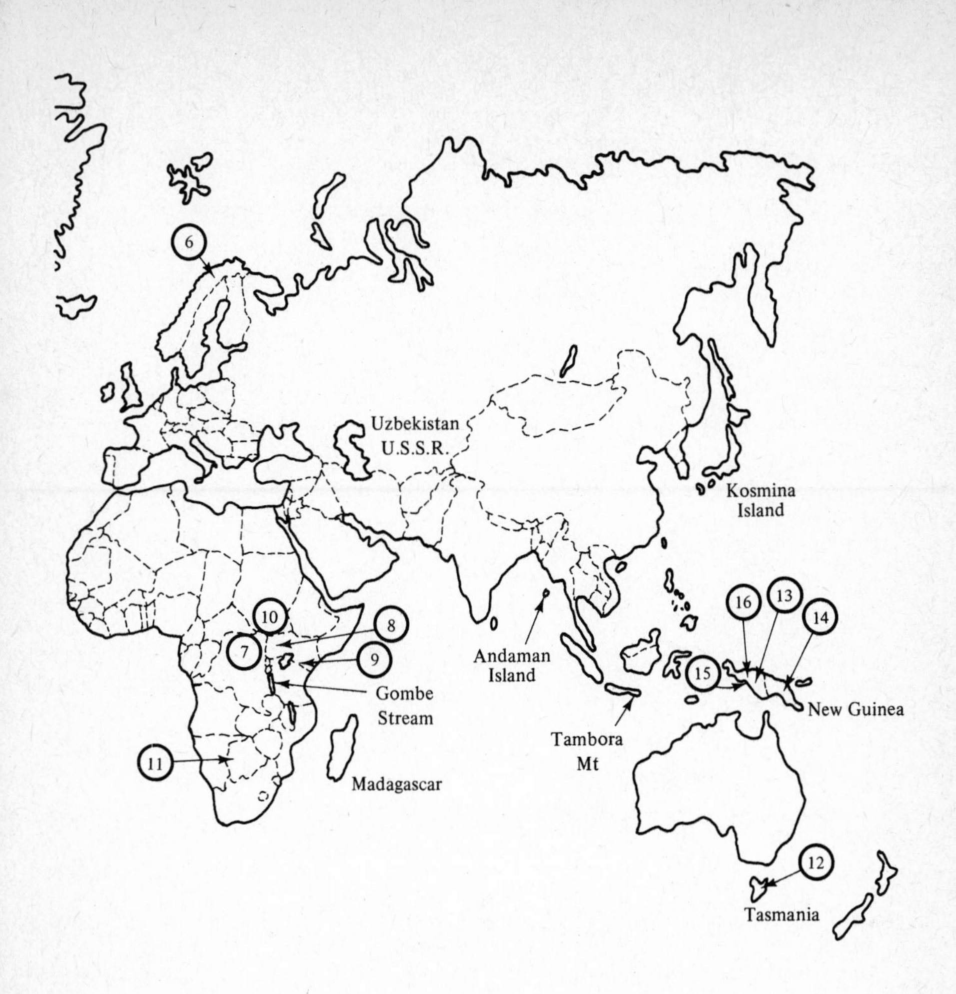
6
Uzbekistan
U.S.S.R.
Kosmina
Island
10
8
7
9
Gombe
Stream
11
Madagascar
Andaman
Island
Tambora
Mt
16
13
14
15
New Guinea
12
Tasmania

one

BACKGROUND AND CONTEXT

chapter 1

Doing Anthropology
The "High Plains Drifters"

IN THE FIELD

The wheat fields on either side of the poker-straight road in western Saskatchewan stretched, as the cliché says, as far as the eye could see. I found myself wishing, on that June day in 1973, that they stretched even farther. I was on the way to make my initial visit to my first real anthropological subjects, a colony of people belonging to a religious sect called the Hutterian Brethren, or "Hutterites." Up to this point, I had not felt much anxiety regarding this visit. Accounts by other anthropologists of contacts with Amazon jungle warriors and New Guinea "headhunters" made my situation seem fairly safe. These Hutterites are, after all, people of European descent who number English among their languages, and, far from being hostile, they practice a form of Christianity that emphasizes pacifism and tolerance.

At this point, though, that didn't help, nor really did the fact that I was being accompanied by the wife of a local wheat farmer who was well known and liked by the people of this colony. I simply had that unnamed syndrome that affects nearly all anthropologists under these first-contact circumstances.

Finally, the road we traveled—which had turned from blacktop to dirt about 10 miles back—curved abruptly to the right, crossed a railroad track and crested a hill, and I saw below us, at the literal end of the road, a neat collection of 20 or so white buildings surrounded by acres of cultivated fields. This was the Hutterite colony, the Bruderhof, or "place where the brethren live."

We drove down the hill and into the colony. Not a soul was to be seen, though. My companion explained that it was a religious holiday that day, a holiday that required all but essential work to cease. Everyone, therefore, was indoors. The colony minister and colony boss, however, had agreed to see me.

We knocked at and were admitted to one of the small buildings that I guessed, from pictures and diagrams of "typical" Hutterite colonies, was a residential building. The interior was darkened in conjunction with the nature of the holiday, and that, combined with

A Hutterite colony: simple lifestyle, large-scale farming.

my nervous excitement, erased all first-moment impressions from my memory. A few minutes later, however, bearings straight and introductions made, I found myself speaking to two men and a woman, explaining the reason for my visit. The men were dressed in the Hutterite fashion—black trousers and coats, white shirts—and they wore beards, a sign of marriage. The older, gray-haired man was the colony minister. The younger man (who happened to be his son) was the colony boss. The woman, the minister's wife, was also dressed in the conservative style that has become almost a trademark of the Hutterites and related groups. She wore a nearly full-length sleeveless dress—a small floral pattern on a black background—with a white blouse underneath. Her head was covered by a polka-dot kerchief, or "shawl."

The three listened in silence as I went through my well-rehearsed explanation. My "contacts," the wheat farmer and his wife, had previously given them an idea as to what I wanted to do, and the whole thing was pretty much set up. But, I thought, if they didn't like me or my explanation, they could still refuse to cooperate. So I started from scratch. When I had finished, they asked me a few questions, far fewer than I had expected: Was I from the government?

(My study used fingerprints, and they apparently knew about that only in the context of law enforcement and personal identification.) Did I know Scripture? (My equivocal answer created no problem.) What would I use this study for? Was I going to write a book? Did I know so-and-so, who had been there two years ago and did all sorts of medical examinations?

I expected, when they were done, that perhaps they would confer with one another or tell me to come back when they had decided. Instead, the minister, who was clearly in charge, simply said, "Today is a holiday for us. Can you start tomorrow?" And so, for the next month, I took part in my personal version of the anthropological fieldwork experience—taking fingerprints, recording family relationships, observing colony life, and getting to know and become friends with the Hutterites of this and one other Canadian Bruderhof.

What exactly had brought me 1300 miles from my college to the northern plains, to this isolated community of people whose basic way of life had changed little over the last 450 years and whose lifestyle and philosophy differ so from those of North American culture in general? Essentially, it was the same thing that takes anthropologists to locations from the highlands of New Guinea to caves in the Pyrenees to street corners in lower Manhattan: the desire to learn something about the nature of the human species.

In my case, I was pursuing a particular interest I had developed early in graduate school. I was curious about certain processes of evolutionary change called *genetic drift*. These had been described half a century ago, but their workings and importance, especially with regard to human populations, were still poorly understood. I'll tell you more about them in Chapter 3.

To examine the actions of these processes on human populations and to determine their roles in human evolution required that I find a human population with a few special characteristics. First, the group should be genetically isolated; that is, most members of the group should find mates within that group. The group should be fairly small as a whole, but it helps if it has large individual families. It is helpful also if the group has knowledge of, and takes interest in, their family relationships and if those relationships reflect genetic as well as cultural categories. (As will be discussed, all societies have systems of family relationships, but few of these systems coincide completely with the biological relationships among the people.) Finally, for my specific purposes, it would be ideal if the individual populations within the whole group were created through the splitting up of earlier populations.

The Hutterites turned out to fit this description very well indeed.

I had "discovered" them through library research on genetically isolated populations. My opportunity to study them was greatly enhanced by a stroke of luck: A fellow graduate student was the daughter of the wheat farmer and his wife who became my contacts and "public relations advisers." Even in science, not everything is planned.

THE HUTTERITES

The Hutterian Brethren is a Christian religious sect founded in Moravia (part of present-day Czechoslovakia) in 1528 by peoples from southern Germany and Austria. They were part of the so-called Anabaptist movement, a religious movement that, among other beliefs, shunned the idea of infant baptism and advocated the idea of a free church not under the control of the state. This made these groups distinct from and disliked by the Catholic and Protestant mainstreams. Many Anabaptist sects were formed during this period, but only three remain today: the Hutterites, the Mennonites, and a Mennonite branch, the Amish, all now living mainly in North America.

One additional aspect of some of these groups' nonconformity was their belief in communal living and ownership. They were "communists" in the economic sense of the word. The biblical passage that forms the basis of the Hutterite lifestyle is Acts 2:44, which reads in part: "And all that believed were together, and had all things common."

But the nonconformity of the Anabaptists also led to persecution. Many members of the various sects were imprisoned, and some were burned at the stake. One of those so executed was Jacob Hutter, an early leader of the group that took his name. This persecution resulted in the demise of most Anabaptist groups, but the Hutterites managed, through continual migration and sheer persistence, to survive. Over the next 300 years they lived in Slovakia (Czechoslovakia), Transylvania and Wallachia (modern Romania), and Russia, coming finally in the 1870s to the United States. Later problems connected with the military draft (the Hutterites are pacifists) and with taxes led many Hutterites to move again, this time to Canada. Today there are about 22,000 Hutterites in about 230 colonies. Most are in the Canadian provinces of Manitoba, Saskatchewan, and Alberta; the rest are in Montana, North and South Dakota, Minnesota, and Washington.

The sect is now divided into three subsects, which have been genetically isolated from one another since World War I. Members

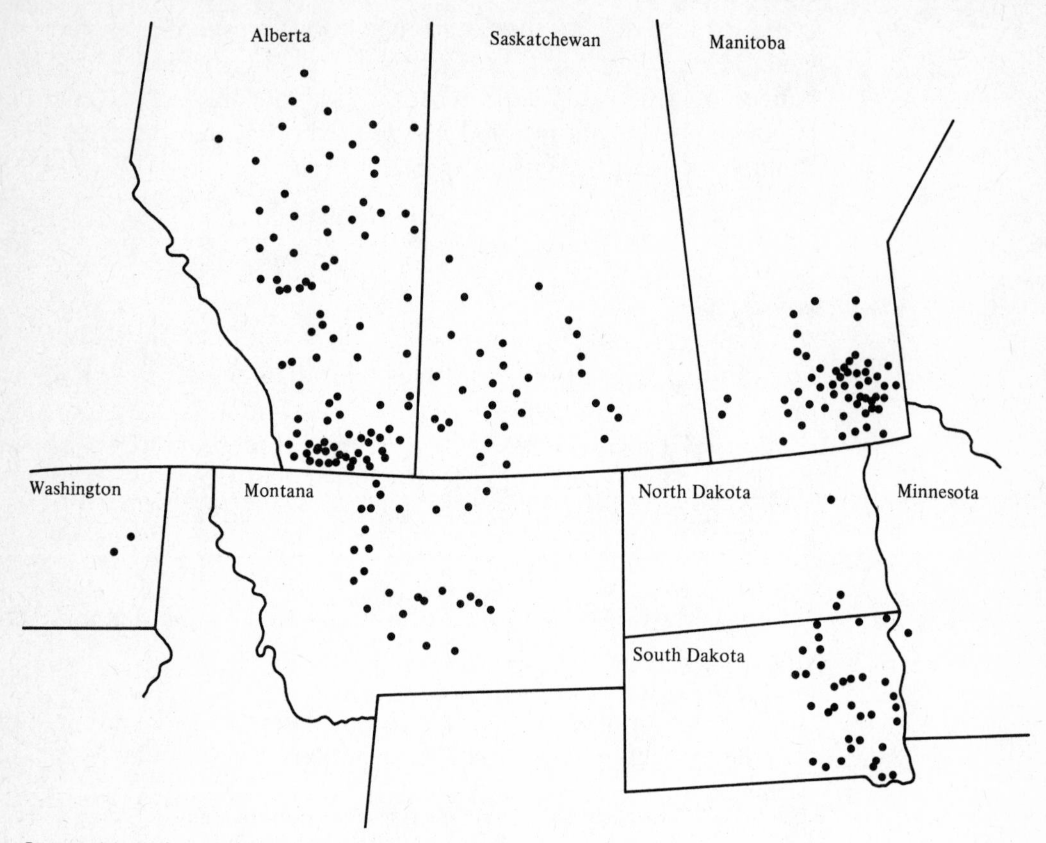

General locations of Hutterite colonies, 1975.

take mates only from within their subsect. The differences among the subsects, however, are relatively minor, limited to such things as clothing styles. Their identity is based on the three original colonies founded by the Hutterite migrants to North America.

The Hutterites live in Bruderhofs, colonies of around 100 people. The lifestyle is communal in every sense of the word: All land, resources, and profits are colony property. An individual's personal belongings are all contained in a "hope chest." Decisions concerning the colony are made by elected officials headed by the colony boss. The colony minister, in charge of the group's religious welfare, is also elected. Work is divided along sexual lines and among a number of specialists—poultry men, teachers, cooks, and so on—but the division is not absolute. There is a definite community feeling about the importance of work and the completion of required tasks. When work needs to be done, there is someone to do it.

The Hutterite economy is basically agricultural, and the specific

Scenes of colony life.

crops and animals raised depend on the geography and economy of the area occupied. Although the Hutterites (like the Amish) shun such worldly items as TV, radio, indoor plumbing, and personal ornamentation, the Hutterites *will* readily accept any modern technology or any contact with "outsiders" that aids them as farmers. As a result of this attitude, and because of the relative wealth of most colonies, you can see people in a Hutterite colony who look as if they've stepped out of the past but who use modern tractors, milking machines, telephones, electronic calculators, fertilizers, and antibiotics.

Children, by law, are schooled at the colony by a state or provincial teacher until the legal age at which they can leave. This is called the "English school." The most important schooling, however, is that given by the colony teacher in the ways of Hutterian life and religion, which are, in reality, one and the same. In addition, practical education is given in the form of an apprenticeship in one of the jobs vital to the colony's existence. This is to prepare the child to become a working member of the colony when he or she is finished with school.

The Hutterites are nearly completely isolated in genetic terms. Few Hutterites ever permanently leave the group, and converts to Hutterian life have numbered only a few dozen since the migration to North America. Moreover, about half of all Hutterite marriages take place between members of the same colony. The rest involve the woman's moving to the colony of her husband, who, of course, must be a member of the same subsect.

Generally, Hutterites restrict marriage to individuals who are second cousins or more distant. In fact, because individuals within a subsect are all fairly closely related, the most frequent relationship between mates *is* second cousins. The average age at marriage for males is 24 years and for females, 22 years. Only about 2 percent of Hutterite males and 5 percent of females never marry.

An interesting phenomenon within the Hutterite breeding structure is the frequency with which sibs (brothers and sisters) marry other sets of sibs. In one sample, 20 percent of all marriages were "double sibship" marriages (two brothers marry two sisters or a brother and sister marry a sister and brother), and 8 percent were triple or quadruple sibship marriages.

Hutterite families are large, but family lines are relatively few. There are only 20 surnames in the sect, and 5 of these are uncommon. The average family size is in excess of ten children. This is the highest substantiated birthrate recorded for any population. In addition, Hutterites maintain a great interest in their genealogies, and they have kept family records with a good deal of accuracy. It is thus easy to trace degrees of biological relationship among various individuals even back to the sixteenth century, a fact that has been important for much research on the group, including my own.

Completing the "match" of the Hutterites to my ideal population is their practice of regularly dividing their colonies, or "branching out," as they call it. When, after 15 or 20 years, a colony becomes so large (about 130 to 150 people) that social and administrative problems arise and there is increasing duplication of labor specialists, a colony will begin the processes of purchasing a new tract of land and dividing its population. Usually the minister simply makes two lists, each with about half of the colony's families. Family units, of course, are never broken up, but the ministers do manipulate the lists to maintain a similarity of age and sex distributions and to ensure that each new colony has the required specialist for each labor position. Family size and degree of relatedness are also taken into account. At last, lots are drawn to determine which list of families will remain and which will move to the new land to found the new Bruderhof.

The two Hutterite colonies I visited in the summer of 1973 were the results of a branching out that had taken place in 1958. Enough time had elapsed for a new generation to be born. Using fingerprint patterns as genetic "markers," I was able to establish degrees of genetic relationship within and between the populations and, most important, to trace changes in genetic makeup through time, from generation to generation. These conclusions would help me in answering some of the questions I had posed regarding the evolutionary processes of genetic drift and their role in human evolution.

ANTHROPOLOGY

Probably when you think of anthropology—in fact, when I think of anthropology—the image that first comes to mind is the sort of thing I've just been describing: the fieldwork experience, when the anthropologist visits a land or a people, usually very different from his or her own. This is the romantic and exciting part of anthropology, the part that provides the public image, the part that makes for interesting films (dramatic as well as documentary). It is also the part that brings out the humanism of the discipline, the ideas about the need to understand, to get to know, to communicate with other peoples, from *their* perspective. Fieldwork is certainly one of the things that attracts people to anthropology as a career.

And fieldwork *is* important. It is the part of the science of anthropology where basic observations are made, where data are collected, where ideas about humans can be tested. But does it tell us what anthropology is really about? Does it define the field?

The first problem you may encounter when thinking of anthro-

Kenneth Feder (right) interviewed at archaeological site.

pology as essentially fieldwork is the great variety of such experiences. My own department provides a good cross section of the many types of fieldwork, all of which are "typical" of this discipline. I've already described my experience of taking fingerprints and collecting various demographic and genealogical data from the Hutterites. Another member of my department here has spent several years living on collective farms in Romania, where he practiced what we call *participant observation*—living with and participating in the lives of one's subjects as well as observing them as an outsider. Still another of my colleagues has spent time observing and researching religious rituals in India.

The two other members of our anthropology department are archaeologists; they study the human cultural past. But one is concerned with the remains of ancient Native Americans who lived in this area thousands of years ago, while the other specializes in the remains of more recent times; he wants to know about the nature of early New England industry—brass mills, glass factories, and the like.

You may already know some other examples. Margaret Mead, for instance, one of the most famous anthropologists, made an early

David Kideckel with Romanian gypsies.

mark for herself by studying the process of growing up in Samoa, focusing on the sexual aspects of maturation. Louis Leakey, his wife Mary, and their son Richard are world-famous for their recovery of human fossils from East Africa that are millions of years old. And Jane Goodall, though not actually an anthropologist, has been doing fieldwork of an anthropological sort for 25 years, studying wild chimpanzees in Tanzania.

How can these studies all be anthropology? What is the common theme that ties together the sex lives of Samoans, the fingerprints of Hutterites, and the behavior of wild apes? The answer to that really tells us what anthropology is all about. For what all of us are doing is trying to answer questions about the human species. We all want to know why we behave as we do, how we evolved to look like we do, why we don't all look the same, and why there is such variation in our cultural behavior. We may start from points as different as modern Romanian farms and 4000-year-old Indian villages. But we would not be doing anthropology unless we applied the information from our studies to those broad questions about our species.

Thus anthropology, as its name indicates, is "the study of humankind." But you might be wondering about many of the other subjects you've taken classes in. Don't history, political science, sociology, and even mathematics all study something about humans? What makes anthropology different?

The answer is that anthropology is *holistic:* It searches for interrelationships among all the parts of its subject. We are a complex species. Like any species, we have an anatomy, a physiology (internal functions), a set of behaviors, and an evolutionary history. But we also, unlike any other species, have culture. We can consciously invent and change our behaviors, and we can think about them. Thus all the other fields I mentioned, and more, are necessary in order to understand fully every aspect of human biology and behavior.

However, also necessary is a field that seeks to understand how all those things are related—how our anatomy and our behavior interact; how our past has influenced our present; how one facet of culture, like economics, is related to some other facet, like religion. That's what anthropology does.

It might help to think of it this way: If you were a zoologist interested in, say, honeybees, you couldn't possibly understand this insect fully unless you understood its anatomy, its physiology, its behavior, its environment, and its evolutionary history. You might specialize in one aspect of its life—say, honeymaking—but to know just what a honey bee *is,* you must understand the interrelationships among all aspects of its life. In that regard, anthropology is a sort of *human zoology.*

But I'll go a step further. One of the things that sets us apart from all other living creatures is our cultural behavior. Indeed, I think it's safe to say that most anthropologists specialize in studying some aspect of human culture. Culture adds a dimension to our species that is beyond the purely biological. A bee can't change its behavior at will; we can. So can we really study ourselves as a zoologist studies some other living thing?

Yes, I think we can. There is a field of zoology that is specifically concerned with behavior and with the relationships between behavior and all other facets of an organism's life. It's called *ethology*, and it is based on the idea that an organism is what it does, that is, that living things survive by behaving, by doing things.

And with behavior as a central theme, all other aspects of a creature's biology necessarily come into play. An animal behaves in certain ways in order to survive in a certain environment. It is able to behave in those ways because it has a certain anatomy and physiology. The nature of an organism today is the result of its nature in the past, its evolutionary history.

So I like to think of anthropology as *human ethology*. We, as a species, are what we do; we look the way we do as a function of how we behave; our behavior is related to the natural and cultural environments in which we live; and these present-day relationships are built on a long history of continuous development and change. This is the approach of ethology, and it seems to me a valid way to study any living organism in a holistic way—whether the organism responds to its environment solely through built-in instincts or can actually create ways to change the environment to suit it.

This, in fact, is precisely what anthropology does.

So let's now embark on an anthropological tour of our species, using the ethological focus on behavior as our organizing principle. We will view humans from the past and humans of the present; faraway "exotic" cultures as well as those, like the Hutterites, who are right next door. We'll look at American culture too. We'll examine the environments in which these humans live, and we'll see how changes in those environments have affected our species. We'll even have to take a look at some other kinds of living things.

SUMMARY

Anthropology can be defined as "the holistic study of the human species." Its central focus is the feature that is unique to humans, cultural behavior. Thus to organize our examination of anthropology, we will use the approach of ethology, the study of living organisms that also uses behavior as a central theme.

NOTES, REFERENCES, AND READINGS

Perhaps the most complete work on the Hutterites is by John A. Hostetler, called *Hutterite Society* (Baltimore: Johns Hopkins University Press, 1974). A fascinating book on a number of communitarian societies, including the Hutterites, is William M. Kephart's

Extraordinary Groups: The Sociology of Unconventional Life-Styles (2d ed., New York: St. Martin's Press, 1982).

The best description I know of the anthropological fieldwork experience, one that makes truly exciting reading, is *Studying the Yąnomamö* (New York: Holt, Rinehart and Winston, 1974) by Napoleon A. Chagnon, about his adventures and scientific work with that now famous South American Indian group. If you like novels, there is a description of an anthropologist doing fieldwork in that form. It's by Elenore Smith Bowen (the pseudonym of anthropologist Laura Bohannon) and is called *Return to Laughter* (New York: Natural History Library, Anchor Books, 1964). Though fiction, it captures, in an accurate and moving story about West Africa, what fieldwork can be like.

If you'd like to know more about ethology, I'd recommend a book from the National Geographic Society called *The Marvels of Animal Behavior* (Washington, D.C., 1972). Not only is it complete and accurate, but also, as you might expect, it is full of wonderful photographs and graphics.

chapter 2

Environment and Ecology
Change in Nature and the Nature of Change

Each of us lives in a world made up of our society and of that society in interaction with all the societies of Earth. We live, in other words, in a sociocultural environment. In addition, even with all our technical achievements, we are still part of another world—the natural world. We are, after all, a species of animal. We got here through the actions of the same processes that have affected every other living organism. Even though we sometimes tend to forget it, we, like all life on Earth, interact continually with the natural environment. We affect it, it affects us, and we are dependent on it.

So before we can discuss humans specifically, we must understand the processes that make all living things what they are, for these processes made *us* what *we* are. We, however, are a complex subject. Our ability to have culture allows us to do things to our environment and ourselves that no other creatures can. Culture adds a whole new dimension to the story. So let's begin by using other living things as examples as we examine the processes of biological change—the processes of evolution.

Consider four pairs of living things:

1. There exists in North America a small fly by the name of *Rhagoletis pomonella*, or, more commonly, the apple maggot. Its common name as well as its Latin species name *pomonella* refers to its habit of boring into apples and laying its eggs there. The apple becomes the source of food for the developing immature insects, called larvae. But there is a problem here: It seems that there are two forms of the apple maggot in certain areas. The larvae of one eat apples, but the larvae of the other eat blueberries. Other than this behavioral distinction, the forms differ only in size (the apple-eater larvae are slightly larger). But their food preferences have important ramifications. Under laboratory conditions it is nearly impossible to get adults of the two forms to mate or to raise the larvae of one form on the food source of the other. In nature, in other words, these two forms probably never interbreed. They are said to be *reproductively isolated*. And this is exactly the definition of a *species:* It is a group of organisms whose members produce offspring only with other members of that group. Members of one species

can't mix their hereditary material or, therefore, their physical characteristics with those of any other species. (That is why species can often be easily distinguished just by appearance.) So the two forms of apple maggot, although they may live nearly side by side in the same location and differ only in food preference and larva size, should be considered as two separate species. In nature, they don't mix their genes.

2. Observe two mammals. One is large, standing just under 7 feet tall. Its skin is a light pinkish beige, and its hair a pale yellow and wavy. Its eyes are blue, and its nose is long, straight, and narrow. The other mammal is considerably smaller, about 4 feet 10 inches in stature. Its skin is dark brown—almost black—and its hair is black and short and grows in tight curls. Its eyes are deep brown, and its nose is broader than it is long. Despite the pronounced differences in appearance of these two mammals, you should recognize them both as human beings, *Homo sapiens*. Unlike the two apple maggot species that looked so similar, these two are clearly members of the same species. If one was a male and the other a female, they could produce live, fertile offspring.

3. The sky at dusk on a summer evening in southern Indiana, where I went to college, was populated by two creatures I never tired of watching. They were both insect eaters and were both marvelously adapted to exploit the great numbers of moths, beetles, and other insects that filled the air at that hour. Both had evolved the same basic answer to the problem of finding and catching the same food source: The bones and soft tissues of their forelimbs were modified to form wings. They both flew. Moreover, they were both warm-blooded and were both covered by an insulating layer to protect their body heat. These similarities had led some people in past times (like the author of the book of Leviticus) to classify them as the same sort of creature. They are, in fact, quite distinct. One is a nighthawk, a kind of bird. The other is a bat, a kind of mammal. The striking similarity of their way of life and source of food is an evolutionary coincidence. The anatomical origins of their wings are very different. Not only are they separate species, but they even belong to separate categories called *classes*, making them about as different from each other as a frog from a human or a snake from an eagle.

4. I give a biochemist friend the results of a chemical analysis of the basic protein makeup of two mammals, as well as some information about their chromosomes (long strands in cells, made up of genes). If I don't identify the mammals, and if I stick strictly to the genetics and biochemistry, my friend may well conclude that these

two are members of "sibling species"—species as similar as the flies in the first example. In terms of the basic chemical structure and the genes that code for it, there are almost no important differences between the two. Yet if I showed my friend the two living, whole animals, she'd have no trouble telling them apart. One is a human, the other a chimpanzee. Recent research has shown that our two species differ in only one percent of their genes. Yet we are, physically and reproductively, quite distinct.

These four examples show that species are not separate, equally distinct entities. There are varying degrees of similarity and difference among living organisms. We all know this intuitively, even if we have never considered it intellectually. We respond to one aspect of this idea emotionally: Many of us have no qualms at all about plunging a live lobster into a pot of boiling water, but few of us would do the same thing to a chicken, and very few, if any, of us would do it to a calf, even though these animals are also sources of food for us and are regularly slaughtered for that purpose. Why do we react in this way? Simply because we recognize that a cow is more closely related to us than is a chicken, and far more so than a lobster. So we tend to project our thoughts, feelings, even our "humanity," onto creatures that are physically more similar to us. Our local "humane" societies would never object to the way we treat lobsters!

What causes species differentiation? And why are there such subtle differences between certain species (like the flies) and yet such marked differences between some members of the same species (like humans)? (By the way, you should have noticed by now that *species* is both singular and plural.) There are two parts to the answer to that question.

First, a specific species looks and behaves the way it does because it is *adapted* to its environment. In other words, it possesses physical characteristics and patterns of behavior that help it survive in a given set of natural circumstances. It is able to find shelter, acquire food, locate mates, and produce offspring, all in step with—perhaps in spite of—the climate, geography, and other inhabitants of the area in which it lives.

Why the different degrees of relationship among species? Well, the process of adaptation is a continual one, since environments are always changing and animals are always moving around. Thus populations of living things sometimes split up, and the subpopulations become adapted to different environments. Species, in other words, can and do give rise to new species. Any two species will have a *common ancestor* somewhere in the past. How far back in time this common ancestor is determines to a great extent just how similar the two species are, that is, how closely related they are biologically. This idea is called *descent with modification.*

Here's a simple example: You are biologically related to all members of your family. But you and your sister are very closely related because you both have two immediate ancestors in common—your parents. You and your first cousin, although related, are more distantly related than are you and your sister. Here the common ancestors are your father's parents or your mother's parents. Species of living things are related in the same fashion—like a branching tree. In fact, we often depict biological relationships with a tree diagram, just as we speak of, and literally draw, "family trees."

The complete process that results in the origin of new species is, as you will see, somewhat more complicated than this, but these two concepts—*adaptation* and *descent with modification*—are at the heart of the matter. Let's look at each of these important ideas more closely.

ADAPTATION

When we consider the adaptation of a plant or animal to its environment, we have two basic questions to ask: (1) To *what* is the organism adapted? (2) *How* is it adapted? The study concerned with the first of these questions is the study of environments, *ecology.*

It is the rare person today who has not heard of ecology, but many people have, for good reason, a misconception of just what it is. Sometime in the late 1960s, I heard one student inquire of another as to whether or not he "believed in" ecology! The second student responded that, yes, indeed, he was "heavy into" ecology. What he meant, of course, was that he was concerned with environmental issues such as pollution of air and water and the extinction of animal and plant species. "Ecology" had become a catchword for concern about these matters. But actually, ecology is not something you can believe in or not. It is a science, one that studies environmental relationships. In the end this does usually lead to an awareness of the dangers of tampering with our world. That, however, is not the focus of the science itself.

Ecology comes from the Greek *oikos*, meaning "house." It studies the "houses," or habitats, of living things. More technically, it is the science concerned with discovering and explaining the network of relationships between organisms and all the various aspects of the environments in which they reside. Now, a moment's reflection should indicate to you that this could be a pretty complicated topic. Imagine all the climatic factors, all the species of plants and animals, all the bits of human intervention—just in your backyard! Obviously, we need some way of organizing such a study, and the organizing concept of ecology is the concept of the *niche* (pronounced "nitch").

An ecological niche (or just plain niche) may be defined as "all the environmental factors with which a particular species normally comes into contact." These are the factors to which a species must be adapted. For some particular species (we'll call it species A) these include: the food it eats, the animals that eat it, the times of day it's active, the temperature of the area it lives in, the place where it finds shelter, the average amount of rainfall, seasonal fluctuation in temperature and rain, and so on. *Anything* that directly affects the life of the organism in question is included in its niche.

Now, that could be complicated enough, but it gets worse. Niches overlap. If species A eats species B, then B is part of A's niche and A is part of B's. If they both happen to be oak-tree dwellers, then oak trees (species C) are part of both their niches. If they are both insects that provide food for some bird (species D), then the bird is part of all three niches. In other words, even if we are concerned with a particular species, we end up having to understand a great deal about the ecology of the other species that make up its ecological niche.

Consider, as a real example, the bats I mentioned earlier. They are adapted in many ways to the particular environment of southern Indiana. Moreover, they are active at night and in the air. So they have adaptations that allow them to fly, to navigate, and to find food under the special conditions of winging rapidly through dark skies. Since their prey also flies, they have to be able to catch it while they are both on the wing, and to do this they have developed special anatomical and sensory structures. But adaptation is not a one-way street. To appreciate and understand fully the bats' adaptation, we have to realize that the insects are adapted to the presence of the bats in their niches. It turns out, not too surprisingly, that some insects that are pursued by bats have an adaptation that allows them to pick up the bats' navigation and food-finding signals (called *echolocation*) and so be better able to avoid becoming a meal. The full story of the bats' adaptation must include a study of the adaptations of the insects on which the bats feed.

Suppose you are interested in monarch butterflies. Studying their niche, you would soon notice that it was sometimes inhabited

Bat catching a frog.

by another butterfly that bears a remarkable resemblance to the monarch. It's called the viceroy butterfly. Is there some connection here? You bet. Monarchs feed on milkweed plants, and a chemical in the plants makes the butterflies distasteful to birds. They are thus protected, at least from any bird that has had the unpleasant experience of having eaten a monarch and has learned to avoid that particular color pattern. Viceroy butterflies, it seems, have taken advantage (evolutionarily speaking) of this adaptive situation. They have evolved a color pattern so like the monarch's that most birds can't tell the difference. The viceroys, therefore, also benefit from this protective device, even though they don't eat milkweed. To understand monarchs completely, therefore, you need to understand viceroys, and birds, and milkweed plants.

One more concept results from this idea of complex systems of overlapping niches. It comes from the fact that if you keep describing overlapping niches, you'll end up with an ecological description of the entire planet. Indeed, if you consider things like gravity, light, and other forces, you'll have to include the whole known universe! We have to stop somewhere, and that somewhere is the *ecosystem*. An ecosystem is not really strictly defined. It depends on the type of organism you are interested in and the number of environmental factors that directly influence it. Generally speaking, though, we

Monarch (top) and viceroy (bottom) butterflies.

think of ecosystems as *types of environments*—an evergreen forest ecosystem, a tide pool ecosystem, an arctic tundra ecosystem, or one that will be important later, an African plains ecosystem. You could, of course, think even bigger. If you were studying blue whales, for example, the world's oceans would be your ecosystem of concern. In short, the set of niches that directly overlap with the niche of the species in which you are interested makes up the ecosystem.

This niche idea relates to humans in two ways. First, we are a biological species that evolved from other biological species. We thus have to understand these sorts of ecological relationships in order to understand our basic nature. Second, the same model can be applied to our current cultural situation. We can each be thought of as living in a particular social niche, which is affected by other social niches, which make up the human *cultural* ecosystem. It is to these niches and this general ecosystem that we are adapted.

Now, the second question: *How* are organisms adapted to their environments? Each species of plant or animal has its own unique set of adaptations to its own unique environmental niche, and these can be described. But is there any general concept we can use to study adaptation, any one thing we can focus on?

We tend, both literally in laboratories and figuratively in adaptation studies, to ''take organisms apart,'' to look at and explain their individual traits. For example, one of my favorite animals is the cheetah, an African member of the cat family. If we ''dissect'' the cheetah, we see that it is covered with fur that is yellow with dark spots. Its body is smaller and more sleek than other African cats, with a unique skeletal and muscle structure. Its spine is extremely flexible. If we were to look at its physiology, we would note certain unique features about the way the cheetah uses energy. In the end, we could list dozens of characteristics that make the cheetah different from other organisms.

But is this adaptation? Of course not. The cheetah doesn't survive by having anatomical and physiological traits. It survives by using them. It survives by doing something, by behaving. And this is true of any organism, even the simplest single-celled animals, even plants. They all function, behave, do something—and this is how they interact with their environments: how they get food, elude predators, find shelter, reproduce. Anatomy and physiology make behaviors possible. A certain muscle structure, a certain digestive system, a particular nervous system—we can think of these as having evolved to facilitate behaviors.

So why does the cheetah have a particular kind of physiology and such a flexible spine and slim body? Among other things, these traits, acting together, allow it to catch food in its own special style: Rather than sneaking up on prey as do lions and leopards, the cheetah runs them down in open country—and does so with bursts of speed that reach nearly 70 miles per hour! The cheetah survives by doing something. Its structure and function make the behavior possible.

As I discussed in Chapter 1, the science of ethology is the branch of biology that focuses on behavior. It is a relatively new field, only 60 to 70 years old, and it began with the sort of idea I just described: that the key to understanding how animals are adapted is to observe them behaving in the wild. This began with a series of individual

A cheetah in full stride.

field studies of all sorts of organisms. Now the science of ethology, having matured, provides us with a central point of reference: It shows us how animals behave so as to survive, and then it allows us to explain more fully how all the features of the animal operate together as a system to facilitate that adaptive behavior.

Moreover, ethology has shown us that behaviors themselves are the results of natural processes. The explanation for the evolution of physical features can also apply to the ways in which organisms act. For example, you may be familiar with the incredibly organized societies of some ants. Ants do some amazing things: They construct complex systems of tunnels and rooms in which they live and reproduce. They divide their labor among a number of different "castes." Some kinds of ants even "herd" other species of insects in order to use substances those insects produce. Now, no one would ever accuse an ant of "thinking" about doing these things. Rather, the ants are genetically programmed to do them. Their behaviors, in other words, are the products of the same processes as their anatomical traits. They can therefore be explained in the same ways. So we may use behavior as a theme in trying to describe and explain the adaptation of organisms.

But you may well ask just how this science of ethology—the biology of behavior—can apply to human beings. After all, we are definitely *not* programmed to behave in the ways we do. We, in fact, are quite unique in that we can think up our behaviors and change them at will if they are not giving us the desired results.

Well, think of it this way: Even though they may have different immediate causes, our cultural behaviors and the strictly biological ones of all other organisms *serve the same function*: They help us adapt and survive in a given environment. Considered that way, the approach of ethology makes sense whether the environment and adaptations are ''natural'' or are created by the organism in question. Moreover, our behavior—our culture—is not something entirely separate from our biology. We are, in a sense, biologically programmed to have culture in the first place, through the structure of our brains. And as I'll discuss later, there may even be some more direct connections between our biological heritage and some of the ways in which we behave. So as long as we keep in mind that there are differences between our cultural adaptations and the instinctive ones of most other animals, the approach, the methods, and the categories of ethology are quite appropriate for the anthropologist studying human adaptation.

DESCENT WITH MODIFICATION

If environments always stayed the same, organisms would not have to change their adaptive characteristics and behavior. All plants and animals would be exactly the same today as they always have been. This, of course, is not the case. Ecological conditions are in a constant state of flux. The geological record shows this for long periods of time. Our own observations make this clear to us as we observe smaller changes such as streams drying up, hills eroding away, old farmland turning to woods, or any of the numerous human actions that alter our environment.

In addition, organisms don't always stay put. Plant seeds get blown by wind or carried by birds to new locations. Animals may wander, or for some reason get pushed, into a new environment. In many, if not most cases, the new environment is too different from the old one, and the organisms don't survive. But there is always a chance that they will be able to adapt to the new conditions. So when environments change, species living in them may change. When a species is split up and portions of the population manage to thrive in new ecological circumstances, new species may come about. Species change over time; this is modification. Over long periods of time, species can give rise to new species; this is descent.

There are two aspects of this idea which must be considered: (1) the *evidence* for continual change through time and (2) the *processes* that bring it about. If you think about it, descent with modification is a bold idea. It says that plants and animals are not stable, unchanging entities. Some species change over time; some become extinct; some give rise to new species. Such a broad, important idea requires a good deal of supporting evidence. And that evidence exists in huge quantities.

I've already noted one basic bit of evidence. This is the fact that plant and animal species are not separate and equally distinct but are, like the members of a family, related to one another in varying degrees. Species, then, like members of a family, have descended or branched from other, earlier species. And there's more.

For one thing, despite the great diversity among living things, there exists a certain unity of life. All living organisms on Earth are made up of cells, all of which have the same basic structure and are made up of the same basic chemicals. Furthermore, all organisms share the same code for their structure and life processes—the genetic code, made up of a chemical called *DNA*. All living things use the same basic set of processes to convert nonliving materials into living tissues; it's called *metabolism*. Finally, living things do not exist independent of one another. In addition to being biologically related, they are all functionally related. They exist within a complex web of ecological interrelationships, each species being dependent on the existence of many other species.

Of course, it's quite conceivable that all species could have arisen (or have been "made") all at the same time, already exhibiting all these similarities and connections. The type of evidence given so far is, as they'd say in courtroom drama, circumstantial. What we need is not only supporting evidence for what *could* have happened but evidence for what *did* happen. And we have this too. It's the evidence from the fossil record. The fossil record is the story of Earth's history and life—very often literally written in stone—and the story it tells is clearly one of descent with modification.

Before we can go into this evidence, one important concept must be made clear. This is the set of relationships known as *stratigraphy*.

If you've ever visited the Grand Canyon or any similar geological formation, or if you just take a good look at the walls of rock along a road that cuts through a hill instead of going over it, you will notice that the sides of the canyon or the wall of the roadbed are layered, like a gigantic layer cake. Closer inspection will reveal that the layers are not all the same. They are of different thicknesses and are made up of different kinds of rock. It should be obvious from this structural relationship of the *strata* ("layers") that they were

The Grand Canyon showing fossil-bearing strata.

not put in place all at the same time but were laid down in sequence, from bottom to top, as different geological events gave rise to different sorts of rock. The stratigraphic record, then, is a record of change through time, and when you consider that in some areas there are hundreds of strata, then it should also be obvious that we are dealing with immense amounts of time.

Now, if we find fossils (the remains of past organisms) in certain strata, we can assume relative dates for them. That is, even if we don't known exactly how old a certain fossil is, we can tell if it is younger or older than some other fossil by noting the stratigraphic relationships. The number of strata separating the fossils can even give us an idea as to how much older or younger one fossil is than another.

Fossils, in their stratigraphic relationships, show us change through time in a number of ways. For one thing, the fossil remains of a particular sort of organism show change. As we'll discuss later, there is a nice sequence of fossils showing the change in the human species over the last several million years. At a broader level, we

Archaeopteryx, about 140 million years old. Possibly a reptile-bird transition. Note the impressions made by feathers.

can see in the fossil record the arising of new variations within a certain type of organism. For example, we know in some detail how modern horses evolved from their earliest known ancestor of 70 million years ago. On a even broader level, we can, in some cases, even see the evolution of one major type of organism from another. It has been suggested that birds and mammals both arose from some early form of reptile. In fact, in both cases we have fossils that give evidence of "transitional" forms between these groups.

The fossil record also shows an increase through time in the number of species. This is precisely what you'd expect if species were related as branches diverging from a common trunk. Finally, there is a trend toward increasing complexity of organisms as you read the fossil story. This does not mean that all types of plants and animals always evolve to become more complex. Some organisms may become "simpler" through time by evolving a smaller size or by losing some anatomical structure they once had. What this does mean is that as time goes by, one finds more kinds of more complex living things. The earliest part of the fossil record contains only the remains of single-celled microscopic organisms. Many-celled creatures appear later, then organisms with shells, then ones that can live on the land, then ones that can fly, then ones that have a constant body temperature and can learn and think complex thoughts. This is just what you would expect if types of plants and animals arose from earlier types. Just as technological items become more complex not all at once but by building onto the base laid down by previous inventions, so too, living things can increase in complexity only by adding new structures or functions onto already existing ones.

So every individual piece of evidence in each of these areas supports the idea that changes in the Earth itself and its inhabitants have taken place over great spans of time and that living things, including us, are related to one another as in an enormous and complex family tree. Within science these ideas are not really an issue today, nor have they been for some time. But precisely how all this happens—the *processes* of descent with modification—is still an important area of research and was the real scientific issue in Charles Darwin's day.

The more we understand about the processes that bring about evolution, the more complex we see it all really is. There are actually a number of processes at work bringing about changes in living things, each acting in its own particular fashion, operating at its own rate, and interacting in particular ways with the other processes. Some of these processes are well understood, some not so well. There are still important and exciting discussions and disagreements over just how each process operates and how important each is to the whole of evolution.

We will cover these processes (and controversies) in the next chapter. In the meantime, though, is there any central process we can focus on, any one important idea that can, in general, answer our question as to how descent with modification occurs?

There is indeed. Though there are other processes of change, this is the one that brings about the changes we're most interested in—the changes leading to adaptation. This is the process that was a major contribution of Darwin and others in the 1850s. It's this that really makes evolution work—or not work. It's called *natural selection*, and it's so important that we should give it its own section.

NATURAL SELECTION

Natural selection is not always easy to understand right off. I had a hard time with it as an undergraduate, and, when I began teaching,

I noticed the same problem among my students. I finally figured out why this is so. As contradictory as it may sound at first, natural selection is hard to understand because it's so simple. Because it's so simple, we have a tendency to try to make it more complex than it really is and to read things into it that just aren't there.

The funny thing is, many of us practice a form of selection when dealing with pets, plants, or livestock. In high school I was quite active in keeping and breeding tropical fish. One of my favorites was a live-bearing fish called a swordtail. I have forgotten the exact details (so I hope experts in the field will forgive me any inaccuracies), but I recall deciding to try to breed a bright red strain of swordtails, and I proceeded as follows:

I started with a pair of the reddest fish I could find and mated them. (Well, they pretty much take care of that themselves!) Then, from the first generation I chose the reddest of the offspring and put them in a separate tank to breed. From the second generation I again selected only the very reddest of the bunch to breed the third generation, and so on. In this way, I hoped to get redder and redder fish every generation until I had a pure strain of bright red ones. (By the way, I ran out of room for aquariums before I achieved my goal!)

Now notice that I was making two assumptions. First, I assumed that reddish swordtails were likely to produce reddish offspring—in other words, that children tend to resemble their parents. But second, I knew that not all the offspring of reddish parents would be equally red. In every generation I had to eliminate from breeding (don't worry, I just moved them) the offspring that were not the reddest, and some of these were not even as red as their parents. In other words, any group of organisms almost always shows *variation* in certain characteristics. Look around your classroom to see that this is so.

To summarize what I did in general terms: I had set up a minienvironment in which one important adaptive characteristic was reddish body color. I then selected from the natural variation of the group the individuals from each generation that possessed an "acceptable" expression of the body color trait. These I allowed to reproduce, and they tended to pass on their body color to their offspring. Thus fish with the "favorable" expression of the trait would increase in frequency (percentage of the whole population), and those with an "unfavorable" expression would decrease in frequency. If I hadn't run out of room, and if all else had worked out OK, in a few generations I could possibly have altered the nature of my swordtail population from an original group whose average body color was reddish orange to one whose average color was bright red. Of course, I would still have to continue to "weed out" any individuals that were not acceptably red from succeeding generations.

Does that make sense? If so, then you have only to take one more step and you've got basic natural selection! But it is an important step, and it's the one that causes the most difficulty in understanding. You see, the example I just gave is of *artificial selection*: An agent, me, was making conscious choices and taking direct action to implement them. We don't have that agent in nature, and trying to put one into natural selection is what gives people problems. So don't transfer the conscious agent; simply translate all the parts of my fish example to a natural environment.

Now the artificial minienvironment becomes the natural environment of a particular ecosystem. The important characteristics possessed by my fish become all the adaptive traits that allow a species to survive in its ecological niche. Selection is no longer a matter of being moved to a different aquarium if you're the wrong color. Now it is based on variation in the expressions of adaptive characteristics and the degree to which the variation affects survival and the ability to pass on one's traits to the next generation.

Wild swordtails from Central America, for example, live in an ecological niche that requires the expression of their adaptive traits within a limited range of variation. These traits would include things like body color, swimming ability, normal vision, smell and other senses, and certain instinctive behaviors. Selection starts right away. Each female swordtail gives birth to many more young than eventually survive, and she helps cut down the number herself by eating any newborn she can catch. Thus swimming speed, protective coloration (wild swordtails are sort of dull green), and perhaps even some "fleeing" instinct are immediately important. As life goes on, the ability to find food, to keep from being food, to ward off disease, to find a mate and reproduce—all these and more "select" the swordtails most able to thrive—the most "fit"—and these are generally the most successful at producing offspring and at passing on the characteristics that made them "fit." Favorable expressions tend to increase in frequency, unfavorable ones to decrease. That's the essence of natural selection.

The adapted population remains adapted because its members are continually going through what you might think of as an environmental "filter." This imaginary filter acts on adaptive characteristics, passing the successful ones on to the next generation and "filtering out" unsuccessful ones. The adapted population stays adapted. No-

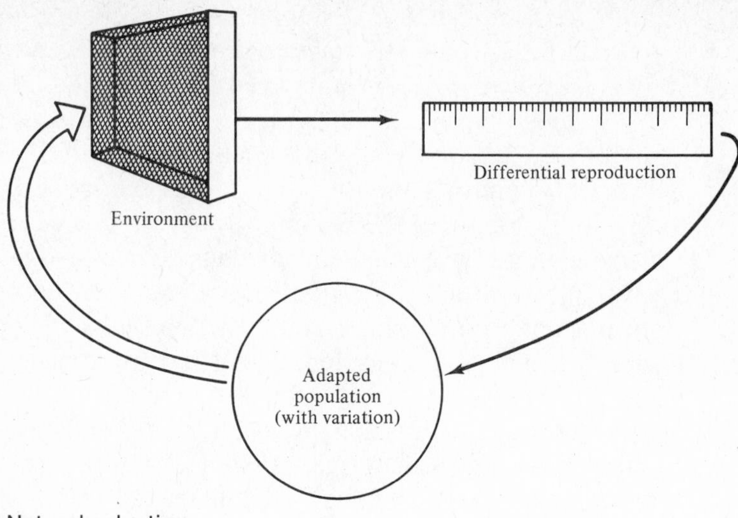

Natural selection.

tice, though, that it still shows variation. With no variation, selection would have nothing to select from! In Chapter 3 we'll talk about why this variation is always present.

Old phrases like "survival of the fittest" and "nature, red in tooth and claw" seem to indicate that selection operates on the level of the individual organism and in terms of whether or not that individual lives or dies. To be sure, if an organism is eaten by another organism, that takes care of its further contribution to the next generation! But life and death alone is not the measure. The measure is called *differential reproduction*. It is defined as how many offspring each individual produces compared with other individuals of its population. This, of course, is partly dependent on length of life. But it also involves health, normal behavior, and "attractiveness" to the opposite sex. An organism can live to a ripe old age, but if it never reproduces—never passes on those traits that gave it a long life—it can be considered "evolutionarily dead."

Now, the explanation so far describes how selection maintains a species' adaptation to its particular ecological niche. We call this *stabilizing selection*. But as we've discussed before, somewhere, sometime, into the life of every species "a little rain must fall," in the form of environmental change. In this case, selection has a different, and perhaps more difficult, job to do. It must readapt the population. Now, different expressions of certain traits may be more adaptive than the old, average ones. These will now be selected *for* under the new ecological conditions, and the old adaptive trait ex-

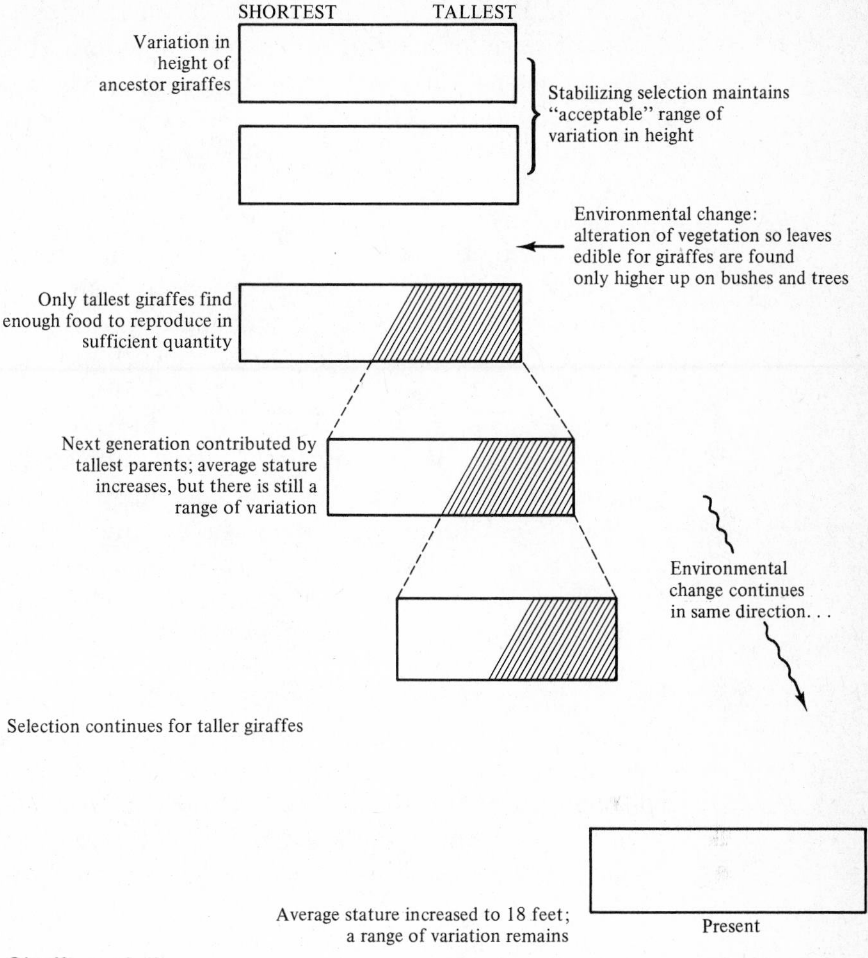

Giraffe evolution.

pressions will be selected *against*. Adaptation through natural selection takes a new direction. This is called *directional selection*. I was guiding directional selection in my swordtails—toward a red fish. If I had succeeded, I would then have had to practice stabilizing selection to maintain the strain.

Real examples of this process are numerous, but let's use one that's of importance historically (see Chapter 3). We are fairly sure that millions of years ago, the ancestor of the modern giraffe was an antelopelike creature, only a few feet tall, that ate vegetation growing on the ground. So how did giraffes evolve into 18-foot giants? (See the above diagram.)

Directional selection brings about much of the change we observe in living things, the change we refer to as *organic evolution*. It is the basic process of descent with modification.

You may want to check yourself at this point: Try to explain how monarch butterflies evolved their particular protective device, then how viceroys evolved to mimic monarchs. If you can do that, you've got it.

One final point about natural selection. It may seem from the giraffe example that selection can work any time it's needed, that it can adapt and readapt, over and over again, any species to any environmental change it may encounter. That's not the case. Remember that there is no directing force at work in natural selection. The characteristics of a species do *not* vary according to what environmental changes may happen in the future. Variation is a result of chance alterations of a species' genetic code (see Chapter 3) and of the trait expressions that have been selected for so far. Therefore, when the environment changes (or when a portion of a population moves to a new environment), selection can operate only with the variation *already present*. It can't make new traits because they're needed. Traits are never present because they may be needed sometime in the future.

Eventually, then, in the life of all species, some environmental change occurs with which the species can't cope. None of the existing variation in adaptive traits gives any individuals enough of an edge to produce sufficient offspring. The species becomes extinct. This is the norm, not the exception. Estimates vary, but it appears that of all the species of animals that have ever lived, 75 to 98 percent are now extinct. Selection has its limitations. It is not an all-powerful, ever-present miracle worker. But it has done some amazing things. Apple maggots, viceroy butterflies, and human beings are all proof of that.

SUMMARY

The structure of living organisms can be examined in terms of their *adaptation* to particular *environmental niches*. The study of environments is *ecology*, and that of the adaptive behavior of organisms is *ethology*. Humans too adapt through behavior, so we, as a species, can also be studied from this perspective.

All living organisms are related to one another as on a giant family tree. This fact and the processes that have brought it about are collectively called *descent with modification*, an idea that is supported by the circumstantial data of comparative biology and by the concrete data of the fossil record. A number of specific processes account for descent with modification, but the central process—the one that brings about and maintains adaptation—is the process of *natural selection.*

NOTES, REFERENCES, AND READINGS

There are many fine books available on environment and ecology. I simply recommend a trip through that section of your library if you'd like more information on these topics. Similarly, for more detail on the fossil record, start in the card catalog under "Fossils" or "Paleontology."

The topic of adaptation is included in any book on organic evolution and ecology. But to get a feel for adaptation in its broadest perspective, I can do no better than recommend the essays of Lewis Thomas, a physician and former president of the Memorial Sloan-Kettering Cancer Center in New York. Nearly all the essays in his first book, *The Lives of a Cell* (New York: Viking, 1974), deal with adaptation on some level. So does the title essay in *The Medusa and the Snail* (New York: Viking, 1979) and an essay called "Seven Wonders" in *Late Night Thoughts on Listening to Mahler's Ninth Symphony* (New York: Viking, 1983).

For some detail on the monarch butterfly story and hundreds more examples of biological "mimicry," see Wolfgang Wickler's *Mimicry in Plants and Animals* (New York: McGraw-Hill, 1968). This, by the way, is the book that finally got me to understand how natural selection works. And natural selection is the topic of the chapter "One Voice in the Cosmic Fugue" in Carl Sagan's wonderful book *Cosmos* (New York: Random House, 1980). If you can, supplement this reading by watching the corresponding episode from the TV series of the same name.

chapter 3

Evolution
The State of the Theory

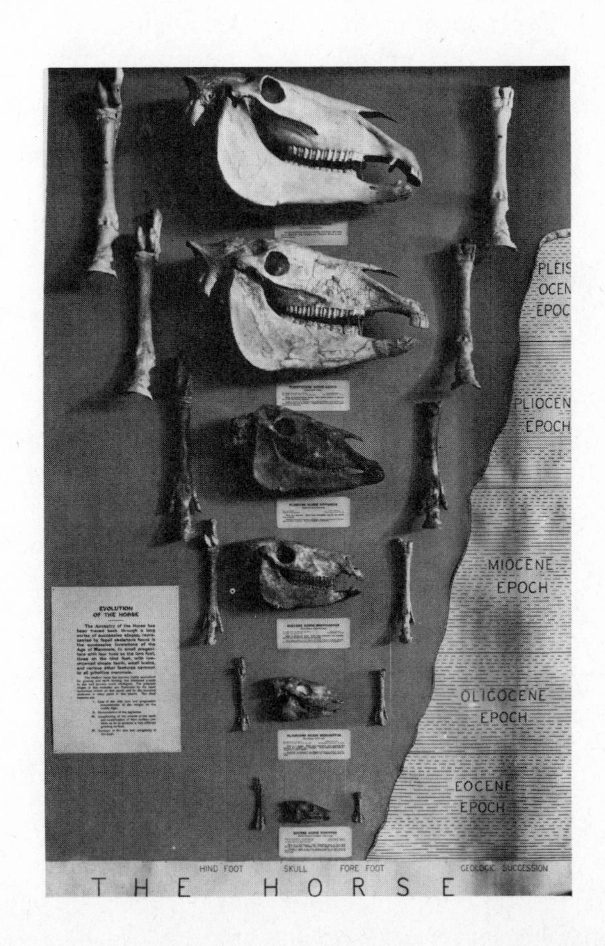

You may be wondering by now what happened to people! After all, aren't they, aren't *we*, the subject of anthropology? Well, as I mentioned, this whole matter of evolution can get fairly complicated, and it's much easier to understand if we look at nonhuman examples before we apply the ideas to ourselves. We still have a way to go. But at this point we can, and should, bring in humans for a moment.

Anthropology concerns itself with people and their behaviors. One of those behaviors is the sort of knowledge and endeavor we call science. Though we often think of science as taking place in "ivory towers" and as being practiced by strange, absentminded, eccentric recluses (and though that sometimes is the case!), science is not something separate from culture as a whole. Cultures, like environments, are *systems* of interacting, interrelated pieces. Even though science searches for that elusive thing called "truth"—something supposedly beyond social and cultural restraints—men and women of science in any culture (even ours) must operate within the context of that culture. The knowledge they have, the knowledge they can acquire, they way they think about their knowledge, the broad view they possess of themselves and the world around them—all these are dependent on the nature of the culture in which the particular scientists live and work.

So for the anthropologist—for anyone interested in science—knowledge of a set of scientific principles must include the cultural history of those principles and an appreciation of the intimate connections among all aspects of culture—even between culture and science. In addition, the discussion of the history of a scientific idea is an aid to a better understanding of that idea. Let's look briefly, then, at the history of the ideas we've been discussing.

THE EVOLUTION OF EVOLUTION

In the last century, a noted naturalist wrote the following:

> Among animals which procure their food by means of their agility, strength, or delicacy of sense, the one best organized must always

> obtain the greatest quantity; and must, therefore, become physically the strongest, and be thus enabled, by routing its opponents, to transmit its superior qualities to a greater number of offspring. The same law, therefore, which was intended by Providence to keep up the typical qualities of a species, can be easily converted by man into a means of raising different varieties.

He later went on to wonder:

> To what extent may not the same take place in wild nature, so that, in a few generations, distinctive characters may be acquired, such as are recognized as indicative of specific diversity? . . . May not, then, a large proportion of what are considered species have descended from a common parentage?

If that sounds like artificial selection, natural selection, and descent with modification, you're right, it is. If you think the naturalist is the famous Charles Darwin, usually associated with the introduction of those ideas, well, that's not the case. In fact, these passages were written by one Edward Blyth (1810–1873), and they were written over 20 years before Darwin published his *Origin of Species*!

How can that be? How could these scientific ideas, supposedly the brainchildren of the great Darwin, have been stated so well, so long before they are usually thought to have been introduced to science and the public? Were these ideas really Darwin's?

We often have the idea that scientific discovery is, as someone once put it, an "Aha!" phenomenon—that great scientific ideas just sort of occur to a great thinker out of the blue. Of course, it doesn't work that way. For the most part, scientific ideas develop slowly as new bits of thinking are added onto previous thoughts, until one day a whole, cohesive theory emerges. Often this synthesis, or the putting together of ideas, is the work of one or a few persons, but it is built on the work of many individuals over many years. Indeed, scientific ideas could be said to "evolve."

The concept of evolution is no exception. Thoughts on the subject can be traced all the way back to some of the Greek philosophers. For our purposes here, however, let's pick up the story in Europe in the 1700s, when the changes that eventually led to our present-day understanding of evolution began to occur. (For more complete discussions of the evolution of evolution, refer to the readings listed at the end of the chapter.)

Biological science, as we would recognize it, was well on its way by the middle of the eighteenth century. For example, in 1758

Carolus Linnaeus published a work that marks the beginning of the science of *taxonomy*, or the naming of organisms. We still use Linnaeus's system today, and we still use many of the names he applied to plants and animals (more on this in Chapter 4).

But all biology at that time was limited by a certain assumption. This assumption derived in part from literal interpretations of the Bible and in part from a simple lack of sufficient data. The assumption has been called *fixity of species*. It refers to the idea that living things have undergone no change since they were divinely created. They were thought to be "fixed" in terms of both their appearance and the number of existing kinds of organisms. Scientists of the time named, described, dissected, and experimented on all sorts of creatures and biological processes, but what they believed they were working with were organisms not only as they were then but as they had always been and always would be.

In the latter half of the eighteenth century, though, things began to change. Fossils, which people had been finding all along, were beginning to be recognized for what they were—the remains of creatures that once existed but existed no longer, or at least not in that particular form. The nature of the stratigraphic record was becoming clear, and it was seen that the Earth itself had undergone enormous change, over what had to be very long periods of time.

The usual picture we get of the story of evolution is that the idea of evolution itself was not accepted until Darwin wrote his book. But that's not accurate. In fact, the records of the geology and biology of the past were well enough understood and accepted by the beginning of the 1800s that what was at issue was not *whether* change occurred but *how* it occurred. Darwin's contribution, in other words, was in providing a reasonable mechanism to explain the change.

Numerous ideas were offered to account for the fossils and for the obvious lack of fixity of species that they demonstrated. One of the most popular of these ideas was proposed by a French biologist, Jean Baptiste de Lamarck (1744–1829). Lamarck's explanation is now discounted; it doesn't work. But because of that, Lamarck has gotten "bad press" that he doesn't really deserve, for the essence of his idea is sound. He said that living organisms are adapted to the environments in which they live. Since the geological record shows that environments continually change, it stands to reason that living things must change their adaptations in order to survive. No problem there! If he had stopped at that point, perhaps Lamarck would be remembered for being one of the first practicing scientists to recognize evolution, clearly and in print, and for establishing adaptation as a central concept.

But that was not to be. Lamarck went on to propose an idea as to how the plants and animals changed in response to changing environments. His idea is called "the inheritance of acquired characteristics," or (to the detriment of his reputation) *Lamarckism*. What he said was that species have an "inner consciousness" that enables them to recognize that some environmental change has taken place. They can then either develop characteristics they already have to a fuller extent or actually bring about new characteristics that would help them survive under the changed circumstances. These new or enhanced traits would then be passed on, in their new form, to the organism's offspring. Thus the "inheritance" of characteristics that are "acquired" during an individual organism's lifetime.

Remember the giraffes we used in Chapter 2 as an example of natural selection? I chose them because they were, in fact, one of Lamarck's most famous examples. Lamarck supposed that the ancestor of modern giraffes was much shorter than at present. Sometime in the past, some environmental change caused the giraffes' food sources to be found only higher up on shrubs and, later, trees. "Recognizing" this change, the giraffes stretched their legs and necks in order to reach their food. Each individual giraffe would thus become a little taller and would be able to pass on the increase in stature to its offspring. Over long periods of time, if the environmental change continued in the same direction, giraffes would increase their height from a few feet to an average 18 feet.

Now that sounds rather plausible, and there was in Lamarck's day (and maybe even today) a certain comfort in the idea that living things can change whenever they need to and through their own consciousness. But it doesn't work. We know of no way in which traits can arise automatically when they are needed, whether it's through the animal's own will or through some action of the environment. Moreover, traits that are acquired during an organism's life cannot be passed on to the organism's offspring.

That needs some elaboration. To be sure, I can bring about changes in my biology. I can lift weights and increase the size and strength of my muscles. I could even be "stretched" and increase my stature! But Lamarck assumed that *any* new or altered characteristic that was needed could arise. So animals and plants could change shape or color or could develop new organs or new behaviors.

Charles Darwin.

That just can't happen. Changes that do take place, such as muscle building or tanning of the skin, are changes that are already "allowed" or programmed by our genes. We can't make something that is not, in a sense, already there. Furthermore, changes, such as larger muscles, that I can bring about won't affect my offspring. My children won't automatically inherit my larger muscles, my permanent tan if I were able to lie out in the sun year round, or anything else I acquire during my lifetime.

So Lamarck's explanation of how change occurred can be discounted. In fact, although people weren't aware at the time of the genetic reasons why, Lamarck's idea was already presenting some problems by the first decades of the 1800s. The search for a mechanism of change was still on. And this is where Charles Darwin comes in.

Charles Robert Darwin was born into a well-to-do British family on February 12, 1809 (the same birthday as Abraham Lincoln). Charles's father, a physician, was a very practical and very religious man. So it was probably from his grandfather that Charles derived his interest in natural history. The grandfather, Erasmus Darwin (1731–1802), a physician and poet, was also a student of nature. In fact, one of his interests centered on the subject then called "transmutation of species"—what we now call *organic evolution*. Erasmus Darwin wrote about such things as the influence of domestication on plants and animals (artificial selection) and the relationship between animals and their environments (adaptation).

As a boy and later as a young man, Charles seemed to lack a direction in life, at least one that pleased his father. He had failed at beginning careers in both medicine and the clergy and obviously preferred roaming around the countryside collecting specimens and wondering about seemingly unimportant things like how species had changed through time. It was with some reluctance, then, in 1831 that Charles's father granted him permission to sign on board the HMS *Beagle* for its voyage of discovery around the world. Unwittingly, the elder Darwin changed the course of the history of science.

The story of the voyage of the *Beagle* is itself a fascinating one. For our purposes here, though, suffice it to say that it provided Darwin with a broad perspective, rarely available to men of this time, on the nature of living organisms. Darwin was able to observe and collect data, literally from around the world, on geological formations and the fossils they contained, on the geographic distributions of species, on the adaptation of various creatures to their environments, and on how individual populations, within a certain kind of organism, varied from one another according to environmental differences. The data not only showed Darwin that organisms changed through time (which was pretty well accepted then) but also hinted that species could give rise to other species. Perhaps it hinted as well at the mechanism that brought these processes about. In addition, the works of certain geologists and social philosophers that Darwin had read introduced new perspectives on natural and social change that also contributed to Darwin's thinking.

Oddly, rather than writing about the "transmutation of species" on his return from the *Beagle* voyage in 1836, Darwin turned his attention to other scientific subjects. He mentioned what we now call evolution only privately to friends and wrote about it only in his personal notebooks and in two trial essays in the early 1840s. We know, however, that he knew the answer shortly after his return home. When his notebooks were published, long after his death, it became apparent that Darwin was convinced that species arise through descent with modification and that the mechanism was natural selection.

Why did he say nothing? Not, as popular knowledge has it, because his idea "proved" evolution; that was accepted by most scientists and much of the general public. Rather, Darwin's silence can probably be explained by his fear that science and society were not ready to accept natural selection. The process, he may have felt, was too "chancy," too dependent on random, fortuitous events. Recall, despite its problems, the popularity of Lamarck's idea, a popularity explained by the fact that inheritance of acquired characteristics said that when a change was needed, it occurred. Compare that with natural selection, where change can come about only if some members of a species *already* possess traits that will allow them to cope with an environmental change. Recall also that in most cases natural selection is eventually not enough, and extinction results. For Darwin, a reclusive, sickly man who shunned public contact and hated controversy, this idea, as confident as he was in it, may have been too radical, at least for the moment.

But history was not to leave Darwin alone yet. In 1858 Darwin received a letter from a young, little-known British naturalist named Alfred Russell Wallace (1823–1913). Wallace, on a collecting trip in Indonesia and suffering from a malaria-caused fever, had glimpsed the basics of a mechanism that might explain, better than Lamarck had, the transmutation of species. Later, working it out in more detail, Wallace felt his idea had merit, and he decided to check it out with the most renowned of naturalists, Darwin.

Upon reading Wallace's letter and his new idea, Darwin's hand was called. For Wallace had stated, in nearly the same terms as Darwin, basic natural selection. Darwin was forced to publish, and the following year, 1859, *On The Origin of Species by Means of Natural Selection* hit the bookstores and sold out in a single day. Possibly to Darwin's surprise, the time was indeed ripe for his idea, an idea that was heralded by the scientific community. "How extremely stupid not to have thought of that!" one scientist is said to have remarked.

By the way, Wallace was not forgotten. Even before Darwin's book came out, a paper by Wallace was presented with one by Darwin at an important scientific meeting, and Wallace continued to work in natural science. Darwin is the more remembered of the two because he was older and already well known when all this happened; because Darwin had been collecting, for many years, data to support his idea and so could publish it almost immediately; and possibly because, later in his life, Wallace strayed from mainstream science and became involved in spiritualism. It should not be forgotten, though, that he derived, independently, the concept of natural selection.

Now, if Darwin and Wallace can be credited with the idea, what about young Edward Blyth mentioned earlier? The two passages quoted are from papers Blyth published in the British *Magazine of Natural History* in 1835 and 1837, long before Darwin published his idea and while Wallace was in his teens! Is natural selection really Blyth's idea?

Anthropologist Loren Eiseley has written persuasively to the point that Darwin almost certainly read Blyth's articles upon his return from the *Beale* voyage and that he, though probably unconsciously, incorporated Blyth's ideas, developed them, and later published them as his own, never giving Blyth any credit.

Was Darwin an inadvertent plagiarist? No, the impeccably honest Darwin would never, I imagine, have done such a thing, even unconsciously. He was too careful, too modest, and too fearful of unpleasantries for that. The explanation to this puzzle lies, again, in the nature of science as part of human culture. The times may have been right in 1859 for the idea of natural selection, but Darwin was probably correct that they weren't right in the early 1840s. Edward Blyth, who was actually a believer in the special creation of species by a divine being, simply didn't understand all the meanings and ramifications of what he had said. He felt he was essentially describing a limited process that helped stabilize species against the constant onslaught of environmental change (stabilizing selection) and that was used by humans in their domestication of plants and animals (artificial selection). He "mused" over whether this process might cause species to split from a "common parentage," but he never elaborated on that idea or developed it further.

Similarly, Darwin, fresh from a voyage he began as a Lamarckian—for there was as yet no other choice—also didn't fully understand what he had read when he saw Blyth's papers, as we know he did. To Darwin, Blyth's statements were probably just additional bits of data, added to the enormous amount he had already collected. In our hindsight, we recognize Blyth's ideas immediately. But Darwin couldn't, because he had yet to piece together all his observations and thoughts, as he always did so carefully, and arrive at his conclusion. That's the way science usually works. Looking back, it's easy for us to accuse individuals of missing obvious ideas, of ignoring people who seem ahead of their time. But like any type of cultural change, scientific discovery and invention (unless forced upon a people from the outside) can come about and be accepted by a society only at a particular point in history, not a minute sooner.

Charles Darwin died in 1882, but not before authoring numerous volumes on various scientific topics, including a second major work on evolution, *The Descent of Man* (1871). In this book Darwin did what he dared not in 1859: He applied his ideas explicitly to humans, and by that time they were accepted with little problem.

But Darwin did die without ever finding out the answers to two important questions. First, he did not understand exactly how traits in living organisms are passed on. Obviously, the ability of successful parents to give their traits to offspring was vital to natural selection. There were at the time some vague ideas about a blending of substances from mother and father, but no substantial theory. Second, Darwin did now know where variation came from. Without variation, selection couldn't operate. He recognized that variation was always present in a species, even after years of selection to the same environment. But as to the origin and maintenance of that variation, he had no answer.

Ironically, the answers to both questions came from the same source, and they were available during Darwin's lifetime. At about the same time Darwin was writing *The Origin of Species*, an Austrian monk named Gregor Mendel (1822–1884), working in a monastery in what is now Czechoslovakia, discovered the basic laws of inheritance. Experimenting with pea plants, no doubt the culmination of many undocumented years of research, Mendel arrived at a number of important conclusions regarding the passing on of traits. First, he realized that rather than being carried in some substance, traits are

Gregor Mendel.

controlled and passed on by individual "particles" or "factors"—we now call them *genes*. Moreover, these "factors" occur in pairs, both members of a pair not necessarily coding for the same expression of a trait. For example, Mendel's pea plants came in two categories for stature, tall and short. From his breeding experiments, he reached the conclusion that there was an individual factor for plant height and that it came in two versions, one for tall plants and one for short plants. An individual plant might have *both* factors in its pair, but in this case the factor for tall plants overrode that for short plants. He called it a *dominant*—and we still do today.

Mendel's second major conclusion concerned reproduction. A plant, he said, passed on to each of its offspring only one factor from each pair. Thus every new plant would have a new pair of factors made up of one factor from each of its parents. In inheritance, factor pairs in the parents are broken up and then recombined in the offspring. Here, then, was the answer to how inheritance takes place and to the question of the source of a good deal of observed variation:

Traits are controlled and carried on individual factors, and these factors are shuffled during reproduction to produce new combinations.

Again, our hindsight makes us wonder why these important discoveries were not immediately incorporated into the biological sciences. But they weren't. The few scientists who did read Mendel's paper on the subject (and this apparently did not include Darwin) failed to grasp the importance of what they had read. Studies of evolution and of inheritance were simply not at the point where Mendel's research would add anything. Mendel himself became abbot of his monastery and ceased his work with plants. Upon his death, the records of his research, which never really had the complete approval of his superiors, were burned.

In 1900, almost 20 years after Darwin and Mendel died, Mendel was rediscovered. Now the time was ripe for his work to make sense. Various researchers had been working on evolution and inheritance, and some were on the verge of discovering what Mendel had. In that year three investigators, working independently, came upon the monk's obscure paper and realized just what they had found.

One of the men was the Dutch botanist Hugo de Vries (1848–1935). De Vries had been trying to explain the rare variations that sometimes appeared in plants (and, of course, animals): things like a single flower of the wrong color or a plant that was far smaller or larger than other members of its species. Breeders called these oddities "sports." De Vries called them *mutations*. Now, with his discovery of Mendel's work, de Vries understood that his mutations were the results of sudden changes in Mendel's "factors."

With this, the final link in the theory of evolution was in place, for mutations explained the source of new variation—where the different versions of the factors or genes came from in the first place. Upon this base is built our current understanding of evolution. To be sure, much has been added, many mistakes have been made, and we are still arguing over details. But we can use what we've discussed so far and go on to describe the state of the theory today.

THE PROCESSES OF EVOLUTION

One wonders what Charles Darwin would think if he could be here today and listen to an explanation of our current understanding of evolution. I think he would be pleasantly surprised to find that natural selection is still at the center of the whole concept. But he would

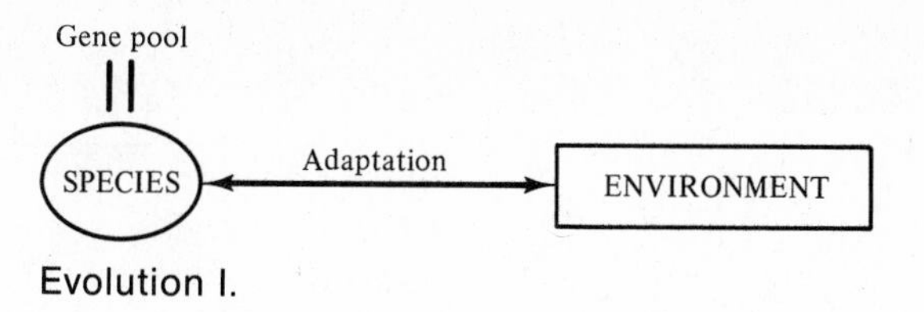

Evolution I.

also probably be amazed at all the new things that have been added. Remember, Darwin didn't know about genetics! I also like to think that he would have no trouble grasping all the new ideas. Evolution is a complicated topic, but if you take things step by step, it all falls into place with beautiful logic.

I've already described the nature of the relationship between any species and its environment: Essentially, unless environmental conditions are in a state of rapid change, any species is adapted to the niche in which it lives. Moreover, the characteristics of the members of that species are determined by their genes, the whole collection of a species' genes being called its *gene pool*.

This set of relationships, however, is not static. Environments are always changing, as the stratigraphic record clearly shows. Species, in order to continue to exist, have to undergo change in their adaptations to keep pace. This is accomplished, when it is accomplished, by natural selection. In addition, the genes coding for a species' adaptive traits are continually changing as well. The processes that bring about genetic change, and the process of natural selection, are collectively known as *evolutionary processes*, and they act as mediators in the relations of genes, species, and environments.

There are five evolutionary processes, and they can be divided into two basic types: random and directional. *Random types* bring about change in no particular direction with regard to adaptiveness. The four processes in this group (mutation, gene flow, founder effect, and genetic drift) act on the genes of individuals and the gene pools of populations within a species. They thus affect the gene pool of the species as a whole. By continually bringing about changes in the genetic nature of a species, they bring about change in the nature of its adaptiveness to its environment.

In general, what these processes do is change *gene frequency*. This term refers to the frequencies (percentages or proportions) of the varieties of a gene present in a population. The number of tall-stature genes in a population of pea plants, for example, versus the number of short-stature genes, will have a direct relationship to the

THE EVOLUTIONARY PROCESSES

Process	Effects
Random	Work on the genes to change frequency
1. Mutation	Are random, undirected
2. Gene flow	Increase genetic variability
3. Founder effect	
4. Genetic drift	
Directional	Works on the adaptive relationship
5. Natural selection	Directed toward better adaptations
	Decreases genetic variability

percentage of tall versus short *plants*. Thus these numbers will say something about the average appearance of the pea plant population.

"Change in gene frequency over time" is *the* definition of evolution. Although on the surface we see the evidence of evolution in the changing appearances of species through time, what is ultimately responsible for that change is the change in the relative proportion of the variants of a species' genes.

Finally, these four processes all act to enhance genetic variability. You will recall that without variation, evolution could not operate. Remember the variation in stature of the original giraffes, for instance. Thus these four processes can be considered as providers of the raw materials for the fifth process, natural selection, which is the only one of the *directional type*.

Natural selection, as you already understand, works directly on the adaptive relationship between a species and its environment. It "selects" for reproductive success those individuals best adapted. Selection does have a direction; it is not random. That direction, of course, is toward adaptation. Natural selection, acting on the variation provided by the other four processes, decreases genetic variability, promoting the passing on of those gene varieties that serve the adaptive needs of the species and limiting or preventing the passing on of those that don't.

Now, let's briefly examine each of the random processes.

Mutation

As de Vries discovered, the material of heredity can undergo sudden change. We understand now that such changes can take place at any genetic level, from a single gene to a whole chromosome. Any such change is a *mutation*.

These random changes are brought about in a number of ways.

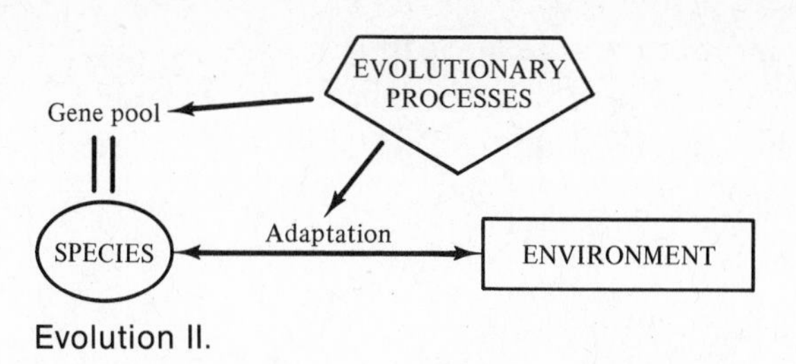

Evolution II.

Cosmic radiation, x-rays, gamma rays from radioactive substances, and certain chemicals are all known *mutagens*. In addition, mutations can take place spontaneously during the normal but very complex processes by which the genes copy themselves during cell division, and when the genetic code is "read" and "translated" into the functional chemicals that make an organism work. These mutations happen all the time. In fact, some have taken place in your body since you began reading this section.

But not to worry. Nature takes care of the worst mutations simply by "killing off" the cells containing them. The point is that most mutations, since they are mistakes, are indeed deleterious (harmful). A mutation, depending on just what gene or genes it involves and how abnormal it makes them, can kill off a cell or produce a slightly abnormal cell. It can bring about illness in the organism in which it occurs or, as in the case of some cancers, can lead to the death of the organism.

There is, however, another side to the story, for all these deleterious effects are the price that living things pay for evolution. Without mutations there would be no new versions of genes and therefore no variation. Just how bad or good a mutation is depends on the nature of the species-environment relationship. But simply put, evolution could not operate without this source of raw material.

Of course, the only mutations that matter on the evolutionary level are those that occur in the sex cells—the sperm and eggs that contain the genes passed to the next generation. A mutation that takes place in, say, a skin cell of my little finger may affect me, but it won't be passed on to my offspring. But a mutation in one of my sperm cells could end up in *every* cell of a child I help produce. That would make a difference.

Finally, there is now good evidence that some very large mutations—those involving large numbers of genes or a small number of very important genes—can result in sudden and extreme changes in organisms. Of course, most such mutations would be lethal. But not all. And when a nonlethal one occurs, it can radically alter the species-environment relationship by producing the beginnings of a whole new species. These mutations are called *macromutations* ("large mutations"), and we'll come back to them.

Gene Flow

This process operates among populations within a species. (Remember, genes cannot be exchanged between different species.) As individuals move from one population to another, genes are exchanged, and new genetic combinations are brought about. Thus the frequencies of the gene varieties change, and genetic variability for the whole species is enhanced, providing natural selection with new "raw materials."

A human example comes from the Hutterites. Half of all Hutterite marriages take place between colonies, and they involve the bride's moving to the colony of her husband. The woman thus brings her genes into the population and contributes them to subsequent generations. This can have a great effect on changing gene frequencies. In one of the two Hutterite colonies I visited, for instance, 70 percent of the female parents came from other colonies, and marriages involving these women produced nearly 60 percent of the children of the next generation. In the second colony, 75 percent of the female parents "flowed" in, and their marriages produced 47 percent of the next generation's children. Changes seen from one generation to the next in a Hutterite colony must take into account this continual mixing or "flowing" of genes among populations, which give rise to new frequencies and new combinations of gene variants.

Founder Effect

Populations of organisms within a species not only mix; they also split up. When a population divides, it produces two or more new genetic populations and thus two or more new sets of gene combinations and frequencies—new variation. Why aren't the two halves (if the population splits in two) the same genetically as the whole original population? When you take a sample from a group of anything, chances are that the sample will not be "representative" of the whole group. This is called *sampling error.*

Try an experiment. Take 100 coins and turn them so you have 50 heads and 50 tails. Mix them up and without looking select ten coins. They will probably *not* be five heads and five tails. The chances are against it. Keep trying and you'll get some idea of the odds involved. Your sample of ten is seldom representative of the whole population of coins.

The same is true for genes in biological populations. Again the Hutterites provide an example. Recall that Hutterite colonies split or "branch out" with regularity. A population divides, half staying in the original location and half founding a new colony. The genetic result, though, is the founding of two brand new populations in terms of the exact frequencies of the gene varieties.

This evolutionary process and gene flow are particularly important for our species as a whole. For most of our history we have been divided into many small populations defined by such things as kinship, religion, and politics. But these populations have always mixed genes, and they have always split up to found new populations. In the last century or so, of course, gene flow has increased enormously because of the great mobility of our species. Thus these two processes of evolution, continually providing new variation, are very important in terms of the evolutionary changes seen in our species over the past 5 million years.

Genetic Drift

Just as genes are not sampled representatively when a population splits, they are not sampled representatively when two individuals produce offspring. An organism passes on only one of each of its pair of genes at a time, and only chance dictates which will be involved in the fertilization that produces a new individual. Suppose each of two pea plants, for example, possesses one gene variety for tallness and one for shortness. (They would, as you recall, both be tall plants.) But they would not necessarily, in their reproductive lifetimes, pass on an equal number of their short and tall genes. It's a matter of chance. It's *possible* that they could pass on only their tallness genes, and so their offspring would have 100 percent tallness genes even though the parents had 50 percent each.

On the level of a whole population, then, where each mating may alter the gene frequencies between parents and offspring, the overall effect could be great, small, or in between. The gene frequencies will "drift" in whatever direction the statistics of probability take them.

This process has the greatest effect in small populations. In a

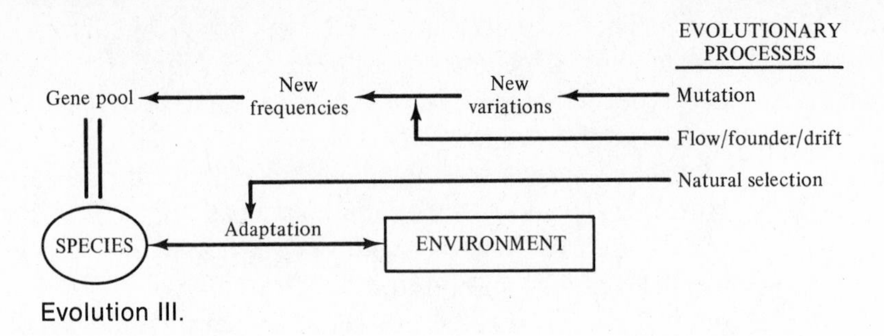

Evolution III.

group, say, of under 100 individuals (the size of a Hutterite colony and of most human populations for most of our species' history), the change in gene frequency produced by one set of parents would have a bigger impact on the population as a whole than it would in a population of 10,000. In a group of large size, a change in one direction might well be balanced by a change in the opposite direction produced by another set of parents.

To one degree or another, these four processes are continually in operation, often in complex interaction, continually providing new genetic combinations and frequencies that the fifth evolutionary process, natural selection, can act on. We have already discussed selection at some length, and all that should be needed to complete the picture of the processes of evolution is to fit selection into the overall scheme that includes mutation, flow, drift, and founder effect.

THE ORIGIN OF SPECIES

If you've remembered all along that the heading of this section was also the title of Darwin's famous book, you may be asking a logical question: Throughout this chapter so far all we've talked about is the modification part of descent with modification. How does the descent part work? Isn't that the real topic of Darwin's book, as the title indicates?

It is indeed the focus of *The Origin of Species*, and the description of how descent works is that book's second great achievement. The process that Darwin outlined to account for modification—natural selection—also accounts for the descent of species from other species. To be sure, all the other processes we've been discussing—things Darwin couldn't have known about—play a part as well. But Darwin's basic idea is central.

Descent of species is based, as is the modification of species, on environment and adaptation. Different environments—that is, new combinations of factors forming new ecological niches—provide new opportunities for adaptive combinations of traits. New combinations of traits—new kinds of organisms—are the beginnings of new species.

This can come about in two basic ways. First, a species may split up, part of the population finding itself in a somewhat different niche. It's the founder effect on the species level. If the new niche is different enough, if enough time elapses, and if directional selection has the variation with which to operate, the population in the new niche can take off on its own adaptive course, eventually becoming so distinct from its parent population that it can acquire the criteria (biological distinctness and reproductive isolation) of a new species. Remember—and this is very important—that this can happen only if the genetic variation in this offshoot population contains genes for characteristics that will allow it to survive and reproduce under the new circumstances. Natural selection can't work magic.

A species may split up due to a huge number of different events. A river may widen or change its course, cutting off a group of organisms from the rest of its species. Members of a species may be carried by wind or water to isolated islands, which would constitute new niches. (As farfetched as this may sound, it does happen. The Galápagos Islands, which Darwin visited on his voyage, were populated by all sorts of creatures in this fashion. The islands are now the home of species found nowhere else.) A geological event, such as an earthquake or volcanic eruption, might divide a species. Or some more subtle climatic change might alter a part of a species' environment, splitting off a portion of the population. For a small insect species, the destruction of a few plants that are important to its niche could divide the group. Or, simply, a species that was rapidly growing and expanding could encounter new niches at the fringes of its range and split off small populations in those niches.

Probably most such environmental changes and population splits are detrimental to the members of the species involved. But when a new species does evolve in this manner, its success is dependent on at least four major factors: a new enough niche; the isolation of the split-off population from the rest of its species; enough time; and, most important, sufficient genetic variation to start the new population off on its new adaptive direction.

The second manner in which new species may originate from a common ancestor begins at the genetic level. Remember macromutations? The vast majority of the time, mistakes of that magnitude

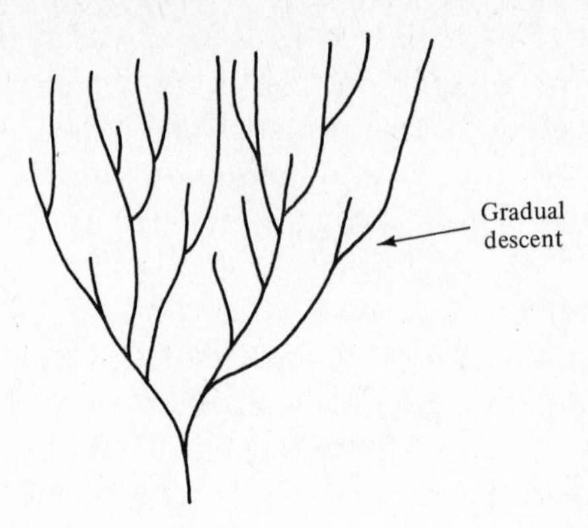

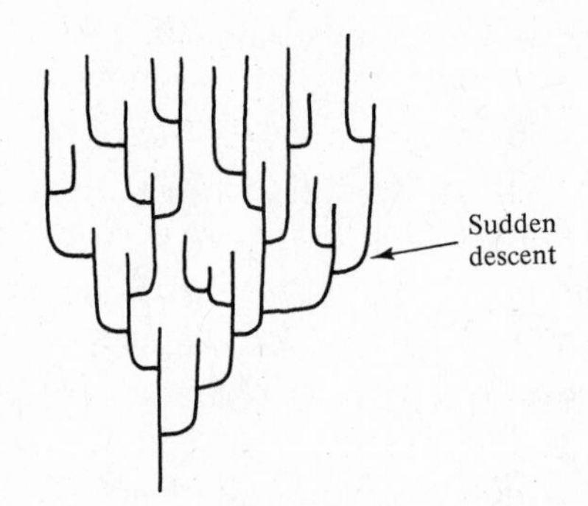

Modes of evolution.

are fatal or at least extremely deleterious. But on the rare occasions when a macromutation results in a very different but healthy organism, it can give a new evolutionary direction a real head start. Of course, even when the resultant organism is alive and well, the perpetuation of its genetic differences is dependent on its success in a new niche. A new direction only keeps going when there is a new niche available to which the organism possessing the new features is adapted. Further natural selection, "fine-tuning" the organism to the new environment, can operate only if there is some degree of adaptation to begin with. Obviously, such occurrences are rare over short periods of time.

However, over the billions of years of organic evolution here on Earth, such things have happened, and it is thought that it may be these macromutations that begin the big changes in evolution, the whole new sorts of creatures. This may explain the beginnings of multicellular organisms from single-celled ones, of animals able to live on land from those confined to the water, of feathered creatures from scaly ones, and of two-footed primates from those who get around on all fours. After all, can the feathers of early birdlike creatures have evolved in a long series of small steps? (Remember, they always have to be adapted, in whatever form, to the environment at the time.) No, in all likelihood, some featherlike structure arose fairly suddenly and was immediately adaptive in some portion of some species' range. Then, and only then, could good old natural selection adjust, enhance, and fine-tune those primitive feathers (and other features), eventually giving us what we know as birds. Recall *archaeopteryx*, a small reptilian creature with virtually modern feathers (see page 30).

These modes of species origin are at present the center of a controversy. There are two schools of thought on the subject. One says that new organisms, whether species or whole new types, arise gradually through the first mechanism discussed, the splitting of species into new environments and the gradual increase in differences brought about by directional selection.

The other school says that natural selection can bring about only minor changes in a species' nature. The kinds of changes that result in new species and new types of organisms must begin as macromutations that bring about drastic and sudden alterations. *Speciation* in this model gets a genetic head start.

It's probably safe to say that the overall evolution of life on Earth involves both types of speciation. But the arguments from these two points of view are what make science work, what will eventually solve the question, and what make science exciting.

Now, to come full circle, how do all these processes account for the similarities and differences between the species in the four pairs that were described at the beginning of Chapter 2? The striking similarity of the adaptations of the nighthawks and bats is a result of a phenomenon called *convergent evolution*. Two species inhabit very similar niches and, through entirely separate routes, evolve similar adaptive mechanisms for dealing with those niches. When one examines each animal closely, though, one finds that the similarity is only superficial. They are quite different creatures, as you would expect.

The two humans that are so different? Here the differences really are superficial. Both are members of the same species and therefore possess far more similarities than differences. The differences they do exhibit are the results of the wide range of the human species and of the varying types of environments humans did and do inhabit. These different environments, both natural and cultural, led to some genetic differences between human groups from various parts of the world. But because we all began as a single species and have always exchanged genes among our populations, no speciation has taken place.

We humans are quite different from chimpanzees in appearance, and a human-chimpanzee pair cannot produce offspring. But our two species are about 99 percent genetically similar. The explanation is macromutation. At this point, we don't know everything that was involved, but it would appear that a few large mutations, or mutations of important genes, took place several million years ago in the common ancestors of humans and chimps, starting the two lines off on their separate evolutionary courses. I'll detail this story in Chapters 4 and 5.

Finally, the maggots. This species distinction may be accounted for in terms of population movement. Some apple maggots may have spread into areas where blueberries were prominent, or some may have just begun laying eggs in blueberries that were found in their range. For reasons yet to be entirely understood, blueberry-raised flies in turn laid their eggs only in blueberries, and the split began.

The five basic processes of evolutionary change bring about alterations in the genes of organisms and in the adaptive relationship between species and their environments. When either the genes or the relationships are radically altered—through mutation, environmental change, or population movements—new species, new types of creatures, descend from common ancestors. Whether the branches diverge as smooth curves or sharp angles (or both), life on Earth is a gigantic, complex family tree.

And at the end of one of those branches is us. It's time now to embark on the anthropological journey—to describe the species that inhabits that branch and how it got there.

SUMMARY

The evolution of evolution—indeed, the evolution of any scientific idea—can only be fully understood and appreciated by seeing it as the product of the cultural context in which it arose. Though science seeks "truths," it always does so within the potentials and limitations of a particular sociocultural environment.

Our modern understanding of the processes that bring about evolution perceives two types of processes in operation: the *random* processes (mutation, drift, founder effect, and flow), which act on the genes of individuals and the gene pools of populations, and the *directional* process of natural selection, which acts on the adaptive relationship between a species and its environment.

New species evolve when existing species are split up and the portions of the population become adapted to new niches. For this to work requires enough time, enough genetic variation, sufficient isolation of the subpopulations, and different enough niches. Species splitting may occur as the result of some environmental change, or it may be initiated by a macromutation that results in a small group of very different organisms. In the latter case, though, there must be some available niche in which the new traits are useful and well adapted.

NOTES, REFERENCES, AND READINGS

Perhaps the most complete book on the history of the idea of evolution is *The Death of Adam* by John C. Greene (New York: Mentor, 1959). It's a detailed and challenging work, but well worth the effort if you're interested in the history of ideas. An easier but no less accurate work is by comedian, physician, and TV personality Jonathan Miller and artist Borin van Loon, *Darwin for Beginners* (New York: Pantheon, 1982). Don't be put off by its cartoon format; there's a lot of good, sound information there. The pictures just make it fun. An examination of the development of natural selection, emphasizing the work of A. R. Wallace, is in Chapter 9 of Jacob Bronowski's *Ascent of Man* (Boston: Little, Brown, 1974). Also try to take a look at that episode from Bronowski's *Ascent of Man* TV series.

The work by Loren Eisely proposing the case for Darwin's inadvertent plagiarism is *Charles Darwin and the Mysterious Mr. X* (New York: Dutton, 1979). It contains the original works by Blyth as well as Eisely's case.

For more original works by Darwin, Wallace, and others, as well as various analyses of the impact of evolution, see *Darwin*, edited by Philip Appleman (New York: Norton, 1970).

I recommend anything and everything written by Harvard paleontologist Stephen Jay Gould. Especially relevant to this chapter are the essays in Section 1 of *Ever Since Darwin: Reflections in Natural History* (New York: Norton, 1977) and those of Section 2 in *The Panda's Thumb: More Reflections in Natural History* (New York: Norton, 1980). The other essays in these two books (taken from Gould's monthly column in *Natural History* magazine) and those in his third collection, *Hen's Teeth and Horse's Toes: Further Reflections in Natural History* (New York: Norton, 1983) all relate to some aspect of evolutionary science, and those dealing with examples of adaptation provide some good background for the discussions in this chapter and in Chapter 2.

For more detailed discussions of all aspects of the subject of organic evolution, I recommend Earl D. Hanson's *Understanding Evolution* (New York: Oxford University Press, 1981) and G. Ledyard Stebbin's *Darwin to DNA: Molecules to Humanity* (San Francisco: Freeman, 1982).

interlude

Anthropology and Science

I have been talking freely about anthropology as one of the sciences and about the scientific method in general. I have also discussed a number of conclusions from science regarding the evolution of life on Earth. But just what is this thing called science? How does the scientific method work? How has it arrived at those conclusions? How is anthropology scientific?

Just as anthropologists often suffer from popular misconceptions, so too do scientists in general. This misconception can be seen in those wonderful old science fiction movies, the ones where some prehistoric monster comes to life and threatens civilization, and the handsome hero, the strange old scientist, and his lovely daughter must save the world. The scientist in those movies is nearly always elderly, usually horribly eccentric, *and* knowledgeable about almost everything. Seldom is it specified what kind of scientist he is. He is simply a scientist, and for the purposes of the film, that means that he knows all sorts of important stuff.

The image we get is of the scientist as an unspecialized, fact-collecting, walking encyclopedia. To be sure, men and women of science do know a lot of information. But that's not the goal of science. The real focus of any science is to *explain* facts. Collecting them is only the first step. This process of explaining facts is called the *scientific method*, and it works as follows.

We begin with some *observation* of natural phenomena. It could be the nest-building behavior of a bird, the light emissions from some distant galaxy, the wing pattern of viceroy butterflies, the social interaction of students in your classroom, or the funeral ritual of a society in highland New Guinea. As scientists, we wish to understand such observations, to know why and how such things occur as they do.

We need, in our search for an explanation, some starting point. So we begin by making what essentially are educated guesses as to possible explanations. These are *hypotheses*. Then comes the essence of science: We must attempt to support or refute each hypothesis. We do this through *testing* and *experimentation*. This may take many forms, depending on the observations and hypotheses involved. But in general we try to collect additional facts about the subject. We try to reproduce our observations and to formulate and carry out tests to see whether and under what circumstances our hypothesis works. We see if we can observe things that our hypothesis would logically predict.

If we find one piece of evidence that conclusively refutes our hypothesis, we consider it disproved. But if the hypothesis passes every test we can come up with, we elevate our idea to the status of a "very good hypothesis": a *theory*.

Notice that I didn't say we proved the hypothesis. Good science is always skeptical, always looking for new evidence, always open to change. The best we can honestly say about a theory is that so far no evidence has been found that disproves it.

It's very important to appreciate just what *theory* means here. It is an idea, proposed to explain some set of natural phenomena, that has failed to be refuted. It is a good idea. *Theory* is a positive term. Too often we hear an idea referred to as "just a theory," meaning, in the popular sense, "just a guess." We all use it this way from time to time. But within science, *theory* means what I've described. The "theory of evolution" or the "theory of gravity" or the "theory of relativity"—all are positive. All these ideas have become central concepts in modern science.

For example, go back to the discussion of descent with modification in Chapter 2. When I listed the evidence for this idea, I was really outlining the scientific method as it is brought to bear on the attempt to explain why species look the way they do and are related as they are. Descent with modification was a hypothesis to explain this, and the evidence listed amounted to the conclusions of all the tests of that hypothesis. Descent with modification is now considered a theory—an idea that has yet to be refuted and that passes every test applied to it.

Now we start over. If we accept descent with modification as a powerful enough idea to be a theory, in a sense it becomes a new observation. Observations need explanations. Darwin hypothesized an idea called *natural selection* to explain this. It is now a theory. And now we are working to test various hypotheses that attempt to explain just how selection works in specific cases, how important it is, and how much it has contributed to the origin of species.

Some hypotheses in this area haven't passed the tests. Lamarck's idea about the inheritance of acquired characteristics, for example, has failed time and again to be supported. It can be considered refuted, at least in that form. The same is true for the idea that maggots arise spontaneously in decaying meat or that Earth is the center of the universe.

Now, how is anthropology a science? Often we hear a distinction made between so-called hard sciences (like chemistry, biology, and physics) and soft sciences (the social sciences like political science, history, and anthropology). The scientific method, however, is a broad idea, not limited to the things we popularly think of as science. Laboratories and test tubes do not a science make. Science is a way of thinking, a method of explanation.

Anthropology, in all its endeavors, uses the scientific method. The specific features of the method differ enormously within anthropology, since the field is so broad and covers such a diverse array of topics. But science is always our methodology.

For example, anthropological *observations* might include aspects of human biological makeup, behaviors of some nonhuman primates, the variation among different societies in a certain cultural feature, or the presence of cultural universals like religion and marriage.

Our *hypotheses* then might take the form of principles from biology applied to the human species, ideas about the genetic bases of behavior, proposals attempting to relate the particular form of a cultural behavior to the nature of a society as a whole, or broad ideas about our species in general to account for the features found in all cultures.

Testing hypotheses in anthropology shows great diversity as well. It may involve more "typical" experimentation—things like lab tests on genetics or medical examinations. But it can also involve research into the fossil record of humans and related organisms. It can entail observation of a particular group of people or a comparison of observations made by several anthropologists of a number of different cultures. Whether the subject is "hard" or "soft," the method used to understand it is the scientific method. This should be clear from what has been discussed so far about evolution. I will show, as we continue, just how the method applies to all other topics within the discipline of anthropology.

But is science the only important kind of human knowledge? Of course not. Some human knowledge can be said to be *nonscientific*. By this I do not mean that nonscientific knowledge is less important than scientific knowledge. I merely mean that it has characteristics opposite those that define science. Specifically, nonscience involves ideas based on faith. Such ideas are not open to testing and explanation through the scientific method. Whereas science enables us to understand the natural world around us, nonscientific ideas deal with more abstract concepts, namely the relationships among people and between people and nature and people and the supernatural. Examples are religious beliefs, ethics, morals, and philosophical precepts.

Such ideas as the existence of a god, the morality of taking a human life, the humane treatment of animals, the number of wives a man may have, and cultural norms regarding proper sexual behavior are ideas that are taken on faith. They hold meaning for a particular group of people at a particular time. They are not statements about the natural world that need to be explained and tested. They are statements about the relationships of human beings.

Both scientific and nonscientific knowledge are necessary for a society of people to survive and function. Science allows people to understand the world in which they live and to take care of basic needs such as the acquisition of food, protection from the elements, and dealing with sickness. Nonscientific concepts help societies stay organized and integrated. They tell us how to behave toward our environment—an environment that includes humans and human culture as well as "nature."

It is important to keep these two realms of knowledge clearly in mind. For although the conclusions presented in this book are conclusions about human beings drawn from science, we will also be discussing differences among human cultures. And each human culture has its own version of this science-nonscience distinction. Each has its own ideas as to what is included in each category and its own version of the conclusions reached for each kind of knowledge. It can get confusing at times. On occasion, when people lack a scientific explanation for some phenomenon—disease for example—they will deal with it on a nonscientific basis. But the distinction, though the specifics vary, can be seen in any culture, and the two types of knowledge make up the basis for any society's way of life. As biologist John Maynard Smith says, "Scientific theories tell us what is possible; myths [nonscientific explanations] tell us what is desirable. Both are needed to guide proper action."

NOTES, REFERENCES, AND READINGS

The quote from Smith can be found in an article of his that discusses the relationship between science and the nonsciences. It's called "Science and Myth" and is in *Natural History* (November 1984). A detailed examination of the scientific method is Carl G. Hampel's *Philosophy of Natural Science* (Englewood Cliffs, N.J: Prentice-Hall, 1966), especially the first four chapters.

An interesting topic—on which we will touch only once in this book but which is both scientifically and socially important—is that of the "pseudosciences", or "false" sciences. These are ideas that confuse the important distinction between science and nonscience. Examples are things like astrology, claims about UFOs and extraterrestrial visitors, ideas about "pyramid power." These attempt to answer questions about the natural world but do so with a set of ideas taken on faith. No testing is involved. There is no attempt to disprove the hypotheses. Proponents of such claims usually seem to make data conform to their idea, rather than the other way around.

There are a number of interesting and informative examinations of pseudoscientific claims. One of the best is the section called "The Paradoxers" in Carl Sagan's *Broca's Brain: Reflections on the Romance of Science* (New York: Random House, 1979). A collection of articles on various pseudoscientific subjects can be found in *Science and the Paranormal: Probing the Existence of the Supernatural* (New York: Charles Scribner's Sons, 1981), edited by George O. Abell and Barry Singer. And there is an entire journal devoted to scientific examination of paranormal claims: *The Skeptical Inquirer* (P.O. Box 229, Central Park Station, Buffalo, NY 14215).

two

THE IDENTITY OF OUR SPECIES

chapter 4

Anatomy and Physiology
The Upright Primate

Entomologists study insects. Ichthyologists study fishes. Herpetologists study reptiles. Ornithologists study birds. Anthropologists study humans. Although we approach our study of humans in the same general way in which all these others study their organisms, anthropologists are limited by their focus on just a single species, *Homo sapiens*. To be sure, we are a complex enough species to warrant a whole discipline. But to do the job right, we need some perspective. We need to see where we fit in the overall biological scheme of things. We need to be able to compare and contrast ourselves with other organisms. We need to answer the question of just what a human is.

Because all organisms are related on that giant family tree of evolution, there are many groups to which we could compare ourselves in our attempt to gain this biological perspective. We will do this briefly with all the important groups. But to narrow it down to the level that will really identify us, we should see how we fit into the group of organisms that makes up our local cluster of branches on the tree. These are the organisms to which we are most closely related in the unfolding story of evolution. As you already realize, this group is the primates, the approximately 150 species that includes monkeys, apes, us, and some other animals you may be less familiar with.

How best to organize this comparison? There are many ways to categorize the features that identify a species. But three seem most relevant to our adaptive approach and ultimately encompass all the others:

1. Anatomy and physiology—what an organism looks like and how its body functions
2. Reproduction—the process whereby species perpetuate themselves (and the main thing that separates one species from another)
3. Knowing how to survive—the behavior of the organism; its adaptations to the features of its ecological niche

Using these categories, and considering ourselves as members of the order Primates, we can identify ourselves as "the upright primate," "the sexual primate," and "the cultural primate." Let's take them one at a time. As you will see, of course (the lesson of ecology), they are all intertwined into one evolutionary story.

NAMING THE ANIMALS

Recognition of some relationship among living things is nothing new. It is probably as old as human intellect itself. But formalizing this recognition was not always seen as important, even to the emerging science of biology at the beginning of the eighteenth century. After all, the plants and animals were then thought to be the unchanging products of divine creation, and an understanding of the evolutionary implications of biological relationships was many years in the future.

One eighteenth-century biologist, however, thought that a formalization was important, even if what he was concerned with was seen as forever fixed. This was the Swedish botanist Karl von Linné (1707–1778). He sought to create a system of names that would reflect the various relationships among all the creatures on Earth. He felt, of course, that he was proposing a way to describe a divine plan. But the system he devised, still used today, meant more than he ever dreamed.

What Linné did was create a system of categories of increasing specificity. The largest category contains within it many smaller categories, and so on, down to the most specific, which contains one item—in this case, one species. Such a system of classification is known as a *taxonomy*, and Linné proposed his taxonomy for plants and animals in his *Systema Naturae*, published in 1758. Another part of his system, by the way, was the use of Latin names. Indeed, he went so far as to Latinize his own name, becoming Carolus Linnaeus, the name by which we know him today.

Our present taxonomic system, based on Linnaeus's original scheme, uses seven basic categories: kingdom, phylum (plural, *phyla*), class, order, family, genus (plural, *genera*), and species. Each organism to be classified is given a name indicating its place within each of these categories and thus its relationship to other organisms. If we look at the taxonomy for four organisms, the system should become clear.

	Human	Chimpanzee	Dog	Wolf
Kingdom	Animalia	Animalia	Animalia	Animalia
Phylum	Chordata	Chordata	Chordata	Chordata
Class	Mammalia	Mammalia	Mammalia	Mammalia
Order	Primates	Primates	Carnivora	Carnivora
Family	Hominidae	Pongidae	Canidae	Canidae
Genus	*Homo*	*Pan*	*Canus*	*Canus*
Species	*sapiens*	*troglodytes*	*familiaris*	*lupus*

We already have some concept that these four species constitute two major groups, a ''humanlike'' group and a ''dog'' group. See how this is reflected in the taxonomic chart. The human and the chimp belong to one order, the dog and wolf to another. Before that, in the higher categories, all four are the same.

Now what happens? Notice that at the next level, family, humans and chimps separate. Dogs and wolves, however, stay in the same groups all the way to the most specific level, species. What all this means is that dogs are more closely related to wolves than humans are to chimps. Even without knowing just what all those strange-looking words mean (we'll get to that), you can easily see the relationships that the taxonomy reflects.

A brief note should be added here with regard to use of these names. Usually, an organism can be referred to by its genus and species names, for this combination is shared with no other living thing. (The species name alone won't do, since these are usually descriptive and can be used for a number of organisms.) Genus names begin with a capital letter; species names with a small letter. And since these Latin (or Greek) names are foreign, they are italicized; thus *Homo sapiens* (Latin for ''man'' and ''wise'') and *Pan troglodytes* (*Pan* from a West African word for the creature, *troglodytes*, the ''cave dweller''—a reference to the erroneous belief that chimps lived in caves.)

Now, as far as Linnaeus knew, he was describing a static, divinely created system of living things. Today, however, we know just how the relationships among organisms have come about—namely, through the processes of descent with modification. And Linnaeus's taxonomic system reflects evolutionary relationships as well as those among present-day creatures. Why? Simply because the degree of similarity or difference between two organisms is a direct reflection of the amount of time they have been evolutionarily separated. It is evolution in different directions—along different

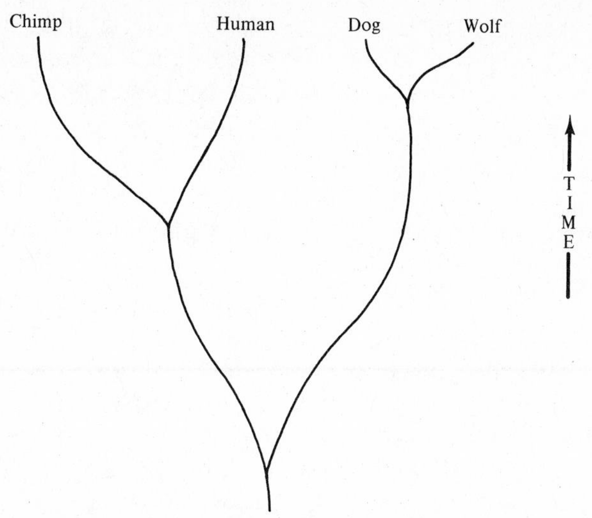

Evolutionary tree of wolf, dog, chimpanzee, and human.

branches—that makes organisms different. So a taxonomy, although it can't give us specific dates for the evolutionary branchings, can tell us something about the *relative* times of the evolutionary episodes.

The dog-wolf group and the human-chimpanzee group differ at the order level. This suggests an evolutionary divergence in the relatively distant past (although not as distant, say, as two organisms distinct at the phylum level). Humans diverge from chimps at the next, or family, level, but dogs and wolves don't part evolutionary company until the last, the species, level. This indicates that the human-chimp split took place much longer ago than did the dog-wolf split. Of course, with actual dates the relative positions of the branchings could change a little, but this is still just about what it would look like.

The actual dates, according to latest evidence, are 5 to 10 million years for the human-chimp split and about 12,000 for the wolf-dog. And this brings up a related point. You may well be asking about wolf-dog hybrids. Can't these two species interbreed and produce fertile offspring? If so, how come they are different species? Well, yes they can (as long as the dog parent is large enough). And the answer to the second question is that, as you recall, speciation is a process. It doesn't take place instantly, even in its most rapid form. Dogs and wolves are really in the first stage of speciation—separate environments. And because the environment of the dog is domestication under humans, we consider the dog and its wild cousin the wolf to be ecologically separate and therefore reproductively isolated from one another. Whether two species *can* interbreed is not as important to the definition as whether they *do* interbreed.

As with Mendel's genetics, Linnaeus's taxonomic system has been added to and refined as new knowledge has been gained. But each man's basic idea is with us today and provides the basis for these two fields of biology.

Linnaeus, of course, lived before genetics, before biochemistry, before ethology, before a theory of evolution. He based his conclusions about organism similarity and difference solely on appearance and what was known of behavior. Considering that, he did a remarkable job, for many of his conclusions are still accepted. Now, however, we have the ability to compare organisms not only for appearance but also for chemistry, details of behavior, and even the genes themselves. Because of this we now see that organism relationships can be a little more complex than Linnaeus imagined. One way in which we have refined his system is by adding new categories to his basic seven in order to capture better the various sorts of relationships among groups of living things.

Here is a taxonomy for the primates. Again, we'll get to the meanings of the words, but you can readily see that some new categories have been added: suborder, infraorder, and superfamily. Members of the Primate order come in two basic types, the two suborders. The second suborder has a major division along geographic lines: Some of these primates evolved in the New World (Western Hemisphere), the rest in the Old World (Eastern Hemisphere). Such a major geographic separation is of obvious evolutionary importance and thus in need of taxonomic categories to reflect it. Finally, there are groups of families among the primates that arrange themselves into larger categories we call superfamilies. (If you think this is complicated, check out a taxonomy of insects!)

The chart, by the way, doesn't include genus and species names. That would make it too complicated. It just lists the common names of a few example primates. At this point, suffice it to say that there are about 50 genera with 150 species of primates. These are not evenly distributed. The family Cercopithecidae has 14 genera; Hominidae has only one genus, and it has only one living species—us, of course.

I said "about" 50 genera and 150 species because taxonomy, like any science, is an ongoing study, and there is by no means complete agreement as to just how all the primates are related. Thus

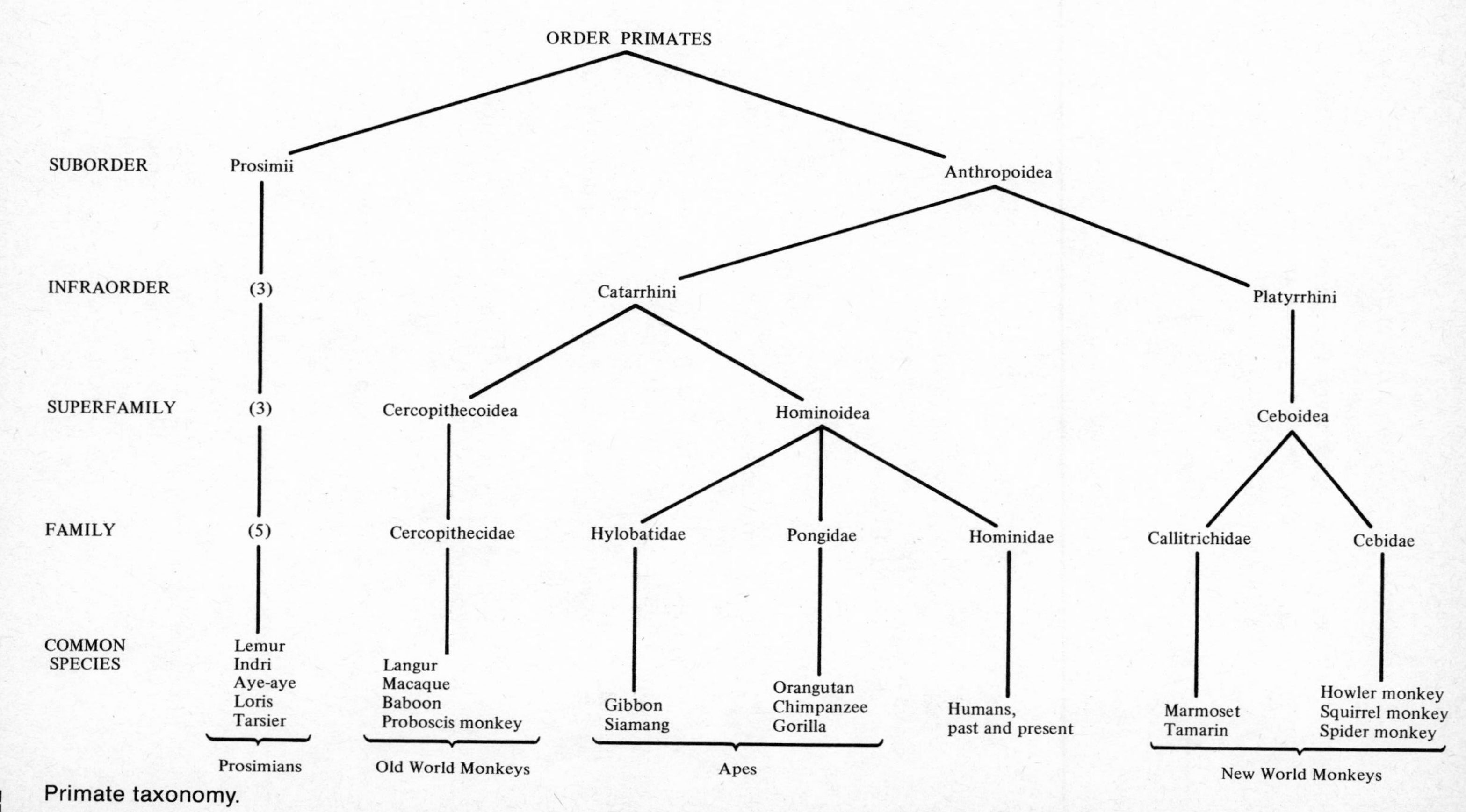

Primate taxonomy.

there are a number of primate taxonomies that differ in details but not in basic setup.

Now, look over the chart and make sure you understand the mechanics of it—what it shows and how. Then let's move on to the primates themselves and some of those names.

INTO THE TREES

> The organization of the anthropoid *Quadrumana* [four-footed walkers] justifies the naturalist in placing them at the head of brute creation, and placing them in a position in which they, of all the animal series, shall be nearest to man.

That statement appeared in the December 1847 issue of the *Boston Journal of Natural History* in an article containing the first scientific description of a gorilla. What is interesting is that even in those days before Darwin's book, science recognized the similarity between humans and the apes and monkeys. In fact, that recognition had been formalized by Linnaeus 100 years earlier when he placed both humans and the known monkeys and apes in the same order, Primates.

But we must now ask, just what is a primate? Why are humans included in this group? How are humans similar to the other primates? How are they different?

Let's begin by placing the primates in a broader biological perspective. It's easier that way to appreciate the characteristics that define them.

Look back at the chart comparing the four species. Note that all four are members of the kingdom Animalia. That seems obvious enough. But what are the other kingdoms of living things? Well, there are five altogether:

1. Monera—single-celled organisms with no internal structures. Called *prokaryotes*. Examples are bacteria and blue-green algae.
2. Protista—single-celled organisms with internal structures. Called *eukaryotes*. Examples are amoebas and paramecia.
3. Fungi—multicellular organisms rooted to a single spot that feed by absorbing nutrients from an external source. They do not photosynthesize. Examples are mushrooms, molds, and mildews.
4. Plantae—multicellular organisms rooted to a single spot that do photosynthesize, that is, form their own nutrients using

carbon dioxide, water, chlorophyll, and sunlight. Many examples, from redwood trees to the grasses.

5. Animalia—multicellular organisms that have means of locomotion, nervous systems, and sense organs. They must secure their nutrients from external sources. Examples are sponges, worms, clams, apple maggots, and humans.

Within the kingdom Animalia are more than a dozen phyla. We, however, are members of the phylum Chordata. Chordates have a dorsal ("in the back") nervous system and a *notochord*, a rod or cord that acts as a support. One chordate subphylum, Vertebrata, has a backbone that surrounds and protects the spinal cord and notochord. We, obviously, are vertebrates.

Within the vertebrate chordates are, as you would expect, a number of classes. In fact, there are seven: the lampreys (a sort of scaleless, jawless fish), the cartilaginous fishes (sharks and rays), the bony fishes, amphibians, reptiles, birds, and mammals. We are mammals, which means that we have hair, maintain a constant body temperature (commonly described as being "warm-blooded"), give birth to live young, nourish the young with milk from mammary glands, and have a complex brain.

At this point I must digress a moment for an important idea. An organism does not reside in a certain category only because it possesses a list of characteristics. All those strange names refer to *types* of organisms—kinds of living things that are adapted in a certain fashion to a certain sort of environment. Adaptation—way of life—is the key here. Thus there can be other creatures that share certain traits with the mammals. Birds, for example, are warm-blooded, and some fishes and reptiles give birth to live young. But adaptively speaking, a bird is still a bird, and a shark that bears its young alive is still a fish.

Moreover, a member of a certain group need not possess all the traits listed for that group. The duckbilled platypus and the spiny anteater, both from Australia, are mammals that lay eggs! Except for this difference, though, they are in every way good members of the mammal class.

The class Mammalia contains about 18 orders, each representing a cluster of branches on the evolutionary tree. There are, for instance, the marine mammals like the whales and porpoises, the rodents, the bats, the seals and walruses, the odd-toed hoofed mammals like the horse, the even-toed hoofed mammals like the cow, pig, and giraffe, the rabbits and hares, the meat eaters, and the primates.

The order Primates is divided into two suborders, Prosimii, the "premonkeys," and Anthropoidea, the "humanlike" primates. The prosimians represent the early primates and possess a number of features not found in the newer primates. For example, most prosimians are nocturnal, or active at night. They tend to have less well developed color vision and less dexterous hands, and some have claws on two of their toes instead of the usual primate nails. Also, because they are nocturnal, they have a better sense of smell than do the anthropoids.

This is not to say, however, that the prosimians are not perfectly good primates. Despite some "primitive" features, they do exhibit the complex of traits that facilitates the primate way of life. This does not mean either that the prosimians *are* the early primates or that all later ones have evolved from a living prosimian. Each living primate is the product of millions of years of evolution. Some have simply changed more slowly or to a lesser extent and so resemble some of the early members of the group.

Below the two suborders, the primates are classified according to all the features that are important in defining evolutionary groups: geography, anatomy, physiology, genetics, behavior, and reproductive isolation. I'll describe the evolution of the primates in the next section.

Now, what are the primate characteristics? They can be conveniently divided into six categories, as follows:

1. The Brain

The two words that describe the primate brain are *large* and *complex*. *Large* is used here in a relative sense. A sperm whale, for instance, has a brain larger than that of any primate (in fact, it's the largest brain known, about 20 pounds!), but relative to the size of its body it's not as large as the brain of even small primates. In other words, primates operate less body with more brain than other creatures. By *complex* we mean that the brain has more nerve connections, larger parts associated with what we would consider "thought," and more ability to take in and use information from the outside. With caution we can say that the primates are "intelligent." Of all primate brains, humans have the biggest, both absolutely and relatively. Our average brain size is 1450 cubic centimeters, more than twice the size of the closest, the 525-cm^3 brain of the gorilla.

A tarsier. A small primate with relatively large brain and large eyes for night vision.

2. The Eyes

Primates are visual creatures. They take in most of their data through the eyes. To facilitate this, primate eyes see in *colors* and in *three dimensions*. The latter, called *stereoscopic vision*, is possible because the eyes face forward and have overlapping fields of vision, and the signals from the eyes are processed in the brain in such a way as to give us primates true depth perception. Watch a gibbon swing from branch to branch or an outfielder catch a fly ball to see just how good this stereoscopic vision is. The eyes of primates are enclosed in a *bony socket* that protects the delicate muscles and nerves. The eyes of other animals are much less well protected. Of course, the area of the brain that processes vision, the *visual cortex*, is greatly expanded in the primates over other mammals. Here, by the way, is one area where prosimians differ; the nocturnal prosimians don't see in color as well as the anthropoid primates. They do, however, have large eyes that take in relatively more light.

3. The Face

The faces of primates, as viewed from the side, are *flat*. Most lack the long, protruding snout of, say, a horse or even a cat or dog. As you might expect, one related feature here concerns the sense of smell. Primates don't smell very well. (Some don't smell very good either!) The smell or *olfactory* sensory areas in the nose are much smaller than in other mammals, and the corresponding area of the brain is reduced. Primates have traded smell for sight as a means of acquiring information. There is, of course, some variation here; the nocturnal prosimians tend to have a better olfactory sense to aid their particular lifestyle. In addition, again connected with facial flatness, the primates have generally a *smaller number of teeth* than other mammals, and the teeth tend to be more *generalized*, that is, not geared toward one specific kind of food.

4. The Hands and Feet

One of the most striking things about the primates is their humanlike hands. Of course, looking at it in evolutionary perspective, we have primatelike hands. The hands of primates are *prehensile*, or grasping. In addition, the feet of many primates have some prehensile ability, in a few cases as much as the hands. This is one respect in which humans differ. The hands of primates are also said to have *opposability*; that is, the thumb can touch, or "oppose," the other fingers. There is a good deal of variation in this feature: Some primates are able to oppose the tips of the fingers, some just the sides of the thumb and first finger, and some must move all the other fingers toward the thumb together, since they don't move well independently. In any case, some degree of this ability is present in all primates, giving them, to some extent, what we call a *precision grip*. The ends of most primates' fingers and toes are adorned with flat nails instead of the claws typical of many other mammals. Some of the prosimians have retained a claw on their second toes. This is called a *grooming claw* and is used for just that. Otherwise, all their digits have nails.

A loris with grooming claw.

Although it is not a hand or foot, some primates have a fifth grasping organ—a tail. We have a popular image of monkeys hanging by their tails, but in fact a prehensile tail is possessed only by a few species of South American monkeys. Those that have it, though, have a very dexterous, strong grasping appendage.

5. The Limbs

The arms and legs of primates are characterized by great *flexibility*. The arms especially, attached toward the sides of the shoulders, are capable of all manner of twisting and turning. The acrobatics of a gibbon or the grace and power of a gymnast on the uneven parallel bars clearly shows this. In addition, for primates that clamber about

A New World monkey with a prehensile tail. Notice also its flat face.

in the trees using both hands and grasping feet, the legs as well are flexible and strong. To help support the stresses placed on the arms and shoulders, the primates have a well-developed *clavicle*, or collarbone. This rugged bone, extending from the outer edge of the shoulders to the sternum, or breastbone, acts as a brace between the shoulder girdle and the center of the body. While most primates are *quadrupedal* ("walking on all fours"), all the primates have some ability to sit, stand, or walk *erect*. For some, this is limited to the sitting position. Others can stand on two legs (are *bipedal*) or even walk that way for short periods of time. Some are erect when hanging by their arms. And humans are habitually bipedal. So although we are the only primates built to stand and walk perpendicular to the ground all the time, all the primates have anatomical differences from the other mammals that allow some expression of this ability. An important result of this is that erectness, when it is used, frees the arms and hands from locomotor functions and allows them to explore and manipulate the environment.

A gibbon brachiating.

A baboon mother and infant.

6. Reproduction

Primates characteristically have *one baby at a time*. Twins are about as common in nonhuman primates as they are in humans, with the exception of lemurs and marmosets, which normally have twins. The primate offspring has a *long period of development and dependency*. It is usually many years before the young primate can fend for itself and many more years before it reaches physical and sexual maturity. This period is proportional to the size of the primate, but in general, all the primates take longer to grow up than other mammals, many of which may be sexually mature within a year or less.

As you can see from this brief discussion, not all the primates possess all the characteristics listed for the order as a whole. Moreover, there are other animals that share some primate features. Birds and insects, for example, have color vision. Some birds, cats, and even frogs exhibit some degree of stereoscopy. Birds and chameleon lizards have prehensile feet. Porpoises have large, complex brains, and some even have the same brain-to-body-size ratio as humans.

So what is a primate? It is an organism that possesses a general complex of characteristics that make it adapted in a particular way to a particular kind of environment. And for the primates, that environment is the trees. The primates are said to be *arboreal*, or tree-dwelling. If you review the list of primate traits, you can easily see how this is so. Primate vision, for instance, is obviously useful when dealing with the complex niche of the trees, where various colors and shapes abound and where you have to worry not only about right, left, forward, and back but also up and down! Having grasping hands and, sometimes, feet allows the primates to move with agility and safety through the branches. The flexible limbs, with support from the clavicles, aid this behavior. Having one young at a time is clearly more efficient than lugging a litter around. Finally—here's the crucial part—the big brain reflects an emphasis on learning as a way of coping with the problems presented by such a complex environment. And the long period of dependency gives young primates the time they need to learn all they must know.

Human beings obviously differ in a number of respects from the other primates. It would be a mistake, however, to think that we are the only different primate. Indeed, there is no "typical" primate. Each species has its own unique variation on the basic primate arboreal theme, its own particular way of dealing with its version of the primate niche. Some of the distinctions of the human primate have already been noted, and most should be obvious to you anyway. But it it important to go over them and make them clear, because the features that make us unique are the features that came about during the evolution of our branch of the family tree. Those features are the outline of the story of the human species.

1. Of all the primate brains, the human brain is the largest, both relatively and absolutely, and it is the most complex. In other words, it does more, takes in more information, and processes that information in a more complex manner. (We'll go into more detail on the brain in Chapter 6.)
2. Human eyes are typical, at least among the *diurnal* (''active during the day'') anthropoid primates.
3. The human face is among the flattest of primate faces, and the human teeth among the most generalized. Our sense of smell is probably no less well developed than in any of the anthropoids.
4. The human hand has the longest primate thumb and thus the best opposability and most precise grip. Our feet, of course, have no prehensile ability whatever. They are completely flat and are related to our bipedal posture and locomotion.
5. Human arms are about the most flexible among the primates, being entirely freed from locomotor activities and therefore used for a multitude of other purposes. In general, the limbs of the human primate, as well as numerous features of the pelvis, the head, other parts of the skeleton, and the muscle system, are all built to facilitate our habitual, terrestrial bipedal standing and walking. As you will see, this seems to be the trend that set off our evolution.
6. Of all slow-developing primate young, the human youngster takes the longest to grow up physically, sexually, and intellectually. This is, of course, directly connected with our large, complex brains and the importance of the information we put into and process in those brains.

Now we must take a look at the physical evidence for the evolution of the characteristics that make up our version of the primate organism.

OUT OF THE TREES

It is difficult to examine the human species adequately without placing it in the context of the whole Primate order. It is likewise difficult

The human primate: biological differences and the cultural dimension.

to look at the story of the human branch of the evolutionary tree without also examining at least a part of the rest of the tree—the part concerned with the evolution of the primates. As with so many other topics, we can begin this one with a question: What about squirrels?

What *about* squirrels? Well, squirrels, along with opossums and a number of other *marsupial* (pouched) mammals, are, like the primates, well adapted to an arboreal niche. But unlike the primates, they all have claws, nongrasping hands and feet, and wide-set eyes with no stereoscopic vision. If these creatures are so well adapted through this set of traits, how can the primate features also be geared to an arboreal way of life? Can two sets of adaptive traits work as well? The traits of the squirrels, after all, are the more primitive, or older, mammalian features.

In 1974 anthropologist Matt Cartmill wrote an article that seems to clear up this problem and alters the simple, traditional explanation that the primate features *arose* as a result of the kind of arboreal adaptation we see today. Cartmill found, as we just did, some other organisms that share important primate traits, and he noted the adaptive use of these features.

For example, the prehensile hands and feet of chameleons and small marsupials are adapted to quick, precise movement through dense bushy undergrowth and to the manual ("by hand") capture of prey, mainly insects. The close-set, stereoscopic eyes of cats, for a second example, help those creatures "zero in" on prey and calculate its position and distance with maximum accuracy. Thus, though the current primate features work just fine in the trees, those features seem more likely to have *arisen* to make possible life in the "slender supports" of bushes and undergrowth and the capture of small, fast-moving insect prey. Later modifications of and additions to this basic set of features then led to the array of well-adapted, tree-dwelling primates we know today and from the recent evolutionary past.

The lesson here is that one cannot simply look at the present-day situation and conclude that these observed relationships tell the whole story. There's more than one way to live in the trees, no way necessarily better or worse or with the same origin. Just different. This is an important concept to which we shall return in considering variations in human cultural adaptations.

Anyway, this adaptive trend began more than 65 million years ago. There is little fossil evidence for this earliest phase of primate evolution, but some fossil teeth from about that time clearly show primate features. The earliest is from what is now Montana—a single, primatelike tooth from what was probably a small rat-looking creature. It lived when the last of the dinosaurs was walking the Earth.

This find, by the way, does not mean that the primates originated in North America. At that time the continents were not positioned where they are today. Continents move, or "drift"—floating, in a way, on the layer of liquid rock below. Some 65 million years ago, what are now North America and Eurasia were joined, and Africa and South America, once joined, were drifting apart. (When mammals were first evolving, in fact, these four continents, along with India, Australia, and Antarctica, were all connected in one continuous land mass we call *Pangea*, or "all lands.") Fossil evidence of the earliest primates indicates that they were found in the northern landmass, made up of North America and Eurasia and called *Laurasia*. We don't know at this point precisely where they began.

These very early primates remind us of modern prosimians, having "primitive" features such as claws and longer snouts. Indeed, if we could see one alive today, until we examined it closely, we might think it some squirrellike animal.

Around 55 million years ago, Eurasia and North America separated. The New World and Old World were formed, and the primates were split into two main groups. By 30 million years ago, Africa and Eurasia had rejoined and North and South America had moved very close together. As climatic changes took place, making the northern areas colder, many animals, including many primates, were able to move to the warmer, southern landmasses.

At about this time, some of the early prosimianlike primates were undergoing further evolution, as new, unexploited niches opened up. They were evolving toward more arboreal, larger-brained creatures—the monkeys. These new, highly successful animals, able to exploit the tree-dwelling environment with great efficiency, became competitors with the prosimians. In the Americas there are now no living prosimians. In the Old World the prosimians are relatively few and tend to live in isolated areas. Most species can be found only on Madagascar, an island that split from the mainland of Africa before the monkeys evolved, providing a safe haven for prosimian evolution.

Continents continued to move, and climates continued to change. As environments were altered, more new, unexploited niches opened up, providing new evolutionary opportunities for the primates. One new evolutionary development is first glimpsed about 25 million years ago. It involved a group of larger-bodied, larger-brained primates, ones who were still arboreally adapted but who may also have spent time on the ground. They were perhaps a little more generalized in their adaptations, a little more flexible in exploiting their niches. These were the first apes.

That first glimpse is provided by a fossil called *Aegyptopithecus* (*pith* meaning "ape," the rest of the name indicating the location of the find). This fossil is one of those called "transitional" because it possesses characteristics of several branches of a group's evolutionary tree. *Aegyptopithecus* displays features of both monkeys and apes. It very likely represents the period when some of the monkeys were undergoing evolutionary change toward this new type of primate.

As with the monkeys, the apes were a very successful evolutionary "invention." Between about 23 million and 14 million years ago, numerous types of apes flourished throughout Europe, Africa, and Asia. These widespread, Old World apes can be lumped together into one taxonomic family, the *Dryopithecidae* (again, *pith* for "ape"; *dryo* for "oak"—the first specimen was found in France in an oak forest). They varied from gibbon-sized to a huge grain eater from India and China who stood maybe 9 feet tall and weighed up to 600 pounds and is called *Gigantopithecus* (no explanation needed).

One of the fossil forms from the latter part of this period is particularly important not only in and of itself but also for the lesson it provides about the nature of the science of paleoanthropology. It is called *Ramapithecus* (after a Hindu mythological hero), and its remains have been found in India, Africa and southern Europe. It is important because the interpretation of the first fossils of *Ramapithecus* to be recovered indicated that it possessed certain features not like those of the apes but rather like those of humans. These were mostly traits of the teeth and jaws, which made up the bulk of the fossil material then on hand. *Ramapithecus* was seen as the first hominid, the first member of the human family. And since the fossils dated from between 14 and 12 million years ago, the beginnings of our family seemed to be ancient indeed.

Now, however, some new finds and new interpretations have apparently changed all that. We still, it seems, are missing the earliest member of our branch of the tree. In the last few years more complete fossil skulls of *Ramapithecus* have been found, as well as some postcranial ("below the head") bones. "Rama," it appears, was not the human-looking, partial biped that early interpretations imagined it to be. Instead, it looks as if it was very much like the modern-day orangutan, a good, solid ape. In fact, *Ramapithecus* may represent the beginning of the orangutan branch. The search continues.

Hominid evolution (left to right): *Homo habilis, Homo erectus, Homo sapiens* (Neanderthal), *Homo sapiens* from 25,000 years ago, modern *Homo sapiens.*

About 12 million years, ago, a major, and, for us, most important climatic change slowly began. Conditions around much of the world became increasingly drier, and the great forests that were home for the dryopithecine apes began to disappear and give way to open plains or "savannas." Many of the apes became extinct. Only those that could cope with the new life, in the now smaller forests, were able to hang on. These were the ancestors of the four modern apes, the gibbon and orangutan of southeastern Asia and the chimpanzee and gorilla of Africa. And in Africa another apelike creature, which we have yet to identify, took a different evolutionary path. It left life in the trees and moved first to the forest floor and then out onto the open, vast, and dangerous savannas that dominated most of the continent.

There is virtually no fossil evidence of this transition, but when we do pick up the fossil record again, about 3.5 million years ago, what we see is clearly human. It was apelike in facial features and had a brain not much larger than a gorilla's. But it had human teeth, it walked around completely upright—something no other primate can do—and it had human hands that a million years later made the first stone tools.

So we hypothesize that as the forests declined, one form of apelike primate, perhaps a little better at bipedal locomotion and a little more nimble of hand and brain, found itself able to exploit the new niche where open forest met savanna, and, later, the savanna itself. Five or six million years later, some descendents of these "ape-men" wrote and are reading this book. Because this evolutionary change is so important—it is, after all, our very beginning—we will go into more detail in Chapter 5 about how we think it actually took place. For now, though, suffice it to say that all the evidence indicates that it did.

From 3.5 million to about 1.5 million years ago, our evolutionary story, as Darwin once predicted, is an African one. No human fossils from that period have been found outside the continent. In Africa, however, the remains of our ancestors are widespread. Fossils have been unearthed from Ethiopia down the eastern portion of the continent to the southern tip. A few fragmentary remains have been found in the north and northwest. And—a most surprising thing to many people—the hominid fossils from this African period seem to represent *two* branches of human evolution! Although there is only one species of human alive today, there apparently were at least two types of people around during this 2-million-year stage.

The members of one branch are placed into the genus *Australopithecus*. Yes, it does mean "southern ape." This is because when these fossils were first discovered and described, in the 1920s, they were thought to be just that (although their discoverer hinted that they were part of the human evolutionary lineage.)

This australopithecine branch is certainly human by the criteria of upright posture, relatively large brain, and dental and other anatomical details. But it became extinct about one million years ago without ever achieving the very large brain or the ability to manufacture stone tools that marked the branch that gave rise to us. The evolutionary trend in this extinct line seems to have been toward larger, more robust, mostly vegetarian hominids. Indeed, some of the remains toward the end of this branch exhibit features of teeth and chewing muscles that resemble those of the gorilla, the big ape specialized for a diet of sometimes tough vegetable matter.

The fossil form, 3.5 million years old, which many anthropologists feel represents the common ancestor of both our branch and the extinct one, is also placed in the genus *Australopithecus*. This is *A. afarensis* (because the first fossil was found in the Afar region of Ethiopia; *A.* because when you've used a name often enough, you don't have to keep writing it!). The "type" fossil, the one that established the features and the name, is the famous Lucy, so called because the evening after she was found in 1974 the Beatles' "Lucy in the Sky with Diamonds'' was on the expedition's tape recorder (anthropologists are only human). In the few years after that, more *afarensis* fossils were discovered in Ethiopia. They are important because they are so complete (40 percent of Lucy's skeleton was preserved) and because they show that without a doubt, we were completely bipedal over 3 million years ago, *before* we had acquired our large brains or the ability to make anything more complex than simple wood and maybe bone tools. In an evolutionary sense, we are indeed the ''upright primate,'' for bipedalism was the first human feature to evolve. And because Lucy, except for her upright posture, is otherwise so ''primitive,'' it doesn't look like we are much older than she—certainly not anything like the 12 million years once claimed.

At first it was not thought that bipedalism could be that old, or the human evolutionary line that recent. But as if to answer those objections, a remarkable piece of corroborating evidence came to light in 1976 and 1977. At a site in Tanzania called Laetoli, a 75-foot trail of footprints was discovered. These prints had been made in fresh volcanic ash 3.7 million years ago by two completely bipedal hominids. The prints are nearly indistinguishable from those of a modern human. This leaves little room for doubt about the interpretation of *afarensis*'s anatomy, locomotor behavior, or age.

The exact place of *afarensis* in the human evolutionary story is still under debate. The most popular current idea says the form is the common ancestor of both the extinct australopithecine branch and the one that evolved into modern humans. A second school of thought says that the split took place earlier and that *afarensis* is part of the extinct branch only. Either idea could turn out to be correct—or neither.

The first evidence for the branch that evolved into modern humans comes from 2.5 million years ago. The evidence is in the form of hominid fossils from eastern and southern Africa that display larger brains, flatter faces, and more modern teeth than their australopithecine contemporaries. In addition, the fossils are found in association with simple stone tools. The people are called *Homo habilis* (*Homo*, a member of our genus; *habilis*, ''the skillful one'').

Why are stone tools so important? First of all, they are the only type of early tool that leaves good evidence. A stick or a bone, even if it has been modified into a tool, may simply not be preserved for over 2 million years, and even if it is, it can be awfully hard to tell if some early human changed it in some way and used it as a tool. More important, though, it is a huge intellectual achievement to take a stone and modify it so as to give it a certain shape that allows it to be used for a particular purpose. To "see," to imagine, a tool within a plain old rock and to be able to conceptualize the process whereby that plain old rock can be turned into the tool involves some very sophisticated thinking. It is the kind of thinking that we do every day but is not found to that degree anywhere else in the living world.

These early stone tools seem simple to us—mostly large, smooth pebbles with a flake or two knocked off one end to make a cutting or chopping edge. But this innovation gave *H. habilis* a real advantage in the harsh savanna environment. Armed with stronger, more durable tools, our ancestors would be better able to protect themselves, to dig up underground plant foods, to shape wood and bone for tools, to chase predators away from their kills in order to scavenge, and, at about this time, begin actively to hunt—at first small animals, later the large game herds so plentiful at that time on the savannas.

We were gradually evolving from just an odd new creature, one of thousands inhabiting the plains, into a successful and formidable factor in the ecology of that environment. And as this tool-making adaptation advanced, it further enhanced selection for the big brains and complex mental functioning that gave rise to it in the first place. The aspects of human evolution were feeding back on one another, each promoting changes in the others. So the brains got bigger, the teeth and jaws relatively smaller and more adapted to a mixed diet, the hands more dexterous.

About 1.5 million years ago, in East Africa, we find the first evidence of a new stage in the human story. It is a stage that lasted over a million years and saw some major advances in biology and culture toward what we now recognize as modern humans. This is the stage called *Homo erectus* ("the human who stands upright"). Yes, we know now that we were bipedal at least 2 million years earlier. But when the first *H. erectus* fossils were discovered around the turn of this century, scientists didn't know that, and these, thought then to be the oldest human fossils, were assumed to be the first upright people. The name has stuck despite its inaccurate implication.

Homo erectus, from the neck down, was virtually modern in appearance, though shorter and more robust than most present-day people. The head still retained some of the ruggedness of the *habilis* stage, but the brain size, though on the average smaller than ours today, now overlapped the modern human range. In other words, the largest *H. erectus* brains were bigger than the smallest *H. sapiens* brains. And since we know that among modern humans, brain size and intelligence have no relation, we can infer that *H. erectus* probably had nearly our intellectual potential.

Their cultural achievements bear this out, for along with these early *erectus* bones from Africa are the tools these people made, tools that evidence a technological and intellectual leap. The tool that characterizes the stage is the *hand ax*. It is an improvement over the old "pebble tools" in being larger and modified all over so as to shape "to order" both its handle and its "business end." It also generally displays finer control over its shaping. It was a popular and useful tool. At several African sites it is found by the thousands.

Our ancestors now had real mastery over that most important aspect of their environment, their food source. Now they could, and did, exploit the vast herds of big-game ungulates (antelopes and the like) of the savannas. And a good adaptation it was, for by a little under a million years ago, we find *H. erectus* not only in Africa but as far away as southern Europe, southeast Asia, and northern China. The adaptations, originally geared to the open plains of Africa, turned out to be good all over, and in the continual search for food, water, and shelter, *H. erectus* wandered from its tropical homeland to the very foot of the great glaciers of the ice ages.

The period of the ice ages, known to geologists as the Pleistocene, is important to human evolution because as our *H. erectus* ancestors were spreading throughout the Old World (and later, as *Homo sapiens*, into the New World), the continual climatic changes brought about by the advance and retreat of the glaciers provided these people with constant challenges to their new cultural adaptation. Everywhere they went they found new sorts of environments, environments that were, however slowly, always changing.

What happened in the Pleistocene is briefly this: For reasons not yet fully understood, the average temperature of the Earth dropped a few degrees. This occurred about four times in the past million and a half years. When that happened, the snow that accumulated on the polar ice caps and tops of mountains in the winter could not all melt away in the summer. So it started to build up. Over the course of tens of thousands of years, the result is the "squeezing out" of huge sheets of ice from the polar caps and down the mountains. These are not the sheets of ice that cover our roads and make driving hazardous. These glacial sheets were sometimes a mile thick! As they moved southward from the Arctic and down various mountain ranges, they literally changed the landscape, goug-

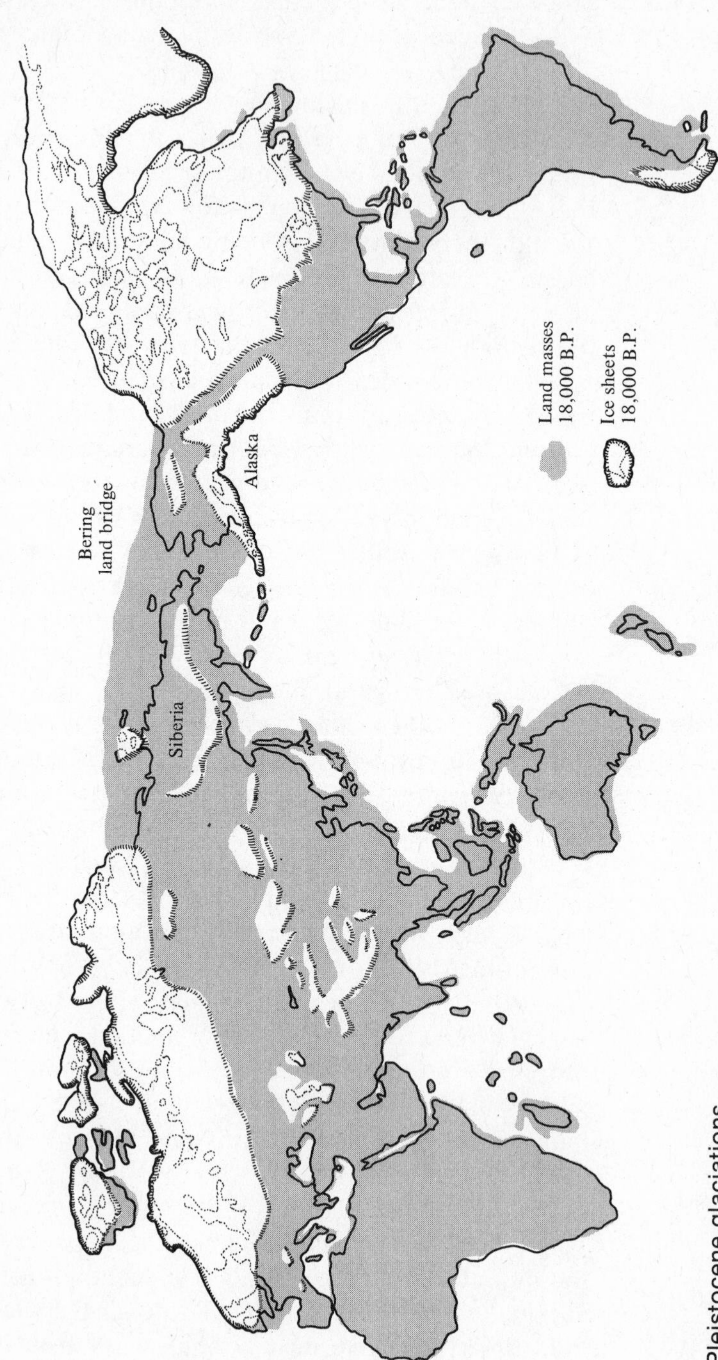

Pleistocene glaciations.

ing out valleys, flattening hills, making new hills out of the debris they pushed in front of them. Long Island, New York, for example, is made up largely of rocks that originated far to the north and were left when glaciers retreated. Moreover, with so much of Earth's water tied up in the glaciers, sea levels dropped, exposing land and creating new migration routes. This is how humans got to the New World—over a land bridge between Siberia and Alaska.

Besides changing the landscape, the Pleistocene glaciations also altered the climatic conditions around the world and thus the kinds of plants and animals that lived in various regions. As you can see from the map, the tropical, temperate, and arctic zones were all compressed into a smaller area than they are now. Then, during the period between glacial advances, called *interglacials*, they expanded again.

This was the world our ancestors faced during a time from over a million years ago to nearly 10,000 years ago—the very time we were becoming biologically and culturally modern.

So as *H. erectus* populations migrated over the Eastern Hemisphere, they were challenged by this environment to think up technological and social inventions that could help them cope and survive. The general result of this, as we see in the fossil and archaeological records, is the beginning of cultural variation among these populations. Tools, the only cultural remains left to us from this time, differed from place to place, as did the physical appearance of the people themselves. In addition, our ancestors were getting away from the single, all-purpose hand ax and were making strides in the manufacture of various tools for specific purposes. We begin to see, as early as a million years ago, the use not only of the modified stone, the *core tool*, but also of the flakes taken off the core. These were probably used as knives or as scrapers for wood or animal hides. Tools for particular jobs, tools to make other tools, tools geared to the needs of the specific group in its specific environment—all the things that characterize our technology today—were on the way. (I'll describe and illustrate early tools in more detail in Chapter 9.)

Another cultural innovation from this time changed us forever: the control of fire. The earliest evidence that humans knew how to control and use fire comes from southern France about a million years ago, and a little later from other parts of Europe and northern China. It is not surprising that the earliest evidence comes from places that, because of the glaciers, were cold. An obvious attribute of fire is its heat. But it can also be used to scare off animals and keep them out of one's cave, for cooking food, for stampeding animals during a hunt, for hardening the points of wooden spears, and for light. This last use, suggests science writer John Pfeiffer, may be the most important in the long run. For the light from a fire lengthens the day. It makes people more independent of the rising and setting of the sun. Literally sitting "around the old campfire" at night, people could exchange information, tell stories, plan activities, experiment with new toolmaking techniques. Fire become a social as well as a practical focus. During this leisure time, people were drawn together around the warmth and protection of this terrifying and destructive force of nature they had tamed. In Pfeiffer's words, when they "tamed fire, they tamed themselves."

The environment-biology-culture interaction continued. Armed with their new and successful cultural adaptation, *H. erectus* faced new worlds, using their skills to consciously invent the means to survive the elements and to gather the available plants and hunt the available animals. In the cold regions, these hunting skills were especially put to the test, as the environments were harsh and the game animals big and dangerous. But *erectus* was up to the task. At a site in Spain called Torralba, about 400,000 years ago, bands of *Homo erectus*, using fire, regularly drove elephants and other game into a swamp, where they killed and butchered them. At about the same time, at a site in France called Terra Amata, similar people built huts of interlocking branches, the first evidence of a dwelling.

The emphasis on cultural answers to the problems of survival thus enhanced selection for traits that would facilitate that sort of behavior. *H. erectus* was already bipedal and had manual dexterity comparable to that of modern humans. The "finishing touch" seems to have been the big brain, and we find the first evidence of that nearly half a million years ago in Europe, and shortly afterward in Africa and Asia. These fossils show a flatter face under a more rounded braincase, which contained a brain well into the size range of modern humans. These are early *Homo sapiens*, members of our species.

A word of caution is needed here. As far as we know from current evidence, our evolution involved one continuous line from *habilis* to modern *sapiens*. To give the stages of that line different species names is not the same as saying that modern humans and chimpanzees belong to different species. There was no point in time when a *habilis* mother gave birth to an *erectus* child. We can't test to see whether a *sapiens* could interbreed with an *erectus*. These names are used because the fossil record comes in chunks, each chunk representing a different time period, and each therefore looking different from the preceding and following chunks. So we label them with different scientific names. Realize, however, that if we could line up fossils representing every generation from *habilis* to us today, we wouldn't be able to tell where one "species" leaves off and the next begins. Real species, as we have discussed, are produced when a branching occurs and is maintained long enough. As of now, it doesn't look as if there have been any of these speciation events in our evolution since the *Australopithecus–Homo* split 3.5 million years ago.

With the coming of *H. sapiens*, it is harder to make generalizations about our evolutionary history. Humans by that time were widespread and thus varied a lot in physical features and cultural adaptations. In addition, fossil evidence from the period of 500,000 to 150,000 years ago is relatively scanty. What we do know, as you would expect, is that control over technology steadily advanced. For instance, beginning about 160,000 years ago, we find that more finely shaped *flake tools* took over in importance from core tools and that a new technique, called *prepared core*, allowed people to predict and control the kinds of flakes they knocked off a larger stone.

Also beginning about 150,000 years ago is an aspect of human evolution that has been, and in some ways still is, rather mysterious and controversial. It involves fossil humans mostly from Europe, the Near East, and central Asia, collectively called the Neanderthals (after the Neander Valley in Germany, where an early specimen was found). Living from 150,000 to 35,000 years ago, these people showed a distinct set of physical features: a long, low skull that protruded in the rear; a large, projecting face; heavy ridges over the eyes followed by a receding forehead; and, in some populations, an average brain size in excess of the modern average. In addition, their bodies were generally more robust and heavily muscled than the typical modern human's.

The first Neanderthal fossils were found about the time Darwin was working on *The Origin of Species*. Early interpretations pictured these people as hunched-over, club-carrying brutes who were "certainly" an extinct offshoot of human evolution. Our stereotyped image of the "caveman" comes from this. In part this misconception resulted from a belief that someone so different-looking could not possibly be our ancestor. In part it came from the fact that one of the most complete early specimens, and therefore the one that became the "type" fossil, was an old man with an advanced case of arthritis and a number of skeletal deformities.

We now know that humans with this basic set of features lived not only in Europe but also in the Near East and central Asia, and similar, though less pronounced specimens have been found in Africa and the Far East. Furthermore, far from being some brutish throwback, Neanderthal populations were responsible for such cultural advances as stone spear points and a large number of well-made specialized stone tools, including "punches" that could have been used in the manufacture of hide clothing and tents. They also made tent and hut shelters and practiced burial of the dead, in some cases with tools and flowers in the graves. They put together some alterlike collections of cave bear skulls that hint at the presence of ritual and religion.

Though some individual Neanderthal populations may have become extinct without leaving any descendants, it is our general contention that this distinctive appearance is simply what some people looked like during this period and that the Neanderthals are members of our species to whom many of us can trace our ancestry and who may have begun some important cultural trends. Indeed, now that we have more examples of people from this time, we see that in general they may not have looked all that different anyhow.

We cannot explain the Neanderthal physical features, nor can we account for why they fairly suddenly disappear from the fossil record, to be replaced by modern-looking humans. Modern traits include a vertical forehead; a small, flat face with a protruding chin; no brow ridges; and a rounded braincase. Humans exhibiting these features are first seen from about 30,000 years ago in Eurasia and Africa. These populations are similar in physical features to modern populations in those regions. Whether they came from outside and replaced the Neanderthals or evolved from them is not known. Nor is it clear whether modern humans arose in one place and spread or were the result of some relatively minor evolutionary changes that took place at about the same time all over the Old World.

At any rate, by 30,000 years ago, biological evolution had reached its modern stage, and cultural evolution began to show advances. Archaeologists begin to find such things as painting and sculpture, large varieties of finely crafted stone tools, and some needles, awls, and harpoons made of bone and antler that had been carved and engraved by tools of stone.

And sometime around this period, humans entered the New World. They came across the Bering land bridge, an expanse of land connecting Siberia and Alaska exposed by the lower sea levels of glacial times. In a relatively short time, people had spread all over

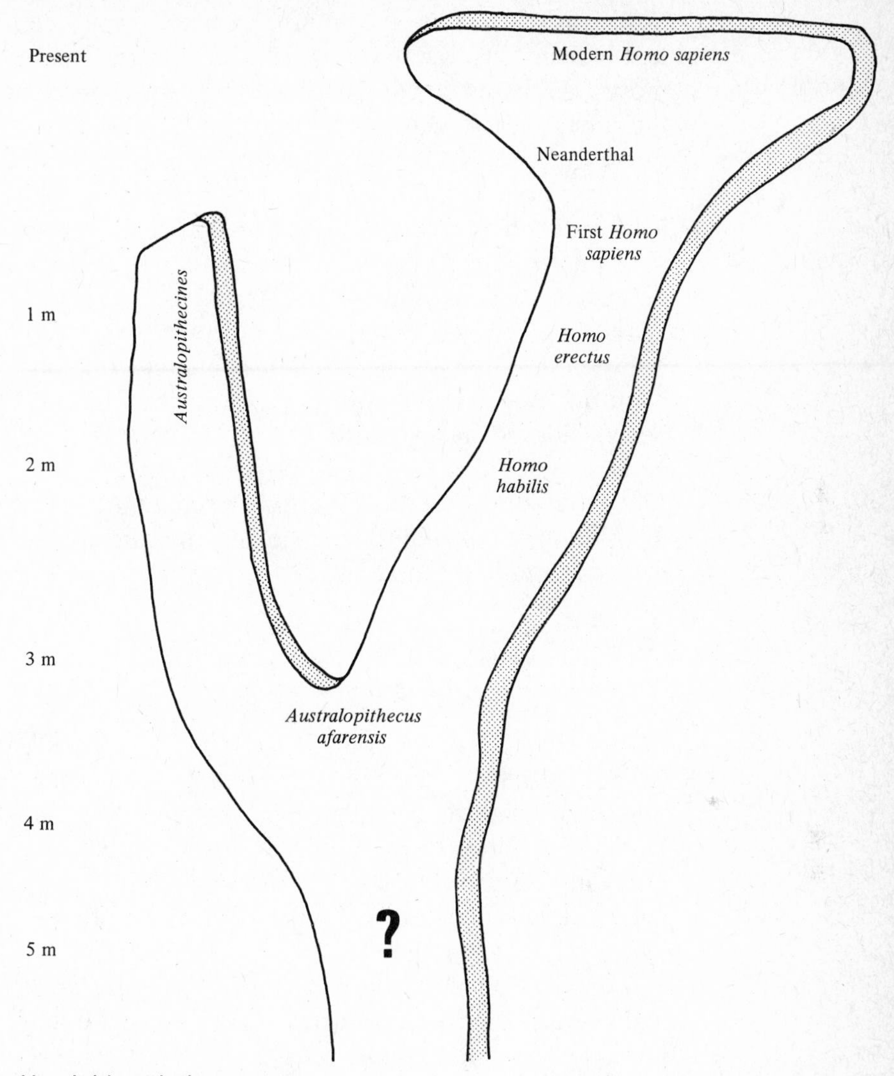

Hominid evolutionary tree.

the hemisphere. Some finds from South America may be as old as 22,000 years.

Culture change then accelerated rapidly, gearing itself to the specific ecologies of the areas involved. In a few thousand years—a short time when compared to the millions we have been discussing—we find the first traces of agriculture, metallurgy, cities, and writing. "History" begins.

This outline of the human evolutionary story has been brief, and it really just scratches the surface. It necessarily got briefer and more sketchy as we advanced toward more recent times. You should therefore be left with a few questions: How do we know about all those tools? What about language? What about social organization, families, economics, and other behaviors? Well, take a breath and lean back for a moment. You recall, the purpose of all this was to account for the physical evolution of the upright primate. Having done that, this outline will now act as a context and background against which to consider some additional items: the other differences between us and the nonhuman primates, our adaptive behaviors, even our present and future as a species. Each of these items will be considered in an evolutionary sense, and this brief outline will gradually be filled in.

Now, how else is this upright primate unique? For the next part of the answer, we must go back to the beginning—the very beginning—and talk about sex.

SUMMARY

Each of the 150 species of living primates has its own unique set of adaptive traits. Ours can be expressed by seeing ourselves as the upright, sexual, and cultural primate.

The relationships among living organisms, and their relative positions on the evolutionary "tree of life" are expressed using a system of nomenclature ("names") based on that devised by Linnaeus in the eighteenth century. The criteria used to classify organisms include physical characteristics, behaviors, and, recently, chemical and genetic traits. But the inclusion of an organism in a category is really determined by its adaptive identity: what kinds of traits does it have, to adapt it in what sort of way, to what sort of environment?

The Primates are a taxonomic order characterized by a number of traits that identify them as intelligent, dexterous, vision-oriented tree dwellers. Humans possess the same basic set of features as do all the primates, but we differ essentially in our upright posture—that is, we are built for ground dwelling. Our other distinguishing characteristics are a result of adaptation to that particular niche.

The evolution of the hominid branch of the primates is reasonably well understood. The available evidence shows that we first evolved in Africa, as a result of a climatic change, and that our adaptive response to that change—the evolution of bipedalism, extremely dexterous hands, and large brains with the cultural behaviors they made possible—eventually allowed us to colonize virtually the entire planet.

NOTES, REFERENCES, AND READINGS

There is a wealth of material on this aspect of anthropology, but I list here some of my favorites that I think you might particularly enjoy. To get a better feeling for the primate order, try *The Primates* (New York: Time-Life Books, 1974) by Sarel Eimerl and Irven DeVore. If you'd like specific details about individual species, see the definitive work by John and P. H. Napier, *A Handbook of Living Primates* (New York: Academic Press, 1967). A good book on the comparison of the human primate with the rest of the order is *The Human Primate* (San Francisco: Freeman, 1982) by Richard Passingham.

The article by Matt Cartmill on the origins of the primates is in *Science* (April 26, 1974). Some articles on the topic of continental drift are collected in *Continents Adrift and Continents Aground: Readings from Scientific American* (San Francisco: Freeman, 1976), edited by J. Tuzo Wilson.

A nice summary of the evolution of the monkeys, apes, and early humans can be found in an article by David Pilbeam in *Scientific American* (March 1984) called "The Descent of the Hominoids and Hominids." The story of the discovery of human fossils, focusing on the recovery and interpretation of Lucy, is recounted in the very readable book by Donald Johanson (Lucy's discoverer) and Maitland Edey, *Lucy: The Beginnings of Humankind* (New York: Simon and Schuster, 1981). Another popular but no less detailed and accurate work is John Pfeiffer's *The Emergence of Humankind* (4th ed., New York: Harper & Row, 1985). It covers, in somewhat narrative style, the entire evolution of our species, plus some of ways in which that evolution can be interpreted and understood.

chapter 5

Reproduction
The Sexual Primate

> The part of the brain that governs the reproductive function, is the cerebellum or little brain. It is located in the lower and back part of the head. The cerebellum also constitutes the organ of amativeness, which, according to the teachings of phrenology, gives love for the opposite sex. Other things being equal, the strength of the cerebellum is proportionate to its size. . . . You will never find the most popular and successful men and women with a small and weak cerebellum, nor a weak, narrow, retreating chin, because they do not have enough love for the opposite sex to form an incentive to be gallant, polite, attentive, winning, etc.

This was written in 1895 by V. P. English, M.D. in his book *The Doctor's Plain Talk to Young Men*. The book seems quite humorous to us today, for it is filled with all manner of outdated information and nineteenth-century attitudes toward sex. For example, we know now that the cerebellum, the part of the brain concerned with coordinating voluntary muscle movement, has virtually nothing to do with reproduction. We also know that phrenology—the "science" of determining human personality and mental characteristics from the shape of the head—doesn't work. And we realize that contrary to what Dr. English implies, our ideas about attractiveness, love, manners, and so on are not species characteristics controlled by the brain but cultural norms, which vary from society to society.

(The book is also interesting for its ideas on the biology of reproduction. Written before the rediscovery of Mendel's work, Dr. English's book contains all sorts of Lamarckian-type concepts about passing on acquired characteristics. It has no information about how inheritance really operates, and it carries the clear implication that the male plays a far more important role in reproduction than does the female.)

Though we may find this book hopelessly naive, and in some cases quite funny, it does demonstrate an important idea: that despite what Dr. English is trying to say, our sexual behavior is not entirely programmed in our brains. Quite the contrary; we can *think* about sex. Instead of automatically responding to external stimuli, as do most other organisms, we decide when, where, with whom, and how to have sex. We decide, as members of a particular culture, what is sexually attractive and stimulating. And what is attractive and stimulating is all tied up with personality characteristics, emotional responses, and learned attitudes. To put it bluntly, we know who we are doing it with, and we care. That we find Dr. English's book a Victorian period piece proves the point. And the ability to think about sex not only makes us different from other organisms, but it also may be the result of important changes that took place at the very beginning of our evolution.

Now, as naive as *this* may sound, we must ask just what sex is and why it is so important.

SEX AND GENETICS

Because we are a sexually reproducing species, as are most species with which we deal or are familiar, we may tend to think of sexual reproduction as the norm. But in one sense it's not. Life began on Earth about 3.5 billion years ago. For the next 2 billion years, so far as we know, the only organisms were prokaryotes, which reproduced asexually ("without sex") by dividing or budding. Thus sex is a fairly recent "invention" in the history of life.

Sexual reproduction first appears around a billion years ago with the evolution of the eukaryotes. And then evolution takes off. Why? Because asexually reproducing species essentially make "carbon copies" of themselves. Except for mutations, most of which are deleterious anyhow, there is no source of genetic variation. As you recall, without variation, evolution can't operate.

With sexual reproduction, two sets of genes are being combined to make a new individual—and that new individual is genetically unique. Genes from two sources are now "shuffled" together during reproduction, giving the evolutionary processes an ample supply of variation. This is why, as soon as sex was evolutionarily "invented," new forms, adapted to new niches, appeared at a more rapid rate than previously. Most of the evolutionary lineages on Earth today arose during the last 30 percent of life's history.

To appreciate fully how this works, we must return briefly to Mendel and his genetics and look at his discovery in a little more detail. We'll use, however, modern knowledge and terminology.

The varieties of one of Mendel's "particles" (genes) are called *alleles*. They arise through the mutation of one form of a gene into another. (Remember, though, that most mutations make something completely nonfunctional.) Every individual has a pair of each gene, and the alleles don't necessarily have to be the same. In many cases, furthermore, one allele is *dominant* over another (the *recessive*). The dominant is expressed, but the recessive is not, meaning that an individual organism may possess some hidden variation.

As an example, let's look at a trait in humans that works just like those of Mendel's peas. It's called the taster trait and refers to humans' genetic ability, or lack of ability, to taste a chemical called phenylthiocarbamide (PTC). This trait is controlled by a single gene, the T gene, which, however, has two alleles: *T*, the dominant, codes for the ability to taste PTC; *t*, the recessive, for lack of the ability. Since every person has a pair of these alleles, there are three possible genetic combinations, or *genotypes: TT, tt*, or *Tt*. The expressions, or *phenotypes*, of the first two combinations are obvious; the phenotype of a person with the last genotype would be "taster," since, even though there is a *t* present, its effects are not expressed because *T* is dominant. (That's why we use a capital letter.)

Now another word of caution before we go on. *Dominant* and *recessive* are loaded words; when used in social contexts, they carry implied value judgments. In genetics, no values are placed on them. All they mean is that when an individual possesses two unlike alleles and one is dominant, the dominant one is expressed. Dominant does *not* mean better, more adapted, more fit, or anything like that. Plenty of deleterious alleles are dominants, and plenty of good ones are recessives. In fact, most alleles of most genes are not even in this nice, clean dominant-recessive relationship. In most cases, alleles are said to be *co-dominant*; they are both expressed in the phenotype to some degree.

To complete the terminology: Genotypes come in two versions, ones with both alleles the same and ones with different alleles. The first state is referred to as *homozygous* (*homo* means "same"), the second as *heterozygous* (*hetero* means "different").

What does this have to do with sex? In reproduction it's these genes that get passed on to the offspring. In asexually reproducing species, both alleles of a parent's pair are passed to the offspring, making that offspring as like the parent as two identical twins. Unless a (nondeleterious) mutation takes place, there is no chance for genetic variation. But if two parents combine their genes in the production of offspring, there is plenty of opportunity.

Of course, if both parents passed on both members of all their gene pairs, the resulting offspring would have twice the proper num-

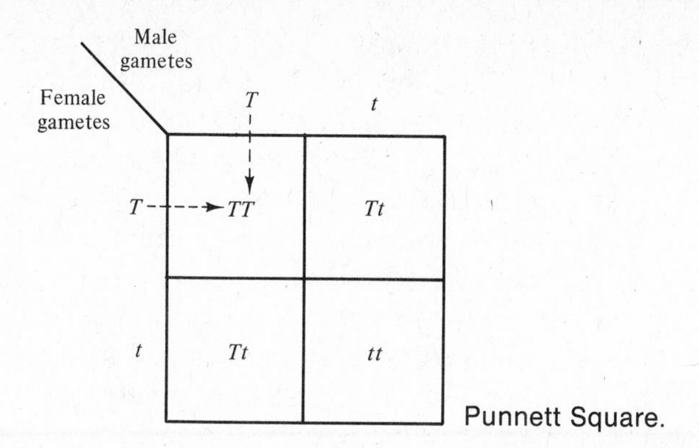

Punnett Square.

ber of genes. What takes care of this is that in the production of the sex cells, or *gametes* (sperm and egg in animals), the gene pairs split up so that each gamete has only one of each pair. Then, when fertilization takes places, the new individual will again have a pair of each gene, the members of each pair coming from different parents. Using a diagrammatic device called a Punnett Square, let's see how this would work if two people, both heterozygous for the taster trait, mated and produced offspring.

The gene pairs are split up in the production of sperm and egg but are *recombined* at fertilization. Thus brand-new combinations are produced. You even stand a 1-in-4 chance of getting a nontaster child from two taster parents. Multiply this simple example by the 100,000 or so genetic pairs that a human is thought to possess, and you can appreciate the enormous potential for genetic variation. That's why sex is so important in the story of evolution.

Now, just what are the features that make us so different in our sexual behavior from other organisms, and how did they evolve?

SEX AND HUMAN EVOLUTION

To understand how we are the sexual primate, we need to understand how mammals in general reproduce. In most mammals, sexual activity takes place only when it can do what it's supposed to do—make baby mammals. And this is because sex is geared to the reproductive cycle of the female. Female mammals produce eggs for fertilization only at certain intervals. These may be closely spaced and regular, or they may be seasonal to ensure the birth of young during times of abundant resources.

This egg production, called *ovulation*, has two results sexually:

It causes the sending of signals that act to stimulate male mammals sexually, and it makes the female sexually receptive to the males. During this period the female is said to be in *estrus* (in popular terminology, "in heat"). This is when sex takes place—as a result of inborn stimuli and responses. At other times, when there is no egg to be fertilized, mammals have much better things to do.

This holds true for all the primates except us. Female primates ovulate, and are thus in estrus, at certain intervals. During estrus, the females give signals that automatically cause sexual stimulation of the male primates. These signals are usually both *olfactory* (based on smell, as in most mammals) and *visual*, involving the swelling and coloration of the skin in the genital area. Those primates you see in zoos that have what look like large, painful growths on their rears are just females in estrus. At these times mating takes place. It may involve a number of males, as in chimpanzees, or just one male that has exclusive "rights" to a female during her estrus period. This second form is seen in baboons, where the males are arranged in a hierarchy in which those that are dominant (there's the term used in a social sense) have more access to estrus females.

This link between sexual activity and ovulation is a mechanism to give a species the greatest possible chance to produce offspring without wasting a lot of time and energy on sex when it will do no biological good. When primates, for example, are not involved in sexual activity during a female's estrus, they have more than enough to do just trying to stay alive.

You should see right away one important feature in which we differ: *We have lost the estrus cycle*. To be sure, female humans ovulate at regular intervals—about once every 28 days, producing an egg that can be fertilized over a period of 3 to 5 days. But there is no sign of this. No signals tell human males that a female has produced an egg ready for fertilization. Some females can tell when they have ovulated, and there is a rise in body temperature; but males can't tell.

Now, if we still had sex only when a female was in estrus, we'd be in trouble! But there are other differences that take care of this. We are, as you are well aware, *continually receptive* sexually. We are not limited to sexual activity only when the proper stimuli elicit the proper responses. We can do it (or not do it) at any time. This is because we have evolved *conscious control* over our sexual activity.

Control over our basic sexual responses, such as hormonal changes and certain physical reactions, is located in older, deeper

A female chimpanzee in estrus.

areas of the *cerebrum* (the "master control" part of the brain)—areas we share with all the vertebrates. But mammals have a new brain area, called the *neocortex*, in which thought processes take place. This is the convoluted, or folded-looking, outer covering of the brain, sometimes called the "gray matter." And we human primates have the biggest, most complex neocortex of all.

Thus before our basic sexual reactions, which are driven by more primitive parts of our brain, can be expressed, they are, in a sense, routed through our neocortex. Here they are mediated, channeled, controlled, and thought about. We thus express ourselves sexually as individual personalities and as members of particular cultures. We respond sexually to individual personalities and according to cultural norms concerned with standards of behavior and attractiveness. We find a person sexually stimulating not because of some automatic signals but because of that person's appearance, personal characteristics, intelligence, socioeconomic status—all the factors by which we judge individual people as members of our society.

Now, as with other things we are discussing, don't think that there is a qualitative difference—a difference in kind—between us and the other primates with regard to sex. There is evidence that our biological cousins do have the capacity to "think" about it. Primates in zoos, for instance, being in an artificial environment and lacking all the stimuli found in their natural habitats, often revert to all sorts of sexual behavior just to give themselves something to do. Since the apes, in particular, have a fairly large neocortex, it is not surprising that they can and do exhibit some conscious awareness and manipulation of sex. But this is generally not important under normal conditions in the wild. There, mating takes place as a result of the inborn signals and responses. The difference is one of degree: Whereas the other primates *can* think about sex, we, in the "natural" habitats of our cultures, *must* think about it. Sex in we humans has evolved away from a series of automatic reactions and is inextricably tied up with our conscious thought.

But now a question arises: If automatic responses work so well for all other creatures, even all other primates, why have we evolved a type of sexual behavior whereby, because sex is not tied to the reproductive cycle, we actually "waste" sex by having it when it will do no good in terms of perpetuating our species? The general answer is that since we have that characteristic, it must have some function. We just have to figure out what that is. And we have an intriguing and quite plausible hypothesis.

The idea comes from anthropologist Owen Lovejoy, who, as is proper, considers it strictly a hypothesis as we have defined that term. It is, however, everything one could want in a hypothesis, for it takes into account all the known relevant data, it follows current knowledge about all the topics it covers, and it emphasizes interactions between its parts—an idea important to modern science. Whether or not it will become an accepted theory will depend on further testing and examination. But because of the features just listed, it warrants a serious look.

The Lovejoy hypothesis begins with a consideration of what are called *reproductive strategies*—how, in terms of number of offspring, a species tries to perpetuate itself. One extreme strategy is found among oysters, which release up to half a billion eggs a year, potentially producing several hundred million offspring. Naturally, if all the offspring lived, the world would be overrun with oysters. But as you can imagine, only a small percentage of the eggs are fertilized, and because oysters don't take care of their young, only a small percentage of those that are fertilized reach adulthood. That's exactly why the oyster is so extravagant in its gamete production. It's like taking 100 snapshots on your vacation to give yourself good odds of getting a few decent ones.

The opposite extreme in reproductive strategy is found among the apes. Quite unlike oysters, apes have only one offspring every five years or so. To try to ensure that that offspring will reach adulthood, they lavish a great deal of care upon it. And since no other offspring are born during that period (because the estrus cycle ceases), the young ape receives undivided attention. This long period of almost total dependency and care is, of course, directly related to the apes' big brains and to the importance of learned behaviors in coping with their environment.

This adaptive strategy, however, has one serious drawback: Should some event result in the death of an ape offspring, up to five years of parental care is wasted. All that energy and all those years spent *not* having other offspring are gone. Five years out of the reproductive period of an ape's life is a relatively long time. If some major environmental change brings about the deaths of many youngsters, the existence of the species itself could be threatened. Lovejoy has suggested, in fact, that the modern apes have gone dangerously far toward this extreme of reproductive strategies.

Now, since we are so closely related to the modern apes, and since the fossil evidence shows that we evolved from apelike creatures, let's assume that our common ancestor exhibited an ape sort of reproductive strategy, having single offspring, widely spaced. Perhaps, proposes Lovejoy, due to some environmental changes, one group of these ancient apes was experiencing offspring deaths to a species-threatening degree. In such a case, what would selection be for?

Well, if—and only if—there was sufficient variation in this characteristic, selection would favor individuals who produced offspring more often than the average. These individuals would increase their potential contribution to the next generation, with a minimum of wasted energy and time if an offspring died. If this hypothesis is correct, there was sufficient variation, there were such individuals, and that trend was selected for.

However (there's always a catch) organisms are *systems*, adapted to environmental *systems*. You can't just change one thing and expect everything to be OK. In this case, having two or even three dependent offspring at one time may have been an answer to the problem of infant death, but it poses new problems itself. Now there are more mouths to feed, and if it was a food shortage that started the whole thing in the first place, this could be quite serious. Moreover, having several offspring to care for makes the females less mobile and thus less able to move about in search of food. Since primates hardly ever share food with one another, things look really bad.

But it seems as though selection found the necessary variations to answer these difficulties. First of all, the problem of mobility could in part be solved through selection for enhanced bipedalism. (I told you things would be interrelated!) Freeing the forelimbs permanantly from locomotor functions allows you to move around and to carry things—food, kids, tools—at the same time. All primates have some bipedal abilities, the apes especially, so this change has the needed initial variation.

But even a bipedal female with a couple of dependent kids can't be too mobile, so we are still not completely out of the woods. Males, however, not encumbered with children, are more mobile, especially if bipedal. So they could walk around, get additional food, and bring it back to the less mobile mothers.

Why would they want to? Primate fathers are notoriously unconcerned with their children. Although most monkey and ape species care about and protect their youngsters as a group, the males probably don't know who their actual biological children are, and even if they do, they don't care any more or less for them than they do for any of their group's kids. So we've got to get the male to want to come back with the food. And what would do that? How about sex?

Now, don't get an oversimplified idea that our earliest ancestor males braved all sorts of dangers to find and retrieve food because they knew that when they got back home they were going to get some sex! It's a *little* more subtle than that! Remember that when we say we can think about sex, what we mean is that much of our sexual behavior is controlled in the neocortex—the conscious part of our brain. Sex is thus all tied up with our cultural concepts, our personal psychologies, and our emotions. We are sexually, emotionally, and personally attracted to an individual, *as* an individual. The movement of sexual attraction from an automatic response to one connected with all these other mental functions may have been evolution's way of bonding male and female into a permanent pair, with ties to each other based on conscious thoughts and resulting in the solution to the problems mentioned.

How did that happen? Well, among some animals there is a built-in behavior called *pair bonding* that brings male and female together to form a permanent reproductive unit. This is seen in such diverse creatures as geese and gibbons, so it's already present in a primate. As our brains were getting bigger and more complex, then, with an increasing ability to think, it would not appear to be too much of an evolutionary trick to add reproductive behavior and personal recognition to those conscious abilities. Thus developed, at the very dawn of human evolution, what we think of as the *nuclear family*, the male-female unit into which children are born and in which children are biologically and culturally nurtured.

All this, if the scenario is correct, probably occurred several million years before Lucy's time, perhaps as some of our common ancestors with the apes were venturing into the open woodlands at the edges of the diminishing forests. And as those forests decreased even further, and the woodlands gave way to savannas, these abilities to walk upright and to operate as a family unit in the production and nurturing of offspring proved adaptive to that environment as well. This phenomenon is known as *preadaptation*: Adaptive features evolved originally in response to one environment, or that are adaptively neutral, happen to be useful in response to an environmental change.

So by 3.5 million years ago, when Lucy was alive, we have a bipedal, savanna-dwelling hominid. If Lovejoy is right, this hominid lived in some sort of male-female-offspring family group that exhibited the efficient and necessary division of labor just described. And

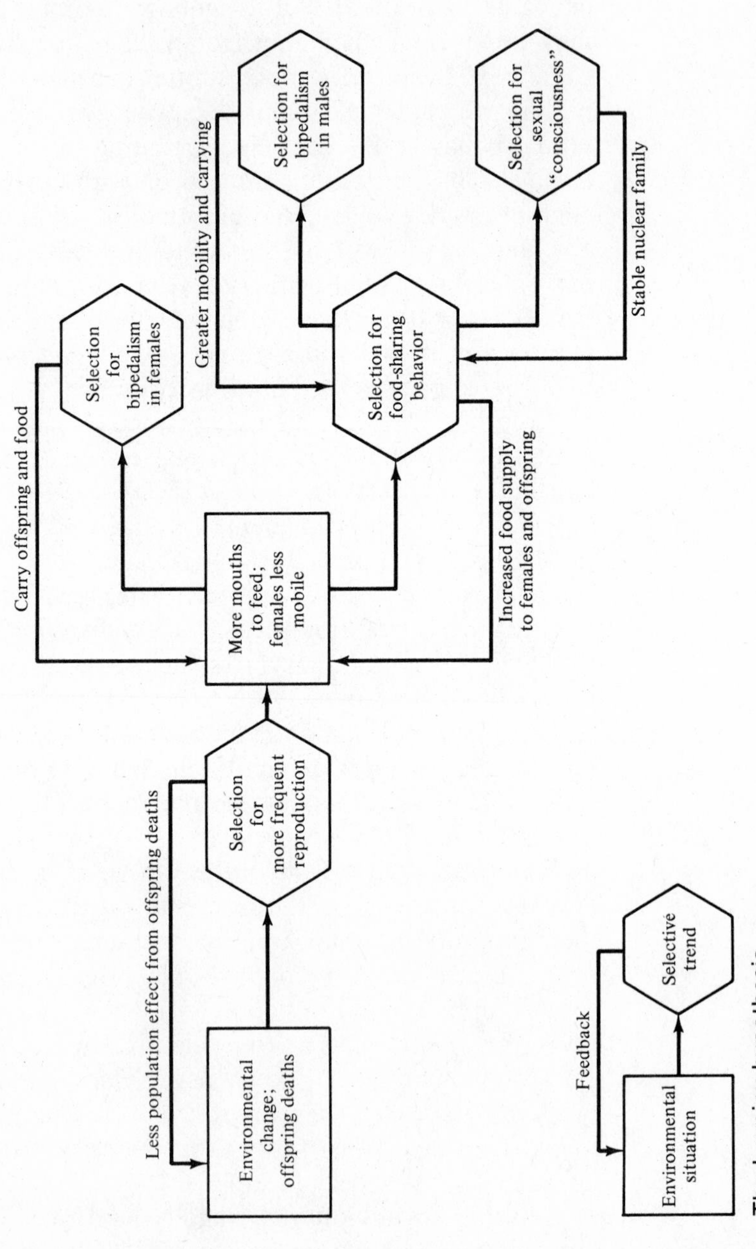

The Lovejoy hypothesis.

those preadaptive traits were a lucky break indeed, as our presence here today clearly demonstrates.

There is, by the way, some hard evidence for this family behavior. In 1975, the year after Lucy was found, the fossil remains of at least 13 *afarensis* individuals were recovered, also in Ethiopia. They appear to have died together, possibly in a flash flood, and they represent both sexes and a range of ages. They have been dubbed, understandably, the First Family.

It should be obvious that Lovejoy's hypothesis is difficult, if not impossible, to examine and test. But it does not contradict what we understand about evolutionary processes and primate biology, and it does nicely account for the evolution of two of our distinguishing features, bipedalism and sexual behavior. It could also be seen as starting the ball rolling toward our third distinguishing characteristic, culture—but more on that in the next chapter. In the years to come this idea will be thought about a great deal and tested where possible. But for now, it provides us with a good working hypothesis, and I, for one, like it a lot.

One way of testing this hypothesis would be to see if despite the cultural emphasis of our sexual behavior, there might be any biological remnant from the time just described, when these behaviors were first evolving. And there seems to be. It is in the nature of our *sexual dimorphism* (''two appearances'').

All sexually reproducing species are sexually dimorphic if for no other reason than that the two sexes need different equipment. But in some species it's hard to tell male from female unless you really examine their anatomy. Can you tell a male robin from a female at a distance? But other species' sexes are clearly distinguished in their external appearance. In another familiar bird, the cardinal, for instance, it's easy to tell the sexes apart. It's easy in humans as well, and the nature of our differences is most interesting.

VIVE LA DIFFÉRENCE

How are men and women different biologically? That sounds like a really stupid question, since those differences are something we think we're acutely aware of. But are we, in this broad, evolutionary sense? Let's look at some of our dimorphic traits.

An obvious one is the difference in hair distribution. We are indeed a ''naked ape,'' having lost most of our body hair in the process of becoming hominids. That, by the way, was probably an adaptation to allow more efficient sweating and cooling of the body as we were doing all that bipedal running around. But we have retained hair in a few places. Underarm and pubic hair I'll get to shortly. There's also facial and chest hair, and this is the sole property of human males. What could its purpose be? It's hard to imagine any adaptive significance other than as a signal. Patches of hair on the face and chest proclaim clearly that the bearer is a male. Lack of these clearly says female.

Now people—even in Lucy's day—aren't *that* dumb. Anybody can tell men from women! But notice where these distinguishing features are: in the front of the body and on the face. Not in the rear, like the anonymous odor and swelling of the nonhuman primates. Humans are not merely males or females but *individuals* who are male or female. And this would seem to support the notion that an important aspect of our evolution was the awareness of our sexual partners as certain people to whom we were attracted in a conscious way.

Also in the front of the body are the female's breasts. Contrary to some popular ideas, the size of a woman's breasts has little to do with the milk production of the mammary glands. Indeed, there seems to be no reason environmentally for the mammary glands of this one primate to be surrounded by fat and connective tissue. The breasts are most likely another signal to distinguish the human sexes. They are in the front of the body, where they are associated with a particular person; they are obviously related to reproduction and nurturing of offspring; and they are rich in nerve endings that connect them to sensations of sexual pleasure.

In addition, there are the overall differences in shape and size of the sexes. Males, on the average, are larger and more heavily muscled, and therefore physically stronger, than females. This is in part an aspect of our primate heritage, since in all the apes males are bigger than females, probably because the males are usually responsible for protection of the group. We may have retained this dimorphic feature for the same basic reason: Greater size in males may have aided their food-getting activities, giving them the greater physical strength needed to make long searches for food, to take food away from other predators, and to keep from being some other creature's meal. In addition, smaller size in females may itself have been selected for to make this food getting more energy-efficient. Smaller organisms eat less and so put less strain on the whole system—a system in which (think back to Lovejoy's hypothesis) getting enough to eat is a central factor.

Sexual Dimorphism. Each culture has its own set of ideals.

Finally, the bodies of men and women just look different. The skulls, especially the faces, show average distinctions, and certain body proportions, notably the relative widths of the hips and shoulders, are different. Evolution has enabled us to tell our sexes apart easily and to do so on the level of the individual person.

Besides dimorphic features, there are also some features men and women have in common that support this idea of a biological heritage for our sexuality.

How about lips? Our lips are everted, which means that the muscle structure is such that the flesh around our mouths is pulled outward. Moreover, the skin covering this area is translucent, allowing the color of the muscle underneath to show through. What do we need that for? Certainly not for manipulating food. Chimps, who have no lip eversion, can do amazing things with their lip area, like separate the halves of a nutshell from the meat and spit the shell out. Our lips may aid in our language, but there is evidence that human language, as we know it, is only a recent invention. No, our lips are probably also a signal, a splotch of color on the face, pointing out a feature that, like the breasts, is rich in nerve endings that are involved in sexual arousal. Nearly all cultures practice kissing.

And—I've saved one of the most amazing for last—what about the other areas where both sexes of the human primate have retained hair: under the arms and in the pubic area? What's that for? Well, those areas may also be ornamental, clearly pointing out regions that are directly or indirectly involved in sex. But in addition, the skin in both those areas is equipped with special *apocrine glands*. These are similar to sweat glands but secrete a substance that, when it decomposes, produces an odor. Being trapped in the hair, this substance decomposes slowly and is able to build up a stronger smell.

This is the smell people in many societies try fanatically to get rid of. But it looks as if, in an evolutionary sense, it's supposed to be there. In other words, we may not have evolved completely away from the primate pattern of olfactory sexual signals. There is, by the way, an interesting sexual dimorphism here too, since females have 75 percent more apocrine glands than men.

Now, are these just leftover biological traits that are meaningless in our modern cultural environments? Or are they, even with our ability to manipulate things culturally, still functional? There seems to be evidence for the latter. For look at what we, in many societies, do with those features. Female breasts are rarely "neutral" characteristics. Among some people, breasts are exposed; among others, they are hidden; among still others, they are covered and then enhanced with clothing. No matter what the cultural attitudes, most all humans recognize breasts as having some sexual significance.

Lips, too, are manipulated culturally by some people. In a number of societies, one form of personal adornment is the application of makeup to the lips to enhance their color difference from the rest of the face. That practice seems to have originated in ancient Egypt, where women also applied makeup to their nipples.

Facial hair? In some cultures men leave it on. In others, they shave it off (what one anthropologist calls a "masochistic rite"). In some groups, beards have a particular meaning, as among the Hutterites, where they are a sign of marriage. What better way to signify the pair bond than by enhancing a sexual dimorphism? In our culture, we have seen beards go in and out of style a number of times recently. Facial hair seems seldom to be an inconsequential characteristic.

Finally, what about the odor idea? Does it sound repugnant that body odor is something we're supposed to have? The idea is certainly not foreign to us. Every day, men and women in many societies put on perfumes of various sorts, in many cases after having washed off their own natural odors. These perfumes are usually used to enhance one's attractiveness to the opposite sex. One very popular scent in the Western world today is musk, which comes from a gland in a musk deer that gives off the odor, probably as a sexual attractant. We get rid of the one nature gave us and replace it with one from a deer!

To be sure, all these traits and our attitudes about them can be manipulated by culture. And some of the traits exhibit biological variation: Many Asian peoples, for instance, characteristically have very little body and facial hair, on either sex. But the fact that these *are* in many cases important traits shows that our biological heritage and our cultures can interact. There is strong evidence that our basic sexual behavior is something that was selected for and established at the very beginning of our evolution. This behavior was "translated" from purely biological to cultural as our species evolved that aspect of its identity, so now there is all sorts of variation with regard to "normal" sexual behavior. But it all seems to be variation on the same basic theme.

All the foregoing concerns details of culture with obvious biological connections. We were, after all, talking about lips and breasts and body hair. But what about some social features that seem strictly cultural, that appear to lack any such obvious biological facet? Could some of these as well be traced back to our biological past?

SEX AND CULTURAL INSTITUTIONS

Among the most interesting of cultural phenomena, and sometimes the most puzzling, are behaviors that are *cultural universals*—behaviors found in all human societies. Because we have the ability to invent our behaviors, and because most behaviors show a great deal of variation among cultures, it seems strange that a few items are found everywhere. These demand explanations, and there are two that may well be explained by our identity as the sexual primate.

The first is *marriage*. Marriage is a set of cultural rules that bring together male and female to create the nuclear family and define their behavior toward each other, their children, and their society. All cultures that we know now and have knowledge about from the past have some form of marriage. Of course, there is a great deal of variation in such things as the number of marriage partners one may have, whom one may marry, how property is owned, and so on. But

A wedding in India.

every society, from the simplest to the most complex, recognizes a need to define culturally a male-female union.

At first that may seem only natural. But that's because it *is* a universal; it's what we're used to. Is there, however, any reason for this kind of setup, especially these days when, for many societies, basic economic needs are taken care of not by the small family unit but as part of a large and complex market system? In our own culture, for example, nearly half of all families are single-parent families, and some of these have always contained just one parent. You certainly need a union of male and female to conceive a child, but after that, anybody can raise and nurture the offspring and successfully make it a functioning member of the group. But except on rare occasions, cultures only accept a union we would call a marriage.

Can the universality of marriage by explained by saying that it is such a good idea that every culture invented it or chose it from among all the possible alternatives? No, not when there *are* other perfectly viable alternatives. Rather, it seems more likely that it can be explained in much the same way as we did some of those sexual dimorphisms—namely, that they had a biological origin and were gradually "translated" into a variety of cultural expressions.

Recall again Lovejoy's hypothesis. It said that a nuclear family—a male-female-offspring unit—evolved at the very beginning of human evolution and was crucial to the success of this new branch. If that sort of behavior was so important to us, and if that behavior was something that was normal and vital for our survival for millions of years, it may be as much a part of our biological heritage as our sex differences. As with these differences, we would have little choice but to operate culturally using the nuclear family as a basis, creating all sorts of variations in specific practice, but always on the same theme. Even single-parent families in our society are really not something entirely new but are just a variation, a miniature nuclear family.

The second cultural universal is the *incest taboo*. A taboo (from a Polynesian word) is a negative rule; it tells you not to do something. The Jewish and Arab prohibition against eating pork would be considered a taboo, for example. The incest taboo is a rule that says you cannot marry persons to whom you are closely related. Just who these people are varies enormously from culture to culture, in many cases (as we'll see later) not even corresponding to biological relationships. But every society does include in the incest taboo the prohibition against sex and marriage between sibs and between parents and offspring. This part is the cultural universal.

There are a few limited exceptions—exceptions that, as exceptions often do, prove the rule. Among certain royal families, most notably the ancient Incas, Egyptians, and Hawaiians, the preferred marriage partner was someone in the family, often a sib or parent or offspring. This rule was an attempt to maintain the family purity of the royal line. But everyone else in these societies lived by the usual prohibition.

Why is this universal? One obvious result of close inbreeding is the potential for the production of defective offspring. This occurs because each of us carries several deleterious recessive genes that are not expressed because they are covered by normal dominants. (Stop here and recall the caution on the use of these terms.) Such deleterious genes are, *because* they're deleterious, rare. But who else in the world is most likely to have them? Your sibs, parents, and offspring, of course. So a child produced by you and one of these people would stand a good chance of being homozygous for one of these genes, thereby expressing the defective trait involved.

Now that's a pretty good reason to come up with a cultural rule that prohibits such matings, and that's the stated reason for our incest laws in this country. However, not every society knows that. Not every society has seen such results happen often enough to make the generalization. Many societies lack the scientific knowledge to do so. (There are, for example, a few groups who don't recognize a clear connection between sexual intercourse and pregnancy.) It seems unlikely, then, that the incest taboo originated as a cultural invention aimed at preventing this biological phenomenon.

Another possible function of the incest taboo would be to prevent sexual conflicts within that most important social unit, the nuclear family. Having sibs, parents, and offspring competing with one another for sexual access to family members would be disruptive emotionally and economically. Having to seek sexual and marriage partners outside the basic unit would limit the potential conflict. But again, could every single society we know have culturally invented the taboo for this reason? After all, as cultural beings we can come up with all sorts of rules of behavior. What's the matter with one that says, "You can marry your sister, but don't fight with your brothers about it"? But except for those royal lines, no one does.

To be sure, the taboo *can* have these important functions for a society. Moreover, many societies require marriage outside the group, using marriage to create social alliances with other societies. But remember the discussion about the primates' possibly not originating as the arboreal creatures we know today? Similarly, the present cultural functions of the incest taboo may not explain its origin. As anthropologist Jane Lancaster puts it, people's *motivations* for a behavior may be different from the *adaptive significance* of that behavior.

As with the marriage example, the explanation may lie in a biological norm becoming translated into cultural rules. It seems that many animals have a biological incest "taboo" that is built into their genes. Many of the nonhuman primates, as well as some other social creatures such as wolves, some birds, and even rats, seem to have a mechanism whereby mating between sibs or between mother and son is virtually prevented. (The identity of the father is often unknown, so father-daughter matings may take place.) The selective significance of such inborn behaviors is probably what I stated: preventing the expression of deleterious genetic combinations and the disruption of the main economic and social unit.

Now since, as we've discussed, a strong, permanent nuclear family may have been basic to our very evolutionary start, and since many primates (including the great apes) already seem to have this biological taboo, it would seem reasonable to hypothesize that our earliest ancestors did too. It seems reasonable then, given the evidence, to see the incest taboo as a biological "invention" that was so important and thus so normal to our species that we were, as we

Kibbutz children.

became increasingly culture-dependent, fairly limited in our cultural variations to that theme. Culture is powerful, though—we can even, as in those royal lines, go so far as to reverse completely the anti-incest behavior.

Finally, is there any evidence that some biological mechanism might still be in operation? Or is our present adherence to our incest rules based solely on our learned behavior? Some compelling evidence for the first comes from studies done among Israeli *kibbutzim*—communal agricultural settlements. In these communities, children of similar age are raised together in day-care centers while their parents are working. Until about 12 years of age, both sexes play, eat, sleep, bathe, and use the bathroom together. They grow up, in other words, as familiar with one another as real sibs, even though they actually come from different families. Israeli anthropologist Joseph Shepher found that there have been virtually no marriages between members of one of these age groups (the actual figure is only 6 marriages within age groups out of nearly 3000 kibbutz marriages)—despite that fact that such marriages are not at all prohibited and in some cases are even encouraged.

It seems as if the social situation in the *kibbutzim* is "fooling Mother Nature." The close proximity and familiarity of the age-group kids is apparently siblike enough to activate some biological mechanism that turns off sexual attraction between real sibs (and presumably between parents and offspring). We can and do make up cultural incest rules to cover many different groups of people, and this variation (as I'll discuss later) has cultural explanations. But the facts that there are incest rules at all and that the sib and parent-offspring prohibition is universal seem to be explained by delving into our biological past. And as in the case of the *kibbutzim*, sometimes even culture can't overcome the remnants of the original behavior.

(It should be noted, of course, that, as I'm sure you're aware, incest does occur in all societies, including ours. But behavior that can be considered incestuous is obviously abnormal and is therefore not an accepted cultural practice. It results from some psychological or biological problem that causes, on the part of the individual involved, the breakdown of the cultural-biological prohibition.)

From our remote beginnings, then, through some of our more obvious anatomical and physiological features, to some cultural institutions so basic we take them for granted, we are indeed the sexual primate.

SUMMARY

Sexual reproduction in general is important in evolution as a supplier of genetic variation, giving selection more on which to act. This principle can be seen by examining the basic laws of genetics as discovered by Mendel.

Sexual behavior in humans differs from that of other mammals, including the other primates, in that we have conscious control over our sexual behavior, rather than behaving according to a built-in set of automatic stimuli and responses. We know whom we are having sex with, and we care. Sexual attraction in us is tied up with all sorts of other cultural concepts of personality and standards of beauty and behavior.

This difference may have evolved as a mechanism to increase the size of, and to strengthen, the basic family unit—by adding a father and by forming a personal, emotional, and economic bond between the parents. Connected to this is the evolution of bipedalism, which helped facilitate mobility and the collection and sharing of resources that were part of this bond.

Although we now define and regulate the family and its relations in terms of culture, we may still carry evidence for the adaptive biological origins of our sexual behaviors. This evidence comes in the form of certain characteristics shared by the sexes, especially some that are sexually dimorphic. Similarly, the social institutions of marriage and the incest taboo may be seen as cultural "translations" of themes that had biological origins.

NOTES, REFERENCES, AND READINGS

There are many good tests available that can introduce you to basic Mendelian genetics. These include genetics texts, as well as a chapter in most books on evolution and anthropology. If you're interested in reading Mendel's actual words (English translation, of course), his "Experiments in Plant Hybridization" is reprinted in *Genetics: Readings from Scientific American* (San Francisco: Freeman, 1981), edited by Cedric I. Davern.

Owen Lovejoy's idea is discussed in detail in the chapter titled "Is It a Matter of Sex?" in Johanson and Edey's *Lucy*, listed in Chapter 4. An expansion of this idea can be found in *The Sex Contract* (New York: William Morrow, 1982) by Helen E. Fisher. More details on sexual dimorphisms and their interpretations are in Desmond Morris's *The Naked Ape* (New York: McGraw-Hill, 1967). Though I obviously agree with Morris on this topic, I also feel he tends at times to oversimplify explanations of other topics such as aggression. So read him with caution and a good sense of healthy scientific skepticism.

Jane Lancaster's distinction between motivation and adaptive significance can be found in her *Primate Behavior and the Emergence of Human Culture* (New York: Holt, Rinehart and Winston, 1975). This book focuses on the rationale for learning about the beginnings of our behaviors by observing those of our closest relatives. It also provides a nice introduction to the study of primate ethology.

Joseph Shepher's study of the *kibbutzim* is titled "Mate Selection among Second-Generation Kibbutz Adolescents and Adults: Incest Avoidance and Negative Imprinting." Don't let the long title turn you off—give it a try. It's in *Archives of Sexual Behavior* (27:259–272, 1971).

chapter 6

Knowing How to Survive
The Cultural Primate

Among the most amazing builders in the world are weaver ants from the Old World tropics. Colonies of these ants construct nests in trees in the form of tents made from the tree's leaves. To do this, teams of ants form living ropes, suspended between the leaves, and pull the leaves together. Then other ants bind the leaves with silk. This they get from their own larvae. Worker ants hold the larvae in their jaws and give them a signal with their antennae that causes them to release the silk from special glands. By swinging the silk-producing larvae back and forth, the workers "sew" the leaves, gradually forming their nest.

A few months ago I decided to build a wall and hang a door in order to create a new room for my study. Having virtually no knowledge of such matters, my first step was to purchase a book all about home improvements. Once I had digested all the necessary information about construction theory, lumber, Sheetrock, and tools, I drew up my plans. Still unsure of myself, I asked a colleague, who is quite experienced in these things, to come over and look at my drawing and proposed construction site. Based on his knowledge, he told me (amazing!) that my plans were fine, and he gave me a few pointers relevant to my specific project. Off I went to buy the required materials and some shiny new power tools, and a few days (and half a container of wood filler) later, I had my new room, complete with a door that really closes. Here I sit, then, at this very moment, looking at my handiwork with a real sense of pride—as any visitor can attest to—and sure that I am now a tried-and-true do-it-yourselfer and ready to build other things.

I think you probably see where I'm headed. Both these examples are quite amazing feats of engineering (well, at least the ants' is), but they are fundamentally different. My project was cultural; the ants' was not. I had to do all sorts of thinking and analyzing to build my wall. The ants didn't think at all about their nest. Indeed, ants have nothing to think with!

This distinction is obvious. It's pretty easy to decide whether a behavior is cultural or not. We've been talking about culture all along in this book, and you've probably had no problem understanding what it means. We all know what culture is.

Or do we? Can you define culture? Can you create a sentence or two that clearly tells why my wall is cultural but the ants' nest is not? If you can't, don't worry; you're in good company. For the whole history of anthropology, one continual project has been to try to come up with just such a definition. There is even an entire book devoted to nothing but anthropologists' definitions of culture. One reason for the difficulty is simply that the phenomenon of culture is so complex. The second reason is that, until recently, we were trying desperately to define culture in such a way as to make it our unique possession. As you can probably guess, it's not.

Now don't think, after this buildup, that I'm going to present you with *the* definition of culture! It's such a complex concept that any one-sentence definition would be superficial. We want a working definition, one that specifically tells why those two building behaviors are distinct. The best way to do that is to list and discuss the characteristics of culture; to show, point by point, how those behaviors are different; and to examine in what ways some nonhuman organisms exhibit cultural behaviors.

THE CONCEPT OF CULTURE

Perhaps the easiest characteristic of culture to see, and the clearest distinction between the two behaviors, is that culture is *learned*. The ants clearly didn't learn how to build nests, even as complex as that behavior is. Rather, the behavior is built into their genes and set off by some series of stimuli eliciting a particular set of responses. My accomplishment, on the other hand, was obviously possible only through learning, and the skills and information I learned were in turn learned by those who taught me, who learned it from someone else, and so on.

Learning used to be considered the only distinguishing feature between our behavior and that of other creatures, but a moment's reflection will tell you that it's not nearly enough. Other animals learn. My dog, for example, has learned not to defecate on the living room rug. But though I taught her that for my cultural reasons, is the behavior cultural on her part? I think not. So what else is different between me and the ants?

A second characteristic of culture is that it involves *concepts, generalizations, abstractions,* and *ideas*. The ants are locked into their nest-building behavior; it must work the same all the time. They don't *know* what they're doing. The behavior is not part of a larger concept. Change one aspect—say, the kind of tree, some climatic factor, or the number of available larvae—and the whole behavior (and probably the nest) falls apart. My wall building, however, certainly involves concepts. My book didn't relate to my wall in particular but gave general ideas about partition building. No external stimuli elicited a wall-building response in me. Rather, I decided, through conscious thought, to do the project. As I ran into unexpected problems while working (there were lots of those), I was able to adapt my knowledge of the general principles to solve them. I should now be able to apply what I've learned from this experience to other, similar tasks.

That sounds good: concepts as a cultural characteristic. But it doesn't absolutely define culture. My dog has some "concept" of the defecation taboo. I certainly don't take her to every house and building we may visit and teach her all over again not to commit that heinous crime in them. No, I'm confident that she has generalized from her training in my house. She has a concept that says something like "don't defecate inside people's buildings." But that still doesn't make her behavior cultural.

We need more. There is, it seems, another dimension to learning. Learning in most organisms is passive. You can learn from trial and error or from imitation, and many organisms do. For many birds, singing just the right song is impossible unless they've heard another bird do it. Singing is genetic, but the exact song must be learned. And remember the birds and the monarchs? The birds had to learn through trial and error about the unpleasant results of eating a butterfly with that pattern.

But learning can also be active, when information is *shared* among organisms, *transmitted* from one to another entirely *extragenetically*, that is, without any direct genetic aspect, as in the birdsong example. The ant's "information" about nest building is, of course, transmitted solely through genes. The information I acquired about wall building was transmitted in an extragenetic fashion.

Now if I bought a new puppy and put it in the house with my present dog, and if I had no input into the situation, do you think the new puppy would learn the defecation taboo? I rather doubt it. Each dog can learn it independently, but one can't share that information with other dogs. The same would hold true for wild dogs in natural situations. Each wolf, for instance, "knows" a lot of specific pieces of information about its environment, but it can't transmit them. Other dogs may learn some fact, say about what foods not to eat, by imitating the behavior of older animals, but they are still learning passively, on their own. It's not culture.

Finally, a characteristic of cultural behavior is the presence of *artifacts*. An artifact is something that is produced or made by artificial means. This book is an artifact; my hormones, although they are continually being produced, are not. An artifact doesn't necessarily have to be concrete. It can be abstract, like the educational institution you're now part of, the religious organization you participate in, or the structure of our nation's government. Artifacts, both concrete tools and abstract organizing principles, facilitate the realization of cultural ideas.

Yes, I know the ants' nest is made; it's something quite concrete. But I said that an artifact must be "artificial." Because the ants' nest building is genetic, it is, in a sense, as natural as their hormones and their body structure. The birds' song? Is that an artifact? Don't make too much out of the learning part of that. Having to hear the right song before a bird can sing it is just to say that the built-in behavior needs the right natural stimulus to set it off. And clearly, there's no artifact that facilitates my dog's behavior of not defecating in the house.

Human culture, on the other hand, not only features artifacts, it is dependent on them. Without artifacts, there is no way I could have built my wall—which, of course, is an artifact itself. I needed books, with written words, produced by publishing houses, purchased with money, to tell me what I needed in the way of materials and tools, which were manufactured by certain companies and which I bought in a store, with money—you get the idea.

So cultural behavior has these four characteristics:

1. It must be learned.
2. It must involve concepts, generalizations, abstractions, ideas.
3. It must be shared through extragenetic transmission.
4. It must be realized through the use of artifacts, both concrete and abstract.

Now, you can put all this into a one-sentence definition if you like, but I find it a pretty awkward sentence, and, anyway, as you've seen, an awful lot of explanation is still necessary. I'll stick with my list and explanatory remarks.

At this point a major question arises. If my dog exhibits a behavior that has two of the four cultural characteristics, is it not possible that some nonhuman organisms, maybe the apes, actually do have behaviors that could be considered cultural? You shouldn't be surprised by now if the answer is yes.

Chimpanzee "termiting."

As we saw with genetic differences, with certain features such as bipedalism, and with the conscious aspect of sexuality, we are not different from our closest primate relatives in kind but in degree. The same holds true for the mental abilities (which we'll discuss soon) that make culture possible. And there are some clear examples of cultural behavior among other primates.

Perhaps the most famous was witnessed by Jane Goodall, the British scientist who has spent more than 20 years studying a large population of chimpanzees in the Gombe Stream Reserve in Tanzania. The chimps there have developed a taste for termites. Except for a short period when African termites sprout wings and fly around forming new colonies, termites spend all their time inside tunnels within large dirt mounds. The chimps have, in a literal sense, solved this problem. Some of them, mostly females, will break a twig off a bush or pull out a long, stiff stalk of grass, tear off any leaves that may get in the way, and snap off any excess length. Then they will insert their "termite fishing stick" into the opening of a tunnel in a termite mound, wiggle it around to cause the termites to "attack" it and hang on to it, and carefully draw it out and have themselves a termite snack. Pretty clever! And it fits our criteria for a cultural behavior.

First of all, it is learned and not programmed in the chimps' genes. It is, as you'll see, far too complex a behavior for that, and anyway, not all chimps do it. It is also shared extragenetically; chimp offspring learn the behavior by closely studying their mothers doing it. It also clearly involves an artifact. But most important, it uses concepts and generalizations. To accomplish this behavior, the chimp must (1) understand the behavior of termites that it cannot see, (2) understand how it can exploit that behavior to get the termites out of their mound, and (3) visualize a tool within a plant and realize the steps needed to modify the natural object to produce the artifact. Moreover, chimps don't need the stimulus of a termite mound (where the insects are out of sight anyway) to elicit the chain of behaviors. They have been seen to make their tool (and different chimps have different styles) and then go looking for a mound. It is clear that they have a concept in mind. When the young chimps imitate the mother's actions, they could not perform such a complex set of behaviors unless they conceptually understood what she was doing. It's not simply a stimulus and a response.

To demonstrate this idea that differences in cultural ability are matters of degree, look at another primate example, this one showing a behavior that might be called "protocultural." On the island of Koshima in Japan, there is a colony of Japanese macaques (Old World monkeys) that has been extensively studied for over 30 years. The scientists conducting the study put piles of sweet potatoes on the beach to get the monkeys to come out in the open. In 1953 a young female they had named Imo began taking her sweet potatoes to a freshwater pool to wash off the sand. In a short time other members of the troop had picked up the idea. Some even washed theirs in the sea, possibly because they liked the salt taste.

But there was more. The investigators also threw rice onto the sand, hoping that it would take the monkeys so long to pick it out that they'd have more time to watch them. But Imo simply picked up a handful of rice and sand, took it to a pool, and dumped the whole thing in the water. The sand sank, but the rice floated, and this she then scooped up and ate. This behavior too, rapidly spread throughout the troop.

Now, this is obviously short one of our criteria; there are no artifacts involved. The monkeys are just manipulating unmodified objects. But it is learned, it is transmitted extragenetically, and it does involve a concept—first on Imo's part and then on the parts of those that imitated her. Sure, raccoons are famous for washing their food. The difference is that the raccoons are programmed to do it. They *all* do it. Not so with the macaques. The scientists saw the

Macaque washing food.

origin of the behavior in one particular monkey and saw it spread. And it didn't spread to everyone. It wasn't a universal trait. Specifically, it seemed to be picked up mostly by the young monkeys; the older ones were more "set in their ways." This, then, is not completely cultural, as we've defined it, but it's well on the way. Culture evolved in stages. So too we see various stages of it manifested in existing organisms.

A final example deals not with actual behaviors under natural circumstances but with behavioral potentials under artificial circumstances. For some time now, people have tried to see if apes could talk. There were a number of attempts at this, but they all failed, since apes simply don't have the vocal apparatus needed to make human sounds. But a lot of humans can't speak either. Many of them use some substitute for spoken language, such as American Sign Language for the Deaf (Ameslan). Maybe, some reasoned, this would work with apes; and guess what? Several chimps and gorillas have become amazingly proficient at using sign language (or some other symbol system), and they use it to communicate in a human language. In other words, all the features that distinguish our communication system from that of other creatures can be used by apes. If you know Ameslan, you can have a conversation with a gorilla! Oh, not about the philosophy of Kant, nor even about the concept of culture. But a real conversation, at the intellectual level of a human child of 3 or 4, with words for abstract ideas as well as for things.

I'll detail this phenomenon in the chapter on language. For now, though, suffice it to say that these achievements indicate that although the apes don't use such a language in the wild, they obviously have the mental capabilities that enable them to manifest the one cultural trait we always thought was ours alone.

So, clearly, other creatures have behaviors that we seem obliged to consider cultural. How, then, are we different? Very simply, in these other animals, behaviors that are obviously cultural are rare. They don't make up the majority of the animal's behavioral repertoire. They are adaptive "icing on the cake." For us, though, culture is absolutely vital. We are dependent on it for our survival. All our behaviors, even though some may have their origins in our biological past, are learned culturally, performed culturally, for cultural reasons. The difference is one of degree, but, if it's any comfort to you, the degree is a great one.

Obviously, though culture is extrabiological, the ability to have culture in the first place is dependent on a biological phenomenon—our brain. Just what is it about our brain, and a little less so about the brain of apes, that makes this ability possible?

BRAINS AND CULTURE

Needless to say, the topic of brain anatomy and function is quite complex, and we're still not completely sure just how it works, especially with regard to things like conscious thought. It's important, however, to understand something about the brain in general to see how it makes our culture possible.

A useful way of looking at the brain, and one that has an evolutionary perspective, is a model devised by Paul MacLean of the National Institute of Mental Health. He calls his model the *triune* ("three-part") *brain*. At the base of the brain, both literally and figuratively, are the oldest parts, the *cerebellum*, which we've already mentioned; the *medulla*, responsible for things like heartbeat, breathing, and digestion; and the *midbrain*, which essentially connects these other parts, called the *hindbrain*, with the rest of the brain. Over the hindbrain and midbrain are the newer parts, the *forebrain*, and this is the part that MacLean sees as coming in three evolutionary stages.

The first and deepest part is called the *R* (for *reptilian*) *complex*, shared, obviously, by all vertebrates of reptile complexity and "higher." This part of the brain deals with such basic self-preservation functions as aggressiveness, territoriality, and social hierarchy. Above this is the old mammalian brain, or *limbic system*. This appears to be the area that controls our strong emotions like fear, rage, altruism (self-sacrificing behavior), and care and concern for the young. Also part of the limbic system are areas dealing with basic sexual functioning and with the olfactory sense. Sex and smell—sound familiar? Something to do with basic memory seems also to be housed in the limbic area.

Surrounding these two parts is the new mammalian brain, or *neocortex*. This is where we "think." Various parts of the neocortex are concerned with perception and deliberation, with spatial reasoning, with vision and hearing, and with the exchange of information between the brain and body. When all these functions act together, we have conscious thought, reasoning, and culture.

Not only are we not certain just how all this operates, but what we do know is beyond the scope of this book. Using analogy, however, I can give you an idea of what goes on in the brain with regard to consciousness and its most extreme expression, culture. My favorite way to put it is to say that with all those functions acting together in various combinations, what we do is "experience events in our brain." That is, we don't respond just to what our senses are sensing at the moment but to what they have sensed in the past, what they may sense in the future, and even to what they would sense in hypothetical situations.

Take the human phenomenon of lying, for instance. Not because I advocate the practice, but because it's something we all do at times and because it's a good example. Suppose someone you're not particularly fond of asks you for a ride home. You don't want to comply, so you lie, saying that you have a doctor's appointment at that time at the opposite end of town.

What went on in your mind? The first thing that happened was that your brain registered the fact, based on stored memory, that you don't like this person. Then, to come up with a way out of the request—something that your brain also told you was necessary—you needed to do an "information retrieval search." Your brain needed to look in its storage area and pull out any piece of information relevant to the situation. Then your brain began putting pieces of data together to concoct a hypothetical event that would sound plausible and would relieve you from the unpleasant task of driving this person home. Having come up with a possible excuse, your brain then tested it: Does it fit all the facts of your lifestyle, personal situation, and so on? Will it in fact provide you with a way out? Will the person believe it? You experience, in your brain, the event of telling the story to the person and of their reaction to it. Maybe one story doesn't seem to work too well; you go back again to concoct and test another one. Having finally come up with one that will seem to work, you then actually tell it to the person, hoping that your brain has done its job. It usually has. And it does all that in a split second!

This basic process applies not only to the questionable practice of telling lies to your fellow humans but to nearly any event in our lives—solving problems, planning our day, learning the rules of our culture, writing and reading the sentences in this book. Our brain has the ability to store massive amounts of information, to retrieve that information, and to manipulate it. We are not stuck with just memories of whole events; we are able to store the pieces of those events as well. We can pull the memories apart, using only the pieces that are relevant, and we can put pieces from various events together in all sorts of combinations to create hypothetical events for solving problems, producing scientific hypotheses, making generalizations about experiences, and, yes, even lying. Keep this process in mind as we move on to subsequent chapters to talk about human cultural adaptations and see how those adaptations would be impossible without brains that work this way.

Now that you understand the biology behind this behavioral characteristic, it's also easy to understand how certain animals exhibit some cultural ability. Especially with regard to humans and apes, we are simply not that different in total biology, including, of course, brain structure and function. Apes have fairly large neocortices too. Their brains can go through the same kinds of processes as ours, just not as complex. In fact, since a neocortex is possessed by all the mammals, it's reasonable to attribute some "thinking" ability to them all. My dog can certainly "reason" on a rudimentary level. (Yes, so can *yours*!) Whales and dolphins are known to be highly intelligent, which simply means that they have complex neocortices as well. We are different in degree, not kind.

This difference can be accounted for evolutionarily. In conjunction with the trends toward bipedalism, conscious sex, and a nuclear family structure, there was also selection for protohuman primates who had larger neocortices, who could "reason" at a more complex level. This would have enhanced the conscious controls over sex, over the degree of personal recognition and interaction with other species members, and over the problems posed by the environment itself—things like getting food and avoiding predators on the savannas.

And there you are! The upright, sexual, cultural primate—all together. Of course, not all these trends were of equal importance at the same evolutionary time. Bipedalism and the change in sexual behavior (if Lovejoy's idea holds) came long before our huge brains. Apparently 5 or 6 million years ago, when these things seem to have started, perhaps just a small increase in neocortex size and complexity would have sufficed. But once off on that track, selection would try to enhance the features that make it possible. Since a big brain was already vital to the system, perhaps an even bigger, more complex brain would make it better. This seems to have been the case, for over the 3.5 million documented years of human evolution, we see an increase in brain size—the result of natural selection "fine-tuning" the system. As bigger brains kept adding to the success of this new species, selection, always having enough variation available, made them bigger. And today we have the very large, incredibly complex brains that typify us.

Now, that's the story of *culture* as a species characteristic shared by us all. But there's another level: *cultures*—the specific sets of rules that govern various societies within this species. How does that work? How do we explain the enormous amount of variation from one culture to the next? How do we go about studying and explaining different cultural systems?

A CULTURAL MODEL

It should be obvious from all we've just discussed that culture at the species level is an *adaptive mechanism*—it is how we survive in our various environments: how we get food, find shelter, organize our groups, and so on.

In this regard it's easy to understand some of the cultural variation we observe around the world. People's cultures are geared to the conditions of their habitats. Eskimos have all sorts of cultural ideas and technologies for hunting seals but not for hunting kangaroos; for Native Australians it's just the opposite. We have all sorts of devices here in our temperate climate that help keep us warm during the winter. Native Americans from the tropical rain forests of Brazil, however, are concerned very little about this.

But what about peoples who live in almost the same sort of environment but whose cultures differ anyway? Philadelphia in the United States and Beijing (Peking) in the People's Republic of China, being at the same latitude, have very similar climates, but the cultures of the two cities are very different in everything from economics to religious beliefs to clothing styles. The climate of highland New Guinea is relatively homogeneous, yet that area is (or was until recent political upheavals) the home of hundreds of distinct cultures. How can we explain this in terms of the adaptation theme we've been following in our study?

Well, culture has two facets. It is the major adaptive mechanism for coping with our basic environmental needs. But at the same time it has become such an important, all-pervasive part of our lives that it has actually become *our environment*. Look around you: Everything you come in contact with, everything you're concerned about, all the solutions to your concerns are cultural. And in that light we can see that most cultural adaptations (once we've taken care of the basic biological needs) are adaptations to culture itself. Most changes in a cultural system are responses to other cultural changes. Culture is *integrated*. So we must look within cultural systems and view them as their own integrated environments in order to understand just how they work and why we see such a great degree of variation.

There are as many specific ways of going about this as there are anthropologists, and there are, as you'll see later, some major schools of thought with regard to basic approach. But I think all anthropologists would agree with what I've said in the preceding paragraph and with the model I'm about to present. It is, to be sure, my own particular way of looking at cultural systems and would be altered a little by other anthropologists. It does, however, capture the basic outlook of the field.

We begin, naturally, with biological humans. We should never lose sight of the fact that despite the power of culture, we are still limited by our biological structure, function, and needs. However, because part of our biology includes a brain capable of culture, there are all sorts of ways in which we can go about fulfilling our basic needs. There are *many possible behavior patterns*. Our task is to figure out why, from all the possible patterns, each society of people practices one particular pattern.

I like to visualize all the possibilities going into a giant filter, like the one in a drip coffeemaker. All the unwanted cultural behaviors are filtered out, but those that are wanted get through and

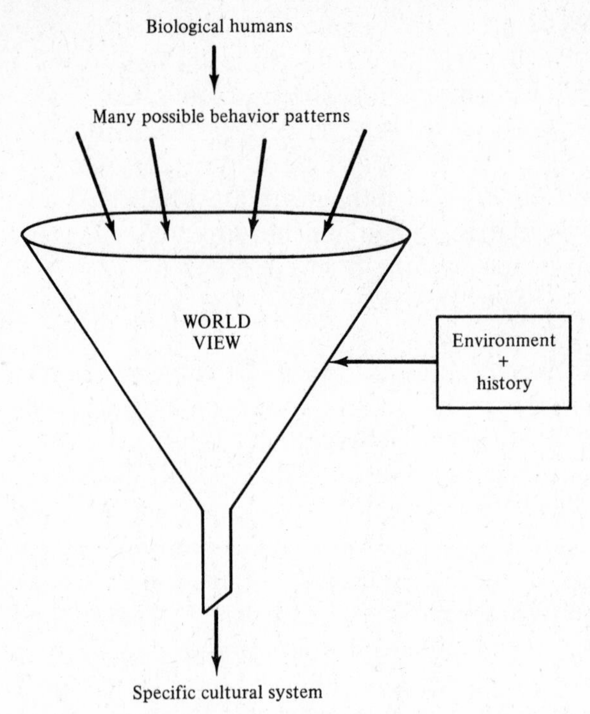

A cultural model.

together become the *specific cultural system*. The problem then comes down to what label to put on the filter. What is it that determines which cultural items are part of the system?

The filter can be labeled "World View." World view is, as one anthropologist put it, a "set of assumptions about the way things are." What sorts of "things"? Well, things like where the world came from, where people and other living creatures came from, how the weather works, why organisms behave as they do, what causes disease, what happens when something dies—basic ideas about the world in which one lives.

I can hear you saying, "I thought he just said culture was adaptive, that it took care of environmental and cultural needs. Real, concrete items. So how can all the parts of a cultural system stem from these abstract world-view assumptions?" The answer is that world view doesn't just appear out of the blue. It may be made up of abstract ideas, but those ideas are based on real traits of a group's environment, both natural and cultural. So the diagram includes the things that give rise to a world view. They are *environment*, by which

I mean the natural features of the society's world, and *history*, their cultural features, past and present.

These two things alone won't work as labels for the filter because not every item of culture is directly related to real, concrete traits of the environment. They are not all as obvious as Eskimos needing ways to hunt seals but not kangaroos. What matters is what a group thinks about its world and its culture, the sorts of attitudes generated by the complex interaction of the natural environment and the cultural history of a people.

Some examples are in order at this point—but not, as usual, without words of caution, in this case two. First, these examples are simplifications. I'll be trying to narrow things down as much as possible in order to show what we mean by world view and how it works. In real life much more would be involved. All aspects of a cultural system interact with all other aspects and with all the facets of the environment and history. Culture is integrated, so a full analysis should include everything. You'll see this clearly in the following chapters, and some of the questions you may have about these examples will be specifically addressed later.

Second, one cannot talk about a society's world view without speaking in religious terms. This is because that's how people talk to one another about their world view. One of the cultural functions of religion is to make the world view real, to put it into words that can be shared by all members of a society. But religion is not the same as world view. Religion is part of the cultural system that comes out of the filter.

Keeping these things in mind, let's compare two rather distinct world views: that of Eskimos with those of certain societies from the Middle East starting about 12,000 years ago.

The environment of the Eskimo is one of the harshest inhabited by humans. Of course, the recent contact between Eskimos and "Westerners" and the adoption by Eskimos of such things as rifles, snowmobiles, and prepared foods have made things a little easier. But before these historical events, the world of the Eskimo was an unstable one, one where the slightest environmental change could literally mean the difference between life and death. Not that the Eskimo was not well adapted; indeed, Eskimos are known for their ingenuity at using natural resources cleverly and efficiently to satisfy their basic needs. But still, the Arctic was not an easy place to live, and the Eskimos saw that world as one over which their control was limited, tenuous, and unstable.

How is this view reflected in Eskimo religion? In other words,

An Eskimo.

how did the Eskimo articulate this world view? Eskimos are *polytheistic*; that is, their supernatural world has many beings. In fact, the Eskimos have a spirit for every natural phenomenon with which they are concerned, including the Eskimos themselves. The spirit world controls directly all aspects of nature and the events of human life. Asen Balikci, an anthropologist who has studied Eskimos extensively, says that they consider the natural world, the supernatural world, and the human moral order as one whole that has existed from the beginning of time. Moreover, since each natural phenomenon is under the control of a spirit, changes in these phenomena are seen to be at the whim of the spirit. The spirits, Balikci says, are "unreliable."

For the natural world to have some stability, for Eskimos to be able to live year to year in such a world, and for them to feel some sense of control, they must constantly be aware of the spirit world and must, at crucial times, perform rituals to placate the unreliable spirits. For instance, it is a common Eskimo practice after a hunt to perform a short ritual begging the forgiveness of the spirit of the animal killed. For if the spirit is not placated, it can choose not to replace the animal and would thus impair the success of future hunts.

Thus the world in which the Eskimos live, their cultural relation to it, and their feelings about it all make up their world view. This world view is articulated and shared through their religious system, and it acts as a "filter," filtering out possible cultural features that would not be consistent with the world view and letting through those that are, those that will support the life of the people in that environment, support the cultural system that makes that survival possible, and support their feelings and attitudes about their lives. Remember, culture itself is also an environment that must be adapted to.

Contrast this with a second example. In the Middle East prior to about 12,000 years ago, people lived the same basic sort of existence as the Eskimos. Not as hard a life perhaps but still one dependent on naturally occurring resources in an environment where humans were pretty much at the mercy of nature. Old religions in the area (as reflections of world views) probably were also polytheistic, with various spirits controlling the important natural phenomena.

But about 12,000 years ago, an important historical event occurred: the invention of agriculture. People who had this cultural ability had control over perhaps their most important resource, food. Think of how that would alter the feelings of a people about their world and their place in it! Their world view would certainly change. And we see this clearly reflected in the three important religious systems that originated in the Middle East: Judaism; its offshoot, Christianity; and Islam.

All three of these religions are *monotheistic*; they recognize one supernatural being. And that being has control over all natural phenomena, including human affairs. But things aren't entirely out of human hands. First, in all these systems, humans are said to be created in the image of the supernatural being, God. As such, humans are given a special place in the world, with special powers and abilities over other creatures. In the Judeo-Christian Bible, for example, it's humans who name the animals; humans are enjoined to multiply and subdue the Earth; animals and plants are stated to have been placed on Earth for the use of people.

Second, humans are not so much at the whimsical mercy of the supernatural as they are under the Eskimo system. In the Judaic-Christian-Islamic tradition, humans can petition God through prayer and action. They can ask God for favors and, if God is pleased, have those requests answered. Humans have some control in their dealings with God.

Farming in ancient Egypt.

This is all a clear reflection and articulation of a world view in which humans see themselves with real ability to know and understand the world around them and to use that knowledge to exercise some real control over their world for their own benefit. The science that allows us in the industrialized world to enjoy all our technological and medical benefits is possible only with such a world view.

Now, don't get the idea that all analyses of culture are this clear-cut. I've oversimplified a little. To analyze fully you would eventually have to include every aspect of a society's integrated cultural system. But to show you that this model can be useful for understanding all sorts of human matters, I give you the following parable.

THE STORY OF THE NECKTIE

In class several years ago, after I had gone over what you've just read, one perceptive student asked, "What about your necktie? It has no practical purpose with regard to survival. Explain that one with your filter!" "Well," I faltered, "sometimes certain cultural practices are so obscure and indirectly related to whole systems that it's nearly impossible to figure them out in this perspective."

Overnight, though, I gave it some thought, and in the next class I proudly presented my analysis. The origin of this specific item—a colored piece of cloth tied around the neck of males—*is* obscure. It seems to have come by its modern form during the reign of Louis XIV of France when, called a "cravat" (from the French word for "Croatian"), it was worn as part of the uniform of Croatian soldiers. It most likely goes back even farther than that.

But the important thing is its meaning in our culture. It is a symbol of status. It is worn in certain situations where one is expected to display one's social status, socioeconomic position, and attitude about the situation. Certain jobs, for example, virtually, if not actually, require a necktie. One must be worn in some restaurants. A man must wear one to job interviews or for court appearances, regardless of which side of the legal fence he's on. And when worn in seemingly inappropriate situations—say, to an archaeological excavation—a tie is a clear sign of the wearer's wealth and high status. This useless and often uncomfortable item lacks any practical purpose but is obviously important as a symbol for ideas.

So what? Well, the whole thing takes on importance when you realize that in some cultures there is no concept of status or wealth differences. Among people classed as hunter-gatherers—people like the Eskimos, who rely solely on naturally occurring resources—it would prove at least inefficient, and possibly fatal, if some people had more wealth and power than others. Rather, in such societies (which we'll discuss in detail in the next chapter) wealth is distributed equally among the members, and there are no recognized differences in social status. Sure, some people may be better hunters than others, or more adept at decision making, but they don't institutionalize and formalize those differences. They can't afford to have anything but a group of people all working together for the common good.

However, in societies that have agriculture—that have control over their food sources—you find a new phenomenon: surplus resources. At least when things are going well, a family can produce more than they need to feed themselves. What do they do with the excess? They probably trade it to someone else for some other resource that that person has a surplus of. Now everyone doesn't have to do everything. I could concentrate on growing wheat and let my neighbor specialize in dairying, and we can both reap the benefits through trade. Moreover, with all this trading going on, we might find the need for someone to oversee the economic transactions—a leader who could lead full-time because those of us he was serving would make sure he had all the necessary resources. And with all that wealth changing hands, all those resource surpluses, and all the specializations in labor, it's inevitable that some people are going to have more than others, both more wealth and more power, the two usually going hand in hand. And there you have status differences.

Our culture, call it Western culture if you will, can trace its ancestry back to early agricultural societies of the Middle East and Europe. Our cultural tradition has long had the concept of status differences built right into it. So the tie itself has a history of its own. But its use as a symbol denoting a differential in wealth and power "ties in" directly with our world view—with our environment and the particular history of the way in which we cope with it.

This, then, is the nature of culture and the way anthropologists go about studying it, both as a specieswide characteristic and as a set of variable behaviors among human populations.

Now that we understand this upright, sexual, cultural primate, we can proceed to look at the individual categories of its adaptations. The categories we'll use would work with any organism; they are the kinds of categories used by ethologists examining adaptative behaviors. They list the major behaviors needed for survival. We are an organism, and the importance of this behavior of ours is as an adaptive mechanism—adapted to the natural environment and to the cultural environment it has brought about. So as long as you keep clearly in mind the nature of culture, you'll see that these categories work as well for us as for any other living thing.

SUMMARY

A cultural behavior is a concept or idea that is shared among members of a population, transmitted extragenetically through learning, and realized through artifacts. Culture is our major adaptive mechanism, a mechanism we absolutely depend on for our survival. But the rudiments of culture can be observed in some nonhuman primates; indeed, chimpanzees who manufacture artifacts are clearly engaged in cultural behaviors, though such behaviors are probably not vital to the perpetuation of their species.

The human brain—the organ that enables us to have culture—may be seen as having different functional levels, the results of different stages of our evolutionary history. All these levels operate together to produce our basic behavioral repertoire. The actual workings of the brain are complex and not completely understood. We can, however, express the cultural functioning of the brain by saying that it is the ability of the brain to "experience events"—present, past, and hypothetical—and to store those events in memory and consciously manipulate their parts.

Culture is a species characteristic. But individual cultural systems differ greatly. To explain, understand, and analyze a given cultural system requires that we see each system as an integrated set of behaviors, all of which are related directly or indirectly to the abstract assumptions about the world we call "world view." World view in turn may be seen as society's response to the kind of environment in which its members live and the nature of their cultural adaptation thus far.

NOTES, REFERENCES, AND READINGS

Ants, with their completely "programmed" social behaviors, make for an interesting comparison with the more conscious behaviors of the primates. For more on these fascinating insects, see the article in *National Geographic* (June 1984) by Bert Hölldobler, "The Wonderfully Diverse Ways of the Ant."

Discussions of the emergence of human culture from the basic primate background can be found in the book by Jane Lancaster noted in Chapter 5 and in Hans Kummer's *Primate Societies: Group Techniques of Ecological Adaptation* (Chicago: Aldine, 1971). For more detail on the behavior of chimpanzees, read the wonderful book by Jane van Lawick–Goodall called *In the Shadow of Man* (Boston: Houghton Mifflin, 1971). A discussion of the Japanese potato-washing monkeys, placed in the context of the Primate order in general, is in Chapter 12 of David Attenborough's *Life on Earth: A Natural History* (Boston: Little, Brown, 1979). The last chapter of that book also talks about the beginnings of the human species and about our communicative ability. Try also to see the corresponding episodes of Attenborough's TV series by the same name.

Carl Sagan talks about the human brain in the chapter called "The Persistence of Memory" in his *Cosmos* (New York: Random House, 1980). A broad evolutionary perspective on the brain makes up his Pulitzer Prize–winning work *The Dragons of Eden: Speculations on the Evolution of Human Intelligence* (New York: Random House, 1977).

Asen Balikci's book on the Eskimos is called *The Netsilik Eskimo* (Garden City, N.Y.: Natural History Press, 1970).

three

OUR ADAPTATIONS

chapter 7

Food
Getting It, Growing It, Eating It, and Passing It Around

FOOD AND HUMAN EVOLUTION

In Part Two I mentioned food in two important contexts. First, it seems to have been the quest for food that started our evolution in the first place. As you recall, some environmental difficulty made widely spaced offspring maladaptive and promoted selection for the more frequent production of offspring. The environmental difficulty may well have involved a food shortage, possibly due to the worldwide drying trend taking place at the time. This led to a further problem with food since there were now more mouths to feed and females were less mobile. The solution was selection for bipedalism and for the dawning consciousness of sex, personal recognition, and ways to manipulate the environment to one's own ends.

Second, in a cultural context, when we were discussing the meaning of the necktie, we compared types of social status differences in terms of the food-getting techniques of the cultures involved. The Eskimos relied on naturally occurring resources, whereas the Middle Eastern groups grew their own food. The food-getting techniques gave rise to and explained the status differences or lack of them.

All this is not really surprising, of course. Food is obviously important. No organism can survive without nutrients to build its structure and run its functions. If there's not enough food, a living thing doesn't really have to worry about finding shelter or reproducing.

This is as true for humans as it is for any creature. Indeed, when we talk about types of human groups, we tend to categorize them in terms of their food-getting techniques, what we call *subsistence patterns*.This is because, as you saw briefly, how a society gets its food has important ramifications for all other aspects of its culture. What food is available and how we can get it clearly has a lot to do with our world view, which affects our whole cultural system.

If you think about it, in fact, you can consider food a moving force behind human history. We've seen how it may be related to the very beginning of our evolution. And as we go through our evolutionary history, we see that it continues to play a crucial role.

For example, the two early branches of hominids, the australopithecines and the one leading to us, were differentiated environmentally largely by food source. The australopithecines exhibited evolution toward a more and more vegetarian diet, while our branch was more *omnivorous*—our ancestors ate anything. This difference is fairly clearly reflected in the dentition of the fossils and in certain other features of the skull.

One important source of food for our branch—the branch forced out onto the open savannas—was meat. There was plenty of meat to go around there, something that was not always true of plants that the hominid digestive system could handle. We probably began our meat eating by scavenging—taking meat away from predators like lions and cheetahs or simply waiting around and helping ourselves to what was left after chasing away the vultures and jackals. But it seems that soon it dawned on our ancestors that they could take a more active role in meat acquisition. After all, chimps have been seen to hunt and kill small mammals on occasion. Moreover, with our growing ability to manipulate our environment, we could conceivably make tools to aid us in this endeavor. Human hunting was added to scavenging and gathering.

This adaptation was really put to the test about a million years ago as humans began to spread out into other Old World continents. As they did, you remember, many of them ran smack into the glaciers and the arcticlike climates they produced. In such climates, plants that can be eaten by primates are scarce, so hunting takes on a greater role in human subsistence. Eskimos, for instance, relied almost entirely on hunting for their food. This emphasis seems to be true for many early humans as well. In glaciated areas especially, we find tools, weapons, and other objects specialized for the hunt—things like stone spear points, harpoons made from antler with rows of barbs, and scrapers for working animal hides. And recall the evidence of group hunting practices from Torralba.

In addition, when hunting of big game takes on such importance to a group's subsistence, it is bound to have an effect on their social order. It has been suggested that this type of subsistence really established the practice of forming a stable, two-parent family unit and a society made up of a cooperating group of these units. This may have been when the biological basis for these habits got translated into cultural norms. Furthermore, such a subsistence pattern would necessitate a formalization of the *division of labor* whereby females, being somewhat less mobile, would take care of gathering plant material and males would do the hunting, the activity that usually took longer, was more life-threatening, and involved travel farther from the home base.

Hunting also seems to have been instrumental in the beginnings of human art. Some of the earliest art we know of, beautiful cave paintings in France and Spain, depicts game animals and hunting scenes. I'll discuss these paintings and their meanings later.

It should be noted here that as important as hunting may have been in our evolution, it can be overemphasized. Old anthropology books can sometimes give you the idea that the human species *began* as big-game hunters who sort of invaded the savannas with their weapons and started killing things. You also can get the idea, reading older descriptions of existing cultures, that in hunter-gatherer groups, the hunting part is by far the more important activity.

Neither idea is accurate. We've already discussed how meat eating probably began in our species. And as far as existing cultures go, except for Arctic groups like the Eskimo, gathering is actually the more important activity in terms of the relative amount of nutrition it brings in. In southern African Bushmen groups, for example, at least 75 percent of the food eaten is plant material gathered by the women. And therein lies part of the explanation for this occasional overemphasis.

Anthropologists have, I hate to admit, been guilty of a little sexism. The field, long dominated by males, has, I think, wanted to see the human species as a macho kind of creature. It was a comforting idea that our very existence and all our physical and cultural features got their start with the hunt. It seemed kind of demeaning to think that we may have begun the carnivorous part of our diet by waiting for lions to finish a meal and then picking over the leavings. Similarly, the idea was often brushed aside that gathering by the women might actually be more important nutritionally. We've matured a lot lately.

But there is a second, and more justified, reason for the misinterpretation. Hunter-gatherer groups themselves tend to emphasize the hunting part of their subsistence despite its sometimes limited role in their nutrition. This is because it is usually the more tenuous of the two activities, the more dangerous, the one less likely to yield results on a regular basis, the one that causes the most anxiety. There are more rituals related to hunting success than to gathering success. So we must be careful not to let our own cultural biases or those of the people we're studying affect our ability to interpret the facts objectively.

Finally, there are some other possible food-related explanations for facets of our evolution. Remember the gradual smoothing out of the facial features and decrease in the size of the teeth that took place in our evolution? And the final change from the rugged features of the Neanderthals to the more graceful ones of modern *Homo sapiens*, especially in the skull? One explanation for these poorly understood evolutionary changes is that our teeth and jaws were becoming less important as tools. As strides were made in stone tool technology, as it became more of a habit to cook meat, and as later, when the glaciers receded, many human groups went from an emphasis on big game to a more mixed diet, the need decreased for large teeth and huge muscles to move them. It has even been suggested that the invention of eating utensils may have brought about some physical alterations in the jaws and teeth.

Food has, of course, continued to play an important role in historic periods. There are countless examples. The potato, for instance, suggested in France as a good, easily grown crop to stave off famine, became such an important part of Irish agriculture that when the potato crop failed in 1845 and 1846, the results were widespread starvation and the emigration of thousands of Irish, many to the United States.

Food has often been used as a tool to manipulate people and events. During war, the two items that opposing forces try hardest to keep from their enemy are ammunition and food. Many a battle has been won or lost as a result of the availability of food supplies. Similarly, a people can best be subjugated by withholding food. During the 1981 crisis in Poland, when food supplies were miserably short, the Polish people placed the blame for the shortage on the government, claiming it was the government's way of putting down the Solidarity labor union movement. Whether this is true or not, the economic situation certainly increased tension within that country, and, not too surprisingly, food supplies increased once martial law was established.

Or consider relations between the United States and the Soviet Union. Despite the military tension and cultural differences, there has been for some time a great deal of trade between the two countries. Especially important are the shipments of grain, particularly wheat, that the United States and Canada sell to the USSR—important because Soviet agriculture, unlike other aspects of its technology, is not nearly as productive as that of the West. The Soviets literally rely on this trade to maintain adequate food supplies.

By the way, the reason for this is too interesting and too relevant to our whole topic to pass up. It seems that in the 1930s a Russian agronomist (a specialist in agricultural science) named T. D. Lysenko proposed a theory for cultivating plants that was based not on what was then understood about evolution and genetics but on Lamarckian ideas. In particular, Lysenko thought he could impart the characteristics of winter wheat to spring wheat by refrigerating spring wheat seeds! As ridiculous as we know this is, the general idea was accepted as official scientific doctrine because it fit Marxist-Leninist social theory better than did the ideas of Darwin and Mendel. Lysenko's ideas, needless to say, didn't work too well, but it wasn't until 1965 that mainstream scientific theory with regard to genetics was reinstated in the USSR. By then, Soviet agriculture was far behind the West's. This is what can happen when scientific theory is determined not by the scientific method but by ideology.

At any rate, it should be obvious that the acquisition of food is a central concern to our species and to the individual populations within the species. And we can thus use subsistence patterns as meaningful categories to organize our examination of cultural variation. We should begin with the pattern that today is practiced by the fewest people but in broad evolutionary perspective is the most important.

HUNTING AND GATHERING

When in 1973 I began organizing notes for my first classes, I recall reading somewhere that there were only 30,000 people in the world who were still hunter-gatherers—approximately the number of full-time students at the university I attended. Figures are hard to come by now, but I would imagine that there are probably none left today—no groups who rely strictly on naturally occurring resources. The modern world has encroached everywhere, bringing with it its technology and medicine and education, as well as its problems and abuses. Populations that acquire some food by hunting or gathering, or both, probably still exist, but it is likely that they also use foods that they or other people have grown.

Although the assurance of food, health facilities, and so on may seem to be a positive development, it does have its negative side. For there are numerous cases of small groups of hunter-gatherer people being moved off their land to make room for farms or roads, being relocated to refugee camps where their culture (and dignity) is obliterated, or, in the worst cases, simply being killed. So it is probably impossible to observe today a true hunter-gatherer culture. Fortunately, there are still people in these populations who remember the way it used to be. There are firsthand anthropological descriptions, and photographs and films. We can, then, get a glimpse into this type of life.

Why is this so important? Aside form the ethical considerations (which we'll take up later), the hunter-gatherer way of life is, in one respect, *the* human subsistence pattern. If we accept the idea that our evolutionary line is, say, 5 million years old and if we add the fact that agriculture has been known for only about 12,000 years, we realize that over 99 percent of human history is the history solely of hunter-gatherers. All our basic physical distinctions, cultural abilities, and cultural practices arose in that kind of situation. It is obviously vital that we understand what it's like to be a hunter-gatherer.

I've already mentioned two characteristics of this subsistence pattern: Such societies tend to have no status or wealth differences, and they are generally polytheistic.

This first trait—the lack of stratification (remember *strata*, "layers"?) within the society—is known as *egalitarianism* (from the same root as *equal*). Although some individuals have skills and talents not shared by others and some have more influence on decision making, there are no *recognized, formalized* status differences, and there are most assuredly no differences in access to resources. As explained earlier the society simply can't afford to have it otherwise. The social order, not to mention the physical welfare of the people, would fall apart.

Hunter-gatherer groups tend to be *polytheistic*, recognizing many supernatural beings. As noted, this is a direct reflection of the world view that is shared by such groups—a world view that sees the environment as unstable and humans pretty much at the mercy of that environment.

Individual hunter-gatherer populations are usually *small*, averaging about 50 persons. It's difficult to support groups larger than this using only what nature provides. Moreover, these groups, which we call *bands*, are usually made up of several families, generally ones that are related. Thus things like the distribution of food are always organized along lines of kinship. Finally, in the realm of demographics, hunter-gatherer bands tend to be flexible in their membership. In times of scarce resources, for example, the band may contain only a handful of nuclear families. But when times are better, several of these small bands may get together to pool their resources

Eskimos, winter.

and talents and form a larger band. The cycles of hunter-gatherer groups are the cycles of nature.

As you might guess, these populations are *nomadic*; rather than staying put all the time, they move around, following the animal and plant foods they rely on. The degree of movement, of course, depends on the degree of seasonal climatic fluctuation and the response of the resources to it. Mbuti Pygmies in the tropical forests of Zaire, for instance, don't have to move around much at all. Eskimos, on the other hand, often have to migrate every season, since the main food source changes with the yearly cycle. The Netsilik Eskimo, from the Hudson Bay area, hunt for seals through the ice in the winter and fish for salmon and hunt for caribou inland in the summer. Imagine the distances they need to travel—and the results if for some reason they fail to obtain enough of each animal.

As you should have figured out, hunter-gatherers practice *sharing* of food and other resources. This is how they maintain their egalitarianism with regard to wealth differences. To be sure, some individuals or some families might be better at hunting or gathering, but in the end the results of everyone's labor must be distributed equally. The distribution of resources is done along kinship lines,

Eskimos, summer.

and the rules of who gives what to whom can get pretty complex, but eventually everyone has an equal share.

Just to show you that there are few hard-and-fast rules in the study of culture, what I just said about equal sharing has a tendency not to be as true for plant foods as for meat in some groups. This is because in those groups, the plants gathered by the women are a more dependable source than the meat brought back by the men. Thus women may give the results of their labors only to their immediate families without adversely affecting the whole group, since all the other women are able to do the same thing.

This division of labor whereby men hunt and women gather is the only type of *labor specialization* found in hunter-gatherer societies. While, naturally, not everyone does everything, there is still no formal specialization—no full-time leader or weapons-maker or cook. Within the appropriate sex role, each person does whatever he or she is capable of. It wouldn't work out otherwise.

Finally, there is *no ownership* of resources or land. One band may normally *forage* (the collective term for hunting and gathering) in a particular area, but it is not considered their territory; they don't fight over land rights. Groups must be able to move around to where the resources are. Keeping an outside group off your "property" may someday backfire on you when your resources fail. So there is sharing between bands within a hunter-gatherer culture as well as within bands.

Although you would be hard put to find any society today that exhibits this specific set of characteristics, enough groups have lived this way in the recent past to allow us to derive the profile just presented and to understand how such people adapt. There are a number of hunter-gatherer populations about which a good deal of anthropological information has been written. I've already mentioned Eskimos, who range from Alaska to Greenland (as well as some closely related groups in Siberia); Pygmies from the forests of Zaire; and Bushmen from the Kalahari desert of southwestern Africa. In addition, we know quite a bit about various populations of native Australians; peoples from the Andaman Islands in the Bay of Bengal; other native American groups, from Tierra del Fuego at the tip of South America to the Shoshone and Cheyenne from the North American West; and the Tasaday, a population of two dozen people isolated for thousands of years in the jungles of Mindanao in the Philippines and discovered by the outside world in 1971.

Because hunter-gatherers live in such a diverse array of environments, and because we as a species have been hunter-gatherers

A !Kung family.

for the vast majority of our history, it is hard to pick one group as a "typical" foraging society. Eskimos, with their almost total dependence on hunting, are rather atypical. The Tasaday, on the other hand, didn't really "hunt" anything much larger than fish and frogs. Maybe it's not really important since all hunter-gatherer groups share the traits discussed, but one group in particular stands out for me as giving us the best glimpse into this way of life. It's an African population, which of course is where it all started. These are the famous !Kung Bushmen.

First, something about the name: The *!* in *!Kung* denotes a click sound. These people have four different clicks as functional *phonemes* (sounds) in their language. The *!* click, for example, is an *alveopalatal* click, made be putting your tongue flat on the roof of your mouth then drawing it quickly away to make a popping noise. Try it. I'll discuss this more in the chapter on language.

In addition, the term *Bushmen*, which is what the Dutch settlers called them, now has racist connotations. We generally try to refer to the !Kung and related groups by a word that another native population used: San, meaning "aborigine." (The San's name for themselves is even harder to pronounce then !Kung.)

One more introductory note: When we write about a population, we use what is known as the "ethnographic present." That is, we speak in the present tense regardless of how the people might exist at the moment or whether they exist at all. In the case of the San, their lives today, as you'll see later, are far different from what will be described. But for the moment we are interested in how they lived when they were indeed hunter-gatherers.

There are about 50,000 who would consider themselves San now living in the Kalahari desert area, which covers much of the border between Namibia and Botswana. The Kalahari, by the way, is not technically a desert because for several months each year it has a good deal of rain. There is archaeological evidence that San peoples have lived in this area for some 11,000 years or more, and other evidence, mostly in the form of rock paintings typical of the San, that they were once more widely spread over the African continent.

The San have a unique set of physical features, the origins of which are unclear. They are short people, the men averaging around 5 feet and the women a little shorter. Their skin color is a reddish brown, distinct from surrounding "black" African populations, and their facial features are youthful-looking, even those of the elderly. Perhaps their most striking feature is their hair. Called "peppercorn" hair, it grows in very tightly curled little tufts. It looks almost as if it has been somehow artificially styled, but it hasn't. Finally, the eyes of many San have the shape and the so-called epicanthic fold that we generally associate with people from the Far East.

The San live in small groups that average 10 to 30 people. Their camps, made up of enough grass huts to accommodate everyone (about 8 to 15), are temporary because the people need to move in search of food and, particularly in this climate, water. The inhabitants of a camp are usually related—a "chain of sibs and spouses," as Richard Lee, one of the recognized experts on the group, puts it. Membership in a group, however, changes with the seasons, as resources become more or less plentiful, and for cultural reasons such as internal conflicts, which are often solved by one family's moving away and joining another camp. The camp, as Lee says, is made up of a group of families that "work well together."

Most of their food comes from some 100 species of plants that they recognize as edible and that the women gather. The most popular plant for many groups is the mongongo nut, a highly nutritious food source containing, among other things, a good deal of protein. Game animals, hunted by the men, are usually ungulates (hoofed animals), which they bring down using arrows with poisoned tips. As I mentioned before, because gathering is the more reliable of the two activities and accounts for the majority of the San's diet, there is a tendency, on their part and ours, to be more concerned with and so emphasize the hunting.

It is interesting in this connection to note that the lives of groups like the San are not always as brutal and harsh as we may believe at first. To be sure, nature is "whimsical," and any unforseen change in the environment can mean the difference between life and death. But when things are going well—that is, when the environmental conditions are stable and are the ones the group is adapted to—a hunting-gathering population actually spends less time than you'd imagine in basic subsistence activities. For instance, when things are going "as planned," the San can acquire the necessary calories by working 20 hours per adult per week. Not bad when compared with our typical 40-hour workweek.

Naturally, the San are egalitarian. There are, for example, no formal leaders. There are individuals who are more important in terms of making decisions about where to hunt or gather or move or in settling conflicts. But these individuals lead by influence and suggestion, not by power and command. The San don't consider themselves led by anyone. One San said that they were *all* leaders. Furthermore, neither sex is seen as the superior of the other.

Resources, too, are generally distributed equally, especially meat. Plant foods, as noted before, may, because of their relative abundance, be kept by the family of the woman who gathered them. But great and elaborate pains are taken to be sure meat is shared equally. Although the hunter who killed an animal is said to "own" the meat, this just means that he is responsible for beginning the distribution, which is done according to kinship lines. The concept of *sharing*—of meat and, not surprisingly, of the arrows used to acquire it—is of central importance to the San's social structure.

The idea of equality with regard to meat is so important that the San have a device for assuring that a hunter who has supplied the camp with a fine, meaty animal will not feel in any way superior or even praiseworthy. The people of the camp, rather than showing their joy at the successful hunt, make negative and derisive comments about the animal killed and display no positive emotional reaction. Lee calls this "insulting the meat." Some men are bound to be better, more successful hunters than others, and this is a social leveling device to cover over a natural inequality.

Lee tells of his personal introduction to meat insulting in his article "Eating Christmas in the Kalahari." It seems that when Lee brought the San he was living with an ox as a Christmas gift, it received insults rather than the praise he had expected. Only when the practice was explained to him did he understand what was going on and see his treatment as a compliment. They were treating him as one of their own, covering over the fact that he had had such a successful "hunt."

There is one interesting exception to the San's egalitarianism. The majority of men have just one wife; we say they are *monogamous*. But a small number of men have several wives, and these men tend to be healers, men who possess a special power allowing them to cure illness. These healers are, of course, not full-time specialists, but they do seem to be recognized as having some status difference from other camp members, and their multiple wives may be a reflection of this. By the way, women are also healers but don't seem to have any special privileges.

San religion is polytheistic. There are two very important, powerful gods who are largely responsible for the creation of the world and for keeping it running. There are also lots of individual spirits, as well as the ghosts of deceased San, who tend to be malevolent. There is also that healing power mentioned before. It's called *n/um* (the / being a dental click, as when you scold someone and say "tsk, tsk"), and it's said to be a substance possessed by male and female healers that they call up through a dance, which then causes them to go into a trance during which they are able to cure illnesses and speak with the ghosts of the dead.

The last characteristic of hunter-gatherer groups I noted was their lack of a concept of land and resource ownership. This is true of the San as well. But it's not the case that different camps of San just roam wherever they want. Each camp has an area that it normally hunts and gathers in, and this area is acknowledged by other camps. If the "home range" of one camp runs out of a resource—say, if their water hole dries up or is contaminated—the people may use the water hole normally used by another camp. The catch is they have to ask permission to do so. Permission is nearly always granted (after all, the tables might be turned the next time). So it's not technically an "owned" territory. It's more a matter of courtesy, functioning to promote an egalitarianism among camps and to stave off any possibility of ill feelings of one camp toward another.

As you can imagine, there is a good deal of variation from one hunter-gatherer population to the next, depending on the specific nature of the environment in which they live. But all exhibit more or less the basic traits mentioned at the beginning of this discussion. The study and understanding of any of these groups gives us a picture of how we existed for most of our evolutionary history. In this sense, everything we are today stems from the foraging lifestyle.

So it was for all our ancestors until about 12,000 years ago. Then there began, in a few populations, what has been called a "revolution." Not one with riots and warfare, but a peaceful one, a change from within a group's own cultural system. It did, however, alter everything that came after. What happened was that someone discovered how to plant seeds.

FARMING

Actually, I've oversimplified for the sake of a dramatic transition between sections. As mentioned before, major changes in any aspect of culture (or biology for that matter) seldom come about instantly. The fact is, no one just one day picked up some seeds, planted them, and invented farming. It came about gradually. We are left, however, with the impression that it was rapid because our evidence is in the form of remains from the past, and such remains rarely show us all the steps involved in a change.

Specifically, our evidence for the transition to a farming way of life comes in two types. First, there are artifacts concerned with the use of domestic plants, things like stones on which to grind grains, pottery in which to store them (sometimes these even still contain some ancient grains), or instruments used to harvest plants. By the time these artifacts were being manufactured in any number, the people using them were already farmers. I will go into more detail about the archaeological aspects of this in the chapter on material culture.

The second piece of evidence comes from our knowledge of the biological differences between wild and domestic organisms, both plant and animal. By comparing, say, wild ungulates with domestic cattle or wild grasses with our familiar wheats and oats and maize (what Americans call "corn"), we can observe certain characteristic distinctions in such things as bone structure of the animals and seed traits of the plants. Looking into the past, then, we search for the earliest evidence of plants or animals found in association with human habitation sites and possessing these features. Again, it is not always possible to find evidence for the individual steps of the transition between wild and domestic organisms.

Moreover, common sense and what we understand about the lives of hunter-gatherers tell us that this cultural change must have

The evolution of maize in Mexico, from nearly wild ancestor (top) to modern cob (bottom).

begun in some populations long before we actually find hard evidence for it. Hunter-gatherers are intimately familiar with the living things in their environments. They must understand the habits of animals and the life cycles of plants in order to survive. People had probably understood for thousands of years that plants grow from seeds of other plants and that some animals can be manipulated. Modern Lapps, from around the Arctic Circle in Scandinavia and the Soviet Union, for example, control wild herds of reindeer but have not actually domesticated them. That control is based on the kind of "ethological" understanding of those creatures that all hunter-gatherers possess about the animals they use. Some of our ancestors may well have done something like the Lapps or have experimented with planting seeds or tending an area where a certain plant grew.

The real question in broad evolutionary perspective is not so much how they did it but *why*. If you were to present the idea of full-scale farming and herding to a real group of hunter-gatherers, they might find the idea rather strange, if not actually funny: "Why should we go to all that trouble when the animals and plants we eat are right out there?'' A good question, because remember, when things are going well, hunter-gatherer populations tend not to spend nearly as much time as we once imagined in their basic subsistence activities.

We are, in fact, still trying to account for the changeover to farming in the areas in which it first occurred. One proposed explanation deals with climatic alterations that were going on about 12,000 years ago: The great glaciers of the Pleistocene were retreating. As they did, large areas of land changed ecologically. Where once people living in those areas subsisted almost exclusively on big-game hunting, now they had available to them the greater variety of foods characteristic of habitats not in the grip of the ice sheets. We know from archaeological evidence that people developed ways of exploiting all the new food sources available to them. We call this ''intensive foraging.'' It may have been in such rich environments that people became extremely knowledgeable about the biology of plants and animals and began to use that knowledge for domesticating them.

But, you must be asking, wouldn't such a climatic change, with an increase in possible sources, just make hunting and gathering easier and more reliable? Farming would seem even less desirable in such an environment. And anyhow, glacial retreats were nothing new. What was different 12,000 years ago?

One difference was population; it was larger. Estimates vary, but around that time there were probably something like 10 million people in the world. That doesn't seem like many by our standards; there are now almost 5 *billion* of us! But at that time, considering that all people were relying pretty much on naturally occurring resources, a large population (relatively speaking) could put a good deal of pressure on the resources in a particular environment. Perhaps such population pressure caused some groups to try to use the knowledge they possessed about plants and animals in an attempt to gain more control over them.

But there are problems with this explanation as well. The early centers of farming, places like the so-called Fertile Crescent (the present-day Middle East, which was then much more fertile), southeastern Asia, and Central America, were fairly rich in wild plants and animals. Perhaps, as archaeologist Kent Flannery has suggested, farming began at the edges of these rich areas. Groups pushed out of the ''optimal'' areas by a rapidly expanding population found themselves in places ''marginal'' with regard to wild food sources.

Their answer to this problem was to apply their knowledge of wild plants and animals to gain control over them and enhance their productivity, thus beginning domestication.

You can see the problems involved in trying to explain such a broad and important event, and research continues. But it is safe to say that the answer lies in some combination of these and other hypotheses and that it probably varies in detail from place to place. We'll look at some of these places more closely in the archaeology chapter. For now, though, let's just accept that 12,000 years ago, the concept of domestication of plants and animals (for whatever reasons) began, spread rapidly, and brought with it other ecological and cultural changes that altered forever the nature of our relationship with the environment and with one another.

We've used the term *agriculture* in previous sections as a general term for farming, but we now must define it in its narrower anthropological sense. There are, you see, two basic kinds of farming, of which *agriculture* in the anthropological sense is one. The other is *horticulture*.

Horticulture refers to farming using only human labor and simple tools such as a digging stick or a hoe. It does not, in other words, use animal or mechanical labor or advanced technology like plows and irrigation systems. Farming with those things is *agriculture*. Just as we did for hunter-gatherers, we can enumerate some of the characteristics shared, generally speaking, by horticultural societies.

First, as compared with foragers, horticulturists tend to live in *larger populations*. The greater control over at least some of their food sources allows them to support a greater number of individuals. In addition, the population is more *sedentary*; that is, it can stay in one area for longer periods of time, since the people can grow food where they are rather than be obliged to go where their food is. Population membership tends to be more stable than in foraging societies, basically because there is less seasonal fluctuation in resource availability. The populations, though larger than those of foragers, are still organized around kinship. They are made up of a group of nuclear families, most of which are probably related.

Relative to groups like us, horticultural societies are basically egalitarian, but because there is now the possibility of surpluses and because there are now more people and thus the need for some kind of overall organization, we see in these groups the beginnings of leaders and labor specialists. There is a tendency to have formal *leadership positions* as opposed to the informal ones found in foraging groups, and there is some *part-time labor specialization*—say,

Horticulture, Ghana.

a man who leads warriors in battle—as opposed to just the sexual division of labor among hunter-gatherers.

We also see in societies with this subsistence pattern the beginning of the concept of *ownership*, on both the family level and the population level. Land on which plants are cultivated may be the property of a family, as are the plants themselves, and a herd of animals may likewise be owned. Despite this, though, the members of horticultural societies still work for the common good, and the products of their labors, though they may be "owned," are nonetheless shared within the group.

At the population level we see the idea of *territory*—my group's land here and your group's there. With growing control over food resources, there is less need to share resources on an intergroup basis and more need to protect one's own resources. Indeed, there is an idea in anthropology that the advent of farming was also the advent of war (*war* being defined as conflict between populations). Put bluntly, when one population had something that another didn't—be it land, food, or animals—the have-nots tried to take it away and the haves tried to keep it.

Finally, the religions of horticulturalists tend to be, like those of foragers, *polytheistic*. But unlike the foragers, the supernatural beings tend to be arranged in a hierarchy; that is, some are more powerful than others. This would seem to be a direct reflection of the people's growing control over nature. They have not yet mastered it, so natural phenomena are still seen as being under some supernatural influence, but they can manipulate it toward their own ends. Their "spirit" is supreme.

Agricultural populations are so defined because they use animal or mechanical labor and plows. Irrigation systems can also be part of the definition. Groups with this subsistence pattern generally have still larger populations than horticulturalists: Due to even greater control over plant food sources, they can support great numbers of people. The populations, quite naturally, are very *stable*, staying in one place for perhaps thousands of years.

With greater numbers of individuals, numbers now into the thousands in some cases, group membership and organization no longer tend to be based on kinship. You are a member of the population if you live there, and the increased complexity of such a group demands some leader or leaders to oversee everything. We refer to this as a *state system*.

With surpluses virtually assured, there can be *full-time labor specialists*. Not everyone has to do everything. If I'm good at growing wheat, I can concentrate on that and trade my surplus wheat to the guy who makes plows for one of the products of his labors. There are also those whose full-time specialty is religious ritual, healing, or, of course, leadership. With more than enough to go around, such specialization is possible. With the great numbers of people involved and the growing complexity of social and economic interaction, such specialization is necessary.

With more than enough to go around and with specialization, some people will naturally accumulate more resources than others. This is *social stratification*—social "layers." As you can imagine, power and wealth tend to be found in the same hands. The more important you are to the working of the whole community, the more

Agriculture, India.

resources you end up with. It follows that *ownership* of various resources is a central concept in such populations.

Religion in agricultural societies may still be polytheistic, but if so it tends to have one high god who presides over all the other supernatural figures, just as humans preside over nature and a leader presides over the human population. As social situations become increasingly complex, the tendency is toward *monotheism*—one all-powerful god over everything, with human beings as the god's most important creation. This is what we see in Judaism, Christianity, and Islam, all of which arose in agricultural societies in the Middle East.

Besides interpopulation warfare, which I've already mentioned, there are a couple other broad results of farming, especially of complex agriculture. When you have a lot of people, all belonging to a politically defined (rather than a kinship-defined) population, who are centrally organized and governed and probably take care of most economic transactions in a central location, you have the beginning of *civilization*. This term, as anthropology uses it, carries no value judgment; it simply means "city making." I have just given a basic description of a city. Indeed, we find in the archaeological record that early settlements we would recognize as cities are all associated with intensive agriculture.

Moreover, with all the information about trade transactions, ownership, and social and economic positions that such a population needs to keep track of, a second result of this type of subsistence is *writing*. Again, the earliest known forms of writing come from early cities associated with agriculture, in this case from the Middle East.

Finally, the need to improve the tools on which the success of such a system is based gives rise to another major cultural innovation: *metallurgy*—the extraction and working of natural metals. In broad perspective, metals, writing, and cities go hand in hand and follow from a economy based on farming with the methods of agriculture.

Keeping in mind our adaptive theme, some obvious questions arise: Why are some people horticulturalists and some agriculturalists? Is agriculture better? Is it a more advanced form, and thus a logical evolutionary result? Are all people who practice horticulture eventually going to become agriculturalists as soon as they acquire the skills?

If you've been paying attention, you should know the answer: You use the subsistence pattern that works. The pattern is geared to the environment in which you live and to the cultural history of your particular group. It shouldn't surprise you to find out that most horticultural societies live in the tropics—areas of sufficient rainfall, abundant plant life, and rich, fertile, easily worked soil. People who cultivate in these areas don't need more complex technology. On the other hand, one tends to find agriculture in areas where more manipulation of the natural conditions is necessary to grow plants. These are places were the ground must be turned and broken up to prepare it for planting, where rainfall is not always enough to nourish plants that are not in their natural habitats, where the soil may have to have its nutrients augmented. A society does what it must to survive. In most cases, though, any more would be a waste of energy.

To be sure, when you acquire the advanced skills and technology necessary to grow plants in the latter kind of environment, you can feed large numbers of people and produce large surpluses. In that sense, agriculture is "better." But there is no inexorable trend toward it. In some areas, like tropical forests, it probably wouldn't

Pastoralism, Afghanistan.

add to your production anyway. And there are negative aspects to it as well, for with such a specific set of circumstances necessary for successful subsistence, more can go wrong. If something happens to your draft animals, if there is not even enough water available to channel through your irrigation ditches, if some internal economic problem makes the required tools unavailable—such things can have devastating effects on your ability to feed yourself. When everything is OK, agriculture works wonders. But it is prone to disruption much more easily than the other two subsistence patterns. So there is no overall "better" or "worse." There is just what works for a particular group in a particular environment at a particular time in history.

Because there are more people today who are farmers than foragers and because such societies are varied and complex, it is difficult to choose one group to exemplify these two subsistence patterns in the way we used the !Kung San. But if you keep in mind that all these subsistence patterns can be considered a basis for all the other features of culture we'll be discussing, the examples we use throughout the book will gradually give you some clear pictures of a number of societies that fall into each of these categories.

There are two more subsistence patterns that we must mention. One is *pastoralism*, the herding of animals. Certainly, nearly all farmers have some animals for labor or food, or both. But pastoralists are people whose herds are the basis for their subsistence and whose cultural system is built around this pattern, to the same degree as the cultural system of the other groups we've mentioned are built around their subsistence patterns. Pastoralists may do some farming, even some hunting and gathering, but these activities are not central to their view of their world.

Most pastoralists are nomadic; the people simply go where there is food for their animals. They are egalitarian with regard to use of pastureland within their group but are territorial with regard to other populations. Also, within their group there is socioeconomic stratification based on ownership of animals. The more animals you own, the more prestige and influence you have. Leadership is present but is rather vague with regard to how it is achieved and who has it. It is probably much like that found among foragers. Labor is divided on the basis of sex, the men being responsible for the animal herds, the women for household tasks. Beyond that there is generally no specialization of labor. Pastoralists' religions tend to involve ancestor worship; that is, their supernatural world is populated by the spirits of their dead. The emphasis is, as you would expect, on human control.

Pastoralists are generally found in areas unsuitable for other subsistence—areas where it would be hard to grow anything and where the wild plants are things like grasses that don't provide human primates with much nutrition but are fine for ungulates. People make do. Examples of pastoralists include the Lapps and their reindeer; cattle herders from the dry savanna areas of East Africa, like the Masai and the Nuer; sheep and goat herders in the Middle East; and yak herders in Tibet.

A final pattern listed by many anthropologists is *industrialism*. This is generally defined as a system based on mechanical rather than biological power. We in the United States are obviously industrialists. Certainly there are social and economic ramifications of such a system—things like very large populations, emphasis on the individual as the unit of labor and on labor specialization, and monotheism in religious expression. But I like to stick with the food theme and to categorize even complex industrial societies like ours accordingly. Despite our industrial base, and despite all the artificial ingredients in our foods, our subsistence is still based on agriculture. Our society still exhibits the general set of characteristics listed for agriculturalists. It is just a *very* complex form of that kind of society. Go over that list and you'll see what I mean.

There is one more major item to consider in this rather long and complex discussion of food. (I told you it was important!) Once a group of people has the food they need and the artifacts to get and process the food and to take care of other technological concerns, and once they can provide all the services necessary to maintain the social structure, how do all those resources get to all the people? How do you make sure that they are distributed? Does everyone share equally? Is distribution of goods and services also related to subsistence?

SOME BASIC ECONOMICS

How do *you* go about getting the goods and services you need? Because you provide society with certain goods you manufacture or services you perform as part of your job, you receive money—a symbolic representation of some value equivalent. This you exchange with other individuals for their goods and services. That all seems logical enough, doesn't it? Is there any other way?

By now you know that the answer to such questions is almost always yes. In fact, within your family, goods and services are distributed in a very different fashion. If I may, for the sake of familiarity, use a stereotype without being accused of sexism: When, say, your father brings home money from his job with which food is purchased and mortgage payments are made, or when your mother performs certain chores vital to the efficient running of the household, they certainly don't expect you and your sibs to repay them with some good or service of equal value. They contribute those things to the family unit, expecting in return only whatever contribution other family members are capable of providing, depending on their age, health, occupational status, and so on. You may certainly perform your own services for the good of the family, and you may even receive some sort of allowance for that. But no one is keeping a ledger of all these transactions to make sure that things balance out. Every family member contributes what he or she can and receives in return the physical and emotional security that family membership provides.

This kind of giving and taking of goods and services, without expectation of immediate and equivalent return, we refer to as *general reciprocity*. It's what happens within your family, and it's what happens within a hunter-gatherer group.

Think about it. Hunter-gatherer groups are families, made up of a small number of nuclear families that are most likely, as we saw for the !Kung San, themselves closely related. Moreover, since the only efficient way to run a population with such a subsistence pattern is to practice egalitarianism, general reciprocity is the only method of distribution that makes sense. Any recognition of what we would consider an "imbalance of trade" would break up the equality of wealth and status that is so vital for foraging peoples. This, then, is another characteristic that goes hand in hand with this subsistence pattern.

There is another sort of reciprocity as well, of course, *balanced reciprocity*. This is where goods and services are exchanged with clear expectation of the relatively immediate return of something of agreed-upon equivalent value. In my example, when I traded some of my surplus wheat for a plow some other guy made, that's balanced reciprocity. This kind of system is what tends to be found in agricultural communities where there are surpluses and labor specialists and where membership is defined more in terms of where you live than your kin ties.

Don't think that a society practices just one sort of distribution system. There can be a distinct difference between what people do within *their* population as opposed to how they deal with other populations. The Mbuti Pygmies, for example, as foragers, practice general reciprocity among themselves. But they also carry on balanced reciprocity with some of their Bantu-speaking neighbors. The Mbuti trade meat they've hunted in the forests for plant foods and various tools that the Bantu have. "Rates of exchange" have been agreed on in advance or may be worked out at the time of the transaction.

As cynical as it sounds, there is an example of balanced reciprocity within our culture: gift giving at Christmas. Despite the ethic we profess to practice that "giving is better than receiving" and "it's the thought that counts," in fact we undergo all sorts of mental trauma at Christmastime worrying about how much to spend on so-and-so's gift so it won't be any more or less expensive than the one we'll receive from that person. It's not explicit or even a formal part of our economy, but it's balanced reciprocity just the same.

When a society gets so large and the economic interactions within it so complex that the trading of the actual items and services becomes difficult, symbolic representations of the value of resources may be used. These can be traded in place of actual products so long as the system is an agreed-upon part of the culture and there is some mechanism for determining and maintaining the value equivalents. This, of course, is *money*, and a distribution system that uses money is known as a *market system*. Ours is basically a market system.

And although the use of money leads to all sorts of complex national and international economics, in broad perspective we can view it as just a form of balanced reciprocity, one that, for convenience, uses symbols for the value of the goods and services distributed.

Between systems that maintain an overall egalitarianism and those that recognize and support social strata is a system that attempts to level out inherent inequalities. When the goods and services of a population are not easily and automatically distributed on an equal basis, this mechanism tries to counteract that. It's called *redistribution*. In this system, surpluses are collected under the direction of some governing body and then redistributed according to need of the recipients.

Perhaps the most famous example of a large-scale redistribution system comes from the Kwakiutl Indians of Vancouver Island. The Kwakiutl would hold periodic feasts called *potlatches*, the point of which was for the holder of the potlatch to try to give away or destroy more food and other goods than his rivals. The whole thing at times got so frenzied that if the potlatch holder was getting behind, he might even burn down his own house as the ultimate display of his status and wealth! Early anthropologists were indeed as puzzled at first as we are by this seemingly wasteful behavior. But upon closer examination it makes sense.

The Kwakiutl were foragers, specializing in salmon fishing and the gathering of wild plants. It was a successful way of life, and the group became large, in the tens of thousands, and widespread in their range, and they moved away from the strict egalitarianism of most foraging societies. Still, they were a single society and were thus concerned about certain inequalities among their people. Specifically, annual fluctuations in the salmon migrations and in the availability of wild plants led to some Kwakiutl villages' having more food than others. The potlatch was a redistribution system—though certainly a bizarre one—to try to level these differences. During this continual giving away of surpluses by the haves, the have-nots tended to receive in the long run, making up for some of their deficiencies.

In addition, since the whole thing was tied up with status seeking (that *was* the overt motivation for doing it), there was continual pressure to produce as much as possible so you could give away more at your next potlatch. The results of it all benefited the entire population.

You may, of course, be wondering why, even though this explanation makes economic sense, the Kwakiutl went to such extremes. Why not just decide that everybody will contribute some of their surplus, which will then be collected by a chief, who will then determine who needs it, and so on? Well, this is a good example of the complex workings of a cultural system—any cultural system. Though the potlatch can be interpreted economically, and though it became a vital part of Kwakiutl culture because it worked economically, the origin of the specific details of the practice are all tied up in the whole of the Kwakiutl world view, which, as you recall, involves not only their present situation but their past as well. It is still unclear just how this practice originated.

A second example of a redistribution system is closer to home: our taxes. The whole idea here is that even though we live in a stratified society, we consider some inequalities to be unacceptable. Part of our tax money is used to provide basic goods and services to individuals who cannot otherwise afford them. On the whole, it really seems to work pretty well, considering the incredible complexity of our society. But it does, itself, involve certain inequities, and this demonstrates the power of an overall cultural system.

We are a stratified society, with the recognition of differences in status and wealth built right into the system. One way in which the system supports such strata is through our complex laws of ownership, protecting what we consider the rights of individuals to possess property and wealth and to hang on to it. So pervasive is this concept that it is difficult to define clearly what is "surplus" to a person. Thus figuring out just what part of a person's wealth goes into income tax is unbelievably complex, as you may well know! In fact, as it turns out, owning things is given so much credit in this society that the ownership of something can actually allow you to contribute less of your income to the redistribution pool. Our intent may be in keeping with certain ethical precepts of our view of the world, but this particular mechanism has certain inconsistencies with regard to our whole cultural system. (I have, in case you were wondering, no solutions to this problem.)

Finally, before we finish, let's go over a few terms for things we've been discussing. These refer to the degree to which a society is stratified. You already know *egalitarianism*—the absence of differences in wealth and status. This is the system found in hunting and gathering groups. Other societies are said to be *rank* societies. This means that they recognize differences in status but not in wealth. The Kwakiutl were a rank society, attempting to level off differences in wealth but doing so in a way that required a recognition of differences in status.

We are a *class* society, recognizing and building into the system formal differences in both status and wealth. A class system, however, is open; that is, an individual has the opportunity to acquire more wealth and status and move to a higher stratum. (Or, of course, one can lose both and move lower.) Another system, however, freezes strata. In this system you are born into your socioeconomic layer and there you stay. Your place in society, both economically and conceptually, is predetermined. Your access to resources, your possible occupations, your potential marriage partners are all decided accordingly. This is a *caste* system, and perhaps the best known example is in India.

As an exercise in thinking about and using all the concepts from this chapter, consider the Hutterites (remember them?). Where do they fit in all of this? What sort of subsistence pattern do they have? How do they distribute goods and services within their society and in their dealings with the larger culture of which they are a part? How is their society stratified? Or is it? Are they just like North American culture as a whole? Later we'll discuss some of these things, but for now see what you can come up with.

Consider this also: If you were a !Kung San hunter who had brought back to camp a nice fat antelope you had killed, you would distribute the meat according to kinship. That is, you would give some meat to certain of your relatives, who would give some to certain of their relatives and so on until everyone had their share. Sounds easy enough. Everyone knows who's related to whom and how. Kinship is basic biology. Or is it? In the next chapter I'll show you how, in some societies, your uncle is the same as your father and your cousin is the same as your sister!

SUMMARY

Perhaps the most important relationship between a species and its environment is the process of food acquisition. For humans, the ways in which societies acquire their food—that is, their subsistence patterns—are so central that we may use them to categorize types of cultures. Thus we speak of a society as being either hunter-gatherer, horticultural, agricultural, or pastoral.

Many, if not most, of the other basic features of a cultural system can be seen as more or less related to subsistence pattern. Generalizations are thus possible with regard to things like basic economics and (as you'll see) kinship and religion. Hunter-gatherer groups, for example, tend to be polytheistic and egalitarian and to practice general reciprocity among themselves. As a society gains more control over its food resources—that is, as it relies more and more on agricultural techniques—it tends to recognize fewer supernatural beings, to become socioeconomically stratified, and to practice balanced reciprocity, perhaps in the form of a market system. Though these statements are generalizations, they do form a basis for analyzing the interactions within a culture of all its integrated parts.

NOTES, REFERENCES, AND READINGS

A general discussion of subsistence patterns, with examples and ideas of related cultural factors, can be found in Vera Lustig-Arecco's *Technology: Strategies for Survival* (New York: Holt, Rinehart and Winston, 1975), and in Part 2 of Frank Robert Vivelo's *Cultural Anthropology Handbook: A Basic Introduction* (New York: McGraw-Hill, 1978).

The hunter-gatherer pattern of subsistence is examined in a book of papers collected by Richard B. Lee and Irven DeVore called *Man the Hunter* (Chicago: Aldine, 1968). Most of my material on the !Kung is from Richard Lee's recent ethnography *The Dobe !Kung* (New York: Holt, Rinehart and Winston, 1984), which includes "Eating Christmas in the Kalahari." Another hunter-gatherer group I mentioned, the Tasaday, are described in John Nance's *The Gentle Tasaday: A Stone Age People in the Philippine Rain Forest* (New York: Harcourt Brace Jovanovich, 1975).

There are many good summaries and examinations of the various hypotheses regarding the origins of agriculture. One that I find useful and can recommend is Chapter 7 of *Pattern in Prehistory: Mankind's First Three Million Years* (New York: Oxford University Press, 1980) by Robert J. Wenke. For more detailed information and primary sources, use his bibliographic listings.

The story of the Kwakiutl potlatch is in Marvin Harris's *Cows, Pigs, Wars, and Witches: The Riddles of Culture* (New York: Random House, 1974).

For more on T. D. Lysenko and portions from his works, see Chapter 9 of C. Leon Harris, *Evolution: Genesis and Revelations* (Albany: State University of New York Press, 1981).

chapter 8

Nature of the Group
Arranging Our Families and Organizing Our People

One of the biggest problems facing the individual anthropologist is the question of *ethnocentrism*. We—that is, people—are all ethnocentric, which means that we feel our particular cultural system is the ''right'' one and that our way of doing things is the ''right'' way. And indeed it is. If every person on Earth didn't live within some sort of cultural system, human life as we know it wouldn't exist. Without some set of agreed-upon ideas and practices, our social fabric would come unraveled. You *should* think your culture is the right one for you.

The problem arises when one makes value judgments about a different culture based on one's own cultural ideas (or worse, when one people force their culture on another). For anthropologists, a major task is to try not to view and analyze the cultures we study from our own cultural perspectives. We must try to practice *cultural relativity*. This means that we try to understand a culture from the point of view of the people who possess and practice it, and we try to realize that no matter how strange some cultural habits seem to us, they work for those people. That's why they exist.

This is not easy at first, but it becomes easier once you realize that you can both be a member of your culture and practice cultural relativity at the same time. Too many anthropologists I have known have tried to deny that they too have cultural attitudes that quite naturally affect their views on what other people do. Such denial is impossible. We are a part of our cultural heritage, just as every person the world over is a part of theirs.

It's OK to react to another society's habits. For instance, you recall I referred in the last chapter to the potlatch as ''bizarre.'' From my cultural point of view, it is. But that reaction doesn't affect my ability to understand the potlatch from the point of view of the Kwakiutl. From their point of view, of course, it makes perfect sense.

So one important part of learning about anthropology and how it studies other cultures is to learn how to look at another society in this relative sense. It takes practice. It means being able to ''get inside the heads'' of other people, to see things from their perspective. We have already begun by examining different sorts of economies. You should now understand egalitarian societies, for example, even though you are part of a class society.

Now we'll look at the part of culture I've always thought was one of the most difficult in this regard. It is the aspect that deals with our family relationships, something that is basic to our lives, both as individuals and as a species. And, for most societies, family relationship, or *kinship,* is the basis for social organization in general. As you might expect by this time, not every society looks at kinship the way we do. If you can understand kinship systems that differ from the one we're used to, you'll have come a long way toward understanding and being able to practice cultural relativity.

First, though, here are some general ideas about social organization.

SOCIAL ORGANIZATION

Many, if not most, organisms live in some sort of society—that is, a group of individuals of the same species living together in cooperative interaction for their mutual benefit. At the simplest level, some single-celled creatures have formed colonies, groups of up to several thousand individuals. In some of these are the rudiments of a "division of labor," certain of the cells, for instance, taking care of locomotion, others of reproduction. Not only is this an example of a simple "society," of course, but also of the beginnings of multicellular organisms.

At a higher level, we have already mentioned the complex societies of ants and other insects. Such societies have strict labor divisions, biologically determined castes, and all kinds of rather incredible group behaviors. So vital is this social interaction to the success of the species that it can truly be said that a single ant, for instance, is really no ant at all. It can't survive on its own. An ant colony, in fact, has been likened to a single giant organism, all the parts playing their specific roles, on which all the other parts, and thus the whole, are dependent.

Such behavior in ants is, of course, purely genetic. The ants can't think about what they're doing; they can't change their behaviors at will. We, at the most complex level of social interaction, can. We've already discussed at length the bases for human society: the evolution of the nuclear family (along with certain biological changes in sexuality) and of the functioning of our brain, which enables us to control much of our behavior consciously to fit specific situations.

But it's a big jump from noncultural ants to cultural humans,

A baboon troop with adult males in foreground for protection.

and to achieve a better perspective on our social nature, it might be a good idea to look briefly at another primate—one that also has a complex society but whose social behvior is not as dependent on culture as ours. The classic example is an African monkey, the baboon.

Largely a savanna primate, the baboon has solved the problems of survival in such a dangerous environment by evolving a highly structured social organization. (Incidently, there are a number of "kinds" of baboons, but since it is not clear just how many actual species there are, and since there is some behavioral similarity overall, I'll generalize.) Baboon society is based on what is known as a *dominance hierarchy.* As baboon males (and to a lesser extent, females) grow up, they achieve varying statuses. These are based on size, strength, courage, and perhaps some undefined quality we can call "charisma." The status differences among individuals are recognized within the "troop," especially those of the highest-ranking males. These are the leaders: They "decide" in which direction the troop will travel, they have access to females in estrus, and they have first rights to a limited food source. They are also the ones who are first to face a threatening predator.

Below a troop's dominant male are a number of subordinate males and then juvenile males who may still be working out their relative rankings. Females have degrees of dominance among themselves but are generally subordinate to most males. This does not mean, however, that they are unimportant, for the focus of a baboon troop is the group made up of mothers and their infants. This is the group that travels at the center of a troop when the troop is on the move, surrounded first by juvenile and then subordinate males, with the most dominant males in the lead and protecting the rear. Should a predator approach—a leopard, for instance—the lower-ranking males quickly move the younger troop members and the mothers and infants to safety, while the higher-ranking males move forward to meet the challenge. This usually works, by the way. A male baboon, weighing up to 100 pounds and armed with 6-inch canine teeth, is a foe even a leopard won't mess with!

The dominance hierarchy is supported through what looks to us like continual violence. Dominant males are always being challenged by subordinate ones. The dominant ones are always asserting their status by chasing and threatening lesser males and females. But rarely does anyone sustain an injury, and in fact, this continual testing and asserting of dominance assures that the system is in its best condition—that the dominant baboons are indeed the dominant baboons—and thus that the troop is as efficient and safe as it can be.

It is interesting to ask, when comparing baboon societies to those of humans, just how much, if at all, the social behavior of the baboons could be considered cultural. I have no doubt that baboons have more conscious awareness of their actions than do ants! After all, as primates they have relatively large cerebral cortices and thus a good deal of reasoning ability. But how much of their social interaction is specifically built into their genes? How much has genetic potential that must be set off by some environmental stimulus? How much is really cultural?

It's difficult to answer, but Hans Kummer, a zoologist who has done extensive research on baboons, feels that at least this social aspect of baboon behavior has very little of a real cultural component. You recall that one test for the presence of culture was variability in a behavioral trait, what Kummer calls *flexibility*. Raccoons, I noted, all wash their food, but the Japanese macaques practice the behavior selectively. Well, although baboons can vary certain behaviors at will in response to new environmental conditions—things like choosing safe places to sleep or picking food sources—the specifics of their social system vary little, if at all. Baboons of one type transported to the environment of another, each having a social system and other behaviors geared to their specific niches, will be able to change some behaviors but *not* the nature of their social interaction. That area is not very flexible, showing that it cannot be considered cultural as we have defined it.

What it does show, though, is that the nonhuman primates can and do have complex social systems and thus that ours, although different in being truly cultural, is not unique on the primate branch of the evolutionary tree. It also demonstrates the possibility that, as with the nuclear family and the incest taboo, some of our social practices may be cultural variations on a biological theme. We'll take up that complex topic again later.

You might also wonder why, for purposes of our comparison, we didn't look at chimpanzees. Aren't they much more closely related to us, with bigger brains than baboons and thus with more reasoning ability? Yes, it's true that chimps seem more aware of their social system. They are somewhat more flexible in their social interactions, and can consciously manipulate social relations. A striking example of this, seen by Jane Goodall, involved a subordinate male who was being chased by a more dominant one. Passing a female carrying an infant, the pursued male grabbed the baby away from its mother and held the infant up between him and his pursuer. The pursuer stopped immediately so as not to chance harming the infant—just what the first male knew (I mean that literally) would happen!

But the overall social organization of the chimps is not nearly as complex or stable as that of the baboons. If this seems strange, remember what we've discussed about adaptation. The chimps simply don't need a baboon sort of system. Living in the forests of central Africa with virtually no natural predators and with abundant food sources, their rather loose system works just fine. But it doesn't provide a very interesting comparison with our own. (By the way, isn't it ironic that the chimps' only real predator is its closest living relative?)

In addition to complexity, the behavior of the baboons is more interesting because they live in essentially the same environment as did our early ancestors. Indeed, it has been said that the savannas have changed so little in the past few million years that, except for the absence of some larger mammal species and the presence of modern humans, an australopithecine or *Homo habilis* would feel right at home on today's savannas. This doesn't mean that our behavior and that of the baboon have the same causes and evolutionary origin. It just means that by looking at how another primate lives in that environment, we might get some clues as to how our remote ancestors survived under nearly the same conditions. From this it would seem that for a primate to survive on the savannas, a stable and tightly knit social organization is essential.

With this general perspective on social organization, we can now examine more closely the social systems of humans. Our systems are different from those of any other creature in that we can consciously invent their specific features and tailor them to the conditions of our environments—both the natural and cultural environments.

We have already begun by noting the relationships between subsistence patterns and ideas about social status and wealth. But we need to look deeper. For example, I said that the egalitarian San distribute food equally according to kinship. How do they know who gets what? What route does the meat follow, and how is this determined? In larger farming societies, how is resource ownership determined? Military alliances? Possible marriage partners?

For most societies (not most people but most groups of people—see the difference?) the social system is based on family lines: your membership in a family and your relationship to other members of that family, relative to the same information about everyone else in your group. This is what we call *kinship*. Now, have your pencil and paper handy and get ready; this is quite a trip!

KINSHIP

For most of human evolutionary history, and for recent hunter-gatherer groups, society was literally family. Social units were made up of small groups of nuclear families that were no doubt related—several biological brothers and their wives and kids, or something like that. Social interaction was thus based on family relationships, and these would have been rather obvious and easily kept track of. After all, there were not a lot of individuals involved, and the intimacy with which people in such a group lived meant that all the biological events—births, deaths, even sexual relations—were known about and observed.

As large populations started to appear with the coming of farming, social interactions got more complex. Now there were more people to deal with, more goods and services being produced and passed around. There were groups other than your own to worry about. There was the need for some sort of leader or overseer to handle interactions within the group. A new social organization was required, one based not on natural groupings but on cultural ones, ones that could be geared to the specific needs and desires of the population concerned.

But do you just start from scratch? Just sit down, dissolve all existing social relations, and make up new ones? Hardly. There already is a model for a social system: the kinship relations around which less complex societies were organized. What happened is that farming populations, needing new and varied schemes of society, created cultural variations on the kinship theme. What family you belonged to, your place in that family, and where your family line fit relative to other family lines still determined your place in society. But the scheme, even though it looked like a biologically based set of relationships, was a cultural one. It may have ignored some biological relationships. It may have created categories that crosscut actual biological groups. It may have lumped, under one name, people of quite distinct biological identities. The model is from biology, but the specific features are cultural.

The base of any kinship system still is, as you should expect, the nuclear family. We have devised diagrams to represent this unit and its extensions, and they work like this: Triangles (or sometimes squares) represent males, circles are females, an equal sign means marriage, a vertical line is descent (the offspring from a marriage), and a horizontal line means sibship (brothers and sisters). A simple nuclear family is depicted here.

In the example, one male and one female are married and have produced two offspring, a boy and a girl. Of course there could be additional spouses and any number of brothers and sisters. Some of the Hutterite families I knew had 12 children! You just extend the diagram accordingly.

The number of spouses one may have varies from culture to culture and is the criterion for the two kinds of nuclear family. The kind we're used to has just one of each spouse. This is called *monogamy* (*mono* meaning "one," *gamy* meaning "marriage"). But a person may, in some societies, have more than one spouse. This is

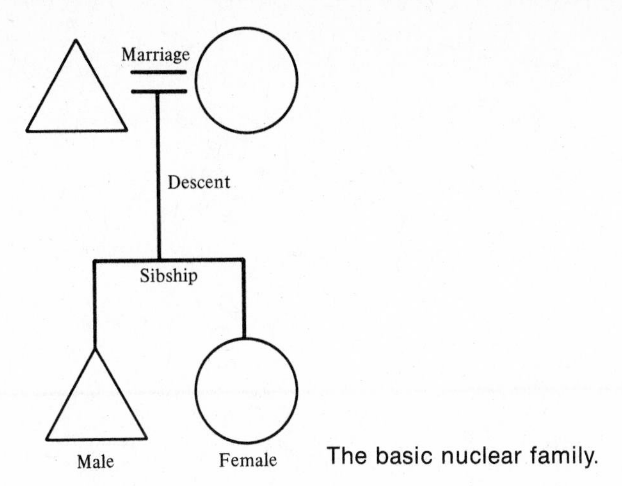

The basic nuclear family.

known as *polygamy.* There are, of course, two versions of this. If a man has several wives, it's *polygyny* (from the Greek *gyne,* "woman"). If a woman has several husbands, it's *polyandry* (*andros,* Greek for "man").

Now here's where we start with the cultural relativity. While we may think monogamy is the "right" version of the nuclear family, the statistics show something else. For, although most people in the world now belong to societies that practice monogamy, most individual *societies,* about 75 percent, practice polygyny to some extent. It is, on a societal level, the most popular form. About one-quarter of all societies are monogamous; only a handful of cultures (according to one study, five) are polyandrous.

Why is that? Even in larger farming groups, the nuclear family is still the basic economic unit. And as long as you can feed all the members of your family, the more members there are, the more efficiently the family will work. You can farm more land with more people. More women can gather more plants. More ties can be established with other families if you have more children, especially girls, to marry off. While one wife is pregnant or nursing, there are still others who can be involved in economic activities. It's simply a more energy-efficient way of doing things—at least up to that point where you have more mouths than you can feed.

Now, why isn't the same true for polyandry? That system would still provide the energy efficiency. But you are not only concerned with number of family members at the moment but in the future as well. And a woman with a bunch of husbands can still only produce at most one offspring every couple of years. But one husband with

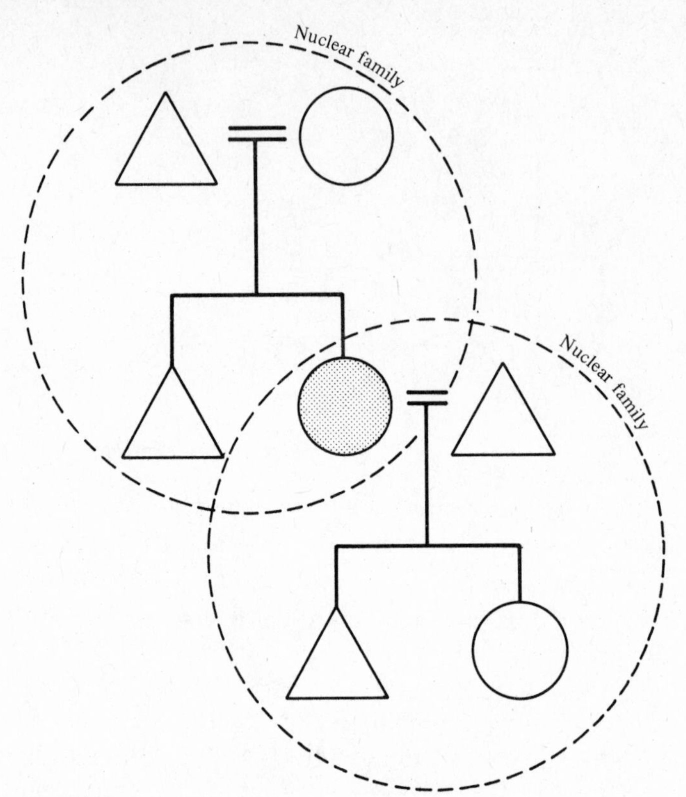

Basis for the extended family and descent line.

several wives can keep producing them. Especially when infant mortality is high, this is the best way of assuring the continuation of the family.

Polygyny, by the way, doesn't mean that all men in a society must or even can have several wives. It just means that it's allowed or encouraged. Often number of wives goes hand in hand with general wealth and power, so access to marriage partners is not equal. (Remember the San healers.) For most societies, then, in which your economic well-being depends on the labors of your family, polygyny is the norm, for sound, practical reasons.

Nuclear families, of course, are not isolated units. They are strung together horizontally to include what we call aunts and uncles and cousins, and back in time to include grandparents and other ancestors. We refer to the horizontal dimension as the *extended family*. The dimension through time is the *descent line*. Consider the daughter from the first diagram. If she marries, she becomes part of two connected nuclear families, the one in which she is a daughter and the one in which she is a wife. Her mother, similarly, is part of two nuclear families, as is the mother's sister, and so on. It is at the level of the descent line that we see the variation that is relevant to our examination of social organization.

If I were to ask you which descent line you belonged to, your mother's or your father's, you would answer that you belonged to both, equally. True, you probably have your father's last name; there may be some legal matters that emphasize your ties to one side over the other; and you may get along better with the people on one side. But in general your place in your family is as the product of, and as a member of, both sides. We call this setup *bilateral* (literally, "two sided").

Well, naturally! How else would you do it? We know all about genetics and biological relationships. What other arrangement would make sense? But (I'm sure you see what's coming) not every society knows or cares about genetics. A bilateral system, even if it seems to fit biology, doesn't fill the cultural requirements of every population. Indeed, most societies (again, not most people but most cultures) organize descent lines in very different ways.

Most groups (about 60 percent) are *unilineal* ("of one line"). This means that an individual belongs to only one side of the family. Depending on the rules of the society, this is either the father's side *(patrilineal)* or the mother's side *(matrilineal)*. This doesn't mean that if you live in a patrilineal society you don't know who your mother is! Of course you do. And you live in a nuclear family unit that includes your biological mother, and you have special relationships with her, both economically and emotionally, that you have with no one else. But if your whole society is organized according to kinship, it means that for any function in which your place in society is important, you are a member of your father's side of the family, not your mother's. Important functions in this regard might include things like property ownership, military alliances, inheritance of leadership or other statuses, or potential marriage partners. In our society, your place in the group as a whole is determined by your residence, your occupation, and your socioeconomic class. In most other groups, though, it's which lineage you belong to.

Membership in a lineage is inherited through the parent whose sex is the basis for the kinship system. In other words, in a patrilineal society you inherit family membership from your father; in a matrilineal society, from your mother. And you can pass on family membership only if you are of the corresponding gender.

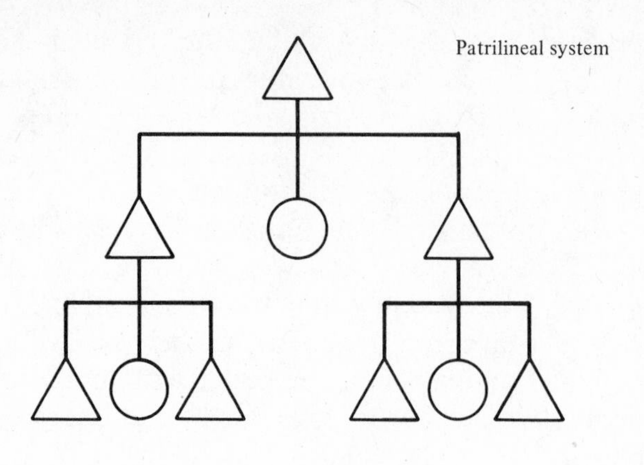

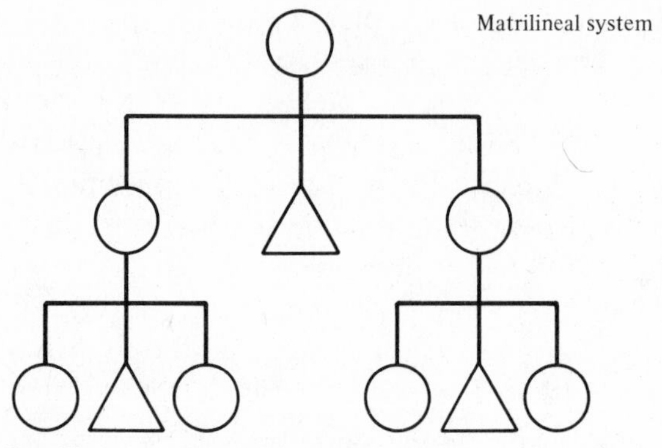

Patrilineal and matrilineal systems.

Now the obvious question: Why? Doesn't unilineality seem to violate logic? No, not if your social structure is organized in terms of kinship. If it is, the practice of having each member belong to just one side of the family makes sense—simply because it makes things simpler. If many of your economic responsibilities, your political and military alliances, and your rights of inheritance are determined according to whom you are related, it makes things a lot easier to cut the potential number of relatives in half. Unilineality makes social organization based on kinship (as in most societies) easier and more efficient. Just why each system originated is an open question. Remember, you can't always infer origin from current function. Nonetheless, this seems to be what unilineality does for those groups who practice it.

Looking at all this in broad perspective, are there any correlations we can make between other things we've talked about and particular kinship systems? Beyond the general function of unilineality, are there any more specific reasons why some groups are matrilineal and others patrilineal? And how about those that are bilateral?

There seems to be some correlation with division of labor in that the gender that plays the dominant economic role sets the emphasis in kinship. If females take care of most subsistence activities, as they do in many horticultural societies, kinship tends to be matrilineal.

For agriculturalists, where the use of plows, even with draft animals, is hard labor, males tend to be seen as the sex associated with the food supply and the society tends to be patrilineal—similarly among pastoralists, where men own the herds and do the herding. In foraging societies, although there is an emphasis on hunting, both gathering by the women and hunting by the men are obviously vital, so the kinship system tends to be bilateral. This also fits with the idea of egalitarianism practiced by hunter-gatherers.

But don't make too much of such correlations. They don't necessarily establish a cause-and-effect relationship. Not all horticultural groups are matrilineal. Some matrilineal societies are foragers. Plow agriculture shows up in some bilateral societies. So ideas about such connections should be seen as no more than "clues" to help us think about how we can explain the variation in kinship systems that we observe.

And this brings up another point: We've discussed the fact, both in biology and in culture, that although you can often understand current relationships among features, you can't automatically assume that those relationships explain the origin and evolution of the features. This is true in the case of cultural traits because culture is not a "thing." It can't react to an environment or to changes in that environment. A culture is something that comes from the minds of people. It's the people who react to the world around them—all the people who make up a society and who made up that society in the past. A culture is the sum of all their individual ideas and decisions, over many years. And people are "only human." As Roger Keesing puts it:

> Cultures do not respond to pressures. Rather, individual human beings cope as best they can, formulate rules, follow and break them; and by their statistical patterns of cumulative decisions, they set a course of cultural drift.

So don't get the idea that sometime in the past, in some foraging society that had just gone horticultural, a group of old, bearded guys sat around and decided that since the women were now doing the majority of the subsistence labor, the group should change to a matrilineal system! Cultural systems evolve. They change through the accumulation of many small individual ideas and acts, all geared to make the system work at a given moment.

You should know, by the way, that besides the three kinds of kinship systems we've covered, there are some others—for example, systems in which an individual may belong to *either* the mother's or the father's side and ones in which an individual is a member of the mother's line for some purposes and the father's for other purposes. These, however, are not as common as the major types we've discussed, so, for this introductory view we can stick with those.

Within the major types of descent organization is more variation: Societies have different specific terminology systems for ordering the exact relationships among individuals. (And just when you thought we were finished with kinship!) There are too many of these systems to cover them all, but a few will give you an idea as to the kinds of variations we find, how we study them, and what they can tell us.

KINSHIP TERMINOLOGY

What do you call the man who is your mother's husband and your immediate male ancestor? "I call him 'Father,' of course. What a dumb question!" Does anyone else share that designation? "Not that I know of!"

You should have guessed by now that it's not such a dumb question. As I'm sure you're beginning to see, not everyone does things the way we do, and categories of family members are no exception.

There are about a half dozen types of kinship terminology systems around the world, of which we'll take a look at three. Because so many people practice each system, we can't use all their linguistic terms like *father, mother,* and so on. But what we can do is use symbols to indicate which people in a kinship diagram fall into the same category. In a diagram of an American family, then, the symbol indicating your father would be shared by no one else, but the one for cousin could be shared by a whole bunch of people. This would show how we use two of our kinship categories. (The idea of using symbols seems an obvious enough solution to the problem of linguistic variation, but since I saw it first in their book, I should give credit to anthropologists Carol R. Ember and Melvin Ember.)

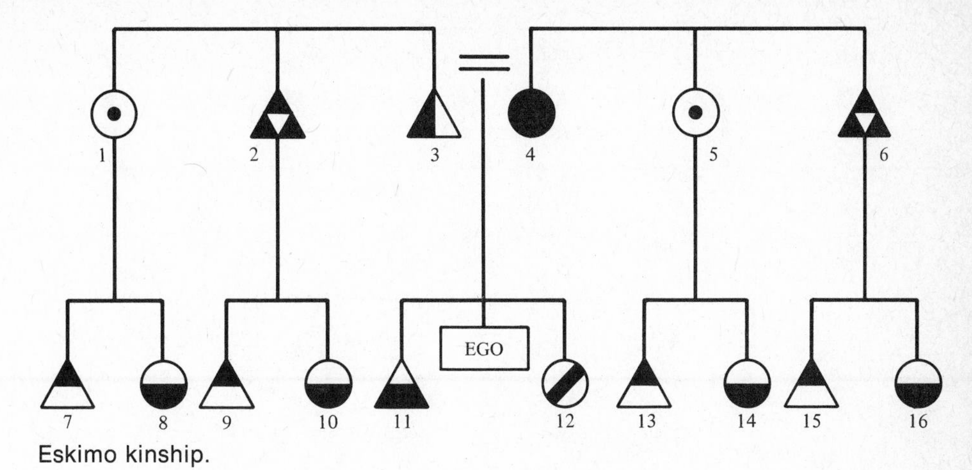

Eskimo kinship.

Terms for members of one's family are, of course, relative to that person's point of view. You call the man we mentioned before "Father," but your mother calls the same man "Husband." You call that kid over there "Cousin Tommy," but your uncle calls him "Son." So each diagram has one person from whose perspective we're viewing the whole system, and we call that person *EGO*.

Let's begin with the system that should be easiest for us. It's the *Eskimo* system, so named because it was described in studies of that group.

To review quickly, what you have here are two married individuals, 3 and 4, who have three kids, 11, EGO, and 12. Each parent has two sibs, one of each sex, and each of these has two kids. To make things simpler, I've left out the spouses of the parents' sibs. EGO, by the way, is of no particular sex, so we can change "its" sex back and forth for different examples.

OK, now the terms. You notice that EGO's biological parents are indicated by symbols found nowhere else on the chart. This means that EGO calls them by terms used for them alone. The parent's sibs fall into two categories, one for males and one for females. In EGO's generation, there are again unique terms for EGO's biological sibs, distinguishing male sibs from female sibs. Finally, all the offspring of EGO's parents' sibs are called by the same term, here with no differentiation of sex (though some cultures using the Eskimo system do make the distinction).

Look familiar? It should. We use the Eskimo system. Just substitute English words for the symbols: father, mother, sister, brother, aunt, uncle, cousin. Easy enough?

The Eskimo system is found most often at both ends of the

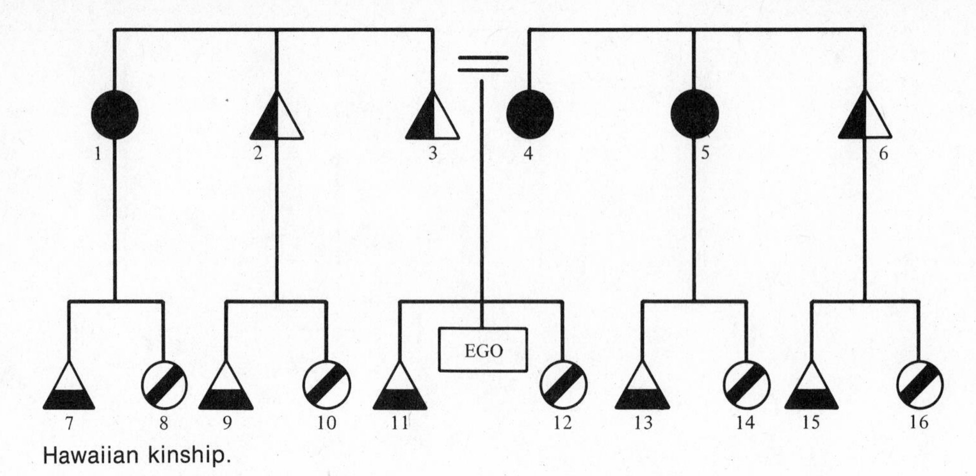

Hawaiian kinship.

scale of subsistence types. It tends to be used by hunter-gatherers and by industrial populations. Why? Look at what is emphasized by the terms: the nuclear family. Within that unit, people are specified. But outside that unit, people fall into a more limited number of categories with no distinction as to side of the family or even, in some cases, sex.

The system goes hand in hand with a bilateral descent line where sides of the family are symmetrical. It reflects an economic emphasis on the nuclear family, as found in foraging groups, *or* a conceptual emphasis on the nuclear family as the only important recognized kinship unit, as in our industrial society. It allows the nuclear family to be set off and allows persons outside the nuclear family to be equally important—or equally unimportant. Thus it's as applicable to our culture as it is to that of the !Kung San.

Probably the simplest system is the *Hawaiian.* In this system persons are distinguished only by sex and generation. No distinction is made for side of the family. This system is found in groups that have bilateral descent lines or one of those systems in which you are a member of either side or different sides for different purposes. Unlike the Eskimo system, also associated with bilaterality, however, the Hawaiian, rather than focusing on the nuclear family, "lumps" nuclear family members and other close relatives into just a few categories. Societies that use this system usually deal with greater numbers of related persons than do foragers. (We, of course, deal with huge numbers of people, but not on a kinship basis.) The emphasis is on symmetry of the two sides, from the parents and sibs outward. EGO's relations to a large number of people are fairly simple and straightforward.

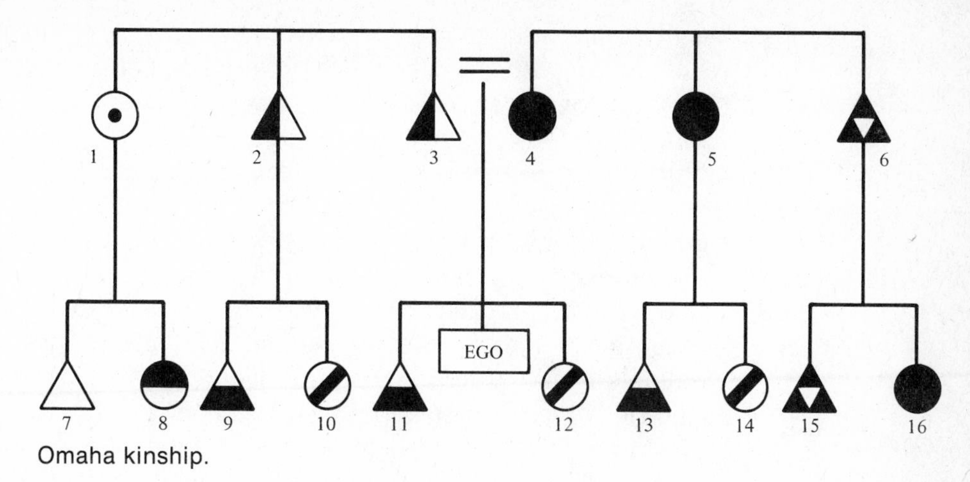

Omaha kinship.

There is another feature, which we have already discussed, that is linked to terminology. This is the incest taboo. Remember that mating between sibs and between parents and offspring is universally prohibited. Though that taboo may have originated with reference to the biological meanings of those terms, in practice it relates to their cultural meanings as well. In other words, any person to whom you refer using the same term that you use for your biological nuclear family members is *the same* as those members, and the incest taboo would apply to them as well.

Look back at the Hawaiian diagram. Who can EGO *not* marry? Everybody. Because everyone on the chart is the same as the members of EGO's biological nuclear family. EGO must find a mate outside his or her family line.

Now, the most complex system—the terminology systems used by unilineal societies. Again, there are several, but a close look at one should show you how it works. This is the *Omaha* system, named after that Native American group.

Pretty strange-looking at first, isn't it? But take things one at a time and it all makes sense. The first thing to do for the moment is ignore numbers 9, 10, 13, and 14. They're special, and we'll come back to them in a minute.

Having left them out, you should notice that on EGO's father's side of the family there are more categories than on the mother's side. In fact, all the members of EGO's mother's family (except 13 and 14—keep ignoring them!) are just male or female, regardless of generation. If we were to add more generations, the situation would still be the same. On the father's side, though, both sex *and* generation are specified. What this tells you is that the Omaha system is usually found in patrilineal societies. As EGO, my important social relations are with the other members of my patrilineage. Thus it is important for me to specify individuals. I am not a member of my mother's patrilineage, though, so those individuals are not as culturally important to me and are specified only by their sex.

But don't confuse personal recognition with cultural categories. Certainly, I know who those people are, and I call them all by their personal names. My mother is not a member of my patrilineage, but I live with her and have close emotional ties with her. She is my mother in every way we understand that term. These categories we're talking about refer to cultural relations—various economic and social rights and responsibilities—that happen to be organized using a kinship model.

Now look at EGO's generation and bring back the people you ignored before. What do you see? Those folks are the same as EGO's biological sibs. People that our Eskimo system considers all the same (we use the term "cousin" for them) are, in the Omaha system, divided into three sets of categories. Numbers 15 and 16 are simply a male and a female on the mother's side—we already went over that. Numbers 7 and 8 are individuals in EGO's patrilineage specified by sex and generation. But 9, 10, 13, and 14, on both sides, are like 11 and 12, who are the biological sibs!

The Omaha system, and another system I'll mention in a second, make a distinction between two kinds of children of parents' sibs: *parallel cousins* and *cross cousins*. Parallel cousins are the children of same-sex sibs; in other words, your father's brother's kids and your mother's sister's kids. Cross cousins are your father's sister's kids and your mother's brother's kids. Got it?

Your parallel cousins in these systems are so distinct from your cross cousins that they are the same as your biological sibs, and thus, of course, fall into that incest category. You can't marry them. Why this distinction? Well, it makes some sense on a cultural level since 9 and 10 are members of your patrilineage but 7 and 8 are not. They are members of *their* father's patrilineage (the husband of your father's sister, who is not on the diagram). This categorization would prohibit you from marrying within your patrilineage but allow marriage to persons who are members of another patrilineage. In some cultures, in fact, where perhaps there are not a lot of people and thus a limited choice of marriage partners, the preferred partners *are* your cross cousins.

But 13 and 14 are not in your patrilineage. Why are they prohibited partners? It may be a matter of symmetry. A distinction so important on one side could hardly be ignored on the other. Anyhow, since your mother's sister is in the same category as your mother, it would make sense that her children would be the same as your own sibs.

There may not be one simple answer to the cousin distinction question that covers all cases. We may just need to look at each example and see how separating parallel and cross cousins works for each society that has the practice. As with so many other things, kinship terminology in a given society is the result of the cumulative effects of years of individual cultural decisions made in response to years of environmental and cultural events. Hard-and-fast rules are difficult to make. For instance, a few groups that use the Omaha system are matrilineal, so our neat analysis won't work for them. Culture, as I'm sure you're beginning to see, is a complex phenomenon.

There are a few more term systems that you can learn about if and when you'd like to delve more deeply into this whole topic (and I hope you're intrigued enough to want to). But just for practice now, consider one other system I alluded to: The *Crow* system is the mirror image of the Omaha and is usually associated with matrilineal societies. See if you can diagram it.

ORGANIZATION ABOVE THE FAMILY LEVEL

Within societies there are a number of organizing principles in addition to those based on the kinship model. For instance, in many societies there are *age sets*—groups of people born within some limited time range of one another. These age-set members remain associated for life and have certain special social and economic rights and responsibilities toward one another.

There are also associations based on gender. *Men's associations,* common in societies in New Guinea, are as important as any other social category for defining a person's social position and socioeconomic relations with other members of the group. We also find various forms of military associations and associations based on occupation, ethnic affiliation, and region of birth.

But as societies get larger and more complex, there is the need for some sort of overall organization. As anthropologist Elman R. Service puts it:

> Kinship . . . can integrate a society only up to a certain point in its growth. After that, the society must fission into separate societies

> if growth continues. . . . Only with the achievement of new integrative means can an increase in complexity keep pace with the growth.

The "new integrative means" he refers to is *political organization*. Such a level of organization, dealing as it does with large populations, may not coincide with cultural boundaries. Whereas members of a culturally defined society share the same cultural world view and speak the same language, members of a politically defined society may practice different cultures. Many African nations, for example, which are political units, are comprised of peoples from a number of different culturally defined, linguistically separate societies. Similarly, members of the same culture may reside in several political communities. I'll talk later about the current situation with the !Kung, whose members now live in at least two African political states.

Political organization serves the same functions as organization on the family level, but it involves more people and more complex interactions. Allow me to defer to another anthropologist for a formal definition of politics upon which I can hardly improve. According to Frank Robert Vivelo, political organization

> refers to the means of maintaining order and comformity in a society. It concerns the allocation of power and authority to make decisions beyond the personal level, i.e., decisions which affect the group . . . as a whole. It provides the structure through which decisions about social policy, and the implementation of social policy, are effected. In addition . . . [it] also concerns the way a society orders its affairs in relation to other groups.

As you would expect by now, the specific features of political organization vary enormously among different societies. We can, however, divide the variation up into a few general types. This scheme was devised by Elman Service and uses four major categories: bands, tribes, chiefdoms, and states.

Band organization is the simplest and is, in a sense, no political organization at all. It is organization based on kinship and is characteristic of hunter-gatherer societies. As you recall, these are small, flexible units with no social stratification in terms of either wealth or power, though there are certain individuals who are informally more influential.

Tribal organization is characteristic of horticultural and pastoral groups. Service has referred to tribes as "collections of bands." The basic organization is still along kinship lines, but now those lines are combined into larger units—called *lineages* or *clans*—and relations exist that unite different kinship units and different residence areas (villages, for instance). Tribes are essentially egalitarian, and there is still no central authority, but the problems facing this larger group are generally more complex than those of a band society and so must involve decisions on the part of the tribe as a whole.

Chiefdoms are the next level up in terms of integration. There is still no central authority over the whole political unit (still referred to as a tribe), but because more people and thus more complex interactions are involved, there are more individual units making up the tribe. There is a need for some form of formal leadership, at least of the main subunits. This leader is the *chief*. Such an organization is found in agricultural and large pastoral groups. The basis of organization is still kinship, since the position of chief is often hereditary. Chiefdoms are socioeconomically somewhere in between egalitarian and class; there are social strata, but there is an attempt to smooth these out through redistribution.

States are characterized by having central authority. In agricultural societies made up of very large numbers of people (including societies we might term "industrial") there is the clear need for all the individual units—though each may be led by its own chief—to be integrated. It is at the state level that we may find individual units from different cultural backgrounds.

Social organization, as you can see, is a large and complex topic. But the general idea is that even though the organizing groups may sometimes be based on biological things like age, sex, and kinship, the actual categories, the rules for membership, and all the ideals of behavior associated with the categories are cultural inventions geared toward taking care of the needs of the group that uses them. And it's in this light that we must try to see and understand them—not always an easy task.

At least, though, when we're examining the cultural lives of existing peoples, we can actually watch culture in action. We can literally ask the people what they're doing and why. We can go back and check out our conclusions.

Not so with the study of past cultures, and most cultures that have ever existed are past cultures, now extinct. Some past people have left behind written records that help us reconstruct their culture. But writing has only been around for 5000 or 6000 years. For all the time before that, our only clues to the lives of people are in the form of the material artifacts they've left behind. Can we hope to understand such abstract things as social organization by looking at ancient garbage? What's the relation between material culture and whole cultural systems? We look next at the work of the archaeologist—the anthropological time traveler.

SUMMARY

All groups of living organisms require some mechanism to coordinate the actions of their members. For most living things, this mechanism is genetic. But when large-brained primates—creatures that rely on learned behavior for survival—are involved, group organization becomes more complex. In baboons, for instance, the personal characteristics of individuals are important in the establishment of the dominance hierarchy that coordinates their societies.

In the human primate, the basis for social organization is, not surprisingly, the basic reproductive and economic unit, the family. For most human societies throughout most of our evolutionary history, social organization has been based on kinship. But even when populations become large, complex, and comprised of a number of biological kin groups, the organizational structure may still be based on the kinship model. Now, however, kin units may crosscut biological lines, and we see all sorts of variations—in one's individual identity as a member of a kin group and in the identity and number of potential marriage partners. This variation must be examined and understood in adaptive terms. The assumption we make is that the form of organization works for the people who practice it and that it is an integral part of their whole cultural system.

When societies become so large and complex that kinship alone can't operate to organize and coordinate them, broader forms of integration must be devised. These are political units, and although many of these still have kinship-based aspects, they are largely based on residence and socioeconomic interaction. Thus the political unit may not coincide with the cultural unit. Once again, we see certain correspondences between this facet of cultural behavior and others we have examined—things like subsistence pattern and economic organization.

NOTES, REFERENCES, AND READINGS

For a fine introduction to all aspects of primate behavior, with a focus on the social aspects, see Alison Jolly's *The Evolution of*

Primate Behavior (New York: Macmillan, 1972). For a discussion of the baboons in particular, including the experiments to determine the cultural component of their social behavior, see the book by Hans Kummer I referred to in Chapter 6.

My favorite introductory book on kinship is by Roger M. Keesing, *Kin Groups and Social Structure* (New York: Holt, Rinehart and Winston, 1975). Figures on the relationship between kinship and subsistence pattern are on page 134 of that book, and the quote is from page 140. The model I used for illustrating kinship terminology is from Carol R. Ember and Melvin Ember's *Anthropology* (3d ed., Englewood Cliffs, N.J.: Prentice-Hall, 1981).

Elman R. Service's categories of political organization can be found in his *Profiles in Ethnology* (3d ed., New York: Harper & Row, 1978). The body of the book is made up of brief ethnographies of four or five example cultures from each type. The quote is from page 3.

The definition of politics I used is on page 135 of the book by Vivelo, cited in Chapter 7.

chapter 9

Tools and Shelters
The Things We Make and Leave Behind

We've probably gone long enough without one of those "multiple-guess" questions.

Which two of the following are in the same category?

a. a beehive
b. the rock used by Egyptian vultures to smash ostrich eggs
c. the chimpanzee termite stick
d. the huts of the !Kung San

They're all tools or shelters, so they are all concerned with the topic of this chapter. The vulture, however, doesn't make its tool, it just *uses* a natural object. So that leaves the other three as things that are *made*. But the beehive, as with the ants' nest we discussed earlier, is really a "natural" object, since all the instructions for it, and the "reason" for building it, are programmed in the insects' genes.

The termite stick and the San huts, on the other hand, are *artifacts*. They are artificially manufactured, based on some abstract idea and geared to facilitate some perceived need. In other words, they are both cultural as we have defined that term. So the answer is (c) and (d).

Now, one more question in our quiz. What's the difference between (c) and (d)? Well, the chimps' termite stick, though it fulfills all our criteria for an example of culture, is aimed at solving a problem related strictly to the natural environment: how to get those termites. The sticks are not part of any larger cultural system. There is no variation in the sticks that reflects any sort of variation on the level of world view. (There is some evidence that individual chimps have favorite plants from which to make their stick, but this seems to be a matter of personal preference, based on who knows what.)

The huts of the !Kung San, though, besides obviously taking care of the need for shelter, are built on a traditional pattern that is based on a long history of cultural decisions. The size and number of huts manufactured at any one time is dependent on the number of people who will use each hut and the number of persons in the group as a whole. These numbers are in turn the results of specific aspects of the San cultural system regarding group size and personal relations within the group. This last factor also determines the placement of the huts within the camp. Who actually does the hut building has to do with the nature of the society's economic and social structure. And the individual features of the dwellings are geared to other aspects of the San technology, things like the number and kinds of possessions to be stored in the huts. (This, by the way, is the huts' use: for storage and for taking naps. People don't actually live in them, as they are small and usually infested with insects.)

To understand San huts you have to understand not only what they *do* but also what they *mean*. This is because, as we discussed before, our artifacts not only take care of our basic environmental needs but also implement and reflect cultural ideas about our relation with the environment and with one another—our world view. Culture adapts to culture as well as to things like climate and food sources.

All the cultural items we've dealt with in the last few chapters are examples of this concept, as was my necktie story. But as a "take-home" question that relates to a familiar artifact, consider that paragon of American culture, the automobile.

The purpose of the automobile is to move people and their belongings around quickly (efficiently and safely, I'm not so sure about). The funny thing is, though, that this basic artifact comes in so many varieties. The four major American car manufacturers produced, in 1983, a total of somewhere around 100 models of automobiles. And then there are all the foreign companies. All those ways of moving you and your things from place to place! The question is, What can you conclude from this about American society, based on all that we've discussed so far? Give it some thought as we continue.

The idea that artifacts are parts of a cultural system and are thus reflections of a society's world view is the basis for the work of the anthropologist who tries to reconstruct past cultures from material remains. This area of anthropology is archaeology.

Of all the areas of focus within the broad field of anthropology, archaeology is perhaps the most distinct. Anthropologists specializing in this area tend to identify themselves as "archaeologists." This is in part because archaeology is the oldest formal specialty within the field, going back as far as the 1400s, when European "antiquarians" began excavating the remains of the classical civilizations of Greece and Rome.

The most important reason, though, is that the archaeologist has such special problems concerned with collecting and analyzing data. Those data, the material remains of past cultures, must usually be dug up—literally. They're most often underground because they're so old, buried over the years by things like flooding, windblown dust, volcanic eruptions, and soil from erosion. To find ancient artifacts, to recover them, preserve them, and study them, requires a very specialized set of technical and theoretical skills, as I'll show you.

But don't think that this makes archaeology something different from anthropology. It's not just finding neat old stuff in the ground and putting it in museums. The archaeologist uses the artifacts as data to try to answer the same types of questions as any anthropologist—questions about the nature of the human species. Archaeology is the anthropology of the past—no more, no less. Let's see how this works in practice.

ARCHAEOLOGY: THEORY AND METHODS

Living in New England, I have on hand one of the best examples of the connection between artifacts and the practical and abstract parts of culture. It's an example that will let us check out some of our methods and conclusions. The artifacts are gravestones carved from the mid-1600s to the mid-1800s.

If you explore old New England cemeteries and find the stones from that period, you will begin to notice that although there are a number of designs carved into the markers, the majority usually fall into three broad types, called death's-heads, cherubs, and urns and willows.

What sorts of things can you tell from these stones? Well, you can certainly tell how old they are. The dates are right on them. And from the epitaphs you can find out something about the people buried beneath the stones: their name, sex, age at death, sometimes cause of death, and maybe something about their occupation, standing in the community, and personality (although, given the context, what's written may be biased!).

Using historical records we can sometimes find out who carved the stone (there seem to have been a limited number of carvers in the area at that time), where the carvers traveled in New England, and even the price paid for the markers. Sometimes prices are even right on the stone!

But the stones can tell us even more. The designs were not carved at random, and they do not exist outside of a cultural context.

New England gravestones: death's head, cherub, urn and willow.

They mean something. And the something they mean relates to attitudes toward death and the afterlife—in other words, to religious belief as practiced in a given cultural situation.

Specifically, the death's-head—a grim, grinning skull—symbolizes a pessimistic view of life and death. It reminds the living of human mortality, of everyone's inevitable end. The epitaphs on these stones tend to stress either these ideas or certain strict Puritan standards of behavior. This is in fact the connection. For the death's-head design is associated with the period of orthodox Puritanism, through the 1600s to the mid- or late 1700s, depending on the area. The famous witch trials of Salem Village, Massachusetts, in 1692, coincided with the peak in popularity of this design.

As orthodox Puritanism declined beginning in the mid-1700s, attitudes about death changed. The emphasis now was on resurrection and the rewards to be enjoyed in heaven. This change is reflected in the replacement of the death's-head with the cherub—a smiling baby-faced angel with wings—and in epitaphs that stress these more positive aspects of death. These new ideas, and the adoption of the new design, seem to have begun in the urban intellectual center of Cambridge, Massachusetts (where Harvard University is and was then) and spread from there. Moreover, the design in this area was associated with graves of upper-class, educated individuals. So we see a connection here between artifacts, religious beliefs, and the nature of intellectual influence in early New England culture. The gravestone designs themselves, it should be noted, originated in England—a further connection.

By the late 1700s, religion had taken on a less emotional nature than it had had under Puritanism. This, in association with a trend toward Greek revival architecture, gave rise to the "classical"-looking urn-and-willow design. The epitaphs now were more in the style of memorials; they said "In memory of . . ." rather than "Here lies buried the body of . . ."

By the mid-1800s, gravestone designs began to show more variation. This was a result of a combination of factors: greater variety of religious expression, a trend toward more individual freedoms, and the immigration of peoples from diverse parts of the world, among others. But in New England during that earlier period, we can see some clear connections between these artifacts and other facets of culture, even ideological ones.

Now, I know what you're saying: "That's fine. But these gravestones are historic. There's no guesswork here. Basic information is written right on the stones! All that stuff about religion is also written down somewhere! Where's the analysis?"

Well, I have several responses to that logical objection before I give you the really old examples you're looking for. First, as surprising as it may seem, there are things we don't know even about cultures with written records—even our own colonial period. People don't write everything down. As we've discussed, people are not always intellectually aware of why they do the things they do. So far as I know, nowhere is there anything in writing that says, "We're gonna carve skulls on our tombstones because we're Puritans and we emphasize strict behavioral rules and stress the idea of human mortality"! So even when we are dealing with historic periods, there are still things that archaeological analysis can tell us.

Second, analyses like those of the gravestones, whereby we *can* check out the connections, form the basis for archaeological analysis in general. In the archaeological record we can't see all the facets of culture in operation. We only find the material remains. So the only thing we have on which to base our hypotheses is the actions of living humans and the written records of the recent past.

For example, we can't see an ancient tool being used, so we can't know absolutely what it was used for. We can, though, see what similar-looking tools are found in existing societies and what they are used for and by analogy hypothesize the same for the old tool in question. This process is called *ethnographic analogy.* It's a lot like the analysis of organic fossils: Until we get really complete records of a type of extinct creature, the only way we can categorize a fossil is by figuring out what living category it most resembles.

So the old gravestones do more than tell us something new about early New England culture. They also give us some ideas about certain aspects of culture in general that may prove useful to us in other archaeological investigations.

Another fascinating example of *historic archaeology* is the excavation of a settlement in Virginia called Martin's Hundred, which was inhabited in the early 1600s. Again, though there were written records available about the area, there were many things not recorded—for instance the layout of the settlement, the exact nature of its buildings, even the type of coffin used to bury the dead. These things were revealed by archaeological analysis of the site. For details, see the book on this site listed at the end of the chapter.

OK, how about something older? There are literally thousands of examples, but one of my favorites concerns a study done by Sir Mortimer Wheeler, one of the most famous of early Old World archaeologists. Using the techniques of archaeological analysis and some basic information from early Roman writings, he reconstructed, in amazing detail, a battle that took place around A.D. 47. In that

Excavation at Maiden Castle.

battle, the Roman commander (and later emperor) Vespasian attacked and conquered a Celtic hill-fort, now called Maiden Castle, in southern England.

Wheeler was able to tell, for example, which side of the fort was attacked, what sorts of weapons were used, and in what particular manner the Romans launched their attack (arrows first, followed by an infantry charge). He could tell that some huts near the entrance of the fort were burned and that the attackers, possibly because they encountered more resistance than they had expected, massacred women and children as well as the adult male defenders. And when the Romans had won the battle, they proceeded systematically to destroy the military aspects of the fort, tearing down fighting platforms, taking apart gates, and toppling stone walls alongside the entrances.

Soon after the battle (perhaps the next night), the conquered people of Maiden Castle buried their dead, in the place where the huts had been burned. The burials were hasty (the Romans were still around), but the survivors remembered in most cases to include in the graves food and drink for the journey to the afterlife. Probably the following day, when the Roman legion had moved on, the people began cleaning up and putting things back in order somewhat, eventually building new roads across the ruins of their old fortifications. They continued to live there (under Roman rule) for about 20 years,

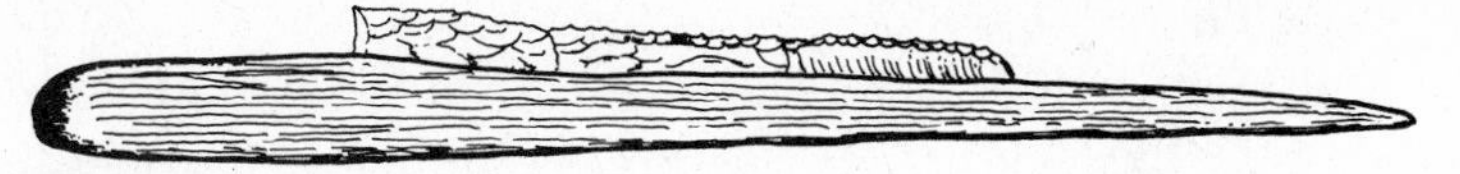

Reaping knife.

when Maiden Castle was finally abandoned and its remaining walls torn down.

How can Wheeler tell all this? For details I refer you to his fascinating book on the subject. But in general, at the site of Maiden Castle, he found such evidence as the iron arrowheads the Romans used clustered on the eastern side. He could tell the order of events by the placement of the layers of artifacts and other features (remember stratigraphy?). For example, the graves were clearly dug through the ashes of the burned huts. The skeletons in the graves were not found in any particular position or orientation, and grave goods varied, indicating hurried burial. The bodies showed signs of the wounds that killed them; it was these multiple and brutal wounds that led Wheeler to use the term *massacre*. Finally, it was clear that at least one stone wall was pulled down when the people abandoned Maiden Castle, sometime in the 60s of the first century A.D., since the remains of that wall are on top of other features and even block one of those roads built after the battle.

So using knowledge of such things as stratigraphic associations, weapons types, architecture and technology, forensic medicine (ascertaining from bodies information such as cause of death), and some things I didn't include about pottery types and old Roman coins, Wheeler painted an amazingly clear and detailed picture not only of the way of life of the people of Maiden Castle but also of a particular event that took place almost 2000 years ago.

But are those written records still bothering you? How about an example from farther back, say around 6000 years ago? Writing was just beginning then, so what written records we do have don't even come close to addressing all aspects of the culture that kept them. In the 1930s, in the Fayum area west of Cairo, Egypt, was unearthed an artifact that consisted of a wooden shaft to which were attached small pieces of flint held in place with mastic (a kind of glue). What was it? Obviously, it wasn't a natural object! But even that conclusion must be based on our knowledge of what sorts of things nature produces as opposed to the modifications humans make to natural things. Furthermore, it was found in the bottom of a coiled basket that had been placed in the earth so that its rim was just about at the level of what was then (6000 years ago) the surface of the ground. Along with our artifact in the basket were some grains of wheat and barley. We know, in fact, using the same sort of reasoning process we're applying now, that these baskets were granaries—places to store collected or cultivated grains. (In this case they had been cultivated.)

So maybe that implement has something to do with harvesting grains. What does it look like? An awful lot like sickles used all over the world today to do just that. If you make one and try it out on some grain-bearing plants (a general procedure called *experimental archaeology*), it works just fine. Furthermore, and clinching our hypothesis, when examined under a microscope, the little flint blades show a luster on their surface just like the luster that results when flint is brought continually into rapid contact with the silica crystals in the stalks of some plants. All of this says that the artifact was used as a sickle, this particular form being known as a *reaping knife*. See how it works?

Now, how about one more example from before written records? Remember the Spanish site of Torralba, where *Homo erectus* used fires to drive animals into a bog so they could be killed and butchered? How have we figured that out?

Well, we know the area used to be a bog because the deposits in which the bones of the animals were found are made up of clay silt. The place is not a bog now, but we know what sorts of features modern bogs have and what sorts of evidence they would leave behind. Similarly, we know what animals the bones belonged to by comparing them to those of modern creatures. And we know that the animals had been hunted by people, since we found some of their butchering tools and since the bodies of the dead animals had obviously been cut up and moved around.

By the way, no bones of humans were found at the site, but we know from previous work that the tools found there are like those made by *Homo erectus* elsewhere in the world. So we infer the connection for Torralba. In addition, the site is the right age, about 400,000 years, for *Homo erectus*.

That fire was used to drive the animals into the bog is inferred from pieces of charcoal and charred wood scattered all over the site. This would not be the case if the people had made individual campfires. These pieces might well be the remains of torches that were carried during the hunt. We also know that the area was used for about ten hunting seasons, possibly in succession. This comes from our knowledge of seasonal changes in plant life and soil composition and of stratigraphic relationships.

We have also been able to figure out in some detail the procedure used to butcher the animals. It seems to have been carried out in three stages: First, the best parts of the carcass were cut off at the kill site. Then, moving to a second place (remember, the whole thing started in a bog), the flesh was taken off the bones and some of the bones smashed to extract the marrow. Finally, at a third place, the meat was cooked and eaten.

This reconstruction comes largely from the analysis of one elephant skeleton. In one place much of the left side of an elephant was found, with bones separated but unbroken. In a second place, bones from the same animal, mostly leg bones and ribs, were located. Most of these had been smashed. And in a third place, many smaller, charred fragments were found.

You can easily picture what happened. The elephant was dismembered at the kill site, where it had been mired down in the bog, with the large, easily removed chunks of meat taken off there. Then, pieces like the legs and ribs were taken to a second place, where marrow was extracted and more detailed butchering was done. The meat was then transported to a place where it could be cut up further and cooked.

There are some more educated guesses we can make about this site. For example, given the number of elephants, deer, horses, and rhinoceroses (yes, they used to live in Europe) that were killed there, it has been estimated that about 100 persons, possibly a gathering of several bands, were involved. The kind of planning and cooperation that must have been necessary for such a venture implies the use of a fairly sophisticated communication system—a language. And from some individual piles of bones, each of which represents some parts of all the animals killed, investigators have inferred a meat distribution system, which indicates an egalitarian social structure. That might be pushing things a bit, but it's only by making such guesses and then looking for further evidence to support or refute them that science progresses.

In addition, since such large quantities of meat were sometimes acquired (as in the case of elephants, which were the most hunted animal at Torralba) it might be guessed that extra meat was dried and saved for future meals. This is what American Indians did with meat from large kills of bison—an example of ethnographic analogy.

Finally, at a site called Ambrona, which is across the valley from Torralba and has many of the same features, archaeologists uncovered a puzzling collection of five elephant leg bones and a tusk that had been arranged in a straight line 20 feet long. Exactly what this was used for no one knows, but one guess is that it might have acted as some sort of support for a shelter made of hides.

Again, you should see the process going on in this archaeological analysis: the utilization of knowledge of modern relationships, coupled with knowledge gained from previous investigations, overlaid with some good guesswork. The process will, of course, vary in detail, depending on the site being investigated and the time period involved. But this is basically how we go about reconstructing the lifeways of any past humans from the evidence they happen to have left behind.

Another word of caution: The examples used here relate mostly to the reconstruction of specific events—an old battle and an ancient hunt. But the task of the archaeologist is to reconstruct entire cultural systems out of these specific pieces of data. And that is in order to do what all anthropologists try to do: answer broad questions about our species—things like the origin of warfare or the evolution of our hunting behavior. The examples I used were meant to be striking things you'd probably remember, and their purpose was to show you how the first stage of the science of archaeology operates.

Now we need to consider just how this evidence is collected so as to provide us with the data necessary for such reconstructions.

When we talk about archaeological excavations, or "digs," we are reflecting the fact that most archaeological sites are literally underground and must be dug up. An initial question then becomes, How do you find a site in the first place?

In some instances, of course, the site is obvious. For example, you can't miss the Egyptian pyramids or some of the large ceremonial cities of ancient Central America. Although all the artifacts were under the soil, the outline of Maiden Castle was clearly visible. In the American Midwest, Indian burial mounds seem to rise out of flat fields.

In other cases, although the site itself may be hidden, evidence of its presence is uncovered accidentally. A farmer plowing a field in Indiana may turn up a sherd of pottery that leads to the discovery of an old Indian village. A crew digging a subway tunnel in Boston may come across the remains of an ancient weir (a device to trap fish swimming in a stream). Wind or water erosion might unearth some artifact long in the ground. Or the vague outline of an old settlement may be noticed from the air, the slight changes in elevation and vegetation not readily visible at ground level.

But the vast majority of the time you simply have to hunt for a site. How you go about this varies greatly, depending on the sort of site you're looking for and the time period involved. In the case of Lucy and her contemporaries, for instance, who are 3.5 million years old and who lived in an area noted for its extensive geological changes, you pretty much have to just wander around until you find something, sticking to places where erosion or some geological change has exposed fossil beds. For more recent periods, though, there are particular procedures used in locating sites. As one example, let's look at the situation in my area, Connecticut.

The basic topography of Connecticut has not changed much since people first lived here. This is because *no one* lived here before the final recession of the glaciers about 10,000 years ago, and the modern form of much of the land in the state is largely a result of those glaciers. So if we are looking for habitation sites of Connecticut's ancient peoples, we can begin with an obvious question: If we were here several thousand years ago, where would we set up camp?

Well, what sorts of areas can people live in and what sorts of resources would they have needed? Clearly, you can't establish a village on the side of a small mountain, so you'd start looking in a flatter area. And you'd look in a place that has close at hand that most vital of resources, water. In the state of Connecticut there are a number of good-sized rivers with broad, flat floodplains that have been around for quite a while. That's a good place to begin.

But where on the floodplain of, say, the Farmington River in central Connecticut do you look? That's a lot of land to cover. Again, you might start with some logical considerations: Forget rocky or hilly places, for example. Second, you might conduct what's known as a surface survey—walk around and see if any artifacts have been exposed by erosion or plowing. We can also use written records. The state archives here contain hundreds of old treaties and deeds, many of which make note of the locations of Indian villages. All that can help.

But in the end the only way to locate such a site for sure is to dig holes in the ground. We call these preliminary holes *test pits*. They are usually around a foot or so square and go as deep as artifacts are found, or, more usually, until it is certain that *no* artifacts will be found. Test pits are located so as to provide the best coverage of the

Floodplain of the Farmington River, Connecticut.

area being examined. If some small area looks very promising, the pits may be concentrated there. Or if it's a very large area, the pits can be placed using techniques of statistical sampling. At any rate, it's through test pits that we usually determine whether we should conduct more thorough excavations in a place or move elsewhere.

If test pits reveal the presence of a site—that is, a place where there are artifacts—and if it appears that there is more material to be found, the detailed work begins. An excavation is much more than just digging up an area and finding interesting old objects. When a site is dug, it is literally destroyed. A table full of artifacts in some lab is worthless unless we know just where the artifacts were located, in geological terms and in relation to each other. Wheeler's conclusions about the battle of Maiden Castle, for example, would have been impossible if all he had to go on were the artifacts themselves. So when excavating a site, detailed and extensive records must be kept of the location of everything. An old cliché says that we should be able to put the whole site back just as we found it!

To control the recording of location, we consider two dimensions at a site. The horizontal dimension is controlled using a grid system. The site is marked off, usually with string and small supports, into a set of squares or grids, and each of these is dug as a separate unit. The size of the grids can vary, depending on the nature of the

The excavation: grid system, vertical control, test pits.

site, but an average is a meter square. As artifacts are found, their placement in the particular grid is noted and drawn or photographed. If the site being dug is something like an old building that is itself divided into horizontal units (such as rooms and hallways), the grid system may not be necessary.

Vertical control, too, may be determined by the site itself—the floors of a building or the rows of stones that make up the walls, for example. Or if the ground we're digging into is highly and clearly stratified, the strata may be our units. But usually we establish them ourselves, digging down in layers of a few inches at a time, so that each artifact may be recorded according to its placement in a certain layer. This vertical dimension is important for determining time and order of events.

The excavation of a site is, of course, only the data-collection part of the process. Once a dig is completed, with all the records in order and all the artifacts bagged and labeled, the analysis begins. Artifacts are measured, photographed, compared with those from other sites. Soil from the site is analyzed for clues to climate and vegetation. Any organic remains are examined to determine the people's diet. Remains of the people themselves, if found, can be investigated for demographic factors like age and sex distribution and for physical attributes and medical data. Gradually, through these and hundreds of other analytic techniques, a picture of the site emerges—a view into the lives of a group of people who are no longer around. This view then itself becomes data, which can be compared with similar information from other sites in an attempt to derive some generalizations about our species.

One aspect of archaeological analysis should be examined a little more closely. All through this book I've been telling you how old things are. Lucy was 3.5 million years old. Maiden Castle was conquered in A.D. 47. Life on Earth began 3.5 billion years ago. How do we come up with those dates?

There are two basic types of dating techniques, *relative dating* and *absolute dating*. Relative dating (which has nothing to do with courting your cousin!) we've already mentioned. This is when you determine whether something is older or younger than something else or when you figure out a date for one thing based on its similarities to another. For instance, stratigraphic relationships give a clear picture of the order of certain events: Those roads were built after the walls of Maiden Castle were destroyed; mammals appear after reptiles in the evolutionary story; the australopithecine branch died out about the time *Homo erectus* was spreading throughout the Old World.

Similarly, we may date things by association. Torralba, for example, gave us no human remains. But other sites clearly set up a correlation between certain tool types and *Homo erectus*. We assume then that *erectus* was the hunter at Torralba. Similarly, it was difficult to give a specific date to Torralba. But we know from other sites that the plants and animals and climatic conditions there were those of about 400,000 years ago.

But where do those specific, or "absolute," dates come from in the first place? There are many techniques for dating a site or items in a site, but most work pretty much on the same principle: If you know how fast some event takes place, and if you can tell how far that event has progressed at your site, you can work backward to tell how old the site is. The two best-known techniques should show you how it works.

The one you've probably already heard of is *carbon dating*. Carbon 14 is a radioactive form of regular carbon, which has an atomic weight of 12. Radioactive means that the form is unstable and that it gradually "decays" into a stable form. The rate at which this decay takes place is called the *half-life*. The half-life of C-14 is 5730 years, which means that in that time one-half of the C-14 will have decayed. In another 5730 years, half of the remaining half (or one-quarter of the original) will have decayed, and so on.

Carbon is an important element in organic molecules; all living things contain carbon and, through respiration and metabolism, exchange carbon with the environment. Most of that carbon is C-12, but some of it is C-14, which is produced when cosmic radiation hits atmospheric nitrogen. When an organism is alive, it contains a certain proportion of C-14, but when it dies, since it no longer takes in any new carbon, all its C-14 begins to decay at its half-life rate.

When we find some organic remains at an archaeological site—some bone or burnt wood, for example—we can test it to determine how much of its "alive" amount of C-14 is remaining and thus tell how long ago it died. For instance, say we find in our Connecticut site a hearth with charcoal. We know how much C-14 that tree contained when alive, but we find now that the charcoal only has one-fourth that amount. That means that two half-lives have passed: 5730 times 2, or 11,460 years. That tree was cut down 11,460 years ago to provide firewood for the inhabitants of the site.

Carbon 14 as a dating technique is only good to about 50,000 years, or about eight half-lives. Beyond that there's not enough C-14 left to test for accurately. So how do we date things that are older—Lucy, for example?

One very useful technique for dating really ancient things, and the one that in fact dated Lucy, is called the *potassium-argon* or *potassium 40* technique. Radioactive potassium, found in volcanic rock, decays into argon, a stable gas, at a half-life of 1.3 billion years. Organic things contain K-40 too, but they lose the argon that it turns into. Volcanic rocks, however, formed during eruptions, have a particular crystal structure that traps the argon that results from the decay of K-40. Using the same reasoning as we did with C-14, we test volcanic rocks for their proportion of argon, work backward, and date the rock. Any fossils found in association with the rock are also that old. Much of the hominid fossil material from East Africa, an area of extensive volcanic activity, was dated in this fashion. This is also really an example of dating by association, since Lucy, for instance, was not dated directly but by the fact that she was found in soil of volcanic origin.

These two, and a number of other dating techniques, supply us with absolute dates for fossil forms, climatic events, and tool types. Based on that evidence, we can then apply those dates to sites or items that can't be dated with the absolute methods. The result, as you've seen, is a pretty good idea of the history of this planet and its inhabitants, including us.

I asked you earlier to think about the automobile in all its seemingly infinite variety. What would those artifacts tell an archaeologist of the future about our culture? Well, the mere presence of the thing in such numbers would indicate, first, that there were a lot of us here and, second, that it was important for us to move ourselves and our belongings around, sometimes over great distances and with some speed. This would be an indication that we made complex economic transactions that involved our entire society as well as other societies. This seems clearly to say ''market system.''

The numerous styles of motor vehicles? First, they indicate that we had labor specialization, for there were obviously different sorts of vehicles for different tasks. But just one type of vehicle, the basic car, came in hundreds of versions, each doing essentially the same thing. That says that we were stratified, that there were recognized differences in wealth and status that were symbolized in part by the kind of motor vehicle we drove around in. Some cost more than others, and those, whether or not they were actually mechanically better, carried more status. See? You can do the same sort of analysis with clothing styles, towns, schools, and so on.

What have all these skills and techniques of archaeology actually told us about our history? Lots, obviously. And this is not the place for all the detail, especially for all the events of recent times for which we have written records—the period we refer to as "historic." But we can look at some important features of the time before history and, as we did with our biological evoution, try to get a feel for the evolution of our culture.

SOME PREHISTORIC HIGH POINTS

People used to talk about biological evolution as if the inevitable result of that evolution was us, as if all branches of the great tree were inexorably increasing in complexity, the end goal being a large brain with humanlike intelligence. Some evolutionary lines were slower in their progress, and some didn't seem to be making much progress at all. But that trend was thought to be the trend of all evolution. You know that that's not the case at all. That concept was a result of what you might call "anthropocentrism"—the idea that we are evolution's highest and best creation, to which all other organisms "aspire."

A similar thing occurred in talking about cultural evolution. Although anthropologists knew better, the way in which they once spoke about human culture history gave the impression that there was an overriding trend toward increasing complexity, culminating in agriculture-based civilizations with advanced technologies. Obviously, this is not true either.

Look around the world. I'm writing this book on a computer, so complex that I comprehend it only vaguely. A few years ago, a member of the Tasaday culture in the Philippines, wanting to cut down a tree for firewood, would do so with a stone ax. Computer societies live alongside Stone Age societies. Yet we are all fully modern *Homo sapiens,* with the same basic biology and intellectual potential.

Culture, as you know by now, doesn't follow some preordained trend. Cultures vary according to the environmental needs and the cultural histories of the societies that practice them. All cultures change, but they do so in different directions and at different rates. We must take this into account when trying to outline the prehistory of our species.

It has been popular to talk about prehistory by dividing the period up into three *lithic* ("stone-age") stages: the Paleolithic (Old Stone Age), Mesolithic (Middle Stone Age), and Neolithic (New Stone Age). The Paleolithic was defined as the period of the Pleistocene glaciers and was characterized by the use of relatively simple, single-stone tools. The Mesolithic was the culture type of people who were able to capitalize on the opening up of lands after the glacial retreat. It was characterized by all sorts of new and, in some cases, compound tools related to intensive foraging. The Neolithic brought in tools made of ground (rather than chipped) stone, as well as pottery and other technology geared toward the new subsistence pattern of farming. Dates were applied to the first appearence of each stage, and the names came to refer to specific sets of tools, called *tool kits*.

Now, that's all well and good, and when someone says "Upper Paleolithic" to me (that period was so long it was itself subdivided), I can picture a certain set of tools and other cultural features and I have in mind a certain time frame. But, those terms were coined with regard to the prehistory of Europe more than anywhere else. That's because when they were first used, Europe was the best-known area archaeologically. They fail, though, to account for different times of appearance in other places, for different rates of change, for different sequences of events, and for different types of tool kits and technologies. And the pigeonholing of 3 million years of human culture into predetermined categories fails to impart a feel for the flow of our cultural history, in all its fascinating variety.

This is clearly not the place to take care of that problem, for all the details of those 3 million years fill volumes. But we can, within the evolutionary context we've already laid out, look at what I see as three of the high points of prehistory. Perhaps through that you can get some idea about what we know of our prehistoric past and about the material evidence on which we base that knowledge.

I'm going to start by asking you the "unthinkable": Please reread the last part of Chapter 4, starting at the coming of *Homo habilis*. This will be your outline of human evolutionary history and will introduce the high points of culture that I'd like to expand on now.

Done? OK, here come the high points.

1. Stone Tools

Stone tools are, of course, crucial. They were the main type of tool for 99 percent of human culture history, and, when they were first invented, they reflected a jump in our ancestors' conceptual control over their environment. But they are also important to us because they are often the only remnant of a past culture that is preserved. Much of what we know about the movement of peoples around the world and of their cultural systems is based on our analyses of their lithic artifacts. Recall that we know it was *Homo erectus* who hunted at Torralba because of the nature of the stone tools found there.

A full examination of even this particular aspect of our culture is far too complex for the scope of this book. The tools come in an incredible array of varieties. But we can make some generalizations.

First, a little about how stones are worked. For the most part, stone tools are made of rock that can be flaked; that is, it chips smoothly, very much like the chipped lip you sometimes find on a soda bottle. Flint and chert are two types of stone that do this, and they were used extensively. To take flakes off a core, you have to hit it with another hard object, usually another stone. If that sounds simple, it's not. You really have to understand the nature of the medium you're working with in order to come close to knocking off a flake in the shape and size desired. I know. I've tried—with disastrous results! There is no better way to appreciate the knowledge and skill of our ancestors than trying to make one of these "primitive" tools.

As technological skills advanced, other implements were used to gain more control over the shape of the stones being worked (or "knapped"). A piece of bone, wood, or—best of all—antler can be used to "pressure-flake" stone, pushing the tool against the side of the stone to get off smaller flakes. Later, two tools were sometimes used to acquire even further control—a piece of antler or bone as a chisel and a rock as a hammer. Finally, a feature often associated with farming societies, rocks were ground, using things like sandstone, to make a smoother, and therefore more durable, cutting edge. This also allowed people to use harder rock for their tool.

The very first stone tools we find are from Africa and are dated at nearly 2.5 million years. They are associated with *Homo habilis*. These early tools are referred to as *pebble tools,* as they were made from stones smoothed and rounded by the action of water. They were simple, relatively speaking—a few flakes had been knocked off to provide a cutting or chopping edge.

These seem to have been all-purpose tools, although there is some variation in shape that might indicate a degree of specialization. At any rate, they lasted for millions of years and are found all over the Old World and into the New, even after they have been replaced as the main tool by more sophisticated ones.

About 1.5 million years ago, in Africa and associated with early *Homo erectus,* we find the first *hand ax,* one of prehistory's most popular tools. Unlike the pebble tools, the hand ax was worked all

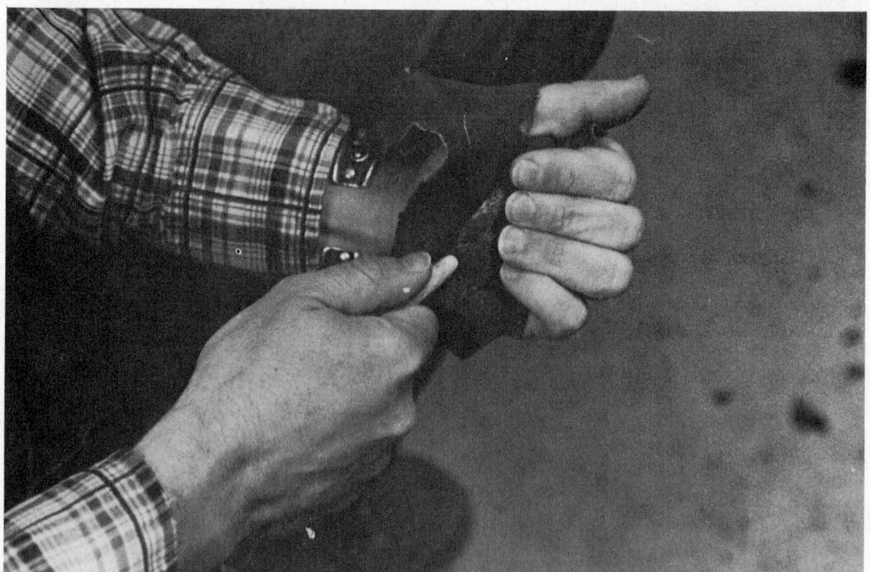

Stone toolmaking: flint knapping, pressure flaking.

Tool types (clockwise from top left): pebble tool, hand axe, blade tool, ground stone tool.

over to provide additional control over shape. The hand ax, found at some sites in the thousands, continued to be made into Neanderthal times and is found throughout the Old World. It seems to have been hard to beat as a tool for heavy work like cutting down trees, digging, and killing and butchering large game animals.

Of course, just what the hand ax was used for must remain conjectural. Most anthropologists feel it was pretty much an all-purpose tool. But recently, anthropologist Eileen O'Brien has suggested that they might have been weapons for killing large animals at a distance, hurled like a discus. Indeed, she had some discus throwers try it, and they proved that they could throw the thing quite far and get it to land accurately and often with its point down. We must always be ready to accept and test new ideas.

Coming pretty much with the hand ax was the idea that the flakes taken off a core were useful too. These *flake tools,* first found in Africa 1.5 million years ago, also persisted for some time in the archaeological record. During their history they were gradually refined, reworked after they had been taken off the core to provide a number of kinds of tools for specific purposes. Things like scrapers, punches and awls, and knives and points were all more efficient than old pebble tools because of their sharper, smoother edges.

The height of flake-tool technology is seen first about 160,000 years ago in both Africa and Europe. This is the *prepared-core* technique, in which a core stone is worked in such a way as to allow a number of similarly shaped flakes to be taken off.

A refinement of the prepared-core technique is first seen in Europe about 40,000 years ago and ushers in an important new tool type used the world over, the *blade tool.* Blade tools are smaller than flake tools, generally sharp all the way around, and made by ''punching'' them off the edges of a prepared core, using a chisellike tool hit with some hammer.

These blade tools were the raw material from which were reworked detailed and efficient knives, scrapers, and punches, as well as spear and, later, arrow points—stone points hafted onto wooden shafts. In addition, *microliths,* small stones attached to some sort of handle (like that reaping knife), were made from pieces of blade tools.

The final step in stone-tool technology, the *ground* stone tool, is first seen from around 9000 years ago in Europe and the Near East and from perhaps even earlier, maybe 20,000 years ago, in Japan and Australia. These earliest specimens were flaked axes and adzes (like axes but with the head perpendicular to the shaft) with ground cutting edges. Soon, though, grinding was used to give the final form to the entire tool.

Grinding is accomplished by rubbing a roughly flaked ''blank'' on a gritty stone like sandstone. Using a finer stone with some wet sand on it provides a polish for the finishing touches. The advantage of ground stone tools is that their smooth surfaces cut better than the rough ones of a flaked tool and that harder stones, less likely to break on impact with something, can be used.

The use of stone tools persisted, even among peoples who learned how to use metals. Many Native American groups, for example, who worked metal for ornaments still had stone weapons and cutting tools. More recently, small flakes of flint provided the spark in flintlock guns, invented in the 1700s. And scalpels for fine surgery (like eye surgery) have been made of obsidian, a volcanic rock also used by our ancestors. It is sharper and wears better than steel. So tools of stone were, and in some places continue to be, major items in humans' tool kits. And for the prehistoric period of our cultural evolution, they are essential bits of evidence in our reconstruction of past lifeways.

2. Abstract Thought

In general, abstract thinking is not unique. As we discussed, chimps can think abstractly, and so can my dog, if only on a rudimentary level. The tools of early humans and the evidence of complex hunting activities such as those at Torralba attest to our ability to think abstract thoughts. But how about really abstract ideas? Things like religion and ritual, social responsibilities, aesthetic appreciation? What evidence do we find for these singularly human features?

Perhaps the earliest hint we get of such kinds of thoughts comes from a cave outside modern Beijing called Choukoutien. The cave was inhabited by *Homo erectus* around 500,000 years ago, and we have not only cultural remains but also the physcial remains of perhaps 40 individuals. Five of those people are represented by skulls, and all five skulls appear to have had the hole in their base (the *foramen magnum*) enlarged by other people. Why? Presumably to get out the brains! And one good reason to do that would be in order to eat them.

Sometimes when cannibalism is practiced by humans it's for emergency nutritional reasons. But when it's practiced as a regular part of a society's culture, it must be viewed as having ritual significance. By ingesting part of the body of a dead relative or a slain enemy, one is thought to gain some aspect of that person's essence or power. Other evidence from Choukoutien indicates that there was plenty of other food to eat, so we can *speculate* (I emphasize that word) that the brain eating there was indeed ritual. And that would seem to indicate the presence of some set of abstract concepts, in this case about an unseen entity possessed by persons and residing in their brains, that could be assumed by other persons.

"Neanderthal Man" was long thought to be some brutish side branch of our evolution. However, besides inventing all sorts of new tool types, the Neanderthals, as we understand them today, also give us *unequivocal* evidence for several specific kinds of abstract concepts. Sixty thousand years ago, a man in what is now Iraq died and was purposely buried. That in itself is new, but in addition, from pollen grains found with the bones, it is clear that he was buried with flowers! In Uzbekistan (part of the Soviet Union) around 50,000 years ago, a boy was buried and his grave surrounded by a circle of goat horns. And in France about 40,000 years ago, what may have been members of a family were all buried in the same location—possibly a family cemetery—and many of the graves contained stone tools.

Such care for the bodies of the dead and the inclusion in their graves of flowers and tools and possibly food could only indicate one thing: belief in an afterlife, a basic ingredient in most religions.

But Neanderthals were also concerned with people in this life. That old man with the bad case of arthritis must have been taken care of by his fellows. His age and infirmity would have made it impossible for him to hunt and find food. In earlier times he might have starved or been killed, but living beyond his peak years speaks of a social conscience among these people. (Things weren't all a bed of roses, however, as there is evidence that the Neanderthals also practiced ritual cannibalism.)

Finally, from this period of human evolution comes evidence of abstract beliefs concerning nature. In caves in France and Switzerland have been found orderly collections of the skulls of cave bears, giant precursors of modern bears. The skulls line covered pits or surround stone "altars." It looks simply as if these people were in awe of the creature (understandable if you see the preserved skeleton of one!) and attributed some sort of power to the beast, power they perhaps thought they could control through ritual. Here again are artifacts that, as far as we know using our procedure of analogy, must represent abstract concepts. There's nothing practical about a pile of cave bear skulls!

Along with treatment of the dead, art is our other best indicator of abstract thought. The first evidence of some sort of artistic appreciation comes from about 300,000 years ago at Terra Amata in France, where the remains of that early shelter were found. Along with the artifacts was a collection of natural pigments in a number of colors. Serving no functional purpose as far as we can tell, they may well have been used aesthetically, perhaps for body decoration—again, a sign of some "concept" beyond those necessary for basic survival.

From 100,000 years ago in Hungary comes clearer evidence of art: an amulet made from a shaped and colored mammoth tooth. But art really begins to flourish with the coming of fully modern *Homo sapiens*. Beginning 30,000 years ago we find, from all over Europe,

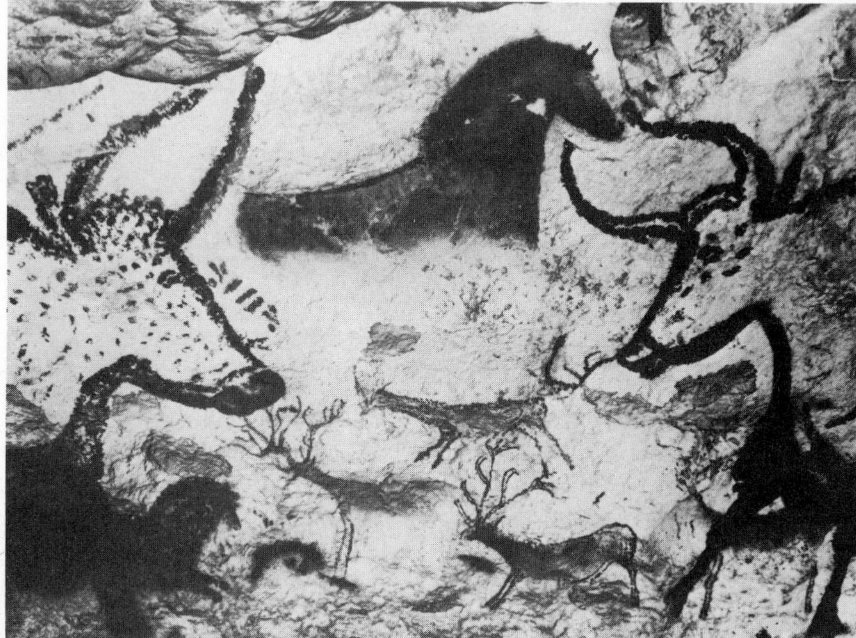

Prehistoric art: Venus figurine from Willendorf, Austria; paintings from Lascaux Cave, France.

little clay figures, called "Venus figurines." The name comes from the fact that these figures are females with their secondary sexual characteristics highly exaggerated and other features hardly visible at all. The thinking is that they were some sort of fertility symbol.

There are, from then on, all sorts of carvings and sculptures, engravings on bone, and even, from a skeleton found in the USSR, the remains of tailored clothing that had been decorated with beads. But perhaps the most striking artwork of prehistory comes from a number of caves in France and Spain starting about 30,000 years ago.

The medium is painting and the subject is game animals. These beautiful, realistic polychrome paintings show bison, mammoths, deer, horses, and other animals we know were hunted then. Sometimes human figures are included to depict a hunting scene. Since these paintings were sometimes done far back in the caves, obviously with light from torches, it's clear that their purpose was not purely aesthetic. Rather, they must have had some ritual purpose—maybe as instructions to young hunters about animals and hunting techniques or maybe as a sort of "sympathetic magic," a hope that the scene depicted would come true in real life. This practice has been observed among Native Australians.

For a more complete discussion of this art and its implications, and for many illustrations, I refer you to a book by John Pfeiffer, *The Creative Explosion*.

So art, burial practices, and ritual symbols give us glimpses into the origins of thought processes and ideas that are characteristically human. They "flesh out" for us the lives of our remote ancestors.

3. Control of Food Resources

Of course, once humans started to hunt and gather, and especially when they used cultural techniques to do so, they gained an important degree of control over their food sources. But nothing like when they started farming. We've already discussed at some length the origins of farming and the kinds of evidence we use to trace its history. What we can do now is look at some specific locations for early farming, some of the specific crops and animals that were domesticated, and some of the specific pieces of evidence used by archaeologists in reconstructing this picture.

Let's begin with animals. As you might imagine, the first animal to be domesticated was our "best friend," the dog. Evidence of domestic dogs, descended from wolves, has been found at sites in Iraq and Israel dating from 12,000 years ago. The Israeli find is of the grave of a man whose left hand clutches the skeleton of a puppy. Other dog remains come from Idaho 8000 years ago. This domestic animal is known worldwide. Dogs now come in all sorts of shapes and sizes, but these early ones, little different from their wolf ancestors, display one telling characteristic: Their teeth are crowded together, a result perhaps of artificial selection for smaller sizes. Though dogs were no doubt used for hunting, their first use, in keeping with our theme, was probably as a food source (another practice that challenges our cultural relativity!).

As I mentioned before, prior to actual domestication, people may have learned to exercise some control over wild herds of animals, like modern-day Lapps do with reindeer. Evidence for this from prehistory is, naturally, indirect, but sites in the Near East, dating back to 18,000 years, show heavy reliance on a single species of wild animal. The inference is that herds of this animal were followed and exploited on a regular basis and were maybe even controlled. Lapps, for instance, capture a male reindeer, castrate it to make it more docile, and then lead it around. Other reindeer, being herding creatures, will then follow it and be readily available to the people.

Beginning around 10,000 years ago, domestic animals show up in abundance all over. Domestic sheep and goats, differentiated from wild ones by such things as horn shape, appear in Afghanistan 10,500 years ago; pigs and water buffalo in Asia 9000 years ago; and cattle in Mesopotamia 8800 years ago.

Evidence for all this comes in a number of forms. There are the biological differences I mentioned, based, as you should note, on knowledge of the differences between modern-day wild creatures and their domestic relatives—analogy again. But there is other biologically based evidence, such as the finding of a large number of bones of elderly animals. This indicates that the creatures were kept, for milk or work, beyond the age at which they would normally be killed if just hunted for meat. This is the case with the early Mesopotamian cattle.

And there's some cultural evidence. From Afghanistan 10,000 years ago come little clay tokens, used, it seems, to keep track of trade transactions, that show symbols for sheep and goats. These animals were clearly part of a person's possessions.

In the New World, settled later than the Old, domestication appears at later dates: 7000 years ago for llamas in Peru, a little later for guinea pigs (yes, you can eat them!) in South America and turkeys in Mexico. Except for the dog, these were the only animals domesticated by Native Americans until they acquired the horse from Europeans. This is explained most likely by the relative lack of animals in the New World that could easily be controlled. With the exception of the South American llamas and arctic caribou, the bison is the only real herding creature here, and their great abundance (before Europeans came) may have made domesticating them unnecessary.

Notice with the animals—and the same is true of plants—that the species first domesticated in each area are species that were native to the area. That may seem obvious enough, but with all the exchanging of material and abstract culture that has gone on recently in the world, it's good to remind ourselves that you don't look for domestication of cattle among American Indians because there were no wild cattle to domesticate. When searching for such things in the archaeological record, we must understand what wild species are and were present and the characteristics of those species.

The earliest evidence for domestic plants comes from the Middle East about 15,000 years ago. The plants involved were two grains, barley and einkorn. This was followed by other grains, particularly wheat, domesticated in the Near East as early as 12,000 years ago and in Asia and Europe 10,000 years ago. Rice appears in Indochina 9500 years ago, and maize (what we call "corn") in Mexico 7700 years ago. The full list is much larger, but you get the idea.

Evidence for domestication of plants, like animals, comes in part from our knowledge of differences between wild and domestic species. Maize, for instance, thought to have been domesticated from a wild grass called teosinte, shows a number of distinctions from its wild relatives in kernel number, overall structure and the presence of a cob.

Other evidence is cultural, in the form of tools used in the planting and harvesting of crops. I already mentioned the reaping knife. There are also stones on which grains were ground to make flour and the stones used for the grinding. We know what they should look like because we've seen present-day people use them. Storage pits and pottery, in which the remains of grains are often found, also indicate the presence of farming. Later, of course, we find evidence of more advanced farming technology, such as plows.

This should give you some idea of what we know about the panorama of our prehistory. It is a knowledge based on the methods and technical skills of archaeology and on what we know about the relations between material artifacts and the cultural systems that use them.

All the things we said about material artifacts can also apply to another facet of human culture. On the surface it's practical, but it relates to all the more abstract aspects of a cultural system. Its specific features are uniquely human, but other organisms have its rudiments. Studying it can give us all sorts of clues about the nature of a given society and its culture. And like material artifacts, it helps make cultural systems possible, helps put cultural ideas into action. It is the biological potential for, and the abstract artifact of, human language.

SUMMARY

Material artifacts are the means humans use to implement their solutions to the problems of survival. We make tools with which to acquire food, shelters in which to live, clothing to keep us warm. But material artifacts are related as well to the cultural environment; that is, the specific form of an artifact may be more adapted to the cultural system than it is to the natural environment. Styles of tools or clothes would be an example of this. Culture is integrated; everything must fit together.

This idea is used by the archaeologist in interpreting the remains of past cultural systems. Understanding the relationships between material artifacts and the natural and cultural environments enables the archaeologist to attempt to reconstruct past ways of life and thereby aid anthropology as a whole in answering the broad questions we ask about human behavior.

Though our image of archaeology usually centers on its data collection phase—the excavation, or "dig"—the heart of this part of anthropology is record keeping. Without a *context* for the data, it would not be possible to see the culture-artifact relationships and thus not possible to achieve the ultimate goals of the field. So the archaeologist uses a set of specific techniques to recover, record, date, and preserve the data recovered, the material remains (often literally the garbage) of a people and a way of life no longer in existence.

The archaeological record of human prehistory is rich and complex. But by looking, even briefly, at some of the high points, we can see that the record tells a story of our species' increasing ability to devise ideas to aid its survival and to implement those ideas by mastering technical skills to produce a vast array of material artifacts.

NOTES, REFERENCES, AND READINGS

The discussion of the relationship between material artifacts and cultural systems takes up one chapter of this book. But the field that studies and interprets this relationship—archaeology—is broad and varied. It covers the whole planet for the whole time our species has been around. I've mentioned in this chapter all sorts of time periods and geographic locations—and consequently have a fairly long list of references to cover all that.

My little exercise on cars is an example of something rather new in anthropology: the anthropological study of American culture—ourselves. More examples of this can be found in James P. Spradley and Michael A. Rynkiewich's collection *The Nacirema: Readings on American Culture* (Boston: Little, Brown, 1975) and in Susan P. Montague and W. Aren's *The American Dimension: Cultural Myths and Social Realities* (2d ed., Sherman Oaks, Calif.: Alfred, 1981).

A more complete anthropological examination of New England gravestones is in an article by James Deetz and Edwin S. Dethlefsen titled "Death's Head, Cherub, Urn and Willow" in *Natural History* (March 1967). A sort of catalog of these artifacts, with lots of pictures, is Harriette Merrifield Forbes's *Gravestones of Early New England and the Men Who Made Them, 1653–1800* (Princeton, N.J.: Pyne Press, 1927, 1955).

The full story of Maiden Castle is in Sir Mortimer Wheeler's *Maiden Castle* (London: Society of Antiquaries of London, 1943). More on the Virginia settlement can be found in *Martin's Hundred: The Discovery of a Lost Colonial Virginia Settlement* (New York: Dell/Delta Books, 1983) by Ivor Noël Hume.

There are a number of good introductions to the theory and methods of archaeology. One that I recommend is William S. Dancy's *Archaeological Field Methods: An Introduction* (Minneapolis: Burgess, 1981). A good discussion of experimental archaeology is in Chapter 17 of John E. Pfeiffer's *The Emergence of Humankind* (New York: Harper & Row, 1985). For a complete accounting of the archaeology of a specific site, see Edwin N. Wilmsen's *Lindenmeier: A Pleistocene Hunting Society* (New York: Harper & Row, 1974).

Descriptions and pictures of stone tools can be found in *Tools of the Old and New Stone Age* (Garden City, N.Y.: Natural History Press, 1970) by Jacques Bordaz. The idea that hand axes may have been used like discuses is in an article by Eileen M. O'Brien called "What Was the Acheulean Hand Ax?" in *Natural History* (July 1984).

About the best book on early art forms and their meanings is John E. Pfeiffer, *The Creative Explosion: An Inquiry into the Origins of Art and Religion* (New York: Harper & Row, 1982).

Some interesting discussions about the origins of agriculture, in addition to those I noted in Chapter 7, are in Chapter 2 of Jacob Bronowski's *The Ascent of Man* (Boston: Little, Brown, 1974) and Marvin Harris's *Cannibals and Kings: The Origins of Cultures* (New York: Random House, 1977).

A wonderful book that gives the dates for all sorts of geological, biological, and cultural events and puts them into an understandable temporal context is by British science writer Nigel Calder. It's called *Timescale: An Atlas of the Fourth Dimension* (New York: Viking, 1983).

chapter 10

Communication
My Brain to Yours and Back Again

When a honeybee, searching for new sources of pollen, finds one, she flies back to her hive. Within minutes a large number of bees will emerge from the hive and, amazingly, fly straight to the new source. Their ability to do this is a result of what goes on in the hive after that first bee flies in.

What happens is that she does a dance! It's called a *waggle dance,* and what it does is communicate to the other bees the exact location of the pollen source. How this works was discovered by Austrian zoologist Karl von Frisch, a discovery for which, in part, he recieved the Nobel Prize.

The waggle dance consists of a number of figure eights. The distance of the pollen source is communicated by the speed with which the bee traces the figures (the faster she goes, the farther the source), by the number of "waggles" she makes with her abdomen, and by the duration of her buzzing during the dance. She tells the direction of the source by angling the straight part of her figure to coincide with the angle between the sun and the food—correcting for wind speed! Because bees see ultraviolet light, this works on cloudy days as well as sunny.

As incredible as this seems, it's just one example of all the ways in which organisms communicate with one another. We sometimes think that we have the only language capable of transmitting such specific pieces of information, but, as usual, that's not the case. The bee dance, as you'll see, even has rudiments of some of the characteristic features of human language.

The important thing here is not to try desperately to come up with a list of features that distinguish human communication but to understand what communication is and how it acts as part of the survival mechanism of living things. At the base of this understanding is the simple concept that communication is the way in which information from the nervous system of one organism is transmitted to that of another organism of the same species. It follows from this that the nature of the communication system is a direct reflection of the organism's nervous system. A bee, for example, is built to perceive the location of its food source, and it has evolved the ability to share that information with its conspecifics (fellow species members). As you might expect, as simple nervous systems evolved into brains, with their more extensive and complex abilities, communication systems, with more to communicate, become more complex as well.

A look at the specific features of our communication system will show just how close this connection is.

HUMAN LANGUAGE

Recall from Chapter 6 the abilities of our brain that allow us to have culture. Essentially, our cerebral cortex can experience events, not only present events but also events from the past and even hypothetical future events. The human brain can do this because it stores massive amounts of information, derived from experience through the sense organs, and stores it in such a way that all the individual pieces of an experience are separately filed and cross-referenced. Thus they can be manipulated—taken apart, modified, put together again in all sorts of combinations. This ability not only lets us play around with experiences mentally but also enables us to make generalizations about them and thus derive abstract concepts.

These mental processes are the kinds of things we talk about, so our communication system must possess features that reflect these processes and make this communication possible. In humans, linguistic abilities are housed in a special area on the left side of the brain, but the functions of that area are basically the same as the functions of the cerebral cortex in general. Look at the main features of human language.

First, we can talk about things that are not right in front of us, things that are not immediate stimuli. We've been doing that all along in this book, for example. This is called *displacement;* the subjects of our language can be displaced in time away from the present.

Second, our language is not made up, as is that of other organisms, of a series of individual signals, each of which has one specific meaning. Our ideas are expressed in units of meaning called sentences, which in turn are made up of smaller units called words, which themselves are made up of various combinations of sounds. This is called *duality* (although there are more than two items involved).

This duality makes possible the manipulation of the units of our language in order to express new ideas, new meanings, new concepts—indeed, virtually an infinite variety of them. This is called *productivity.* Just as we manipulate the thoughts in our brain, so too we manipulate the mechanism we use to share those thoughts. If we couldn't do that, we couldn't share them, and culture, by definition, must be transmitted and shared.

Finally, since we do communicate abstractions, it would be impossible for our language to be made up of features that are *iconic,* features that resemble the things being talked about. The pictures in this book are iconic. These words are not. They can't be! What would an iconic expression for the concept of *world view* look like?

These words, and their spoken counterparts, are symbols. Their relation to their meanings are *arbitrary.* That's why every language in the world can have a different symbol for the same item or concept. The words are just culturally agreed-upon representations of those items and concepts.

Apply these features to the communication system of the bees. There is a degree of displacement involved in their "language" since the flowers are not right in front of the bee who's "talking" about them. She must "remember" their location for the few minutes it takes her to get back to the hive. Similarly, the bees receiving the message must remember it long enough to get to the flowers. But you'd never see a bee dancing a message like "Hey, remember that bunch of daisies that were over there last year?" Nor can they dance about the future.

Neither is there any duality in their system. Each movement has a meaning of its own, and that's it. Thus there can be no real productivity. To be sure, the bees can communicate about a variety of distances and directions. But that's all they can talk about. Finally, the bee system may seem arbitrary—the dance doesn't look like a flower or a map to it—but it's not really symbolic. The speed of the dance corresponds to the speed with which the bees can fly to the pollen source, and the angle of the straight part of the figure *is* the angle of the sun. That's a lot different from our saying, "Fly 300 yards at 10 degrees east of north." Those symbols can have meaning only because we have agreed that they do.

What all this amounts to is the same as saying that the features of our language are cultural, though of course the ability to have language is biological. Our language is something we must *learn.* We are no more born knowing how to speak English than we are knowing the cultural rules of American society. Our language involves *abstractions:* It uses abstract, arbitrary symbols to speak about abstract concepts. It is passed on to future generations not in the genes but through cultural *transmission*. And it is facilitated through the use of *artifacts*—written words in literate cultures, but also the spoken words themselves. They are artifacts, literally made by humans.

But the biological basis for our language ability must not be underemphasized. We have to learn the features of our native language, but that learning itself seems to be something that has a biological facet. If you think about it, you'll realize that before you even opened one of those grammar books in elementary school and learned what a past participle was, you could already speak your native language with a good deal of fluency. You made some mistakes, of course; we all do. But those were generally exceptions to the basic rules of your language's grammar.

What happens when we are children is that part of our brain is furiously working to take in data about our communication system and to formulate the generalizations about it that will enable us to use it. You don't have to sit down with a child on a regular basis and pound into its head all the rules of grammar. The child will learn that all by itself, simply by having heard the language spoken. And there's some evidence that this ability decreases with age. It becomes, for most of us, harder to learn new languages once we're in our teens and older. And children who have been deprived of human social contact and thus of the opportunity to hear and use language have a very difficult time making up for the deficit later on. Language ability is in our biological makeup, and so, it seems, is the ability and procedure for learning it.

Look, as evidence of this, at the grammatical mistakes children make. They are usually due to exceptions to basic rules, exceptions that must be specially learned. A child who says, "I seed the rabbit," in a language that usually forms the past tense by adding *–ed* is being perfectly reasonable and is actually demonstrating an understanding of a rule of English grammar.

The study of all the arbitrary pieces of human language is called *descriptive linguistics,* and it is a whole field in itself. But in order to give you an idea as to what is involved and how language differs from culture to culture, let's just touch on some of the essential aspects.

The basis for any language is, of course, the set of sounds that make it up. These sounds are called *phonemes,* and each language has its own phonemic "inventory." For instance, the language of the !Kung contains four phonemes that we refer to as *clicks*. They are real sounds, just like any we use in English, and the difference between one click and another can make the difference between one word and another.

Languages also differ in the number of phonemes (English has 46) and in phonemic distinctions. Two of the most often cited examples of this involve distinctions, or the lack of them, in English and Chinese. The *t* phoneme in the words *tack* and *stack* are, to us, the same. But to a speaker of Chinese they are two different phonemes. Say them out loud and notice that the *t* in *tack* has a puff of air after it (called *aspiration*) but the one in *stack* doesn't. That's the difference—an important one in Chinese. On the other hand, the first phonemes in *lock* and *rock* are different to us but are just variations of the same phoneme to Chinese and Japanese speakers. The supposedly humorous linguistic stereotype we see in old films and on TV is based on this.

The arrangement of phonemes also differs among languages. For instance, remember the Mbuti (say it with two syllables) from central Africa? That *mb* combination in the initial position is something we don't have in English. Nor is the *nkr* in the name of Nkrumah (also two syllables), the former president of Ghana.

Finally, the pitch and stress placed on a word can act as a phenome, making the difference between one meaning and another. In Chinese there is a word basically pronounced *ma*. But there are actually four variations in pitch (rise or fall of the voice) placed on this combination of phonemes that among other things, can make the difference between saying "mother" and "horse"—something you might want to be very careful about!

Phonemes don't have meanings themselves, but they can make a difference in meaning within the context of the basic meaningful units. These meaningful units are called *morphemes*. A word is a morpheme; it means something. But not all morphemes are words. The word *words,* for instance, is made up of two morphemes: the morpheme *word,* which has a particular meaning, and the morpheme *–s,* which means "make the preceding morpheme plural."

Morphemes may come in several versions. For instance, there is a morphemic item in English that, as a prefix, makes negative the word to which it is attached. This morpheme comes in four versions: *im–*, *in–*, *ir–*, and *un–*, as in *im*possible, *in*credible, *ir*responsible, and *un*reasonable.

Moreover, pitch and stress can act as morphemes, changing the meaning of a set of words. In Russian the difference between a statement and a question does not have to be in word order, as it is in English. The changes in direction of pitch as you say the words of the sentence make the difference. Compare the following English and Russian sentences:

I am going to the post office.
Am I going to the post office?

Ya idu na poatch-tù. (statement)

Ya idu na poatch-tu? (question)

Finally, morphemes are strung together to make up the basic means for conveying whole ideas, the sentence. Each language differs in its rules for the order of morphemes in a sentence, and this is called *syntax*. For instance, if we want to negate the idea expressed in an English sentence, we have to put a negating morpheme in front of an appropriate word: *I don't love you*. But in German, the negating morpheme *nicht* at the very end of the sentence can do the same thing: *Ich liebe dich nicht*.

As an example of the power of the rules of language—rules that we intuit as children before we ever learn them formally—Noam Chomsky, a linguist from M.I.T., offered the following sentence:

Colorless green ideas sleep furiously.

Although it doesn't really make any sense, we easily recognize the sentence as grammatical. All the morphemes (like *green* and *–less* and *–ly*) and the words they make up are in the right places and order. Compare it with this version:

Furiously sleep ideas green colorless.

That doesn't sound right at all.

These then, are the basic pieces of our language systems, pieces that, within certain rules, are broken up, shuffled around, and recombined to facilitate the communication of our thoughts—thoughts that have been through the same kinds of manipulations.

At this point, two questions should come to mind: Just what is it that brings about the differences among human languages? And how did human language evolve? We'll take up the second question first.

Chimpanzee "greeting" expression and posture.

LANGUAGE AND EVOLUTION

We can generalize and say that the features characteristic of human language make ours an *open* communication system. Because of its duality and productivity, it is almost infinitely creative.

The communication systems of nonhumans, on the other hand—even the nonhuman primates—are said to be *closed;* that is, there are certain calls or other signs that have certain meanings, and that's it. The only way to add to such a system is somehow to evolve a new call or sign with a new meaning. For example, chimpanzees have around 15 calls, along with facial expressions and gestures, which convey such things as the presence of food, fear, excitement, anger, submission, threat, and perhaps even "laughter." But the meanings of these calls and signs are limited, and no one has ever seen any evidence of them being combined or strung together to convey new meanings.

So the question becomes, How did the closed system, which no doubt was possessed by our ancestors, turn into an open system? Linguists Charles Hockett and Robert Ascher, in a long article called "The Human Revolution," have proposed a simple model of how this may have taken place. In it (and here I'll simplify even more) two closed calls are both found, by one of our ancestors, to be appropriate for communicating a certain situation. But instead of using both calls, this inventive ancestor combines a part of each to make up a brand-new call that "means" the presence of both the ideas conveyed by the old calls.

If the call for "food" is made up of the sounds ABCD, and the one for "danger" of the sounds EFGH, then when a lion was seen standing over a newly killed antelope, both those calls might be used. Or you could be "productive" and use ABEF—"food but danger too." This might make the combination CDGH mean "no danger but no food either" and ABGH mean "food and no danger." The system is now open, and all the other calls and their parts may become phonemes that can be combined into various morphemes and those into words and sentences. To be sure, it didn't happen this quickly and simply, but it must have entailed a process very much like this.

When did this transition take place? That is, of course, impossible to tell because it occurred far in the past and it happened over a long period of time—like most of the other changes we've discussed. We are left then with indirect evidence, which comes in two forms.

First, there is the logical approach, accomplished by trying to figure out just what sort of language ability would be necessary to facilitate the cultural practices of early humans. For instance, the australopithecines could have had a family structure with internal cooperation and sexual division of labor and pair bonding, even without the complex open communication system we have today. Baboons do!

But to possess ideas about some power residing in the human brain that can be acquired by eating it, or to organize an elephant hunt that entails a number of bands all chasing the creatures with lit torches into a bog and killing them—well, that might require something a little more complex, since abstract ideas and future events are involved. So it might be reasonable to guess that *Homo erectus* possessed a real human language.

The second approach is anatomical. We know, mostly from studies of brain injuries, quite a bit about the parts of the brain associated with linguistic abilities. Damage to specific areas of the brain results in difficulties with specific aspects of language. If we could detect the presence and extent of those areas on the brains of fossil humans, we might be able to get some idea as to the evolutionary stage of their language.

This is done by taking what are known as *endocasts,* casts of

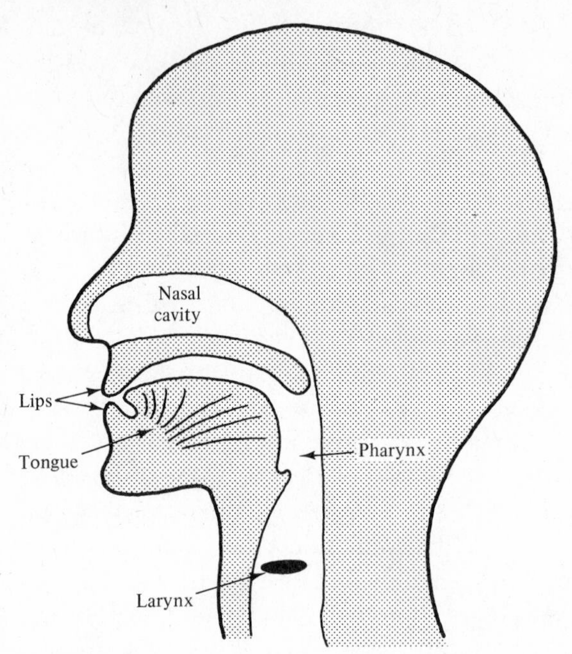

Human vocal tract.

the insides of fossil skulls, which would, of course, give a pretty good idea of the size and shape of the brain that was once in them. Anthropologist Ralph Holloway, the foremost practitioner of this study, has claimed, guardedly, that he can see in the endocasts of *Homo habilis* evidence of Broca's area, a part of the left side of the brain associated with speech. This feature, however, may also be present in nonhuman primates, and its presence is not necessarily an indication of its function. These studies continue.

More productive, perhaps, are attempts to reconstruct the vocal tracts (tongue, pharynx, larynx, nasal cavity, and vocal cords) of fossil humans to try to determine the nature of their speech. Since human language is a spoken one, and since there are certain features common to all languages (like the use of consonants and vowels), this would seem to give a reasonable estimate of overall linguistic ability.

Based on the known relationships between the vocal tract (which is all soft tissue) and the anatomy of the skull and bones of the neck, several investigators have been able to reconstruct the vocal tracts of a number of our ancestors, using complex computer programs. In addition, relationships are known between the shape of vocal tracts of human adults, human newborns, and apes and the kinds of sounds each of these can make. From such relationships we can estimate the kinds of sounds made by our ancestors.

Using this sort of reasoning, anatomist Jeffrey Laitman has concluded that the vocal tract of the australopithecines was like that of most mammals—unable to modify the passage of air so as to make vowel sounds. (They could, however, swallow and breathe at the same time, something our dogs can do but we can't!) But the vocal tract of *Homo erectus* was beginning to show changes in the direction of the modern situation and could, according to Laitman, have produced vowels. The completely modern vocal tract form, he says, is not found until about 300,000 years ago. This coincides nicely with the cultural evidence. But similar studies of later humans, particularly the Neanderthals, have added the information that even that late, some humans may not have been able to make the variety of vowels present in modern human languages and therefore had not fully achieved our present linguistic capability.

Such studies are intriguing but must be viewed with caution. First, just because today we use certain sounds to transmit our thoughts doesn't mean that those same thoughts (or ones of similar complexity) couldn't have been transmitted with a different set or number of sounds. The evidence seems to focus on vowel sounds. The number of these varies quite a bit among modern languages, and things like regional accents are usually based on differences in vowel pronunciation. Compare the speech of Ted Kennedy with that of Jimmy Carter, for instance. Vowels are part of all languages but display a good deal of variation. Some Polynesian languages, for example, have only three vowel sounds. Isn't it reasonable then that a language could work just fine with as few as one? As noted before, we should be careful when extrapolating backward in time from a current situation.

There are, in addition, many humans today who can't speak at all and yet who can use human language in some other form. They can write, but that's just a representation of spoken language. They can also use sign language, which lacks things like phonemes but can convey ideas every bit as complex as those conveyed by the spoken word, every bit as efficiently. So, although articulate speech probably evolved along with human language (it is the "normal" situation), we should be careful when making specific assumptions about certain connections—things like the number of vowel sounds the Neanderthals used and the degree to which they could express abstract concepts.

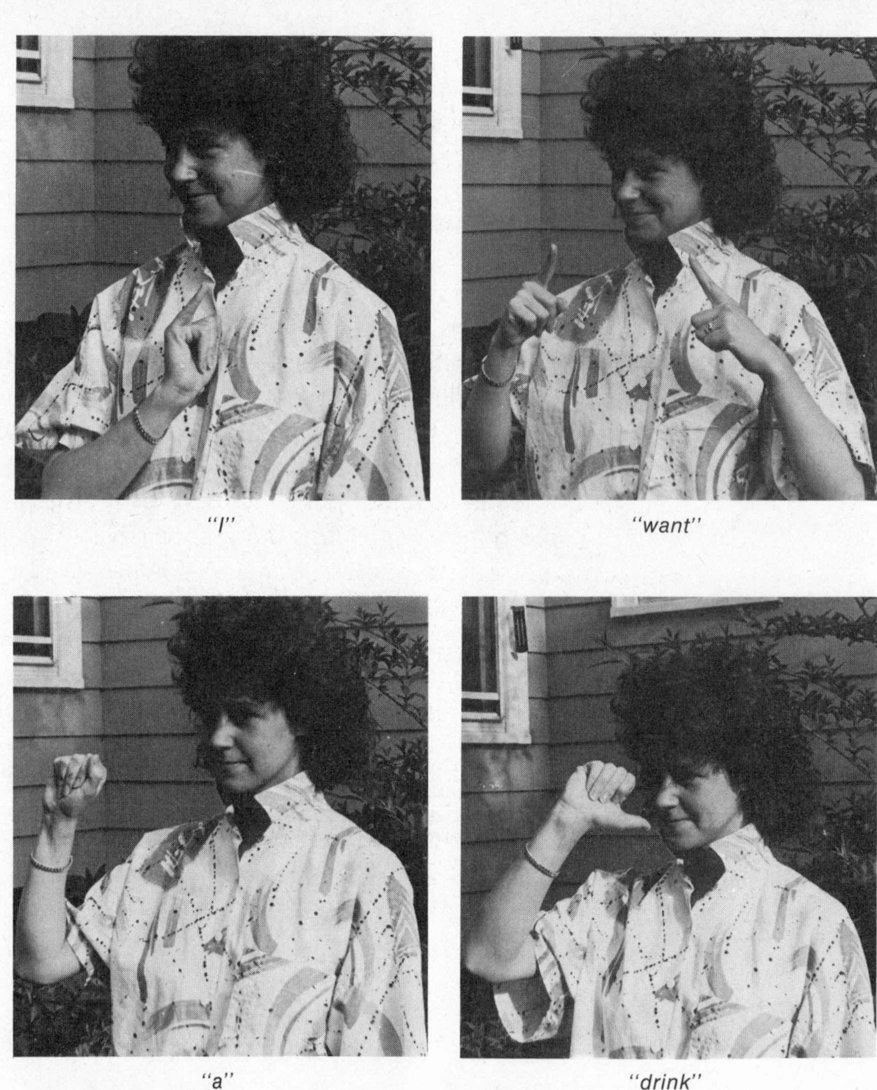

"I" "want" "a" "drink"

A sentence in Ameslan: "I – want – a – drink."

Sign language brings us to our next consideration with regard to this topic of language evolution: the "talking" apes. A number of attempts were made in the past to teach chimpanzees to speak. Such attempts were, of course, based on the similarity between them and us, so these investigators should perhaps be given credit for that recognition. But the attempts were doomed to failure from the start. Chimps lack a vocal tract capable of modifying sounds as we do, and their lips and tongues are not structured like ours. A chimp named Vicki, for instance, trained in the 1950s, was able to "speak"

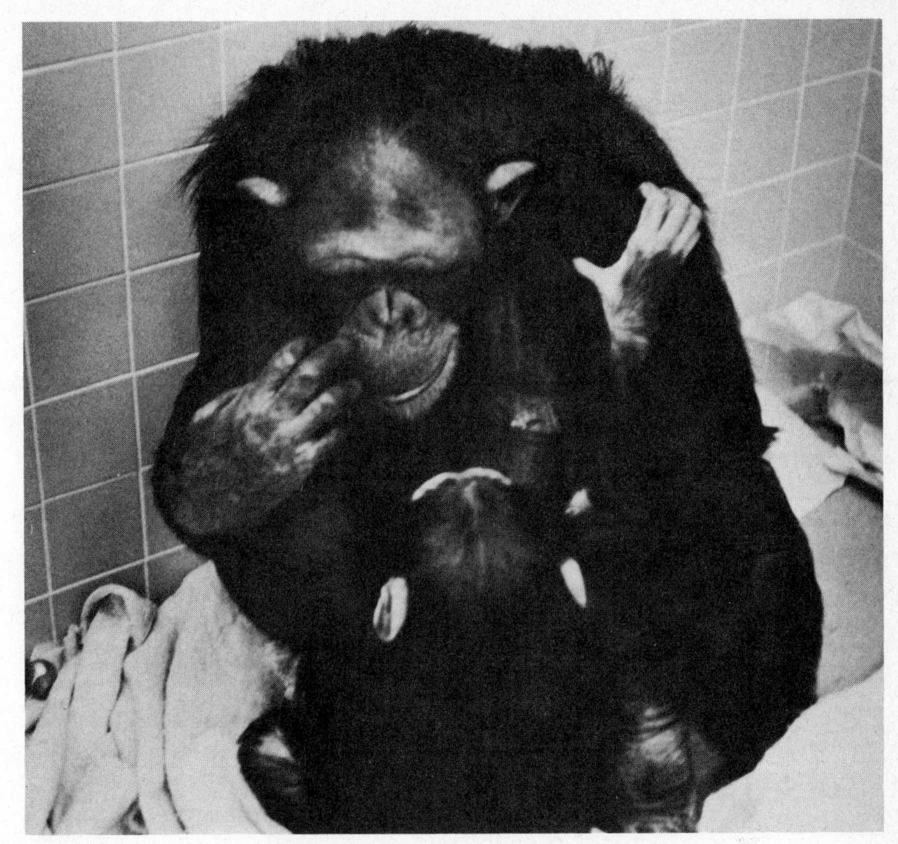

Washoe signs "cry" to her adopted son Loulis.

only a few words, things like *mama, papa,* and *cup*. The vowels in these words were merely puffs of air, and Vicki was forced to hold her lips together with her finger to make the *m* and *p* sounds.

In 1966 a pair of psychologists, Allen and Beatrice Gardner, realizing that not all humans are capable of speech and that therefore that ability itself is no indication of linguistic capabilities, tried a new approach. They acquired a young chimp, whom they named Washoe (after a county in Oklahoma), and began to teach her American Sign Language (Ameslan). This is the language used by many deaf persons, and it conveys ideas with every bit as much detail and efficiency as the spoken word.

The details of the story of Washoe and other chimps trained by the Gardners and their colleagues can be found in the book by Eugene Linden, but suffice it to say that Washoe learned hundreds of signs, was able to use them in sentences, could obviously understand and communicate abstract concepts, and could combine signs to cover new items and concepts not in her vocabulary. Some of the chimps who followed Washoe can sign to each other, and others can sign back to humans in response to spoken English.

All this was not without controversy. A number of other scientists interested in the phenomenon felt that there were not enough experimental controls in Washoe's situation; she was treated pretty much like a human child, and all the data about her language ability came from direct, subjective observations by human observers. To try to correct this problem, another chimp, Sarah, communicated using colored plastic symbols that didn't at all resemble the things or ideas they represented. Sarah had to make complete sentences, which included punctuation, by arranging the plastic pieces in precisely the correct order for an English sentence. Thus "reading between the lines" by the observers was eliminated.

Still another chimp, Lana, communicated via a computer using a keyboard with symbols. Again, her sentences had to be complete and in the proper order. In this situation, moreover, the computer recorded all her "utterances," so hard data were available. To the surprise of many, both the Sarah and Lana experiments supported the Gardners' conclusions that chimps can be taught to use a communication system with all the characteristics of human language: displacement, duality and productivity, and arbitrariness.

There are skeptics who feel that the chimps are not really producing their own words and sentences but are merely using their trainers' signed statements and questions as cues, parroting back what the humans see as proper responses. This is, however, a minority viewpoint, and, as if to answer such objections, we now have the signing gorillas, Koko and Michael.

Trained by primatologist Francine Patterson, Koko and Michael are claimed to have vocabularies of some 400 signs, which they use in all the ways humans use words. Koko, for instance, signs to herself when alone, just as human children babble to themselves. Besides just using her signs in proper order for the rules of English syntax (amazing enough by itself), she can also make jokes, like insisting that a white towel was red before revealing the presence of a small piece of red lint clinging to it—and then grinning about it. She can produce new words, like *white tiger* for zebra, an animal for which she had no word. She can lie, for example, blaming a colleague of Patterson's for damage to a sink that she had inflicted herself. And she can use language for that most human of uses, cursing—as when, mad at Patterson, Koko called her a "dirty bad toilet." Hardly elegant, but something no other nonhuman can do!

Koko signs "Smoke," referring to her kitten, Smoky.

Lest we still had doubts, there is Michael's story. In a recent episode of the TV science series Nova called "Signs of the Apes, Songs of the Whales," Patterson claims that Michael spontaneously signs a story, something about men coming and hitting gorillas and there being "red" all over. It might not seem very meaningful, except that (unfortunately) the way young gorillas are captured is by first killing the adult members of their group. Michael may be telling the story of his capture in Africa. If so, not only is he talking about something from the past, he is also telling about an event that occurred before he learned to sign!

Exactly what the apes are capable of linguistically is still to be determined, as is the precise nature of their acquired language. But it seems safe to say that even if their signs are not quite up to par with our language, they are at least awfully close. "Fine animal gorilla," says Koko.

Now, another question. In the wild, chimps and gorillas, so far as we know, use a closed call system. Why is it that they have brains that are able to learn and use an open communication system, one that we always thought was our unique possession?

Remember that although our language ability is contained in one localized, specialized area of our brain, the basic "wiring" in that area is much the same as that throughout our cerebral cortex. After all, as we've been discussing, language is just the way we transmit our thoughts to one another. Given that the brains of apes have the same sort of "wiring," even if not as complex, it's not too surprising that they can be taught human linguistic behavior to some extent.

Why do they have brains that can "experience events" and manipulate thoughts in the first place? As we've discussed, the primates are creatures that survive in part by learning about their environments and by understanding and remembering what goes on in them. Second only to us in this regard are the apes. What's going on in their brains has to do with the habitat they live in and the relationships within their groups—the same kinds of things that are rattling around in our skulls.

So again, by studying this ability in our closest relatives, we can get a hint as to how it may have developed in our ancestors. We see language almost as a natural result of a large, complex brain. The apes seem just short of having thoughts so complicated as to require a humanlike language to communicate them. Thus, even though they are capable of learning such a language, they haven't invented one. We, though, could not survive without language, so complex are the things we must share with one another. Between these two states is the story of the evolution of our language.

Language, of course, is another cultural universal. But as with the other cultural universals, and with any cultural practice, there is an enormous amount of variation from society to society. Can we explain this? What is the connection between language and culture?

LANGUAGE AND CULTURE

There are something like 3000 languages spoken in the world today. Some of these, like the cultures that use them, are becoming extinct as the modern industrial world spreads over the planet. No doubt a large number of languages we've never heard of have already become extinct.

As with biological species, and as with cultures in general, languages are related to one another. Languages can be arranged taxonomically according to similarities and differences. One language, a *common ancestor,* can give rise to several new languages. A tree can be drawn, showing the evolutionary relationships among languages.

To give you an example of one such taxonomic grouping, let's look briefly at the *Indo-European* language family, one of about a dozen major families. Within this family are several branches: *Indic; Iranian; Armenian; Slavic; Greek;* the *Romance* languages, including Spanish, French, and Italian; *Celtic,* like Welsh and Gaelic, rapidly falling out of regular use; and *Germanic,* which includes the Scandinavian languages, German, and English.

This classification is based on similarities and differences among these languages in such things as grammatical rules, phonemic inventories, and vocabulary. By examining such items we can begin to understand the evolutionary histories of these languages—which one gave rise to what other ones. It is not an easy task, for language is fluid. It changes rapidly and is easily influenced. The French, for instance, who have a national academy that makes decisions about the language, now commonly use such English derivatives as *le weekend.* In the United States, although we are a Germanic-language-speaking country, we regularly use a number of French words. You should be able to come up with a few. And the Japanese have adopted America's favorite pastime, along with its name, which they call *besu-boru* (the final *u* is silent).

We, of course, accept and are familiar with the degree of linguistic variation in these Indo-European languages. Most of us speak one or more of them. What we lack is an appreciation for the enormous variation found around the world. I've heard people described as "speaking African." It would probably amaze the person who said that to find out that there are some 800 languages spoken on the African continent. On the island of New Guinea, which is smaller than the state of Alaska, there may be (or have been in the recent past) as many as 1000 languages spoken.

What our surprise at these facts shows is the importance of language to a culture and its people. Those of us who grew up speaking English think of it as "normal." It's difficult for us to conceive of really conveying thoughts and ideas in another tongue. Language is central to the success of our culture. It is how we learned our culture in the first place, and how we will pass it on. Truly to understand another language is truly to understand the culture it represents. And that's a monumental task.

An ongoing project since the beginnings of anthropology has been to figure out just what the relationship is between a cultural system and the language that its people speak. Can everything about a language—its phonemes, its morphemes, its rules of syntax—be related to the culture that uses it?

There have been a number of attempts to discover such relationships and to formulate rules for generalizing them. These studies have met with failure. There seems to be no practical reason why the French have gutteral *r*'s and the Russians roll theirs. Why German can tack *nicht* to the end of a sentence, but English can't tack on *not*. Why clicks as phonemes are found mainly in southern Africa. Like genes, the specific features of languages seem to undergo flow, drift, and mutation—random changes not related directly to cultural adaptation.

What *is* connected to cultural systems rather directly, though, are words. What people call things tells us what sorts of categories they have. How they express ideas tells us how they view their world. We have already done one exercise in this—kinship terminology. Although we were using graphic symbols instead of actual words, our symbols did represent word usage, and the study of which people were called by what term told us something about the cultures that practiced each system.

This phenomenon of grouping things according to a society's world view is called *folk taxonomy.* The study of such phenomena is usually known as *ethnosemantics,* or "cultural meaning." Here's the classic example.

In English, the white, crystaline stuff that falls from the sky in winter is called "snow." We have all sorts of subheadings of snow, depending on how and in what way it's important to us. As I look out on my snow-covered driveway, what I'm concerned about is "heavy snow" versus "light snow." Kids, facing the prospect of school, want to know whether it's "deep snow" or not and, if it is, whether it's "wet" or "dry," because that will determine its utility for snowballs and snowmen. Skiers listen to reports for word of "powder" or "granular snow." But these are all subcategories of "snow," and they are by no means universally agreed-upon in terms of meaning. I have no idea what a skier means by "granular."

The reason for this sort of "snow" taxonomy is that snow is relatively unimportant to us. In terms of real life-or-death survival matters, snow doesn't matter. We deal with it culturally with a good deal of success. Not so for the Eskimos (at least prior to their acquiring snowmobiles and the like). For these nomadic hunters, the exact nature of that white stuff was vitally important. It meant the difference between finding game or not, between easy and difficult travel, between being able to build an igloo or not—all literally life-or-death concerns.

This is reflected in their folk taxonomy for what we call "snow," that is, in the words they use for snow and its variants. In fact, the Eskimos have no single word for that type of precipitation. Rather they have ten words for the various types and states of that natural phenomenon. These are not ten subcategories of snow; they are separate concepts.

The details of this classification, and some of the biological and cultural ramifications, are covered in the delightful book by Williams and Major called *The Secret Language of Snow.* But to give you some idea how it works, these are the categories they list:

1. *Annui,* falling snow
2. *Api,* snow on the ground
3. *Pukak,* snow that can cause avalanches
4. *Qali,* snow that collects horizontally on trees
5. *Kanik,* rime (like when your breath freezes on a cold window)
6. *Upsik,* wind-beaten snow
7. *Siqoq,* swirling or drifting snow
8. *Kimoagruk,* snowdrift
9. *Qamaniq,* bowl-shaped hollow around the base of a tree
10. *Siqoqtoag,* sun crust

On the other hand, the Jivaro from Ecuador (most famous for their shrinking of human heads), who live in the Amazon Basin forests, are said to incorporate the phenomonon of snow into a single concept represented by a single term. It refers to the Andes Mountains, with which they are familiar but which play no direct role in their lives. The term includes the mountains, the snow, the idea of altitude, lower temperatures, and so on—in short, it means something like "the way it is up there."

Other folk categories have been studied as well. Color terms, for example, vary greatly from culture to culture. Some groups, like the much-studied Dani from highland New Guinea, have only two color terms, roughly corresponding to *light* and *dark.* In Western societies, however, we have dozens of recognized, agreed-upon colors. It's not that the eyes and brains of us and the Dani are any different. We both perceive the same visible spectrum. What's different is the cultural importance to each group of distinguishing these perceived differences. The explanation for such diversity is still pending. But it may well have something to do with the nature of a group's art: how complex and realistic their art is and thus how necessary it is to have names for the various hues. We have very complex and realistic art styles; the Dani have almost no art and rely on natural objects like feathers and mud for body decoration.

Number systems, too, vary. If I were to ask you to list for me all the numbers we recognize, you'd rebel. The task would never end. But for a Dani it would be easy. Their number system consists of "one," "two," "three," "many." Again, there is no perceptual or intellectual difference between us and them. It's just that it is not necessary for them to tally or keep track of the number of anything beyond three.

Don't, however, get the idea that you can simply relate these things to a certain area of the world or to a certain level of cultural complexity. It's far more involved than that. For instance, other highland New Guinea groups, who are on the surface quite similar to the Dani, have number systems using a base of 27 or 28, and one well-known New Guinea society, the Kapauku, count into the thousands. As with all cultural phenomena, the interrelationships can be quite obscure and complex, and with the specific features of language they seem especially so.

But in broad perspective, we see language as part of a society's cultural system, and we assume that its features, even if we can't explain them all, are related to that system more or less directly. In this broad perspective, we can certainly discern overall connections.

The Hutterites, for example, are essentially trilingual. They speak English to outsiders like me. They use German for religious ritual, and it is the language in which all their literature, both sacred and secular, is written. To one another they speak "Huttrish," their unique dialect.

All this makes perfect sense. The Hutterites originated in a German-speaking region, and their conservative outlook would almost dictate that they would hang on to the language that was first used to communicate their thoughts and cultural ideas. Moreover, the German they use is "High" German, an old form of the language. English is utilitarian; the Hutterites now live in English-speaking areas of North America. Their own dialect, with which they communicate information about everyday things, has a practical history. It includes words derived from the languages common to all the areas in which the Hutterites have lived. Even with my meager linguistic abilities, I was able to perceive some English, German, and Russian in their dialect. For example, they called me *der fingerprint mensch,* a German-English mix. In fact, their dialect uses words and phrases not just from those major languages but from specific dialects of those languages, learned during the Hutterites' 450 years of migrations.

So language is an intimate part of any cultural system. It is the mechanism whereby each of us, as a youngster, learns the basics of our system, and it is the means we use to communicate to others, in the present and in the future, the ideas and norms of our culture.

Thus the features of a language, at least the words and their meanings, are a reflection of the basis of any cultural system: its world view.

One of the things we talk about is especially important, for it is a direct statement of world view. It is the way we pass on and maintain the view that is the basis of our culture. It is our means for understanding our relationships with our environment and with each other and for translating that understanding into articulate rules of behavior. It is religion and the secular systems derived from it.

SUMMARY

A communication system functions to transfer information from the nervous system of one organism to that of others of its species. It is therefore a reflection of the structure and function of that nervous system. Thus human communication—language—has characteristics that enable us to share information and ideas that are cultural. The features of human language reflect the features of our brain that make culture possible. Thus human language is very different from the communication of even our closest relatives.

Studies are now in progress to try to determine just when human language evolved. We can get some idea as to how it evolved, though, by comparing our communication to that of chimps and gorillas. The fact that under certain conditions these apes can be taught to use a human linguistic system shows us again just how similar our species are in terms of mental abilities. In addition, since apes don't use such a system in the wild, these studies also show us how intimately connected are language and culture.

The specific connections between a language and the culture that uses it are not, as previously believed, on the level of sounds and grammatical structure. There are, however, direct connections between the world view of a society, the words the people use to talk about that world, and the categories into which those words are organized. On a broader scale, as I showed with the Hutterites, the particular linguistic origin of the words used can reflect something about a society's cultural history.

NOTES, REFERENCES, AND READINGS

More on honeybees can be found in the section called "The Work of Being a Bee" by Aubrey Manning in *The Marvels of Animal Behavior* (Washington, D.C.: National Geographic Society, 1972).

A short but informative book on the definition of culture from a linguistic perspective is Ward H. Goodenough's *Culture, Language, and Society* (2d ed., Menlo Park, Calif.: Benjamin/Cummings, 1981). The individual features of human language are covered very concisely in Peter H. Salus, *Linguistics* (Indianapolis: Bobbs-Merrill, 1969) and in an article by Brian Stross, ''The Nature of Language,'' in *Language, Culture, and Cognition: Anthropological Perspectives* (New York: Macmillan, 1981), edited by Ronald W. Casson.

The evolutionary perspective on our language makes up Chapter 8 of Richard Passingham's *The Human Primate* (San Francisco: Freeman, 1982) and is the topic of Philip Lieberman's *On the Origins of Language: An Introduction to the Evolution of Human Speech* (New York: Macmillan, 1975). The famous article by C. F. Hockett and R. Ascher, ''The Human Revolution,'' is in *Current Anthropology* 5 (1964): 135–168. Jeffrey T. Laitman's work on the vocal tract reconstructions is recounted in ''The Anatomy of Human Speech,'' *Natural History* (August 1984).

A nice, readable book that covers all the ape language experiments is Eugene Linden, *Apes, Men, and Language* (New York: Penguin, 1974). The linguistic achievements of Koko and Michael are discussed, with lots of pictures (including one Koko took of herself!), in Francine Patterson's article ''Conversations with a Gorilla'' in *National Geographic* (October 1978).

Discussions of folk taxonomies can be found in the section called ''Folk Classification: Relativity and Universality'' in the Casson book mentioned above. And the book on snow is *The Secret Language of Snow* (San Francisco: Sierra Club/Pantheon, 1984), by Terry Tempest Williams and Ted Major, illustrated (wonderfully) by Jennifer Dewey.

chapter 11

Maintenance of Order
The View from Within

Network television shows, not known for their profundity, do provide now and then a gem of a line. My favorite is from the comedy series *Taxi*. In one episode, the other employees of the Sunshine Cab Company ask Latka, the "foreigner," why his wedding ceremony is so bizarre and complex. Latka answers that in his country there is a saying that what separates man from the animals is "mindless superstition and pointless ritual."

Don't we in fact often think of the beliefs and rituals of other peoples as mindless and pointless? Even some beliefs and rituals found in our own culture—ones that we don't happen to practice—we think of in this way. It's a "natural" reaction. And there's a good reason for it.

We see the basic beliefs of others, and the ways they express those beliefs, as "mindless and pointless" because *ours* are so important to us. Other people may dress differently from us, and we may see other modes of fashion as a little strange, but that's not really so important. Basic beliefs are. And that is because these beliefs, as we've discussed, are a direct reflection of our world view—the set of assumptions and attitudes that give rise to and hold together the cultural fabric of our lives. Except for personal survival, nothing is more important or more central to our existence.

Such expressions of world view can generally be termed *religion,* although in complex and culturally heterogeneous societies, secular *laws* take the place of religious concepts as rules for human behavior. Still, as we shall see, such laws are themselves often just secular statements of religious principles.

As tempting as it is to come up with your own definition for a concept, sometimes you can't top one that already exists. For religion, the definition that I think best captures the functions I've mentioned is by anthropologist Edward Norbeck from his book *Religion in Human Life: Anthropological Views*. Norbeck defines religion as a

> distinctive symbolic expression of human life that interprets man himself and his universe, providing motives for human action, and

> also a group of associated acts which have survival value for the human species.

Moreover, he sees the roles of religion

> as explanatory, and in many ways psychologically reassuring, and as socially supportive by providing validations for existence, motives for human action, and as a sanction for orderly human relations.

Religions, or "legal" systems that derive from them, are our way of making the world view real. They provide us with a means for communicating world-view assumptions. They give us a medium for formulating values of behavior that correspond to the world view. And they provide a framework for putting those values into action in our everyday dealings with one another and with the world around us. Furthermore, they are the way in which we impart our world view to future generations. Little wonder that *our* religion seems so "natural" and *theirs* so strange!

But as with any facet of culture, our overriding assumption is that a religious system makes sense for the people who practice it. We already saw this when we examined the basic features of the Eskimo religious system as compared with those of the early agricultural Middle East. Let's now look more closely at religion and related cultural phenomena and see in what ways cultures are similar and different in their expressions of this important behavior.

RELIGION AND RELIGIOUS SYSTEMS

We've already mentioned, using Norbeck's words, what religion does. But just what *is* it? Religions, as you'll see, vary greatly from society to society (something you should be used to by now), but the one trait they all have in common is the *supernatural*. Religion is a set of behaviors pertaining to the supernatural, which has all the functions noted before.

By "supernatural" we mean something—a force or power or being—that is outside the known laws of nature. Thus one difference among societies is in which phenomena are dealt with by "religion" (a nonscience) and which are dealt with using "scientific" knowledge. (You should recall this distinction from the discussion in the Interlude.) Most North Americans, for instance, deal with disease in a scientific fashion. But for the Fore (a New Guinea group I'll talk about soon) disease is explained as the work of sorcerers—a supernatural explanation. This is the case even though the Fore go about their farming activities using knowledge that would be considered scientific. It can get a little confusing at times, and understanding another society's religion really tests one's ability to practice cultural relativity.

Not only is a belief in the supernatural universal among religions (indeed, it defines religion), but religion itself is a cultural universal. As with the other universals we discussed, this requires an explanation. Does it, as the others seem to, have some biological basis?

There would not seem to be any practice among nonhumans (and thus possibly among our ancestors) that could have been translated into this particular cultural behavior—nothing like pair bonding (marriage, in cultural terms) or avoidance of mating with sibs (the cultural incest taboo). Rather, the biological "basis" of religion can be found in our big brain. Such a brain, with its complex functions and abilities, evolved as our species adapted by understanding its environment and by using that understanding to manipulate the environment for survival. But the potential to understand does not guarantee the understanding of everything. Some natural phenomena might be within the intellectual grasp of a group of humans, but others are not. These, however, need to be explained, too. And this is where forces outside of nature come in.

For example, our species has had a "science" of making stone tools for millions of years. The abilities of the human brain were brought to bear on the problem of modifying natural objects into artifacts, and they were quite successful. But what about a phenomenon like death? Or the weather? Or the movements of the stars? We have only recently *begun* to understand these things in a scientific fashion, because that sort of understanding requires all kinds of groundwork in the form of data, experimentation, theory, and technology.

These things were important to our remote ancestors, who sought to explain them. They needed to feel some control over the features of their world, even if only in the form of "understanding." So the supernatural was invoked. The phenomena themselves were beyond the natural "laws" that the people understood. It stood to reason, then, that the explanation for them was also to be found beyond nature. Their view of the world was put into concrete terms, terms they could communicate to one another, terms that helped determine their reactions toward these phenomena.

Recall, as an example, the Eskimos. They explained the seemingly random changes they saw in their environment as the work of individual spirits with individual control over their physical embodiments. What the seals did was determined by the seal spirit. If the seals were to do what the Eskimos needed them to do in order to hunt them, certain behaviors geared toward appeasing the seal spirit were required. The Neanderthal cave bear "cults" probably had a similar basis.

Death, the greatest natural mystery, is nearly always dealt with using stories of an afterlife, the body or some aspect of the deceased usually going back to where it came from. In all cultures, care is taken, in the form of a ritual, to make sure the person gets there, and often, as in ancient Egypt, quite elaborate procedures are involved. There are other ramifications as well, for in many societies, in order to get to the proper place after death, one must behave in a certain fashion while living. Thus the explanation for this most fearful of natural phenomena not only interprets something about humans and their world. It also supplies a reasurring story, it provides a motive for human actions, and it acts as a sanction for orderly human relations—all the functions appearing on Norbeck's list.

The universality of religion, then, is a result of the blessing of our big, complex brain with its ability to understand the world around us and the curse that that big brain can't understand *everything* and is acutely aware of that fact.

As we have done throughout this book, we should ask again if there are any antecedents to human religion to be found among nonhumans, any clues that some other creatures might dimly ask some form of the questions that religion answers. There is only one, and it's pretty vague. But it's also rather tantalizing. It comes from our friends and "cousins," the chimps.

During a rather violent thunderstorm at the Gombe Stream Reserve in Tanzania, Jane Goodall observed what she termed a "rain dance." At the height of the storm, several male chimps took turns running to the top of a hill and then hurtling down it screaming, jumping into trees along the route, tearing branches from the trees and waving them around. When a male had reached the bottom, he returned to the top to start over, during which time other males performed their dance. All this was observed by a gallery of females and youngsters lining the sides of the route. This was not a common event; Goodall saw it only a few times during her more than 20 years at Gombe. But it was a striking and somewhat thrilling occurrence.

Just what the rain dance means to the chimps is probably impossible to figure out—unless, through sign language, we could *ask*

Neanderthal burial, artist's conception.

one! (And if that worked it would certainly verify the chimps' ability to use human language—but don't hold your breath.) But one is tempted to imagine the dance as being a reaction to the anxiety that the chimps feel toward what must, even for wild creatures, be a somewhat frightening phenomenon. Maybe they are just performing what ethologists call a *displacement activity,* like our whistling in the dark. Or maybe they are trying to scare away the storm that is scaring them. If that's the case, their dance indeed has the rudiments of a religious ritual. The question, for the moment, is open.

Returning to humans, we should now take a look at the ways in which religious expression varies from culture to culture. Religion may be a cultural universal, but, like any cultural expression, it shows an enormous amount of variation in the way in which it is geared to individual cultural systems and in how it changes to keep pace with them. There are, of course, as many specific religious systems as there are cultures, but we can get an overview of the variation by noting the general ways in which these systems vary.

I have already mentioned the distinction between *polytheistic* and *monotheistic* religious systems and the clear connection between these and some general types of world view. Again, polytheism tends to be found in societies, like the foraging !Kung, that interact with their environments on a more personal level, where people are one of many natural phenomena and are at the mercy of the others. In addition, groups practicing polytheism tend not to have political systems with one particular, formal leader. The supernatural reflects the natural in terms of social organization as well.

Monotheistic systems are found in groups that have gained some distinct control over their habitats, groups like the Middle East agriculturalists. Such groups tend to have a hierarchical political system with formal leaders and followers.

As usual, such a two-way distinction doesn't always work out exactly. It has been said, for instance, that true monotheism is rare. For example, Christianity is usually considered monotheistic, there being a single, all-powerful deity. But that deity comes in three forms, the "Holy Trinity," which is distinguished by three separate linguistic terms: *Father, Son,* and *Holy Ghost* or *Holy Spirit*. (You should recognize this as another example of a folk taxonomy, evidenced by language). Moreover, the Virgin Mary has virtually been deified by some Christian branches, and all sorts of angels and saints are included in the supernatural "cast of characters."

Judaism, on the other hand, from which Christianity branched, is a truly monotheistic religion—taking care of the notion that being an early Middle East farming society dictates exactly the kind of religion a group will have. You should know by now that it's seldom that easy. This difference in the recognized number of supernatural beings between Judaism and Christianity probably has to do with the wide spread of the latter and the diverse number of cultural systems that adopted it (voluntarily or otherwise), each system giving the religion a slightly different twist. Remember, world view is a combination of environment plus history.

The nature of the supernatural also differs, and we can categorize three kinds of beings or forces. The first is sometimes called by a Polynesian word, *mana*. It refers to a force possessed by a nonliving thing or by a person. Charms, like lucky rabbits' feet (mercifully now out of fashion) or Italian horns have *mana*. So do some sacred black and green stones venerated by the Dani of New Guinea. People can have *mana* as well, as do those San who possess the healing power *n/um*. And many cultures have taboos against contact with certain objects, like the ''unclean'' foods listed in the Bible. These have negative *mana*.

Other supernatural beings are beings of *human origin:* ancestors and ghosts. Recall the importance of ancestors to the !Kung San. And the lives of the Dani are ruled largely by the ghosts of their ancestors. Such supernatural beings are important among peoples for whom the kin group is the major social, political, and decision-making unit. Thus, not only are living humans important; so too are the spirits of deceased humans. The real and the supernatural mirror one another.

Finally, there are supernatural beings of *nonhuman origin*. These are the ''gods,'' the beings who created themselves and then made the world and all its creatures, including people. These beings may be in the form of a single, all-powerful deity or a number of individual spirits, like those that control the natural features of the Eskimos' world.

As you can see, a culture can have a combination of these types of supernatural beings. The San, for instance, have both human ghosts and spirits of natural phenomena to deal with on a regular basis. They also recognize those two powerful gods who created everything in the first place and generally keep things going. What the anthropologist must do is look at the specific nature of the beings and forces recognized by a culture and the ways in which the people deal with them. In this way one can see how these forces act, for that culture, to fulfill all those roles that religious beliefs play in human life.

Supernatural beings also differ in *personality*. Some are benevolent; some are malevolent; some are even mischievous. This in part may be connected with how a group of people perceives their environment: Is it harsh (like that of the Eskimos)? Or is life fairly easy (as it is for the Dani)? Indeed, for the horticultural Dani, basic subsistence seems so easy that their main supernatural beings, ancestoral ghosts, are mostly known for their mischievous deeds, their distinctly good and evil acts being rather informal and variable.

It has also been suggested that the personality of the supernatural may correspond to a society's child-rearing habits. If they treat children gently, their gods are gentle gods. If they are strict disciplinarians, the gods are gods to be feared. Notice how in Christianity the deity is referred to as "God the Father" and the followers as "His children." Gods are often linguistically classified as parents.

Also showing variation is the degree to which the supernatural *intervenes* in the daily affairs of people. Generally speaking, the more scientific knowledge a people has, the less direct is the influence of the gods. Natural phenomena, including human actions, are attributed to natural forces. The degree and kind of intervention may also be related to the complexity of the social order. Especially where there are inequalities in wealth and power, rules for human behavior that come directly from the supernatural may help to maintain the existing order.

The kind of person who specializes in taking care of the religious knowledge and welfare of a people varies as well. Here we may define two basic categories. The first are part-time specialists, usually called upon only in times of crises like illnesses. These people are called *shamans* (after a Siberian word). Shamans are also distinct in that they receive their powers directly from the supernatural. They are, literally, "chosen" for their task. This type of religious specialist is found usually in egalitarian foraging or simple horticultural societies where there are no full-time specialists in anything and where religious knowledge, so vital to survival, is known and practiced by everyone. Only very special situations, like curing, require some extra help.

More complex cultures have *priests*. Priests are full-time specialists and train for their profession, learning what is passed down by other humans. They are the repository of religious knowledge and thus are the persons who know best what the gods say, how best to interpret their words for human implementation, and how best to get in touch with the gods. Where shamans have real supernatural power, priests have knowledge.

But with such important knowledge often comes power of a more down-to-earth nature: political power. In some cultures it can be difficult to separate the political system from the religious system, the political leaders from the religious ones. This was true among the ancient Aztecs of Mexico, for instance, and to a great extent in medieval Europe.

Finally, the ways in which people get in touch with the super-

San shaman in trance.

natural show incredible variety. People may pray, in a congregation or alone. The prayer itself may be individual or may involve group recitation of prescribed words. Some form of eating may be involved—everything from a feast to the taking of communion, the symbolic ingestion of the body and blood of Christ.

Sacrifice is a common way of pleasing the supernatural. It may take the actual killing of an animal or a human to do this (the latter also being found among the Aztecs), or it can just involve some sort of abstinence, as Christians practice during Lent. Music, noise, and dance are also ways of attracting the attention of the gods, as is art—drawings or some symbol representing the supernatural. And in some cases, people feel closer to the supernatural during some sort of transcendent experience, often brought about by taking drugs. The Jivaro do this. But such psychological states can also be brought on by fasting, by exhaustion, or by physical abuses like self-mutilation. The Dani, for instance, cut off joints on a couple of fingers of some of the female relatives of a person who has died. And in James Michener's *Hawaii* there is a vivid description of a man mutilating himself following a relative's death. Walking on fire, self-flagellation with whips and chains, and piercing the cheeks with long skewers all fall into this fascinating category.

Two other terms should be mentioned in this consideration of variation in religious expression: *magic* and *sorcery*. Magic refers to situations where people feel they have control over the supernatural, rather than the other way around. Instead of pleasing the supernatural through acts or asking for favors through prayer, magic seeks to manipulate the spirits. This manipulation can be for either good or evil; if for evil, it is called *sorcery* or *witchcraft*.

These practices on a regular basis are found in less scientific societies, where many natural phenomena are explained through the action of the supernatural. What magic and sorcery do is give the people a feeling of some degree of control over certain important events. The Fore see disease as the result of sorcery, that is, as the result of humans acting with the help of supernatural agencies. A result of this kind of explanation, of course, is that since the diseases are caused by humans, other humans can take actions against them. A sense of control is achieved.

A belief in sorcery and witchcraft, of course, doesn't disappear with cultural complexity and science. There were several periods in Europe between the thirteenth and seventeenth centuries when witches were accused and burned by the thousands. And I noted in an earlier chapter the famous Salem witch trials in Massachusetts in 1692. Even lately, ideas about witches and magic powers and psychic abilities have risen in popularity once again. Though they don't play the part in our culture that they do in less complex societies, belief in such things is most certainly an aspect of modern American life.

This, then, is what religion is and some of the general ways in which it varies from culture to culture. The wealth of this variation and the richness of religious expression within cultural contexts is a whole field in itself. It is thus something of which we can only scratch the surface here. What we can do, though, is take a closer look at one particular religion. We can see how at least some of its major features relate to the overall cultural system of its followers and how these features have changed through the course of history. We can then explain some of its variations.

It's easier in a way to look at the religion of some "exotic" group of people. We can analyze it from afar, dissociated from any emotional connection to it. But that's too easy. Let's instead discuss a religion that most of us either practice or are at least quite familiar with, one that, in a broad historical context, helps make up the moral and ethical outlook of American society. It's also a religion about which we have extensive written records. Let's look at Christianity.

RELIGION AND CULTURE

Christianity can only be viewed in this way in its identity as a branch of Judaism, because that's how it originated. Judaism, a monotheistic religion with connections we've already discussed, dates back, as a religious tradition if not a formal religion, to the time of Moses, probably the thirteenth century B.C. The first Jewish empire was founded by David, in Palestine, in the sixth century B.C. David was considered a *messiah,* which originally meant one who had great holiness and power. Shortly after David's death, though, his kingdom was conquered, and there followed hundreds of years of oppression of Jews by some half dozen other nations. The last of these, the Roman Empire, virtually brought an end to the Jewish homeland in A.D. 135.

A result of this long period of colonialism and economic oppression was the development of the idea that someday, if the Jews kept their covenant with God, a somewhat different messiah would come. This messiah would lead the Jews in a military conquest of their oppressors. This idea peaked during the period of Roman rule, which began about 40 B.C. During that time, a number of "messiahs" appeared and led groups of Jews in what anthropologist Marvin Harris calls "guerrilla warfare" against the Romans. At first little more than a nuisance, these uprisings soon became a threat to the Romans, and the Jews involved were typically executed when they were captured—which they nearly always were.

It was into this political environment that Jesus was born. He is seen today, of course, as a peaceful messiah, but there is good evidence that he was, in his time, part of the military messiah tradition. A complete treatment of this topic can be found in Marvin Harris's provocative book *Cows, Pigs, Wars, and Witches: The Riddles of Culture,* but, briefly, there is no reason to think that Palestinian Jews of 2000 years ago would have followed any claimed messiah who advocated peace with the Romans. No precedent whatever existed for that. The goal of the Jews was military overthrow.

Jesus, of course, was captured and crucified—the standard form of execution for such rebels. This had ended the brief reigns of Jesus' predecessors, but a number of his ardent disciples claimed that, rather than proving that Jesus *wasn't* the true messiah, his death was merely a test of his followers' faith. If they kept the faith, he would one day return. So while most Jews still awaited a military savior, a small cult of Jewish Christians began to spread, preaching this variation of Jewish doctrine but still maintaining its ties with the religion at large. Over the next 30 years (Jesus was killed in A.D. 33) the cult had spread as far as Rome itself and had begun to be taken up by some non-Jews.

This last feature began a split between the Jews of Palestine, where the new Jewish Christians still considered themselves Jews, and those outside the homeland, where the "Christian" part was emphasized. The separation became complete when, after the Jewish uprisings had become a serious problem for the Romans, a major military campaign was launched, under the leadership of Vespasian and his son, culminating in the destruction of the temple of Jerusalem in A.D. 70 and the famous fall of the fortress of Masada in 73. You should, by the way, remember Vespasian from the story of Maiden Castle in England. (The Romans really got around in those days!)

Incredibly, the military messianic tradition persisted quietly for the next 60 years and arose again in earnest in A.D. 132. This uprising resulted in the founding of an independent Jewish state, which lasted until 135. In that year, the Romans mounted a fierce and bloody campaign that ended in the destruction of Jewish settlements, the deaths of hundreds of thousands, and the taking of more thousands into slavery. But the victory in Jerusalem in 70 really showed the might of the Roman Empire and brought about the cultural changes we're concerned with.

With the temple (the heart of Judaism) destroyed, connections between Jews and the Jewish Christians were severed. The Palestinian Jews had to cease, or at least not actively pursue, the messianic trend—for a time anyway. The Jewish Christians, though, responded differently. Especially in other parts of the Roman Empire, including Rome itself, it was simply not wise to continue following the cult of Jesus as it then existed, particularly since the belief was that he was coming back! So the nature of this messiah changed. He became a peaceful savior, bringing salvation not in this world but in the next—hardly a threat to the Romans. It was about this time that the first of the Gospels, that of Mark, was written. The Gospels tell the story of Jesus and outline his teachings—confirming his emphasis on heavenly rather than earthly reward, though retaining some of his militant statements as well. Christianity, as we recognize it today, had begun.

Numbers of communities banded together to await the Second Coming and to preach the teachings of this new religion. Some of this early history is recounted in Acts of the Apostles in such passages as 2:44: "All that believed were together and had all things common" Sound familiar? It's the passage on which the Hutterites base their communal lifestyle. We can now see that style as a direct descendant of that of the first Christians.

The origin of Christianity, then, can be understood as a branching off from the long-standing traditions within Judaism, brought about by a particular set of historical circumstances and by people's reactions to them. The basic tenets of the religion are a reflection and an affirmation of a particular world view—a view generated by all the aspects of the founding group's environment and history.

Over the next nearly 2000 years, the history of Christianity becomes quite complex, as the basic idea spreads throughout the world, is adopted by all sorts of societies, takes on all sorts of variations, and undergoes historical changes. Suffice it to say that there are now three recognized major branches of Christianity: Roman Catholic, Eastern Orthodox, and Protestant, each, especially Protestantism, with a number of subbranches.

Each of these branches and subbranches can itself be understood anthropologically in terms of its origin and its place within the culture of its followers. But to see how this works, let's skip over the major divisions (though their stories are very interesting) and look at two specific and very different branches of Protestantism.

The first we've already gone over at some length. This is the religion of the Hutterities. You recall that the Hutterities were founded as part of the Anabaptist movement, a religious movement of the early 1500s that involved a number of groups but had as its themes the repudiation of infant baptism (from whence the name), a literal interpretation of the Bible (especially the New Testament), and a dislike for state-controlled religion.

That the Hutterites are Christians, instead of some other religion, is historical. They arose within basically Christian Europe. You would not expect them to come up with something entirely new. It is more likely that they would vary the existing tradition to suit their cultural requirements.

At the time of the Anabaptist movement, a major change was taking place in Europe in terms of people's ability to acquire information. Specifically, the printing press, invented by Gutenburg about 100 years before, had put the Bible in the hands of the common citizen. Now, for literate persons (mostly townsfolk and artisans) or persons who knew someone who could read, there was no need to rely on the church or the state for knowledge about the content and interpretation of the Bible. Some people began to think for themselves about religious issues, and the Anabaptist ideas just noted were three of their important conclusions.

Such conclusions, however, were not viewed kindly by the state, which was, at this time, inextricably linked to the church. Repudiating infant baptism had been considered heresy for some time, and this was used to punish the Anabaptists and other sects. But their real "crime" was actually their threat to the state's hold over the religious lives—and thus the economic lives as well—of its subjects. Many of the religious rebels were tortured and burned at the stake, including, as I mentioned, Jacob Hutter, whose followers took his name in tribute.

Living communally, apart from society at large, was not an original part of the Anabaptist belief system. It became necessary, in the face of continual persecution, to separate themselves and to develop a social system that was self-sufficient and had a good deal of internal strength and cohesion. The self-sufficiency was possible because many of the people were, as I said, literate urban artisans and craftspersons. So the early Hutterite communities began to produce their own food and manufacture their own houses, clothing, and other artifacts. The agricultural life, of course, has lasted to the present. So too has the craftsmanship. One can still find shoemakers, carpenters, and bookbinders in a Hutterite colony.

The ideological basis for such economic and social communism was found, not surprisingly, in the Bible. The social system of the Hutterites—having "all things common"—is modeled after the communities of early Christians, who gathered together, separate from the larger society, to follow the teachings of Christ while awaiting his return—just as the Hutterities do.

Now, compare the Hutterites' version of the Christian tradition

Anabaptists forced to jump to their deaths.

with that of another North American group. This branch is generally less well defined than the Hutterites and is quite variable, but we can focus on its most extreme form. It's called the Holiness Church, and its followers the Holy Ghost People. Sometimes, for reasons that will become clear, they are referred to in a derogatory fashion by outsiders as the "Holy Rollers."

Holiness churches started in the first decade of this century in Tennessee and are now found mostly in Appalachia—Georgia, the Carolinas, Virginia, West Virginia, Kentucky, Tennessee, and Ohio. The basis for their form of Christianity comes from the Gospel of Mark, 16:17–18. Jesus is speaking to the disciples:

> And these signs shall follow them that believe; In my name shall they cast out devils; they shall speak with new tongues; They shall take up serpents; and if they drink any deadly thing, it shall not hurt them; they shall lay hands on the sick, and they shall recover.

The Holy Ghost People feel that if they believe strongly enough, the Holy Ghost will enter their bodies. The manifestations of this

"Taking up serpents" in a Holiness Church.

are, as predicted in Mark, "speaking in tongues" (a babbling, rolling sort of speech), convulsive dancing and trancelike states, the ability to "lay hands on" the sick and cure them, and a "call" to handle venomous snakes or drink poison.

The snakes used are local rattlesnakes and copperheads. The poison is a dilute strychnine solution. The meaning of these acts, always performed at the height of the service when the music is loud and many persons have the Holy Ghost, has to do with professing one's faith: "God will protect me from this dangerous act, so strong is my belief. But if I die from it, that is God's will and I will accept it." Persons bitten by the snakes or who become very ill from the poison will not accept medical aid. At least 20 persons associated with this religion are known to have died in this century from snakebite. As a result, the practice is outlawed in most of the states listed. It goes on, however.

Besides these biblically sanctioned features, there are some others that characterize and distinguish Holiness churches. There is, for example, no formal minister, no one who is trained and ordained to conduct the services. The leader of the service is chosen much like the !Kung San choose the man to ask about where to hunt. It is based on outgoingness, charisma, speaking ability, or perhaps just whoever gets up and starts.

What goes on during the service, moreover, is individual rather than group-oriented. People pray with their own words, kneeling if they want, or standing, dancing, or lying down. This makes sense, of course, since possession of the Holy Ghost is an individual thing. It doesn't happen to everyone, and to those to whom it does, how they manifest the experience is up to the Holy Ghost, treating them each in its own way. So a Holiness service appears rather chaotic once it gets going. There are quiet periods when collections are taken or when individuals "testify," telling personal stories about their experiences with the Holy Ghost. But the main event finds some participants playing music, some praying, others dancing, "laying hands on" fellow church members to cure illness or simply to share the Holy Ghost experience, and some holding snakes or drinking poison.

Finally, the attitude of the Holy Ghost People toward their relationship with God is unique in Christianity. Most Christians' prayer is in the form of a request to God. But as one man puts it in a film of a Holiness service, these people feel that "if you believe, God is *obligated*" to answer your prayer. To put this into anthropological terms, they are nearly practicing *magic*. God is still supreme and can do with his followers whatever he chooses. But a strong enough faith on the part of the people "obligates" God to them. Furthermore, since the Holy Ghost choses the persons through whom it will manifest itself, we might almost consider these people to be *shamans*.

How can we interpret this somewhat unusual version of Christianity? Again, the fact that they are Christians lies in the history of the culture of which they are a part. But the particular practices of the sect would seem to be explained mostly in broad economic and social terms. The Holiness church is largely a phenomenon of poor, rural Appalachia. People in these areas are among the least economically well off in America. They are small-scale farmers, merchants whose clientele is local people, or employees of coal-mining companies. They don't, in other words, have the kind of control over their economic welfare that Americans are "supposed" to have.

Not many of us do. But the image of American affluence that comes across in books and magazines and, later, on TV is quite different from the lives led by the folks in poor, rural America. Having little more than this image with which to compare themselves, they feel rather out of step with the mainstream of American life. The religious expression they practice gives them a sense of *control.* They have a "oneness" with God in their possession of the Holy Ghost, which can actually act through their bodies. And simply by believing strongly enough, they can even obligate God to them.

Moreover, in an environment economically at the bottom of America's social stratification, the Holiness service is an opportunity for a little egalitarianism. There is no formal or even informal hierarchy. Everyone is important. Everyone expresses himself or herself as an individual. The only difference between people—the possession of the Holy Ghost—is a difference that can be eliminated by strong belief. Possession of the Holy Ghost is open to all.

There may be another function of this type of belief and ritual, one that I am still thinking about but is a focus of a book on the Holy Ghost People by anthropologist Weston LaBarre. He feels the Holiness service may provide a mechanism for sexual expression. No one is having *sexual* intercourse at the service, but *social* intercourse between the sexes is taking place. And this is something not done regularly in conservative societies like the ones in which we find Holiness churches.

Open sexuality is not a part of these peoples' lives, yet it is a characteristic of American society as a whole. If you don't believe it, watch TV for a couple of hours, commercials as well as programs. Again, there may be a feeling of being out of step with an important aspect of American life. Or it may be that the conservatism of the social setting is at odds with some "natural" human tendencies. At any rate, a look at a Holiness service, as in the film *Holy Ghost People,* reveals a good deal of touching between members of opposite sexes, and not always between members of a recognized couple. (I've seen the film at least 50 times and know the people pretty well!) The idea is to pass on and share the presence of the Holy Ghost. There is no overt sexuality involved. But the touching and dancing may function to provide some outlet for sexual identity and expression that are normally repressed.

Again, don't think that sometime in the past some people got together and said, "You know, we're really sexually repressed, so let's start a religion where we can touch a bunch of women we're not married to!" As with most other cultural (or biological) changes, these practices developed gradually—they evolved—and their current functions don't necessarily account for their origins. Nor are the people always consciously aware of those functions.

In that regard, though, the foregoing analysis of the Holiness church is lent support by the fact that it is of fairly recent origin and started in just the sort of place in which it is now usually found. In this case current function seems to be original function.

From this examination of Christianity in general, and of two of its branches in particular, you should have an idea as to how we apply our basic ideas about religion to analyzing specific situations. Each system we looked at, large and small, was based on traditions, themselves based on some general principles regarding what types of religions one tends to find in what types of cultures. Then the individual features of the system were explained by delving into the culture histories of the societies involved and into the peoples' reactions to social, political, and economic situations that make up the tapestry of history. You should see religion as a part of a cultural system, intimately connected to all other parts.

But if religion acts to provide motivations and sanctions for human action, what about societies that are so complex and technological and scientific that religion has ceased to be at the center of human life? What maintains order within those societies?

LAW

We can lump other order-maintaining systems into one category and call them *legal systems*. Legal systems are secular—that is, not religious. But they perform many of the same functions religious systems do: They define the premise on which are based human interactions within the society, they outline specific behaviors that correspond to this premise, and they provide rules for handling disputes about and transgressions of these behaviors. Though secular, they are often based on the religious principles that correspond to the traditional world view of the culture in general.

Take our own society. If the foregoing is true, the basis of our legal system should be the Judeo-Christian religious tradition. What is at the center of that tradition with regard to how humans ought to act toward one another? If you boil it down, it can be stated by the so-called Golden Rule: "Do unto others as you would have others do unto you." Or, "Judge not lest you yourself be judged." Or, "Let he who is without sin cast the first stone." What it all amounts to is that a person should treat others as he or she would like to be treated.

What is the essential premise of our legal system? Nowhere is it better stated than in the Declaration of Independence:

> We hold these truths to be self-evident, that all men are created equal, that they are endowed by their Creator with certain unalienable Rights, that among these are Life, Liberty, and the pursuit of Happiness.

Then, in the Constitution, after laying out the foundation of a government formed to

> establish justice, insure domestic tranquility, provide for the common defense, promote the general welfare, and secure the blessings of liberty . . .

are listed, especially in the first ten amendments, or Bill of Rights, some specific ideas aimed at protecting the rights named in the Declaration and at punishing (though fairly) those who trespass on the rights of others.

Viewed in this way, our system of government—our legal system—is a translation of Judeo-Christian religious principles into secular terms and the formulation of specific laws to implement those principles in the practical world.

"Well, of course," you're saying. "Is there any other sort of system than one that protects those rights?" Sure there is. Though it would be accurate to say that all people seek to be alive, free, and happy, just how cultures define those ideals in practical terms differs greatly.

For the Dani of highland New Guinea, for instance, the taking of human lives is a regular, formalized occurrence that makes up a central focus of their existence. The Dani have a system of ritualized warfare that involves killing of an enemy to placate the ghost of a slain member of one's own group. In other words, "You killed one of my guys, so to put his ghost to rest, I have to kill one of your guys, which will mean that you'll have to kill one of my guys . . ." And for purposes of revenge—so important is this concept—a woman or child may be killed instead of a male warrior.

Not that we don't have our share of murders and wars, but a

system like the Dani's seems absolutely "barbaric" to us. It's difficult to maintain one's cultural relativity when examining the Dani system, so foreign is that part of their culture to our basic principles. What we must remember anthropologically, though, is that there is a reason for their system and that through it they are "pursuing happiness" as they define it. But it is, to get back to the question at hand, a very different overall outlook. You might say that they "do unto others because others have done unto them." Our system—both the legal one and the religious tradition upon which it is based—seems "normal" to us *because* it is ours. But there are other ways of seeing things.

The chapters in Part Three have discussed the major categories of human adaptive behavior. We have discussed the possible origins of our behaviors as well as the cultural variations we observe in them. And we have talked about how we as anthropologists go about trying to understand these behaviors.

If that were all there was to it, my job would be a lot easier—and so would yours! But there's more. We don't look at cultures as bunches of people who are eating and communicating and maintaining order. A culture is a whole, integrated system with all those individual features and all the people involved working together in complex interaction. Although any anthropologist would agree basically with my filter diagram, we don't all agree on exactly *how* all those things interact in terms of the human motivations behind them and the immediate functions they provide. Have we so successfully taken care of practical needs that all our actions have only symbolic meaning? Or do we still do things for down-to-earth practical reasons? Or both?

Furthermore, has our successful cultural adaptation left biology behind? Or are we still, and will we be forever, biological organisms? And just how much can we say about these biological bases for certain cultural behaviors?

It's time now to put all this stuff together and discuss some general ideas about human ethology.

SUMMARY

World view is an abstract set of conditions and assumptions about those conditions that is at the integrative center of any cultural system. But world view requires a mechanism to give it reality, to allow it to be transmitted among a people and to future generations, to provide answers to questions about the world, to translate its assumptions into values that regulate human behavior, and to formulate rules of behavior that put those values into action. These are the functions of religion and of secular legal systems.

Religion, distinguished from secular systems by its dealings with the supernatural, is, like any facet of culture, highly variable from soceity to society. It is, however, a cultural universal, that universality being explained by the need for a mechanism that helps people to understand the complex world around them and to coordinate their actions accordingly. Many features of the natural world can be explained scientifically, but many cannot and thus require explanations that are "nonscientific." There is also the need to regulate the various levels of human interaction—to tell us how to behave.

As one of several aspects of cultural behavior, we can find correspondences between variables of a religious system and other features of the culture of which it is a part. Since history also affects world view, we find that we must look at the historical dimension of a religious system in order to understand its origins and basic characteristics.

In many if not most societies, some of the rules of life have evolved away from the strictly religious and have become phrased in secular terms. In societies, like our own, where the answers to world view questions are largely scientific and rational, the vast majority of our basic rules are secular laws. Laws perform the same functions as religious systems, at least with regard to defining the premises for human action and outlining the specific actions that correspond to those premises. Laws also take care of disputes about those regulated actions and provide for the punishment of those who transgress them.

Even where a society, like ours, is regulated almost exclusively by a secular legal system, there is often at the basis of that system a religious tradition, the religious rules having been "translated" into secular ones.

NOTES, REFERENCES, AND READINGS

My favorite work on this facet of culture is Edward Norbeck's *Religion in Human Life: Anthropological Views* (New York: Holt, Rinehart and Winston, 1974). It defines religion and its roles and gives numerous ethnographic examples. The quotes I used from it are on pages 6 and 23.

The description of the chimpanzee "rain dance" is from *In the Shadow of Man* (Boston: Houghton Mifflin, 1971) by Jane van Lawick–Goodall.

My discussion of the origins of Christianity is largely from Marvin Harris's *Cows, Pigs, Wars, and Witches: The Riddles of Culture* (New York: Random House, 1974). For additional information on this, see the reference section of that book.

Again, for the most complete work on the Hutterites, you can't do better than the book by John Hostetler I mentioned in Chapter 1. For the point of view of one of the original Hutterites, Jakob Hutter himself, see *Brotherly Faithfulness; Epistles from a Time of Persecution* (Hutterian Society of Brothers, Norfolk, Conn.: Deer Spring Press, 1979).

The Holy Ghost People are described and analyzed in detail in Weston LaBarre's *They Shall Take Up Serpents* (Minneapolis: University of Minnesota Press, 1962). It gets a little heavy on the symbolic, psychoanalytic side, but it's well worth the reading.

Religion is a rich and varied subject because, since world views differ from one society to another, the part of culture that deals directly with world view differs as well. There is, therefore, a great deal of anthropological literature on the topic. For a nice cross section of that literature, see *Reader in Comparative Religion: An Anthropological Approach* (3d ed., New York: Harper & Row, 1972), edited by William A. Lessa and Evon Z. Vogt.

For a similar collection on the topic of law, focusing on its function in handling disputes, try *Law and Warfare: Studies in the Anthropology of Conflict* (Austin: University of Texas Press, 1967), edited by Paul Bohannan.

four

THE EVOLUTION OF OUR BEHAVIOR

chapter 12

The Ethology of *Homo sapiens*
Pigs, Wars, Slow Infections, and Sorcerers

Anthropologists are in agreement, and by now you should clearly see, that all the facets of a cultural system are integrated—connected to one another by a complex web of interactions, both at a given point in time and over the course of time. I have tried to show this by pointing out some of the interrelations involved in the individual aspects of cultural adaptation.

But now we must try to put it all together. We must look at all our data and attempt to come up with some generalizations—some hypotheses to explain our species' behavior, to provide us with a model for analyzing this behavior, and to help us understand, in broad perspective, why we act as we do.

Is there, to begin with, any overall idea about the functions of culture, any theme that would help us in our search for explanations of culture phenomena? If you think back, you can see two aspects of what culture does: It adapts a society to the natural environment in which it lives, providing food, shelter, and so on. But it also adapts the society to itself, to the cultural environment. Remember, a culture must operate as a *system* of interrelated parts. Put another way, a cultural behavior can have practical value, or it can have symbolic value. It usually has both.

The necktie in our culture, for example, now serves a symbolic function: It is a sign of relative social status. That's my motivation for wearing one in certain social situations. But the tie itself decends from something that was probably practical: It was part of a military uniform and therefore a denotation of rank. And the phenomenon of displaying rank and status is connected to some basic ideas about something that is very practical: how you get your food.

Similarly, the focus of Hutterite culture—communal living—began for the practical purpose of helping the first Hutterites survive in a society that was bent on persecuting them out of existence. So important has this feature of their culture become that it is symbolic of their whole life style. Everything they do, they do in terms of the community. Each Hutterite is, first and foremost, a member of the community. If you look at Hutterite history, though, you see that this symbol has continued to have practical adaptive functions too, for the persecution that plagued the early Hutterites didn't end, and perhaps the one thing that has enabled them to survive for over 400 years has been their sense of community and the way in which they bring that sense to bear on their everyday social and economic pursuits.

So the practical and the symbolic both seem to be functions of any cultural phenomenon, if viewed in broad enough perspective. But there are varying schools of thought within anthropology with regard to just how important each of these functions is. Some anthropologists emphasize the symbolic, feeling that most cultural features serve cultural needs. Others maintain that nearly everything we do has a practical—usually economic—explanation.

There are too many individual anthropologists for me to give you all the variations on this issue. So let's look at what are perhaps the extreme forms of each, and then I'll see if perhaps they can't be reconciled in light of all we've discussed so far.

The opponents are British anthropologist Mary Douglas and the American Marvin Harris. And for the "battlefield," let's go back to that most basic of human concerns—food, specifically those lists of "clean" and "unclean" foods in the Bible.

SO WHAT'S WRONG WITH PORK?

Everyone's aware that, traditionally, Jews are forbidden to eat the flesh of swine. So too are Muslims. Indeed, for these religions, pigs are considered unclean creatures: "Of their flesh shall ye not eat, and their carcasses shall ye not touch . . ." But you may not be aware that this taboo is just part of a whole list of foods considered unclean by the ancient Hebrews. You'll find this more interesting, I think, if you begin by reading the list yourself, from the source. You will find the list twice, in Leviticus 11:1–47 and Deuteronomy 14:1–21. Read them both, as each has some specific information not included in the other.

It takes a little patience to sort out all the generalizations from these two chapters, and wordings vary, depending on the version of the Bible you have. So here's a summary.

Among the important animals that are OK to eat are those that have parted or cloven hooves *and* chew the cud. (For those of you who, like me, are city kids, chewing the cud refers to the habit of some ungulates of regurgitating partially digested food and rechewing it so as to digest it more thoroughly and thereby extract more nutrition from it.) Creatures listed in this category include oxen, sheep, goats, and various wild deer and antelope.

However, any creature that only has *one* of these attributes is unclean and cannot be eaten. The camel chews the cud but does not have a cloven hoof. The coney (hyrax) and the hare don't really chew cud but look like they do, and neither has anything like a hoof, so they are included in this category. (What hares are chewing, just in case you thought cud chewing was strange enough, is fecal matter! Eating it again releases additional nutrients.) And the pig, which has a cloven hoof but does not chew the cud, is prohibited by the same general criteria.

Water creatures have an easy taxonomy in this regard. If they have fins and scales, you can eat them. If they don't have both, you can't. Thus a trout is OK, but an eel or a shark (no scales) or a clam or lobster (neither) is unclean.

The longest specific list of prohibited creatures is for the birds. I need not repeat it here. But if you know anything about birds, you'll see that most of those considered unclean are birds of prey or scavengers—eagles, hawks, owls, ravens, and vultures. (Notice that bats, which are mammals, are listed as prohibited fowl—an interesting zoological error.) Leviticus says nothing about which birds may be eaten, and Deuteronomy says only "of all clean fowls ye may eat." But how do we know which are clean? What are the criteria for clean fowl? What is the basis for the distinction? Well, let's go on for now.

All insects (your Bible may say "creeping things") are prohibited, except those that have "legs above their feet" (that is, jointed legs) to leap with. These acceptable insects include locusts, beetles, and grasshoppers. Yes, people eat bugs! It's actually not all that uncommon. (Notice here that the insects are described as going "on all four." As it is unlikely that the ancient Hebrews were unable to count, I attribute this to an error of translation. "On all four" must mean something like "not bipedally" and is not a reference to a specific number. The numerous translations the Bible has undergone have resulted in a number of such problems.)

There is an unspecified mention of things with "paws." Presumably this would include mammals like the wild cats and dogs (and maybe domestic ones as well).

Finally, there is a list of "creeping things that creep upon the earth." These are specified as weasels, mice, tortoises, ferrets, chameleons and other lizards, snails, and moles. Here, behavior—some manner of "creeping"—is the criterion, rather than a zoological category. In addition, there is a general prohibition against eating anything that has already died, even if it is one of the clean creatures.

Now, how do we explain these taboos? You can discount right away the conventional wisdom that pigs are "unclean" because they are literally dirty and carry disease. They are in fact no dirtier than any other domesticated animal, nor are they the only animal that can be a source of disease. Moreover, the parasite usually associated with pigs, the trichina worm, is rare in hot climates, can be controlled with proper cooking, and was only discovered in the nineteenth century. In addition, of course, many of the other creatures labeled as unclean are perfectly fine, safe sources of food. There's obviously some other explanation.

British anthropologist Mary Douglas emphasizes the symbolic functions of cultural practices. Once beyond the obviously practical (things like the acquisition of food), the functions of most acts of culture, she feels, are aimed at conforming to, and thus reinforcing, our basic assumptions about our world, our world view. So she sees these food taboos as essentially reflections of some broad idea, serving some abstract cultural need rather than a practical one.

Douglas's argument is detailed in her book *Purity and Danger.* Most of the taboos, she feels, are aimed at preserving humans' "holiness," which she takes to mean "wholeness and completeness." Thus things in this world should not be confused. Things must be uniform, integrated, conforming: "Holiness requires that individuals shall conform to the class to which they belong. And holiness requires that different classes of things shall not be confused."

It follows from this general principle that one of the most vital aspects of our world, our food, should be categorized in such a way that the categories (or "classes") are clear and that creatures conform to the characteristics that define their class. If they don't, they are not holy and thus "unclean" for humans.

So, Douglas says, water creatures that lack fins and scales fail to conform to the criteria defining this class of organisms. Creatures that have "four feet" (or more, presumably) but that fly are also unclean; they fail to behave accordingly for legged land creatures that "should" be walking or jumping. This is why locusts and grasshoppers are OK. Animals with "paws," she says, are unclean because they have "hands instead of front feet" and so "perversely use their hands for walking." And all those "creeping" creatures are taboo because of their "indeterminate form of movement."

The list of unclean birds doesn't seem to work well with this interpretation. A raven is not fundamentally different from, say, some perching bird like a robin, which is, I assume, OK to eat. Douglas takes care of this problem by suggesting that the list may be poorly translated, the translators using names of modern species for old Hebrew and Greek names of quite unrelated creatures. If the list could be retranslated, she offers, we might find the unclean birds to be birds that can't fly or that swim and dive as well as fly and that therefore are "not fully birdlike."

Now, before we get to her discussion of the cloven-hoofed, cud-chewing creatures, let's examine her idea so far. To be sure, the listing of creatures that can and cannot be eaten or even touched serves an important symbolic purpose. It maintains the "holiness" of those who adhere to its principles. It reminds them constantly of their relationship with God. "By rules of avoidance holiness was given a physical expression in every encounter with the animal kingdom and at every meal," says Douglas.

But though the categorization itself may serve this function, Douglas's interpretation still doesn't explain why the animals are categorized as they are in the first place. *Who says* creatures with fins and scales are the "proper" kind of water animal? Indeed, there are more kinds of marine animals without these two traits than there are with them. Who decided that a huge number of insects (maybe most) are not "correct" land creatures because they have feet but also fly? What's wrong with creeping? And paws?

And I'll bet you didn't notice what's missing from the list of clean and unclean foods: plants. Nobody listed plants! Surely there are plants that are bad to eat and plants that fail to conform to some "taxonomic" norm. Clearly, there's something else going on here. A clue to it can be found in Douglas's discussion of livestock.

Here the criteria for cleanliness are clearly based on cultural matters. She says, "Cloven-hoofed, cud-chewing ungulates are the model of the proper kind of food for a pastoralist." Why? Not because of some overriding set of traits, as with the other categories, but because the rules are an "*a posteriori* [after-the-fact] generalization of their habits." The rules, in other words, reflect what the people were already doing with regard to eating the flesh of animals. And we must assume that with something as vital as food, what they were already doing had practical reasons behind it.

This is where the other view of cultural analysis comes in, as expressed in its extreme form by Marvin Harris. Harris is a "cultural materialist," someone who sees cultural patterns not as "random or capricious" but as based on "practical circumstances" and "ordinary, banal, one might say 'vulgar' conditions, needs, and activities."

People may do things for reasons that are symbolic on the surface, but beneath it all, their cultural practices are based on down-to-earth, "mundane," usually economic matters. Says Harris:

> Practical life wears many disguises. Each lifestyle comes wrapped in myths and legends that draw attention to impractical or supernatural conditions. These wrappings give people a social identity and a sense of social purpose, but they conceal the naked truths of social life.

Harris's ideas on cultural materialism are detailed in a technical book by that name and in two popular books, *Cows, Pigs, Wars, and Witches: The Riddles of Culture* and *Cannibals and Kings: The Origins of Cultures*. Here, in contrast to Douglas, is what he says about the dietary laws.

Harris would agree with Douglas that the laws are after-the-fact generalizations of already existing habits. And the habits in question revolve around the fact that the people among whom these laws originated emphasized farming as a source of food. You recall that the Middle East was one of the areas where agriculture first appears in the archaeological record. Part of the reason for its emphasis in that area is that, given the ecological conditions there, farming is a much more efficient source of nutrition than is herding. You get, Harris says, about ten times the number of calories back per calorie expended in farming as you do in raising livestock. Moreover, as the emphasis on farming increased in the area, it brought about ecological changes itself, turning forests into grasslands, which themselves sometimes converted to deserts. This also made most hunting a costly proposition in terms of nutrition returned for energy expended.

This emphasis on farming explains why plants are not given clean and unclean labels. So central was the raising of plants to the ancient Hebrews that there was no need for any reinforcement of the habits or reminders about which plants to grow and which to avoid. That information was a given.

Thus the practical concern of cost versus benefit for various sources of food is, says Harris, at the heart of the matter. People gradually stopped hunting for wild creatures, especially those that provided little meat and were hard to catch. They also were careful about the animals they did herd; such animals had to be useful alive as well as on someone's dinner plate. Otherwise, the cost in energy was too high.

This last consideration explains the prohibition on the pig. Pigs are useful only for meat. They are hard to herd—indeed, they are not creatures that herd naturally. They cannot digest cellulose and thus are not grazing animals suited to the natural fauna of the Middle East. In fact, their digestive system is much like our own (that's partly why we use fetal pigs for dissection in biology lab), so they actually compete with humans for the same sources of plant food. And they are hard to raise in hot, dry climates because they don't sweat. They need a source of moisture in which to roll around to cool their bodies. If no other source is available, they will use their own excrement—the source of our notion that they are "dirty." It was, in short, not a good idea for the ancient Hebrews to raise pigs, and they gradually stopped doing it.

How do we know that they ever did raise them? We have archaeological evidence of that fact—bones of domestic pigs. The factors described here came about as a result of a gradual ecological change, brought on in large part by human agricultural activities, to which people gradually responded in both practical and abstract terms—the interaction of environment and history again.

What about the animals that *were* herded—sheep, goats, and cattle? All these are animals that can survive in the Middle East climate and can be easily controlled. In addition, they serve functions other than as sources of food. They all provide milk. Sheep have wool. Cattle can be used for work and, when dead, as a source of leather for clothing. The benefits of herding such creatures outweigh the costs.

Some wild creatures are also listed in this cloven-hoofed, cud-chewing category. Harris feels that whether they are clean or unclean depends on the same basic criterion: cost effectiveness. Wild deer and antelope are relatively easy to hunt and do provide a good deal of meat. Hares and hyraxes, on the other hand, are hard to find and kill and are not worth the effort anyhow.

To round out this part of the list, we have the camel, an animal so useful for transportation and other work that to eat it would have been most detrimental in terms of energy efficiency. The same could be said of the horse and donkey. The latter was used widely in the area, but neither is included in the lists (maybe because neither actually chews the cud), though Harris says that rabbinical scholars have normally added them. Again, their use alive was so important that eating them was out of the question—so much so that it may simply not have been necessary to list them.

The hunting idea seems also to apply to the birds and water creatures listed as unclean. Such bird as eagles and vultures were hard to catch and not very nutritious (or very tasty, I'll bet). And there might be another factor, not mentioned by Harris, which relates to practical health concerns and concepts of cleanliness. Recall that the prohibited birds are mostly birds of prey or scavengers. They eat other creatures, including ones that are already dead. The eating of carrion is something that is specifically prohibited by the laws.

The inefficiency of most hunting can be invoked as well to explain the taboo against finless, scaleless aquatic animals like clams, eels, and marine mammals—none of which were very common in the area anyway. The idea also explains the animals with "paws" and those that "creep": These would not have been very energy-efficient sources of food.

Neither would most insects. But those that are OK—locusts and grasshoppers—are big, "meaty" bugs that are most abundant and easily captured when they are swarming and eating people's crops! There is surely some practical sense to eating them, and folks did.

Now we seem to have two quite diverse points of view here: Douglas, who feels that the explanation of the laws lies in their symbolic value for the Jews, and Harris, who thinks they all stem from practical considerations. I think they are both right and that their difference is that each emphasizes a different aspect of the same story. When you read them carefully, you see that they realize this too.

Harris explains the *origins* of the laws as religious expressions of preexisting practical habits. Douglas as much as acknowledges this in that passage I quoted. But *that* they are expressed in terms of loose zoological categories labeled "clean" and "unclean" may be explained by the need for people to order their world and to do so in a way that makes sense culturally and symbolizes basic cultural ideas. These categories are "folk taxonomies." And Harris admits that some of the prohibited creatures, especially some of those in that rather diverse "creeping" list, may have been prohibited

> not for ecological reasons but to satisfy random prejudices or to conform to some obscure principle of taxonomic symmetry intelligible only to the priests and prophets of ancient Israel.

Now, once the laws are in place, serving to maintain certain practical habits, they may also function, since they are in religious terms, to remind the people of their identity and relationship to the supernatural, even after their practical functions are no longer important. Harris again:

> Food taboos and culinary specialties can be perpetuated as boundary markers between ethnic and national minorities and as symbols of group identity independently of any active ecological selection for or against their existence. But I don't think such beliefs and practices would long endure if they resulted in the sharp elevation of subsistence costs.

A cultural pattern serves those who practice it in both practical and symbolic ways—the same cultural feature possibly doing both at the same time or changing its focus through time. Both these functions must be considered when attempting to analyze a cultural system.

So what about whole cultural systems? How does this work when looking at more than just a group's dietary laws? As examples, let's examine more closely two fascinating stories from New Guinea.

PEACEFUL WARRIORS AND CANNIBAL FARMERS

That both my examples come from New Guinea does not mean that the analytical process I've just described is applicable only to "primitive" tribal peoples from the western Pacific. It can be applied to any culture; that's one of the points I've emphasized all along. It's just that these two examples are my favorites and are so interesting that you're not likely to forget them.

The Dani, whom I've already mentioned several times, live in the western half of the island of New Guinea, called West Irian or Irian Jaya. I say "live" because we use the "ethnographic present." The fact is we don't really know what's become of the Dani since the borders of Irian Jaya, part of Indonesia now, have been sealed off to outsiders. It may well be that the Dani as a culture no longer exist. So the description I'm about to give refers to the group in the early 1960s and before.

There are maybe 100,000 people who speak the Dani language, but the group we're concerned with, about 50,000 individuals, lives in the Grand Valley of the Balim River, an area of about 250 square miles. This population was first studied in the 1950s. The most complete recent ethnography is by anthropologist Karl Heider, called *Grand Valley Dani: Peaceful Warriors,* from which I got the title for this section.

The Dani are horticulturalists, using only digging sticks and human labor to break the ground, plant it, and care for and harvest their crops. They deviate from the classic definition of horticulture in that they use irrigation ditches. (As I said, there are always exceptions to any of the nice, neat categories we define.) The major crop for the Dani, making up some 90 percent of their diet, is the sweet potato. Almost their only source of meat comes from domesticated pigs. (In contrast to the Middle East, highland New Guinea is an ideal place for pigs—not too hot, with plenty of moisture, and, because of the extensive growing of sweet potatoes, plenty of food for both people and pigs.)

In general the Grand Valley is a nice place to live. The average temperature year round is about 70 degrees Fahrenheit, and there is plenty of rain. Although there are seasonal fluctuations in rainfall and temperature, there are virtually no growing seasons, so crops may be grown continuously. And the elevation is high enough so that many common tropical diseases are not present. You'd think that people in such a place would live happy, peaceful lives. Well, happy, yes; and the people themselves are described as "gentle" and "nonaggressive." But peaceful, hardly. For as I've mentioned, the Dani are continually at war.

The Grand Valley Dani are divided into about 12 alliances, which are subdivided into a total of about 50 units called confederations. There has existed, for how long no one knows, a state of ritual war between various alliances. The idea is that the ghost of a person slain in war demands revenge, which requires that the life of an enemy be taken in return, and so on. Round and round it goes.

The opportunity to take lives is provided by large battles. These take place by mutual agreement on the "no-man's-land" between alliance territories, usually only on days when the weather is nice. The weapons used are long (13-foot) spears and bows and arrows. These weapons are typically poorly made, and a warrior who is paying attention can usually see the things in flight and avoid being hit. When a man is hit, though, if he is killed or even badly wounded, the battle ceases, for there is concern that no more than one life be taken in revenge. It all has the appearance of a huge game—though one with high stakes.

If several of these battles fail to result in the death required, the group needing the death may resort to ambush. Here, an unwary woman or child can be the victim and will serve the purpose of revenge as well as a warrior. When a person has been killed, all other activities cease and both sides hold celebrations: one a dance of joy that their slain member's ghost has been avenged, the other a funeral, with all the display of emotion that we'd expect, especially when the deceased is a child.

Upon reading about the Dani, or upon seeing Robert Gardner's marvelous film about them, *Dead Birds* (so called because the Dani see themselves as birds, which are mortal, as opposed to snakes, which shed their skins and so are immortal), many people see such a cycle of death as incongruous given the relatively "temperate" (as Heider says) conditions of their environment and their personalities. Why do people who seem to have no real economic hardships and who feel the same emotions of grief and sorrow as anyone else have a cultural practice that *assures* that violent death will take place on a regular basis? Moreover, the men seem obsessed by war and death, most of their daily activities being centered around watching for the enemy, making weapons, and weaving bands decorated with shells that are traded only at funerals. How can we explain such a system?

First, I must repeat a caution from earlier: We have here a classic "Which came first, the chicken or the egg?" situation. Just because I have to relate the features of this cultural analysis in some order doesn't mean that that is the order in which they took place or that what I mention first is the cause and what I mention second is the result. We're talking about an evolving system, one that developed through time, with all its features interrelated. What might have been a functional relationship in the past may not hold true in the present. And without any written records of Dani history, the best we can do is point out the functional relationships that were observed over only about a ten-year period, from the first studies of the Dani until 1963, when the Indonesians took over West Irian from the Dutch and began to alter forever the lives of the native peoples of that country.

You should know first that the ritual war is not the only kind the Dani fight. They also have periodic "secular" wars. These are rare, occurring maybe every ten years or more—so rare, in fact, that Heider, when he first studied the Dani in 1961, didn't know they existed. The secular wars take place for secular reasons, usually arguments over wives or pigs (both are commodities and signs of status to the polygynous Dani) or some other matter that gets out of hand and cannot be resolved peacefully. Conflict resolution is something the Dani don't seem to be very good at.

Secular wars are usually fought between confederations within an alliance because it is between such groups that the economic and social relations occur about which conflicts arise. Secular wars are not played by any "rules." The idea is to kill members of the enemy confederation and take their goods and land. The last such war we know of was in 1966, when some 125 people, of both sexes and all ages, were massacred. It was this war that prompted the Indonesians to step up their attempts to "pacify" the Dani—which they did using armed police and military units.

War as we normally think of it is thus possible within the Dani cultural system and has been part of it. These secular wars, though, are few and far between. The ritual war is continuous. It might almost appear as if the ritual war "fills in" the time between "real" wars—and to an extent, that's the case.

The ecological conditions of the Grand Valley make basic subsistence a fairly easy task, given the technology the Dani possess. With, relatively speaking, a minimum amount of labor, sweet potatoes can be grown in sufficient quantities to feed everyone, and this vegetable seems to be nutritious enough to make up the bulk of the diet. Similarly, the pigs, raised and cared for with little in the way of labor and time, provide the additional sustenance available from meat. The majority of the food-related labor, in fact, is done by women and children. The men usually break new land for a garden, the hardest work involved, but after that the farming is the responsibility of the women. Children are largely responsible for herding the pigs. The men, as a consequence, have lots of spare time.

Now, don't get the idea—and I know you know what I'm about to say—that the men dreamed up this elaborate game to relieve their boredom! It's not that simple. It's more accurate to say that an important *function* of the ritual war, and part of the reason it persisted as an aspect of the culture, is that it gives the men something to do. It provides a focus for their activities. It gives them a social and personal identity. It's exciting. But that's probably not *why* it originated.

After all, you wouldn't pick such a solution to boredom out of the blue. It would be more reasonable to assume that it derived from some already existing habit—namely, the secular wars. These wars came about, and were made possible, because there are a large number of people, living isolated in a given area, who are spread out over that area in individual units. Thus there is a sense of "mine" and "thine." Moreover, the subsistence pattern is successful enough that the beginnings of social stratification are seen. Differences exist in number of pigs possessed, in amount of land farmed, and in number of wives. Conflicts can easily arise over these things as well as over matters such as relative power and influence and social status. Polygyny itself carries the seeds of tension, because the common phenomenon of "co-wife resentment" can sometimes send one wife back to her parental village, which in turn causes ill will toward her kinsmen on the part of her husband.

In other words, these conditions, and the Dani's reactions to

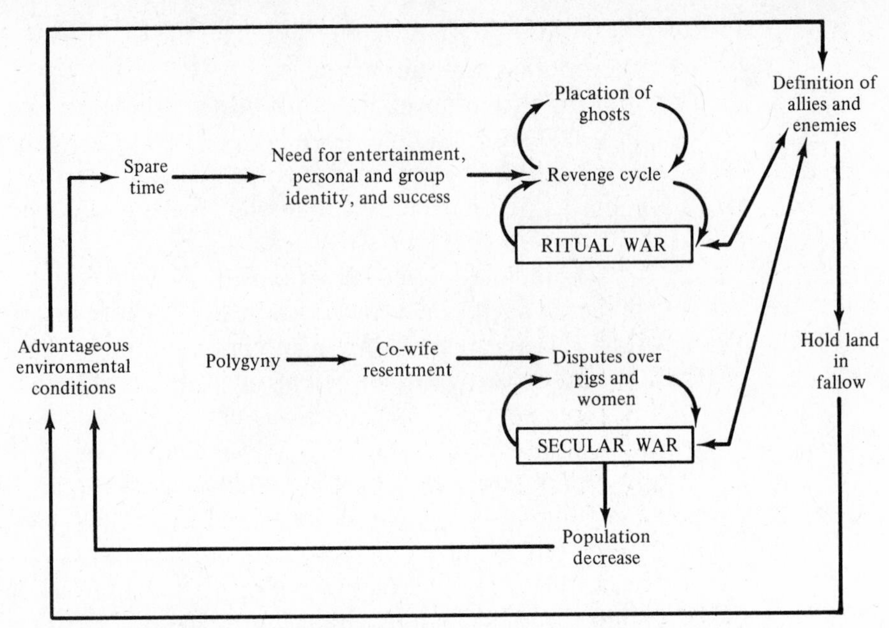

Holistic summary of Dani culture.

them, set the stage for a concept of tension and conflict as a normal (or at least not abnormal) state of affairs. There were territories established, statuses acknowledged, and wealth unequally distributed—all the things we *don't* see among egalitarian foragers, who tend to be peaceful at least among themselves.

So the ritual war is somehow derived from—is an extension of, a symbol of, a metaphor for—the secular conflicts and the conditions that brought them about. The exact relationship we'll probably never know. But the ritual war "caught on," in part because of its identity as a derivative of the other war, in part perhaps because it filled the time and ended up providing a theme for Dani life.

The importance of the ritual fighting is evidenced by its justification in the Dani religious system. The habit was translated into religious sanctions. If you were to ask the Dani why they fight, they would not say "because we're bored" but "because the ghosts must be avenged." The practical and the symbolic are in intimate interaction.

Are any other relationships in operation here? Well, during the ritual war, a "no-man's-land" exists between the rival factions. This land is not planted, although when alliances were different it may have been, and when they shift again, it may be farmed once more.

And following a secular war, there is usually a good deal of shifting of people, alliances, and land. This phenomenon of shifting alliances allows areas of land to lie fallow for a time. This lets their nutrients build back up and may add to the overall success of Dani farming. Whether the Dani are aware of this, and whether it really makes an ecological difference, we don't know. But it's one route of investigation (which we can probably never take).

Another economic relationship exists as well. War increases the number of ceremonies—those directly concerned with warfare as well as the funerals that result from it. Ceremonies are important not only for their symbolic meanings but also as events during which food is consumed and goods are exchanged. Pigs, for example, are normally eaten only in some ceremonial context, so the more ceremonies, the more pork can be consumed. The increase in ceremonies, then, may have the positive effect of keeping Dani wealth in circulation.

Now, you would think, when the Dutch and then the Indonesians came in to "pacify" the Dani and put an end to the ritual warfare cycle, that lacking such an integral part of their culture, the whole of Dani society would fall apart. Something with so many interrelations and to which the Dani devote so much time and concern must be something they can't do without. But that's not what happened. The Dani took the imposed change quite calmly. They continued to sit in watchtowers, to find occasions to eat pigs, and to carry around weapons. Taking away the war made little difference in their lives.

What we see here is a complex interaction of both the practical and the symbolic working together in various combinations through time and resulting in the manifestation seen as Dani culture in the early 1960s. What I've outlined, as you can imagine, is only part of the story, just the main parts (for details, see Heider's book). And though we see how all the parts *can* interact, we really can't be sure how they *did* interact. Obviously, the calm with which the Dani accepted pacification tells us that there's something else going on in terms of the relation between what seems to have been a vital phase of culture and the cultural system as a whole.

At any rate, though, it's through piecing together and describing sets of interactions like this that we approach an understanding of another cultural system and thus of culture in general.

For a second example, let's move over to the eastern half of the island, to the now independent nation of Papua New Guinea and the society called the Fore.

There are about 14,000 people who consider themselves Fore (pronounced "Fo-ray"). The example in question, however, refers to a subgroup of about 8000, the South Fore. These people, like the Dani, are horticulturists and pig herders. Also, like the Dani, their major crop is the sweet potato, although there is a greater variety of minor crops than is found among the Dani. In addition, the Fore do more hunting than the Dani.

As with any culture, the Fore, when first studied, exhibited a set of cultural features that made them unique. But they exhibited something else as well: a unique disease, found occasionally in surrounding groups but concentrated among the South Fore. Their name for the disease, and the one we have adopted, is *kuru.* It is a degenerative disease of the central nervous system. Its symptoms follow an almost unvarying pattern, starting with loss of balance, followed by lack of motor coordination, slurred speech, abnormal mental behavior (such as uncontrollable laughter), and finally complete "motor incapacity" and death. It takes on the average a year for this sequence to progress.

When first discovered among the Fore, not only was kuru found to be nearly unique to this group, but also its cause and mode of transmission were a mystery, and it displayed a strange distribution. Between 1957 and 1968 there were 11,000 deaths from kuru, accounting for about 80 percent of Fore deaths. But by far the most common victims of the disease were adult women, in whom it was nearly eight times as frequent as in adult men. Following the women, children of both sexes were the next most common victims. There was clearly a lot to explain.

Again, I'll refer you to a book for all the details of this quite complex story. The book is an ethnography of the Fore by Shirley Lindenbaum called *Kuru Sorcery: Disease and Danger in the New Guinea Highlands,* and I think it is one of the best examples available of a holistic anthropological study. Here, though, are the major features, the discovery of which earned Carleton Gajdusek of the National Institutes of Health a Nobel Prize.

The first problem to solve was the cause of the disease. At first, because it was pretty much isolated among the South Fore, it was thought to be genetic. But there is no genetic mechanism that would make women, and children of *both* sexes, the most frequent victims, and the disease seemed too frequent to be genetic. You would expect a 100 percent fatal disease to be rapidly selected out of existence.

The answer came from veterinary medicine. It was reported to those investigating kuru that a similar disease was known among sheep and goats. It's called scrapie, and it's classed as a "slow infection''—one with a long and variable incubation period. Kuru turned out also to be a slow infection, with an incubation period of anywhere from 2 to 23 years. That means that you can contract the disease as a child but may not exhibit the symptoms until you are in your twenties.

At first the agent of these ''slow infections'' was thought to be a virus, but recent work has shown that scrapie and another human neurological disease, Creutzfeldt-Jakob disease, are caused by organisms called ''prions.'' These prions are made up mostly of protein, and—amazingly—seem to possess no DNA or RNA! Apparently, they somehow use the genetic material of the host cell to reproduce themselves. At any rate, prions are also thought to be the probable agent of kuru and possibly of Alzheimer's disease.

How was kuru transmitted? The agent appeared nowhere else in the Fore environment except among the people themselves. They were clearly getting it from each other. But since the active agent hangs around in the nervous system, transmission through the air or from physical contact with someone who had kuru doesn't explain it. Somehow people were coming into contact with actual nervous tissue of kuru victims. Yes, they were practicing cannibalism! And this practice was done largely by women who had with them, of course, their children of both sexes.

Now, it's not the eating of the flesh that transmits the disease. You catch it by touching the brain tissue of a kuru victim—brains being one of the more important parts eaten—and having the agent enter your body through a cut or sore in your skin or via the mucus membranes around your eyes and nose. As women were ''preparing'' the bodies for consumption they, and their kids who were close by, had plenty of opportunity to contract kuru. And since the bodies eaten were those of close relatives, the uniqueness of the disease to the South Fore is also accounted for. Where the agent came from in the first place, of course, we don't know. But once it's around, these cultural features explain its transmission and distribution.

Those are the basics—but naturally there's more. Why were they practicing cannibalism? And why only the women? Cannibalism, to the Fore, is done for reasons somewhere between ritual and nutrition. Rather than feeling that they are gaining some power from the deceased, they seek to acquire a ''fertilizing'' effect. As Lindenbaum states, ''Dead bodies buried in gardens encourage the growth of crops. In a similar manner human flesh, like pig meat, helps some humans regenerate. The flesh of the deceased was thought particularly suitable for invalids.''

But when we step back and look at broader relationships, we

may see this practice as having perhaps a more material origin. It appears to have been taken up by women—possibly "revived" from past times—to supplement their diet in what was fast becoming a protein-poor society. And men, who are dominant in Fore society, had first access to what meat was available. Indeed, the cannibalism does seem to have nutritional functions.

Now we go on to more connections. Why was the society becoming protein-poor? Complex economic changes brought about by the Australian government (which then controlled Papua New Guinea) had turned these one-time foragers and simple horticulturalists into settled farmers, with an emphasis on the sweet potato and the pig, as well as some cash crops as part of involvement in a larger economic system. This way of life, and the larger, more sedentary populations it had produced, had gradually depleted the forests and the game they contained, making protein increasingly scarce. Moreover, now that they were part of a larger economic system, these fairly egalitarian people began to exhibit stratification in both wealth and status. Large-scale historical changes had affected the specific environment of the Fore, initiating (or at least promoting) the practice of cannibalism, which for the Fore had symbolic meaning on the surface. And this in turn transmitted and increased the frequency of a devastating disease.

This cycle caused other changes. The Fore, as I mentioned, explain serious diseases as the work of sorcerers, people who for one reason or another bear a person ill will and act to cause that person harm. As kuru increased, the Fore began to fear that their women would all die and that they as a society would perish. And they naturally explained this in terms of the acts of many powerful sorcerers. Who were the sorcerers? People who were not faring well in the new economic stratification. So the increase in frequency of the disease coincided with the coming of economic differences and rivalries. The invocation of sorcery to explain disease fit right in.

In addition, it seems as if the wives of the "Big Men"—those who had the most wealth and power—had more access to human flesh than the wives of the less powerful, so kuru was more frequent among families of the Big Men, who naturally saw themselves as being victimized by those of lesser status and wealth. Where did the Big Men turn? To their own sorcerers or "curers," who performed magical acts to counteract the sorcery that had caused the disease. This was not done for free, however, and wealth began to pass from the Big Men, who had most of it, to lesser men, in the form of fees to the curers or even bribes to the accused sorcerers themselves.

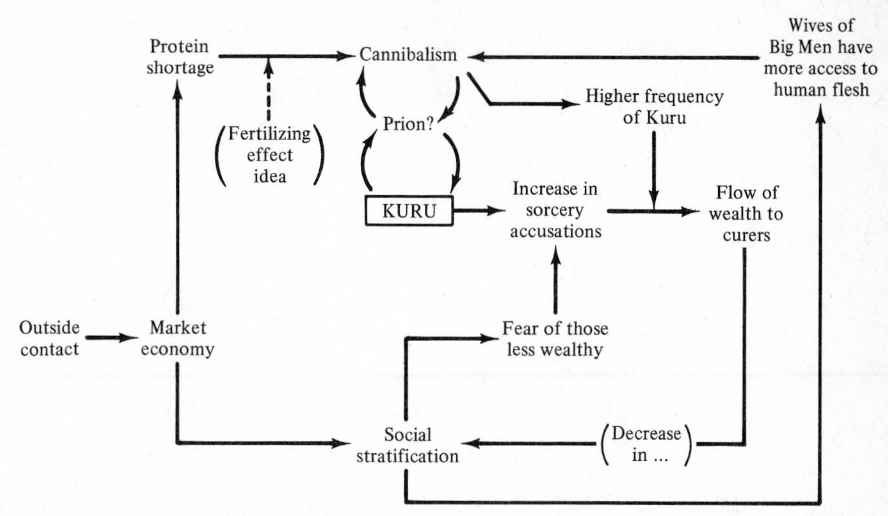

Holistic summary of Fore culture.

Lindenbaum calls this a "redistribution economy," and it acted to smooth out some of the differences in wealth and status.

As with Dani warfare, we see in the full explanation of kuru a complex interaction between the practical and the symbolic, both facets needing to be accounted for and understood. This is the only way we can hope to understand specific cultural "riddles," individual cultural systems, and human culture as a whole.

The two examples from New Guinea and the information about food taboos show the intimate connection not only between different facets of culture but also between culture and biology. We had to examine the biology of pigs, for example, and the workings of a bizarre little organism in order to explain some cultural systems. But are there any more direct connections between biology and culture? Is our behavior, for instance, totally determined by culture, or does it have a biological basis? If so, just how much influence does it have over our actions?

BIOLOGY AND CULTURE

On the cold, stormy evening of January 13, 1982, during the Washington, D.C., rush hour, Air Florida flight 90 out of National Airport apparently iced up during takeoff and moments later crashed into the Potomac River, killing 78 people. Only a handful of the plane's passengers survived, and one of those probably owes her life to a young man named M. L. Skutnik.

Skutnik, stopped on his way home from a government job by the chaos resulting from the crash, was watching the rescue operations when he noticed a woman survivor in the water unable to grab onto a lifeline. Removing his coat and shoes, he dived into the icy Potomac and saved her life.

In June of the following year, Kansas City Chiefs running back Joe Delaney saw three young boys floundering in the water of a Louisiana lake. Delaney jumped in to try to help them. Unfortunately, one of the boys drowned. So did Delaney; he couldn't swim.

These heroic deeds fall into a larger category called *altruism*—acts performed for the benefit of others that are potentially detrimental to the person performing them. The question that comes immediately to mind is why anyone would perform such acts. Why did those two men do what they did?

Maybe they were responding to cultural ideas. But there would have been no retribution—legal or moral—if they hadn't acted. Their deeds were extremely dangerous. Nothing was forcing them to act. No one would have blamed them if they hadn't.

Perhaps what they did was an automatic response to some biological instinct, coded in their genes. But one of the strongest instincts is that of personal survival, and both these men put their lives in jeopardy for people they didn't even know. So maybe, then, their deeds were the result of some complex interaction between cultural ideas and built-in behaviors.

Such questions are part of the broad area of study—and controversy—that tries to figure out just how much our behavior can be attributed to biology and how much to culture. As you might imagine, there have been, for many years, two extreme points of view on the matter; we might call them *biological determinists* and *cultural determinists*. The first feels that human behavior is biologically determined, though somewhat mediated by culture. The second group feels that humans are born pretty much as "blank slates" behaviorally and that culture "writes in" everything that needs to go on those slates.

This "nature versus nurture" controversy has been going on at least since Darwin's time, but its modern manifestation in science begins with the publication in 1975 of a book by Harvard entomologist (insect specialist) Edward O. Wilson called *Sociobiology: The New Synthesis*. Wilson argued, persuasively and really inarguably, that the behavior of organisms, like their physical features, is coded ultimately in their genes. Behavior thus undergoes selection and so must be explained in terms of adaptation and the successful passing on of genes to future generations. No problem there.

But in the book's final chapter, Wilson applies his thinking to human behavior. Perhaps under all the cultural causes, explanations, and rationale for human behavior, there is a biological basis. Perhaps human cultural patterns make sense not only on a cultural level but on a biological, adaptive one as well. That is, maybe the reasons for some of our cultural behaviors have to do with natural selection, the passing on of genes.

The reaction to Wilson's book was swift and sometimes vicious. At worst Wilson was accused of being a racist and sexist or at least of promoting potentially racist, sexist theories. The reasoning behind such claims is thus: If human behavior is genetically determined, the *differences* in human behavior must be genetically determined, so people from different races and cultures and the two sexes, being *genetically* different, are thus unequal on a very basic biological level.

Arguments in print (and, no doubt, in some of the hallowed halls of academe) ensued. But as people have had time to think it over more rationally, the controversy has quieted down. We now see this area of study as a reasonable one indeed, even if some of the specific ideas are still in the early-hypothesis stage.

The fierce reaction was somewhat understandable, though at times not particularly in keeping with the idea of scientific open-mindedness. Starting in the 1960s, a number of books were written that in a very unscientific fashion made all sorts of proposals about biological bases for our behavior. These books, controversial and often quite well written, captured the public's imagination, and legitimate behavioral scientists were concerned about countering their unfounded claims. They became very touchy about such things.

Perhaps the best-known example of this sort of literature is the work of playwright-turned-anthropologist Robert Ardrey, especially his first two works, *African Genesis* and *The Territorial Imperative*. Ardrey's claim was that all the violence humans commit toward one another can be traced to the fact that we are descended from "killer apes"—our australopithecine ancestors who roamed the savannas bumping off animals and sometimes, to defend their territories, one another. The "killer instinct," he said, is in our genes. The best we can hope to do culturally is channel that natural aggression into less fatal endeavors than war, murder, and rape—activities like sports, for instance.

I have to admit that those two books are what got me interested in anthropology. They were well written, stimulating, and intriguing. But once I began my formal study of the field I saw the errors inherent in such claims as Ardrey's. There is, to begin with, a big difference between killing an animal for food and dropping bombs on some other country's citizens. Genes for one don't make you do the other. One may well have a large biological component; the other has cultural reasons. Moreover, it is scientifically naive to think that aggressive behavior leading to such diverse things as hunting and war is based on some simple genetic mechanism that can be selected for and passed on like the gene for the taster trait. Some behavior *is* genetic—as for ants' nest building—but it certainly must be coded for by the actions of many genes in complex interaction. Finally, such ideas fail to take into account the power of culture to mold and vary people's behaviors—the kind of things we've been discussing for the last hundred pages.

In addition, the period of the 1960s and 1970s was one in this country that saw a growing awareness of and concern for equality and human rights. The world has a long history of abuses of human rights based on perceived and often concocted ideas about biological differences among human groups. "Such-and-such a race is naturally dumber than we are, so they can't hold the same jobs or attend our schools." Things like that. So anything that sounded even vaguely like such ideas or that could be misused to support such ideas was immediately suspect. But now that things have calmed down, we can look at the scientific side of the issue more dispassionately and perhaps find a reasonable model on which to base studies in this field.

The basic idea of Wilson and others generally labeled as "sociobiologists" is that behavior is genetically based and thus makes sense in the same adaptive ways as physical features. We've already discussed that, and few would argue with it. To demonstrate the point, sociobiologists give examples of behaviors that at first seem to make no adaptive sense and then explain how they work.

Take altruism (being careful not to assume that the use of a human term implies human motivation). There are lots of examples of this from the animal world, but I'll use another of my favorite creatures, the prairie dog.

Prairie dogs spend much of their time out of their burrows grazing on the open plains. It's a dangerous occupation, for the environment also supports such predators as hawks and coyotes, whose job it is to eat prairie dogs. When a prairie dog spots such a creature, it stands up on its haunches and gives a bark, which is taken as a warning by the other members of its group to "hit the dirt" (literally). The thing is, the prairie dog that gives the warning, by doing so, makes itself visible and vulnerable. It's often the one that gets gobbled up.

Now, assuming (safely) that this behavior is genetic and not the result of some set of prairie dog ethics, we have a problem: If the prairie dogs that behave in this way have a higher mortality rate than the average, how do the genes for the behavior get selected for? They don't seem to pass the test of differential reproduction.

But who *are* the prairie dogs that these altruistic ones are saving? They are its close relatives. Thus they share many of its genes—including the genes for the warning behavior. So even if the one prairie dog doesn't pass on any of the genes it personally possesses, it is in effect, by aiding its kin, passing on some of its genes, just in different "packages." In this way the genes *can* be selected for.

This phenomenon is called *kin selection* and is based on the fact that close relations share percentages of their genes. My sister and I, for instance, have around 50 percent of our genes in common. (You should be able to see why.) Suppose I get killed saving my sister from some danger. Although my "package" is gone, I am still helping some of my genes get passed on.

Darwin, by the way, wrote about this concept. He applied it to the problem of neuter insects—worker ants and bees, for instance, that are sterile and thus can't pass on the genes that code for their neuterness and all their behaviors. Darwin, of course, didn't know about genes, but he said in *Origin of Species* (page 259 of the first edition) that

> a slight modification of structure, or instinct, correlated with the sterile condition of certain members of the community, has been advantageous to the community: consequently the fertile males and females of the same community flourished, and transmitted to their fertile offspring a tendency to produce sterile members having the same modification. . . . I believe that natural selection, by acting on the fertile parents, could form a species which could regularly produce neuters . . .

It seems like every time you come up with a good idea in evolutionary biology, Darwin said it first!

At any rate, using such complex and seemingly hard-to-explain examples, Wilson and others have amply demonstrated how behavior works like any other adaptive feature. But what about human behavior?

I think part of the reason Wilson was a target of the same kind of attack as theorists like Ardrey stems from a misunderstanding. As used by legitimate scientists, "biologically based" does not mean "biologically determined" and thus inevitable. Wilson gives top priority to culture as the immediate basis for our actions. But he proposes that behind those actions might be some biological origin, with, maybe, remnants still kicking around in our genes. After all, we are biological creatures, and we didn't somewhere in our evolution just give up all our biological features and take on our identity as the cultural primate. Everything we are today has *evolved* from something in the past.

You may realize by now that we have already discussed at some length examples of a model that brings together the two extremes of this argument. It is an idea that reasonably takes into account all the important facets of our study: the power of our cultural abilities, our identity as a biological organism, and all we know about evolutionary biology and the nature of culture. Remember marriage and the incest taboo?

As biological creatures we are born with, and genetically endowed with, certain *potentials* as well as *limitations*. Our cultural behaviors take off from this basic groundwork. Our big brains allow us to have almost unlimited thoughts, but our bodies, despite any amount of cultural tinkering, will never fly unaided by artifacts. The structure of our hands makes possible Andrés Segovia's guitar playing (or Eddie Van Halen's!) and my typing, but there's nothing we can do without artificial means to increase our normal number of births from the primate heritage of one at a time. Potentials and limitations.

The same holds true for behaviors. Culture provides variations on "themes." And those themes have been set by our evolutionary history. It stands to reason that some of these themes might be fairly specific—such as pair bonding and avoidance of mating with close relatives. These, as we've discussed, may have been so important adaptively that they placed a strict limitation on our behavior. That's why our cultural translations of these behaviors—marriage and the incest taboo—are cultural universals. Culture *is* the motivating factor for just how the behavior is manifested. Culture can even, as among inbred ancient Egyptian royalty, reverse the behavior. But it's still all variations on behavioral themes that were set up before we became the cultural primate.

Furthermore, although we don't have a gene (or genes) for pair bonding, for example (what some of those popular writers might suggest), we do respond genetically in ways that may be left over from the time when our pair-bonding response was still strictly biological. I refer to our sexual behavior: the conscious control, the loss of the estrus cycle, the continual receptivity, and the parts of the body that are centers of visual and tactile sexual stimulation. Although we modify them culturally, we certainly didn't dream up those things as part of culture!

Seen in this fashion, then, certain cultural behaviors may be assumed to be variations on specieswide biological themes. Certainly, most specific cultural features *cannot* be treated this way. My necktie, for example, has no biological antecedents that I can think of! It is purely a cultural matter, though, as we saw, a fairly involved one. But for cultural behaviors that are universal to the human species, such a model as I've outlined offers a reasonable explanation for their universality and their origin and adaptive meaning.

Oh, yes, what about Skutnik and Delaney? Is this idea applicable to their deeds? Try this: That they were able spontaneously to put their own lives at risk to help a fellow species member may well be an action based on the same biological program that causes the prairie dog to perform its altruistic deed. But the prairie dog was programmed to do that in order to promote the passing on of its genes via its close relatives. The two men *didn't know* the people they went to rescue.

Maybe, as with the case in the *kibbutzim,* culture has "fooled" nature. Those two men may be among those who take seriously our cultural idea that "all men are brothers." Naturally, they don't feel emotionally the same about all people. But their belief in that cultural abstraction was enough to trigger the altruism response and lead to what by any criteria were irrational acts—but acts full of positive cultural meaning.

The ethology of *Homo sapiens,* like that of any creature, looks for adaptive explanations for behaviors and the physical features that facilitate them. Human culture makes the ethological study of us more complex, but not different. For culture *is* the way we adapt, and, now, it is the environment to *which* we adapt, using the artifacts of culture. But all these relationships must be seen as the current manifestation of millions of years of evolution, an evolution that began before culture. The interactions operate at a point in time as well as through time. As Ruth Bleier says in her recent book *Science and Gender:*

> For each person [and for the whole species], brain-body-mind-behaviors-environment form a complex entity the parts of which are inextricable from each other; the parts and the whole are ceaselessly interacting and changing and carry within themselves the entire history of their interactions.

SUMMARY

When trying to analyze cultural behaviors and cultural systems, it is imperative to keep in mind the two dimensions of culture. Culture has both symbolic value and practical value. It has present function and original significance. It adapts people to the natural environment as well as to the cultural environment. In Jane Lancaster's phrasing, it has both motivation and adaptive significance. And while these two dimensions may coincide (it's easy to figure out why Eskimos don't hunt kangaroos), they may also be quite different. Fully understanding a culture is dependent on understanding both dimensions and the ways in which they interact. They both always play a role.

Thus the analysis of Middle Eastern food taboos combines both Douglas's focus on the symbolic with Harris's focus on the practical. And our explanation of the cultural systems of the Dani and Fore involved the complex interplay of both those dimensions.

In addition, we may see these two dimensions in a broader perspective: function and motivation as cultural features and adaptive value and origin as biological ones. Searches for such relationships have been controversial, and some proposed connections along these lines have been downright unscientific. But since we have evolved physically from other organisms, it stands to reason that we can have evolved behaviorally as well. And so the bases for some of our behaviors may be explained biologically, even though the current reasons and motivations for them are entirely cultural.

NOTES, REFERENCES, AND READINGS

Mary Douglas's approach to the analysis of culture can be found in her *Purity and Danger: An Analysis of Concepts of Pollution and Taboo* (Balitmore: Penguin Books, 1966) and *Natural Symbols: Explorations in Cosmology* (New York: Random House/Vintage Books, 1973). Marvin Harris's ideas on cultural materialism are detailed in *Cultural Materialism: The Struggle for a Science of Culture* (New York: Random House, 1979). This is a technical and rather difficult work, but for two intriguing and readable accounts, see his *Cows, Pigs, Wars, and Witches: The Riddles of Culture* (New York: Random House, 1974) and *Cannibals and Kings: The Origins of Cultures* (New York: Random House, 1977). The quotes I used are from page 5 of the former and pages 202 and 206 of the latter.

The most current work on the Dani is Karl Heider's ethnography

Grand Valley Dani: Peaceful Warriors (New York: Holt, Rinehart and Winston, 1979). The kuru story is detailed in what I think is one of the best examples of holistic anthropology available, Shirley Lindenbaum's *Kuru Sorcery: Disease and Danger in the New Guinea Highlands* (Palo Alto, Calif.: Mayfield, 1979). This is "must" reading for anyone who wants to see just how anthropology should operate.

An article detailing the work on prions and giving the possible explanations as to how they work with no genetic material is "Prions" by Stanley B. Prusiner in *Scientific American* (October, 1984).

The book that started the whole modern controversy over sociobiology is Edward Wilson's *Sociobiology: The New Synthesis* (Cambridge, Mass.: Harvard University Press/Belknnap Press, 1975). Whatever your views on sociobiology itself, this book remains one of the best there is on animal behavior. It also contains a 65-page bibliography on the subject. A shorter and slightly less technical book on the same topic is *Sociobiology and Behavior* by David P. Barash (2d ed., New York: Elsevier, 1982). And for a collection of works on sociobiology—old and new, pro and con—see *The Sociobiology Debate* (New York: Harper & Row, 1978), edited by Arthur L. Caplan.

Perhaps the prime example of those oversimplified, unscientific, but ever-so-popular works purporting to explain human behavior is Robert Ardrey's *African Genesis: A Personal Investigation into the Animal Orgins and Nature of Man* (New York: Atheneum, 1961). He followed it up with three more, but that one will give you the idea.

The quote with which I ended the chapter is from Ruth Bleier's *Science and Gender: A Critique of Biology and Its Theories on Women* (New York: Pergamon Press, 1984). This book is most relevant to a topic that I'll take up in the next chapter. I picked up the quote in a review of the book by Stephen Jay Gould in *The New York Times Book Review* (August 12, 1984), which itself is interesting and related to several of the topics of this chapter.

five

THE SPECIES TODAY, THE SPECIES TOMORROW?

chapter 13

Variation
Different Looks, Different Behaviors

For the last six chapters, we have been immersed in the particulars of human cultural behavior and in the attempt to make some comprehensive statements about our behavior in general. Now we must step back even further and once again take a look at the species in its entirety, much as we did when discussing our biological evolution.

To begin, imagine yourself as an extraterrestrial astronaut anthroplogist exploring Planet Earth for signs of intelligent life. You'd obviously find it here (although just how ''intelligent'' is sometimes debatable!). Reporting to your home planet, what do you suppose would be the most striking features that you would want to relate about this newly discovered species? Well, in broad perspective, after giving a basic description of its physical features and general behavior, you'd probably report the following: This bipedal, sapient species is (1) widespread and very numerous, (2) highly variable in physical features and behaviors, and (3) due largely to (1) and (2), in deep trouble.

Let's begin with (2): human biological variation and its cultural manifestations and ramifications.

OUR BIOLOGICAL DIFFERENCES

We don't all look alike—not even identical twins. Our unique physical individuality is a result of our genetic individuality, there being (I once read) more potential combinations of human genes than there are elementary particles in the universe! (How many that is I don't know, nor can I really conceive of such a number. Suffice it to say it's vast). In the case of identical twins, who pretty much share the same genes, there are still differences brought about by the interaction between genes and environment. Twins may start out with the same genes, but those genes never manifest themselves in quite the same fashion in both individuals.

Furthermore, we humans obviously come in two major types, male and female. We've already discussed this dimorphism at length, and we'll come back to it shortly.

You can easily tell what general areas of the world many of these people are from.

Finally, there are broad geographical differences among humans. You can often tell what part of the world a person comes from and maybe, since we arrange ourselves in culturally defined units, what society that person is part of. We conceive of people as "looking" Japanese, or Russian, or American Indian. We have, in other words, an idea of *racial* categories.

Just what these racial categories are—and are not—we'll come back to. But for now, how is it that we can tell such things about people in the first place? It is simply because we, as a species, exhibit variable physical traits, called *polymophisms* ("many forms"). We vary in everything from skin color to blood type to fingerprints, and many of these traits show regularities in regional distribution. The study of polymorphisms is one of the most interesting and most socially important in anthropology, and we may organize it around three general questions about the traits: how?, what?, and why?

To understand *how* a species comes to exhibit polymorphic features, think back to what you know about adaptation and ecology. Organisms are adapted to their environments. It stands to reason that the more widespread a species is geographically, the more ecological situations it must adapt to and thus the more variable will be its biological traits. Since more than a million years ago, when some of our ancestors first ventured off the African continent, humans have inhabited all sorts of environments. And since much of the adaptation to these diverse environments occurred before we had a very complex culture, that adaptation was largely biological.

As we gradually evolved the cultural ability to buffer ourselves against "natural selection," many of our biological adaptations became meaningless—at least in terms of survival in a natural environment. But not in terms of the cultural environment, for an important part of each individual society we formed was the concept of being a "normal" member of that society—normal not only in behavioral terms but also in terms of appearence. Remember that mating at this point was based on all sorts of cultural ideas, and those would include certain standards of sexual and personal attractiveness. What's attractive and, therefore, normal? Naturally, what is already normal. Thus some physical features commonly found in a certain area, having arisen quite likely as biological adaptive responses to the ecology of that area, would tend to stay in the area and become characteristic of it.

There is really nowhere now that we *don't* live, so it's not surprising, despite all our recent moving (and mating), that we display a good deal of physical variation and that that variation shows some geographical regularity. We're both Americans, but you'd have no trouble deciding that my ancestry is mostly European and that Muhammad Ali's is mostly African.

Now, *what* are the human polymorphisms, and *why* do they vary as they do? They are any variable biological feature, and there are thousands of them. For some we know precisely how they are genetically coded; for others we have no idea. For some we can explain why they vary as and where they do; for others the best we can do at this point is say that the variation is random. In many ways this study is still in its infancy.

For examples of what we do (and don't yet) know, let's look at three interesting human polymorphisms. For starters, let's examine the polymorphic trait that is one of the most obvious and has been at the center of many of our racial problems: skin color.

Skin color in humans with normal genetic endowment ranges from very light pink to nearly black. We know that the chemical processes that result in a person's skin color are coded for in a number of genes, but we don't know how many. With a trait like this, that doesn't fall into a small number of discrete (either–or) categories, it's hard to tell. Moreover, the environment plays a role

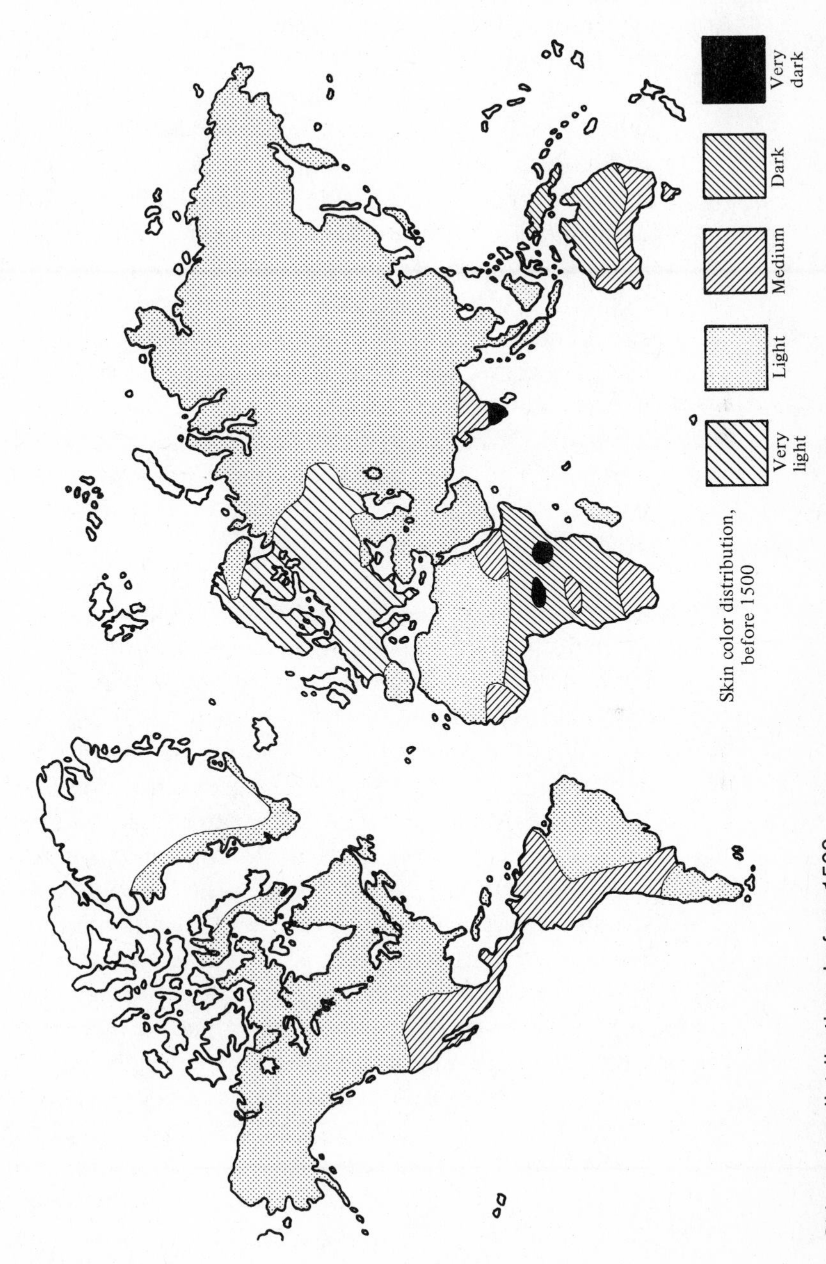

Skin color distribution, before 1500.

too. Amount of sunlight can alter the shade of one's skin, as can things like age, diet, and health. But despite our ignorance in that area, we do have a fairly well accepted hypothesis for why we have different skin colors in the first place and why they are distributed as they are.

The first step in trying to explain a polymorphism is to see whether you can find any regularities in its regional distribution. This is tough these days, for we are a mobile species, and we do buffer ourselves with culture against many of the selective factors of our environments. But if you look not at cosmopolitan urban populations but at indigenous (native) peoples, you might still get an idea of the "original" distribution of a trait. For skin color we see that, generally speaking, the closer a population lives to the equator, the darker its average skin color. The farther away from the equator, the lighter the average skin color.

Now, what is it about the equator that might be important to humans? The first thing that comes to mind is temperature. But that varies not only with latitude but also with altitude. So there are some pretty cold spots close to the equator—the beginning of the Andes, for instance, right on the equator, or the Himalayas, about the latitude of Florida. But another factor, sunlight, would not vary like this. Sunlight is more intense at the equator and less so as you move away from it. This is because the sunlight strikes Earth at a more direct angle at the equator.

What's important about sunlight? Two things: Too much of it can burn skin and underlying nerve and circulatory tissue, leading sometimes to cancer. But at the same time, humans require sunlight for the synthesis of vitamin D, important for proper bone growth (too little causes rickets). Putting this in evolutionary perspective, it would appear that, among the earliest humans (who you recall lived in equatorial Africa), dark skin was selected for to block out some of the intense solar radiation and thus protect those tissues. (This is why humans have a tanning response to increased amounts of sunlight.) The sunlight was still intense enough that sufficient ultraviolet radiation got through to manufacture vitamin D. In those populations that gradually moved away from the equator (mostly north, of course; look at a map), not only was dark skin no longer necessary for protection, but light skin may have actively been selected *for* to let in more of the less intense sunlight for vitamin synthesis. Skin color may be seen as a "balancing act," having to take into account both protection of important tissues and the manufacture of vitamin D.

Gradually skin color has become less important in terms of these factors. Culture has provided protection from too much sun through shelters and clothing and, now, all sorts of sun-screening lotions. And the addition of vitamin D to foods, especially milk, has eliminated the problem of rickets in northern latitudes, at least among people to whom those foods are available. This is a fairly recent phenomenon, though, as there is evidence that the European Neanderthals had a high incidence of rickets, due perhaps to their not having as yet evolved the lighter skin color adapted to such a climate. Now, however, because of our cultural "buffer," we see people of all skin colors living all over the place with little or no physical problem.

But we still see enough of the former distribution to be able to discern the generalization and come up with our hypothesis. Why? First, because not everybody moves around and mixes their genes. Most people tend to stay put. But also because of those cultural barriers and norms I mentioned. What is typical in terms of physical appearance for an area is what tends to be thought of as "normal" for cultural standards of attractiveness and beauty. So physical features, even if they originally made sense biologically, come to make sense culturally as well. And this acts to strengthen further the regularity of the trait distribution.

A second polymorphism is also one with which you should have some familiarity: blood type. Actually there are some 30 different blood group systems that we could look at; that is, 30 traits of the bloodstream that can be tested for and for which we understand the genetic basis. But the one we'll examine is the well-known ABO system.

As you're aware, humans come in four "varieties" for this blood group: type A, B, AB, and O. (By the way, the Rh system is another trait altogether and is listed along with your ABO type only because of its clinical importance. There's no connection.) Anyway, your ABO type refers to the presence or absence of chemicals called *antigens* on the surface of your red blood cells. You can have the A antigen, or the B, or both, or neither. This trait is controlled by a single gene, so we say it is *monogenic*. That makes skin color *polygenic*. The single gene involved has three alleles: A, B, and O. These are not separate genes but alleles of one gene.

Since everyone has a pair of genes, and since there are three alleles, that makes six possible genotypes: AA, AO, BB, BO, AB, OO. But, as we said, there are only four phenotypes:

Genotype	**Phenotype**
AA, AO	A
BB, BO	B
AB	AB
OO	O

You should be able to see the relationship among the alleles, namely that A and B are both dominant over O and codominant with each other.

That's how the trait operates genetically, and, in fact, we know many more details about it. But why does it vary? Although we can make some statements about geographical distribution, that distribution seems erratic, cutting across continents, climatic zones, and "racial" boundaries. The highest frequencies of type A, for example, are found in such places as Australia, Europe, and a few pockets in North America (which in these studies means native North Americans). Type B has its highest frequencies in Asia, although, surprisingly, it is rare among Native Americans who are, of course, of Asian origin. Type O is most common in the Americas (90 per or more), with somewhat smaller frequencies in such diverse places as central Africa, Australia, and Siberia. There seems to be no regularity with regard to any climatic feature.

There are some statistical connections between blood types in the ABO system and frequencies of certain diseases—things like stomach cancer, bubonic plague, and smallpox. For example, in areas that have a history of plague, type O is found in lowest frequencies, indicating perhaps that persons with type O have a greater susceptibility to that disease. And hospital studies show a significant correlation between stomach cancer and persons with type A. However, such statistics can be deceiving, and there has yet to be established a causal relationship. That is, if these statistics are indeed telling us of some actual connection, we don't yet fully understand what it is. At present the adaptive importance of the ABO blood group polymorphisms eludes us.

It may be, as some feel, that ABO blood types are of no adaptive importance. If this is the case, their distributions are the result of random processes of evolution—those that take no particular direction with regard to the environment. For example, that Native Americans are high in type O rather than B, which is the most common

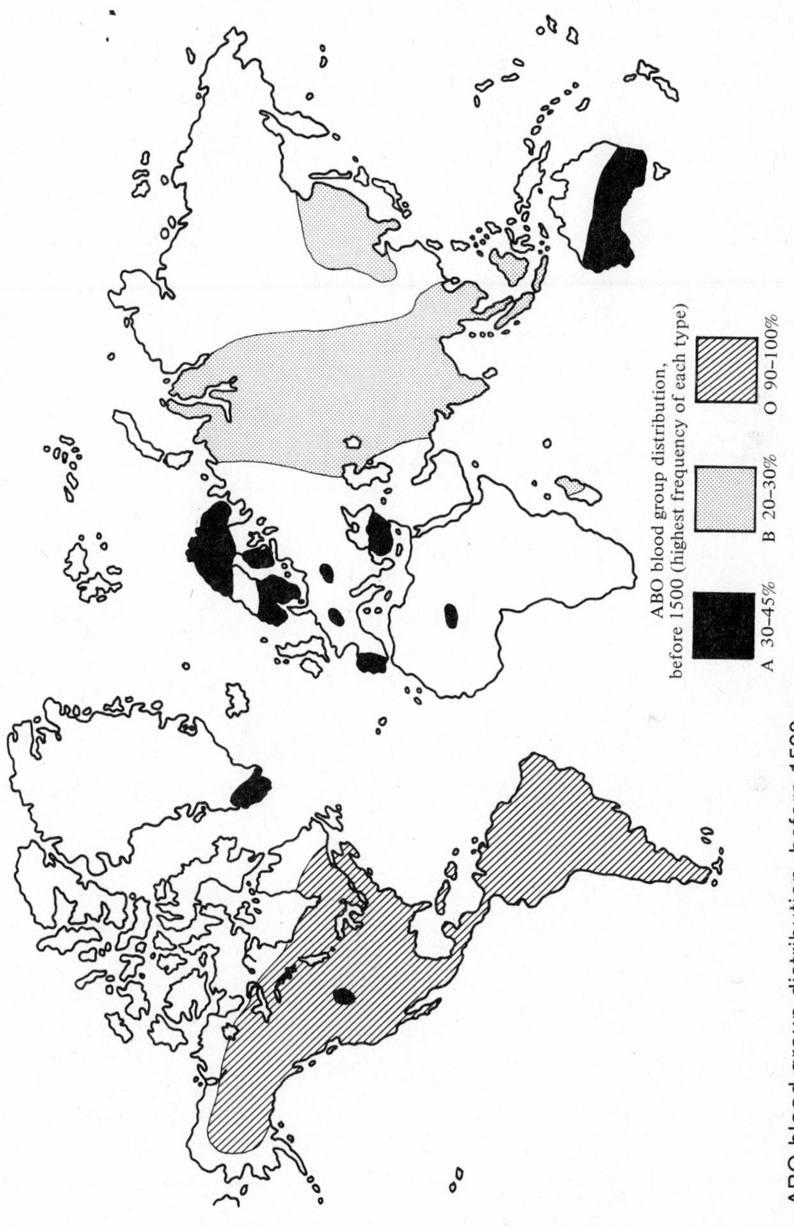

ABO blood group distribution, before 1500.

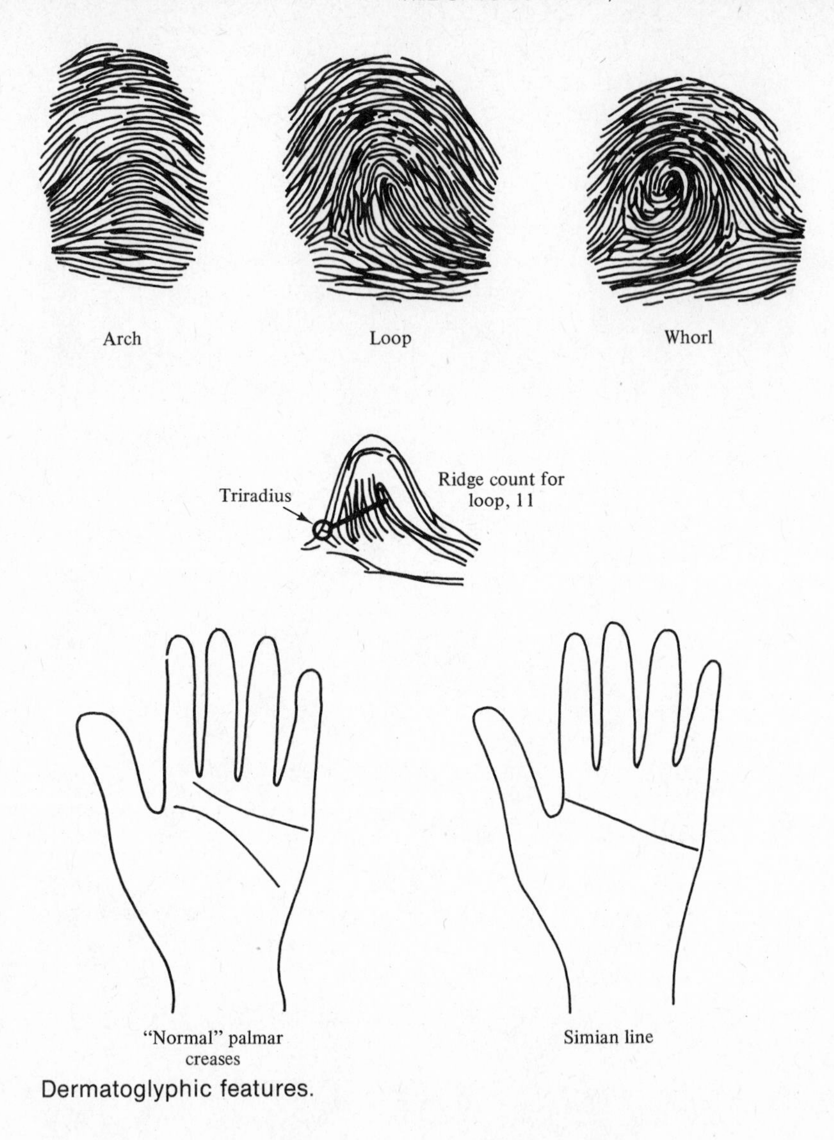

Dermatoglyphic features.

throughout Asia, may be a result of a founder effect. The groups that migrated to the New World over the Bering land bridge happened to be high in O, thus imparting that characteristic to succeeding Native American generations. Recall that O is quite high in the Siberian section of Asia. Maybe most Native American populations came originally from there. There is another school of thought, however, that feels that *no* trait can be adaptively neutral and that blood groups must mean *something* in terms of the environment. As with so many other things in this field, research continues.

For blood type, then, we know a lot about the genetics but little about the adaptive significance. This is just the opposite of skin color, for which we have a pretty good adaptive explanation but about which we know very little genetically. And, to show you the variety present in variable traits, let's look at fingerprints—about which we know neither.

Prints on the fingers, as well as on the palms, toes, and soles of the feet, are collectively called *dermatoglyphics* (''skin carvings''). No two persons are alike in the particular features of their prints; this is why they are so useful for personal identification. But there are also dermatoglyphic features that fall into a number of discrete categories and show geographic variation. They are thus human polymorphisms.

For one thing (and to make things easier, I'll stick to the fingers), fingerprints come in three basic patterns: arches, loops, and whorls, with a few subcategories of each. In addition, patterns of the last two types have a size, determined by their *ridge count.* This is the number of lines between the center of the pattern and the *triradius,* the point at which the lines defining the pattern separate.

From studies of family lines, comparisons of twins, and data from various populations, we know that dermatoglyphic features are under some genetic control, but with a good deal of environmental influence. This environmental influence takes place before birth, as the fingerprints develop between 6 and 21 weeks after conception. But just how the genes work or how many are involved, we don't as yet know. It appears that pattern size is under more direct genetic control than is pattern type, but the exact relationship is unclear.

What about the *why* of this polymorphism? It is unlikely—and here comes a new concept—that the variations in dermatoglyphic features themselves are of any adaptive importance. The reason we have prints in the first place is to increase friction and to enhance the sense of touch; monkeys with prehensile tails have ''tailprints.'' But an arch is probably no more adaptive in an environment than a loop, nor is a big pattern more ''fit'' than a small one.

However, there are correlations between the frequencies of certin features and some disorders of known (or suspected) genetic origin. For example, a *simian crease* (so called because it is common in apes) is found with unusually high frequency among persons with Down's syndrome (once popularly called ''mongolism''). This disorder is caused by the possession of three of the 21st chromosome, instead of the normal pair. This doesn't mean that all Down's people have a simian crease, nor that if you have one you'll get the syndrome (which, being genetic, cannot be caught). But it does point out the possibility that the genes that help code for dermatoglyphic features are also those that, when defective, lead to various disorders. The genes themselves, then, are quite important, even if one of their manifestations is adaptively neutral. Just as some traits are polygenic—controlled by several genes—so some genes or gene complexes can control several, perhaps unrelated, traits. This is called *pleiotropy.*

These and many other polymorphisms are the subjects of study by anthropologists, who are trying to determine their genetic bases and adaptive significance. In addition, though, even while we are in the process of such studies, we can use what we do know about these traits as tools for answering some larger questions.

For one thing, polymorphisms have long been the basis of attempts to define human racial categories. These we'll discuss soon.

They can also be used as "genetic markers" for studies of populations and evolutionary processes. It's rare that we can actually define a population in terms of its genes, but we can compare two or more groups in terms of their phenotypes and thus approximate their genetic similarities or differences.

This is what I did with the Hutterites, using dermatoglyphics. You recall, I was interested in genetic drift and the founder effect. To study the extent to which these processes brought about genetic differences between colonies and between generations, I needed to compare those units in genetic terms. Dermatoglyphics—which besides being interesting are easy and inexpensive data to collect—provided such a comparison. Even though we don't yet understand exactly how they are coded for, we do know they have a genetic basis. So through the use of some sophisticated statistical analyses (done on a computer), I derived several mathematical statements about the relative similarities and differences among the various population units of my study. These were assumed to approximate the degrees of genetic similarity and difference and so were useful in trying to answer the broader questions I had about the two evolutionary processes in which I was interested. Similar studies are done all the time with other polymorphic traits—the monogenic ones like blood groups as well as the polygenic ones like skin color and various body measurements.

Explaining the polymorphisms can lead to understanding of broader ideas. One of the best examples of this is the genetic disease known as *sickle-cell anemia*. Sickle-cell is popularly thought of as a disease of blacks. This is because one part of the world in which it is found in high frequency is central Africa. But it is also found in southern Europe, the Middle East, and Southeast Asia.

Sickle-cell is a disease of the blood in which the red blood cells, normally shaped like discs with depressed centers, change shape (many of the shapes looking like sickles) and, in their new form, fail to carry oxygen efficiently enough to nourish the body's tissues. Severe pain, and often death, is the result. What's puzzling about the disease is its high frequency in those parts of the world. If it is often fatal, or even if it severely limits the contribution of its victims to the next generation, you would expect the gene for the disease to have been selected out. But it hasn't been. For some reason it has been maintained, despite its maladaptive nature.

Sickle-cell is a monogenic trait. It is the result of the mutation of a gene responsible for the production of hemoglobin, a chemical involved in oxygen transport. The mutation causing sickle-cell is recessive, but not entirely so. Persons who are heterozygous for the trait—that is, who have one normal allele and one sickle-cell allele—may exhibit symptoms of the disease to a lesser extent, usually as a result of some environmental trigger (like low oxygen at high altitudes), or not at all. Thus the heterozygote condition is less advantageous than no sickle-cell at all but not as bad as being homozygous for the mutant allele. What might maintain this mutant allele, then, would be some advantage conferred on the heterozygotes, who don't normally die of the disease but who, if they mate with another heterozygote, pass the allele on to three-quarters of their offspring. (Work it out with a Punnett square.)

Again, going to the geography, we find the answer. All areas with high frequencies of the disease are also areas where malaria is a serious problem. And it turns out that heterozygotes have an immunity to malaria: The sickle-cell allele causes their red blood cells to be unable to carry the malaria bacteria. Under such environmental circumstances, being a heterozygote is much better than being a homozygous dominant (they get malaria) or a homozygous recessive (they usually die of the anemia before reproductive age). The allele is thus maintained. We call this phenomenon a *balanced polymorphism,* and understanding it may lead to our explaining the presence of some other maladaptive traits found in unusually high frequencies.

By the way, culture also enters into the picture. Many of these sickle-cell areas are ones in which irrigation is an important part of agriculture. The irrigation ditches provide breeding places for the mosquitoes that carry the malaria bacteria from host to host. Thus this cultural practice enhances the whole system, strengthening the adaptive importance of the heterozygote condition.

These, then, are some of our polymorphic traits—some of the

ways in which we differ—and some of the ways in which we can use our knowledge of them.

WHAT THEY MEAN

> I advance it, therefore, as a suspicion only, that the blacks, whether originally a distinct race, or made distinct by time and circumstance, are inferior to the whites in the endowment both of body and mind.
>
> THOMAS JEFFERSON

> There is a physical difference between the white and black races which I believe will forever forbid the two races living together on terms of social and political equality. And inasmuch as they cannot so live, while they do remain together there must be the position of superior and inferior, and I as much as any other man am in favor of having the superior position assigned to the white race.
>
> ABRAHAM LINCOLN

Jefferson? Lincoln? Though these statements, quoted in Stephen Jay Gould's *The Mismeasure of Man,* shock us today, they do make a point: that our attitudes toward human differences change with time, as our history and environment evolve. Race, and what it means, obviously has some cultural component, tied up with a society's world view.

But race is real, isn't it? After all, people look different. And those differences allow us to place people within geographical, and even ethnic, contexts. As I said, it's clear to anyone that Muhammed Ali and I belong to different races.

Ever since there was something called anthroplogy, one of its focuses has been the attempt to determine just how many races of humans there are and what defines those races. Polymorphic traits, in all sorts of combinations, have been described, analyzed, and subjected to statistical analyses, with the result that over the years anthropologists have come up with anywhere from 3 to 300 human races! Something's not right. And that's because, *on a biological level,* races don't exist!

Yes, people vary. And yes, we can make geographic generalizations about the distributions of some traits—so much so that we can often tell, quite accurately, where people are from. But those polymorphic traits simply fail to assort themselves into a given number of nice, well-defined, discrete categories. The only unique biological category we have within the human species is the individual, in which case there would be 4.8 billion races!

Understanding this requires some examples. Take skin color. I pointed out earlier the generalization about skin color and latitude. That exists. But skin color doesn't change abruptly as you move from one continent to the next, from one "race" to the next. It changes gradually. The shades of skin color grade into one another. There are no boundaries between one color and the next. Indeed, there are no discrete categories of colors to begin with, just gradual change from almost black to light pink. Moreover, if you think about the generalization, dark skin is an equatorial phenomenon, not an African one as our stereotype suggests. Dark skin is found in Africa, in the Middle East, India (where some of the darkest-skinned peoples live), Southeast Asia, and the islands of the western Pacific. The Dani from New Guinea and the Mbuti from Zaire may have the same color skin, but to put them in the same race doesn't make much biological sense.

How about adding more traits? Maybe a race is defined by a combination of traits? You'll find the same thing happening. You'll discover the same trait combinations from diverse parts of the world. And you'll find so much variation within one of these carefully defined races that your combination doesn't hold up as a defining criterion.

Our culture, for example, recognizes an "African" or "black" race. But Africa is a big place. People native to that continent come in all shapes, sizes, and, yes, colors. And you can find some of the same combinations of traits elsewhere, for instance, among the Dani (whom some of my students have identified, before I told them, as African). The same is true, of course, among the "European" or "white" race: There exists a great deal of variation within the "race," and trait combinations "characteristic" of European whites are replicated in other geographic areas.

Indeed, no matter how many traits you add, no matter how much analysis you do with genetic markers and gene frequencies, any attempt to map out the world into distinct racial groups is doomed to failure. There are geographical regularities to be sure. But these are generalizations. There simply are no clear-cut boundaries; no distinct, unique biological units; no races. In fact, attempts to define these nonexistent groups have taken away from the things that we really need to know about human variation: those hows, whats, and whys we discussed earlier.

Now, I'm sure you see that intellectually. But you're probably

Variation within a "race"; similarities between "races" (clockwise, from top left): an Italian-American and a Scottish-Canadian, Asmat mother and child (New Guinea), and Ugandan women.

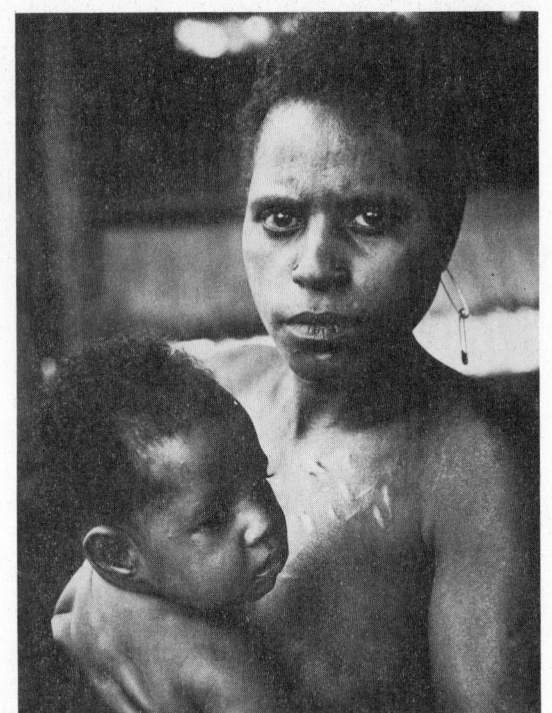

still wondering about Muhammad Ali and me. We are thought of, and think of ourselves, as belonging to certain racial groups. When I say I am "white," that means something to people; the same is true when Ali says he's "black." Just what is race, then?

Very simply, race is a *folk taxonomy*. As with snow, numbers, and kinship, a society's racial categories are based on what the people know and how important it is to them. For fairly isolated societies, the racial taxonomy is quite simple: "us humans" and everyone else! What such societies (like the Tasaday) call themselves means just that: "humans" or "the people."

But as a society comes in contact with people of different cultures and appearances, it needs to incorporate this new information into its folk taxonomy of human differences. This is precisely how we came to recognize the racial groups we do today in the United States. Our taxonomy is derived from the information available to, and the attitudes of, Europeans during the period of exploration and imperialism. Beginning in the 1400s, European exploration, done largely by sea, made contact with new peoples on the edges of continents—western Africa, India, the Far East, North America, and the Caribbean. Europeans thus began to acquire some appreciation of the degree of human variation in the world, but their sample was limited—a little here, a little there. And since the peoples they contacted were so widely separated geographically, they were bound to appear quite distinct in physical appearance and cultural behavior. It understandably looked to Europeans as if the people of the world came in a small number of distinct varieties.

Furthermore, much of the reason for exploration was the acquisition of new territories, of spices, gems, and other material goods, and of labor. So there was a built-in attitude about the peoples contacted: They were seen as at least "less civilized" than Europeans, sometimes even as "less human." (After all, went the explorers' thinking, it was the Europeans who found *them!*) Their "purpose" was to be exploited (not always in an "evil" fashion, but exploited nonetheless) for the benefit of the civilized world. To justify the exploitation of those peoples, these attitudes were reinforced by explaining the differences in terms of the newly emerging sciences of evolution and anthropology. The categories and those attitudes toward them became a fixture of Western culture.

To be sure, when I say "justify" and "were reinforced," I don't necessarily mean consciously. These things occurred gradually, as do most cultural changes, in order that the various parts of culture—the material parts as well as the abstract parts—can be consistent with one another. But so important were these worldwide economic relations to Europe that such attitudes, and their incorporation into current science, seem almost inevitable.

Linnaeus, for example, who founded the science of biological taxonomy, correctly placed humans with the other primates and gave us the name *Homo sapiens*. But he also divided us up into five subspecies or races: Americans, Europeans, Asians, Africans, and a catchall for mostly legendary humans, Wild Men. Sound familiar? And in keeping with the cultural context of his time, Linnaeus freely mixed, in his descriptions of each race, biological, cultural, and "psychological" factors. For instance, the European race was described as fair, sanguine (cheerful), brawny, gentle, and inventive, with yellow or brown hair and blue eyes. They were covered with clothes and governed by laws. On the other hand, the African race he described as black, phlegmatic (sluggish), relaxed, with black, frizzled hair, silky skin, and flat noses. Africans were crafty, negligent, anointed with grease, and governed by caprice (whim).

You can clearly see in those descriptions both a tendency to generalize (from what we now see as inadequate data) and to reflect the cultural attitudes of Europe at the time. Even Charles Darwin was not immune from being a product of his culture. While stating in no uncertain terms in *The Descent of Man* (1871) that all humans are members of the same species and have descended from a common ancestor, he nonetheless says, referring to the people of Tierra del Fuego and other "savages":

> For my own part I would as soon be descended from [a monkey or a baboon] as from a savage who delights to torture his enemies, offers up bloody sacrifices, practises infanticide without remorse, treats his wives like slaves, knows no decency, and is haunted by the grossest superstitions.

From this folk taxonomy have our current racial classification, and many of our current attitudes, descended. And though we can objectively understand how such taxonomies come about, they can—especially in scientific societies like ours—lead to two related problems.

The first is that such folk categories, seeing as how they are derived from and are part of our world view, take on a reality of their own, beyond their inherent reality. Thinking, as we do, that we base our cultural practices on practical, rational, scientific principles, it is only natural for us to grow up assuming that these racial categories *must* reflect such reasoning; that is, that they must be categories that exist in the real world and have a concrete basis. Thus we infer real differences between groups of people we classify as belonging to different races. As I hope I have shown, variation does exist, but it does not assort itself into nice, neat clusters.

This poses a real dilemma for us these days. For while we are trying to rid ourselves of our racial prejudices (and we all, as part of this culture, have them), we are unable to ignore those historical categories, because we think of them as more than just parts of our particular cultural heritage. Nor should we ignore them, for we have made determinations about people's educational, economic, and occupational opportunities based on their racial background. To overcome that, we need to do such things as keep track of how many people from each category are getting jobs, are entering college, and so on.

Though it would be nice simply to purge such ideas from our minds, in the practical world that won't work. The ideas are too much a part of our society, and they have for too long been the basis of many socioeconomic policies, decisions, and attitudes. I have, needless to say, no solution. But a first step, I think, might be just what anthropology is trying to do, just what I have described: understand exactly what these folk taxonomies are and what they do and don't mean.

Even though these kinds of problems are "logical" and understandable, some others are not. These come about when the distinction between biological differences and cultural categories is intentionally confused for the purpose of subjugating a group of people. There are countless examples, but almost all take the following form: The "race" in power in a society tries to show that certain biological characteristics of the racial groups not in power "prove" the inherent inferiority of those races. Thus their social position is determined not by society but is "predetermined" by their genes. It is a clever and often quite effective way of rationalizing and stabilizing a current social, political, and economic situation.

So over the years, and even today, brains are measured, intelligence tests given, fertility data gathered—all aimed at proving that members of a particular race "deserve" to be where they are because they are less intelligent or less fertile (and therefore less "fit"). Darwin must be rolling over in his grave to see his idea so misused! For a detailed discussion of such abuses, you can do no better than the book by Gould I mentioned, *The Mismeasure of Man*. But let me expand a little on two general categories.

First—and one of the most galling to evolutionary scientists—is the idea that certain groups, because of their cultural level, are less evolved. Again, there are lots of examples, but one of the most

Tasmanians.

striking is the treatment of the natives of Tasmania. Living in a Stone Age culture when discovered by Europeans, they were judged to be at a lower evolutionary level than the Europeans, with the result that they, and their culture, were persecuted to extinction. They were even hunted for sport!

This sort of thing morally outrages most people. But we must at the same time delve further into the basis for the behavior. Specifically, why do some societies have complex cultures, while others live in the Stone Age? The answer is not evolutionary level. Such differences are explained by the principles of adaptation and by the concept of *diffusion*.

With regard to adaptation, you recall that a society bases its cultural system (to include its material culture) on its world view. This in turn is a reflection of the kind of environment in which a group lives, in combination with their particular cultural history. Simply put, a society uses what they have on hand to provide them with what they need. They can use only what raw materials nature supplies. They can acquire and use only those they have the technology for. They don't waste time and energy securing items that are useless to them.

Furthermore, a society relies on contact with other societies for the majority of its cultural items. It has been estimated that only 10 percent of a society's cultural "inventory" originated within that society. The other 90 percent came from other cultures. Items *diffuse* from their culture of origin to others, which "borrow" them and adapt them to their own needs. Thus a population isolated from much contact with others is left very much to its "own devises." This explains the Stone Age culture of the Tasaday, thought to have been isolated for some 2000 years. On the other hand, cultures that change quickly are ones that have ample contact with other peoples. We find farming, cities, and writing so early in the Middle East because that area was a major migration route since the days of *Homo habilis!* People living in that area came into contact with numerous other cultural systems, and this provided raw materials and impetus for change.

But in addition, this idea of "simple" and "complex" cultures is itself oversimplified. For when we look at even the least "complex" society, we still see a group of people superbly adapted to their environment through the use of innovative, creative cultural ideas and artifacts. It is only when we set up a comparison, from our cultural viewpoint, that these terms have meaning.

The second "mismeasure" concerns the relative intelligence of races. I mentioned the measuring of brains, done in South Africa, for example, aimed at showing that a given race has smaller brains and so is dumber. That's clearly just bad science, for we know that brain size within the normal human range (about 1000 cm^3 to 2000 cm^3) has no correlation with intelligence. But what about more "scientific" measures of intellectual ability, like IQ tests?

In the United States there is an average of 15 points difference in the IQ of white and black children. This statistic is inarguable.

But the cause of this difference has been attributed by some to a genetically based difference in intellectual ability between persons of these two races. One author even claimed that the races possessed different *kinds* of intelligence.

Now think about that for a minute. First of all, such claims are biological; but are those races biological categories? Of course not; they're folk taxonomies. Moreover, do IQ tests measure some kind of innate intelligence? They certainly may point out some biologically based learning disability, but in general IQ tests measure the ability to take IQ tests! I don't mean that as sarcastically as it sounds. I simply mean that IQ tests test knowledge and reasoning ability, which have largely been acquired through culture. Thus differences in IQ reflect for the most part various differences in cultural background: access to knowledge when young, encouragement to learn, quality of education, and so on. Looked at this way, is it surprising that American black kids, on the average, don't score as high as the average American white kid? And this interpretation is supported when white kids from poverty areas are compared to affluent black kids. You can guess how the IQ scores compare then.

Finally, it has been suggested by some that whites possess intellectual abilities geared toward problem solving and abstract reasoning, while the abilities of blacks are focused on memorization, rote learning, and trial-and-error experience. This argument denies to a large number of people the very abilities—to solve problems, to formulate abstractions and generalizations—that are a hallmark of our species. In an evolutionary sense, that claim makes no sense.

Not everyone who makes such claims is a racist or a bigot. Many are sincere, dedicated researchers. And no legitimate research should be stifled just because it may point out something unpopular or may be perverted and misused by less well meaning people. *Any* knowledge can be misused. But when scientific-sounding research is as scientifically poor as some of these studies on race and IQ, it is particularly dangerous and open to misinterpretation and abuse. We must be alert and critical of such studies. We should never ignore them because we don't like what they say; nor should we simply accept them because they "sound" like science. One of my goals in this book is to impart to you some of these critical skills and the desire to use them.

"Race" is a difficult enough problem. But there are two other areas of human variation that we should also note briefly and are also sources of scientific, social, and moral controversy.

GENDER AND HEALTH

Our species has, I trust you recall, two sexes. These are two real, distinct biological categories. Males and females differ because of the presence or absence of a whole chromosome, made up of hundreds of genes. Specifically, females have a pair of X chromosomes, consisting of genes concerned with female characteristics as well as some others for traits like color vision and blood clotting. Males have one X chromosome (because they need those other genes) and one Y chromosome. The Y is not the other member of a pair of Xs. It is a separate chromosome, smaller than the X and made up of different genes—mostly genes for male characteristics. Unlike the situation with "racial" groups, which have no distinct biological identity, with sex we clearly have two genetically distinct units and thus the possibility of all sorts of physical and maybe even mental differences besides the physical ones we're all aware of.

A good deal of current research is looking into the possibility of such differences. For instance, there is some evidence that the brains of men and women may function differently. Males, on the average, may have better spatial reasoning skills, and females, on the average, may be better at linguistic skills.

Some researchers also contend that the brains of females are better at communicating between their right and left halves. The right side of our cerebral cortex is concerned with things like spatial associations, the left half with language. Some evidence exists that females have more integration between those functions and therefore make more conceptual connections between visual and lingusitic items. Males, on the other hand, tend to be specialized for one or the other function. These and other examples are examined in detail in the entertaining book by Durden-Smith and De Simone, *Sex and the Brain*. Such research, it should be pointed out, is still in its earliest stages.

Real differences, however, are not the problem. They exist, whether we like them or not, and it's important that we understand what differences we are, and are not, dealing with in the first place. Rather, the problem is what we, as cultural beings, *do* with those differences. What matters are our cultural variations on the biological themes, our gender identity and role within the cultural system.

These ideas—how we feel about the social position and cultural roles of men and women—vary from society to society. Among the Dani, women are, in a sense, possessions. In our society, women run for public office. Hutterite women can hold no official office in a colony, but, I discovered, they exert a great deal of influence over colony social and economic decisions. Gender identity and role vary to fit in with the workings of a given cultural system.

In our society at this time, for example, we are trying to change our sexual identities and roles. Traditionally, women in American society were relegated to such roles as homemakers, nurses and secretaries, roles viewed as merely "support" occupations. Educational opportunities were limited, and it was not until 1920 that women in the United States could vote. We are currently sensitive about anything, no matter how scientifically sound, that suggests any sort of sexual differences, especially if it concerns intellect or behavior. That is because the previous social order so often invoked purported biological differences as justification for its narrowly defined sex roles.

For example, some of the same people who were, with predetermined conclusions, busily measuring brains of various races were doing the same with the brains of men and women. Women, being on the average smaller and shorter then men, have smaller brains. We know now that this has no relation to intelligence. But if you think it does (as people did in the past), and, especially, if you *want* to think it does, the data from such research can be a power social tool for rationalizing and stabilizing the relative positions of women and men.

This confusion of the biological and the cultural is still an area of social, ethical, and conceptual controversy today. As with race, though, one important step toward a solution is to understand just what differences do and don't exist and what they do and don't mean in terms of potentials and limitations. Only then can we culturally accommodate the differences we can't do something about and try to overcome those we can.

A similar problem exists with regard to the cultural positions of persons handicapped by some illness, disability, or genetic abnormality. The addition of this topic to the consideration of human differences was suggested by a former student, who is also a case in point.

This young women had cerebral palsy. Confined to a wheelchair, she had very little control over her movements and required almost total care. Her speech was so slurred that it was intelligible only after a good deal of practice. What's interesting is that many people, she told me and I sensed, assumed that her mental state matched her physical one—that she was as intellectually handicapped as she was physically handicapped.

That turns out in this case to be anything but true. This woman is an intelligent and gifted writer (accomplishing that by means of a word processor manipulated with a rod attached to a helmet—what she calls her "handy cap"). But that's not the point. The point is, as with the other things we've discussed, that it is easy for us to confuse the biological with the cultural or one biological feature with another.

Indeed, handicaps, although real biologically, are treated differently in different cultural systems. Albinos, for instance, are feared and often killed in some societies and revered as specially blessed in others. The mentally retarded are outcasts in some groups but thought in others to harbor hidden talents and knowledge. Some physical handicaps are minor inconveniences among some people but serious problems among others.

Remember that culture is an environment, and the "fitness" of a trait is measured only with regard to a particular environmental situation. My nearsightedness is easily accommodated by my culture; I wear glasses and assume that they put me at no particular disadvantage with regard to passing on my genes. But imagine a nearsighted *Homo erectus!* Or even a nearsighted person in a recent foraging society. In fact, visual defects are found at a much lower frequency among groups like the Eskimos than among industrialized peoples. Such defects have clearly been undergoing negative selection in such populations.

So with handicaps of various sorts, the important thing, again, is to understand what they do and don't mean biologically and behaviorally and then to accommodate or overcome them in the context of a particular cultural system. The woman I mentioned before—as part of our attempt to achieve equality for all our citizens and to help each person live up to his or her potential—now lives in her own apartment, aided by a number of part-time assistants and by some technical devices that allow her to use the phone, open the door, and so on. Our cultural environment has come to acknowledge the relative limitations of her disability along with the potentials still available to her and is beginning to make both a part of the cultural system as a whole. Along with this comes—though slowly at times—changes in our cultural attitudes about the meaning of such differences.

This kind of understanding—of handicaps, of the sexes, of "race"—is interesting in itself. But it is also vital, given the ways a lack of understanding can be and has been misused and the human suffering that results. As Stephen Jay Gould says:

> We pass through this world but once. Few tragedies can be more extensive than the stunting of life, few injustices deeper than the denial of an opportunity to strive or even hope, by a limit imposed from without, but falsely indentified as lying within.

SUMMARY

Our species is a variable one; we exhibit many physical and chemical polymorphisms. An important current focus in anthropology is the study of the genetic bases, geographical distributions, and adaptive significance of our polymorphisms.

A one-time focus of anthropological studies on human variation is no more: the attempt to define, classify, and count human racial groups. We understand now that on a biological level, races—as clearly defined, genetically unique populations—don't exist. Such units are constructs of a particular cultural system; they are folk taxonomies. As such, they have meaning within that system but should not be taken as universal, biologically meaningful units.

A major social problem that arises out of this confusion of the biological and the cultural is the misuse of biological ideas in an attempt to rationalize and maintain cultural categories, attitudes about them, and socioeconomic hierarchies based on them. This problem can manifest itself as out-and-out racism and bigotry, but it can also simply be a "natural" need on the part of people to order their world and maintain their style of life. In either case, it can be a dangerous and harmful problem. Overcoming it is dependent on understanding biological differences, be they "racial," sexual, or health-related, and accommodating or overcoming them culturally so as to provide all persons the opportunity for equality and the chance to realize their potentials. Though anthropologists are not in the business of telling other societies how to arrange their cultures, these goals don't seem too much to ask on behalf of all human beings.

NOTES, REFERENCES, AND READINGS

Many fine books are available on the general topic of human variation and race. Two of my favorites are Stephen Molnar's *Races, Types, and Ethnic Groups* (Englewood Cliffs, N.J.: Prentice-Hall, 1975) and

Kenneth A. R. Kennedy's *Human Variation in Space and Time* (Dubuque, Iowa: Brown, 1976).

Two short but informative books on the genetic bases of human characteristics are *Elements of Human Genetics* (2d ed., Menlo Park, Calif.: W. A. Benjamin, 1977) by L. L. Cavalli-Sforza and *Human Genetics* (2d ed., Englewood Cliffs, N.J.: Prentice-Hall, 1969) by Victor A. McKusick. For a nice discussion on the relation between environment and polymorphisms, see D. F. Robert's *Climate and Human Variability* 2d ed., Menlo Park, Calif.: Cummings, 1978).

The argument that race is a folk taxonomy rather than a biological reality is covered by the articles in *The Concept of Race* (New York: Macmillan, 1964), edited by Ashley Montagu. I particularly recommend the pieces by Brace, Ehrlich and Holm, and Barnicot. The sad and disturbing story of how racism and bigotry brought about the extinction of the Tasmanians is covered in *The Last of the Tasmanians* (New York: Barnes & Noble Books, 1974) by David Davies. The most famous (or, perhaps, infamous) work proposing racial differences in intelligence is Arthur R. Jensen's "How Much Can We Boost IQ and Scholastic Achievement?" in *Harvard Educational Review* 39, no. 1 (Winter 1969). This is a long, scientific-sounding, and potentially convincing argument—until you apply to it modern genetics, statistics, and anthropology. Then, as I've outlined in the chapter, it falls utterly apart.

The new studies on various differences between men and women, including those on mental differences, are entertainingly discussed in Jo Durden-Smith and Diane DeSimone's *Sex and the Brain* (New York: Arbor House, 1983). An older work that covers the same topic (as it was understood then) and includes ideas about the cultural ramifications of sexual dimorphisms is Ashley Montagu's *The Natural Superiority of Women* (New York: Macmillan, 1974). Though he's dead serious about the natural (biological and psychological) superiority of women, his goals in the book are to show that "natural superiority does not imply social inequality" and to "bring the sexes closer together." The relation of the sexes in anthropological perspective, examining sex roles in different types of cultures, is the topic of Ernestine Friedl's *Women and Men: An Anthropologist's View* (New York: Holt, Rinehart and Winston, 1975).

Finally, I strongly recommend the book by Stephen Jay Gould, *The Mismeasure of Man* (New York: Norton, 1981). It is about the attempts to classify people according to intelligence and how such classification maintains social inequalities and limits human potential. The quotes I used from that book are on pages 32, 35, and 28–29.

chapter 14

Culture Change
Processes and Problems

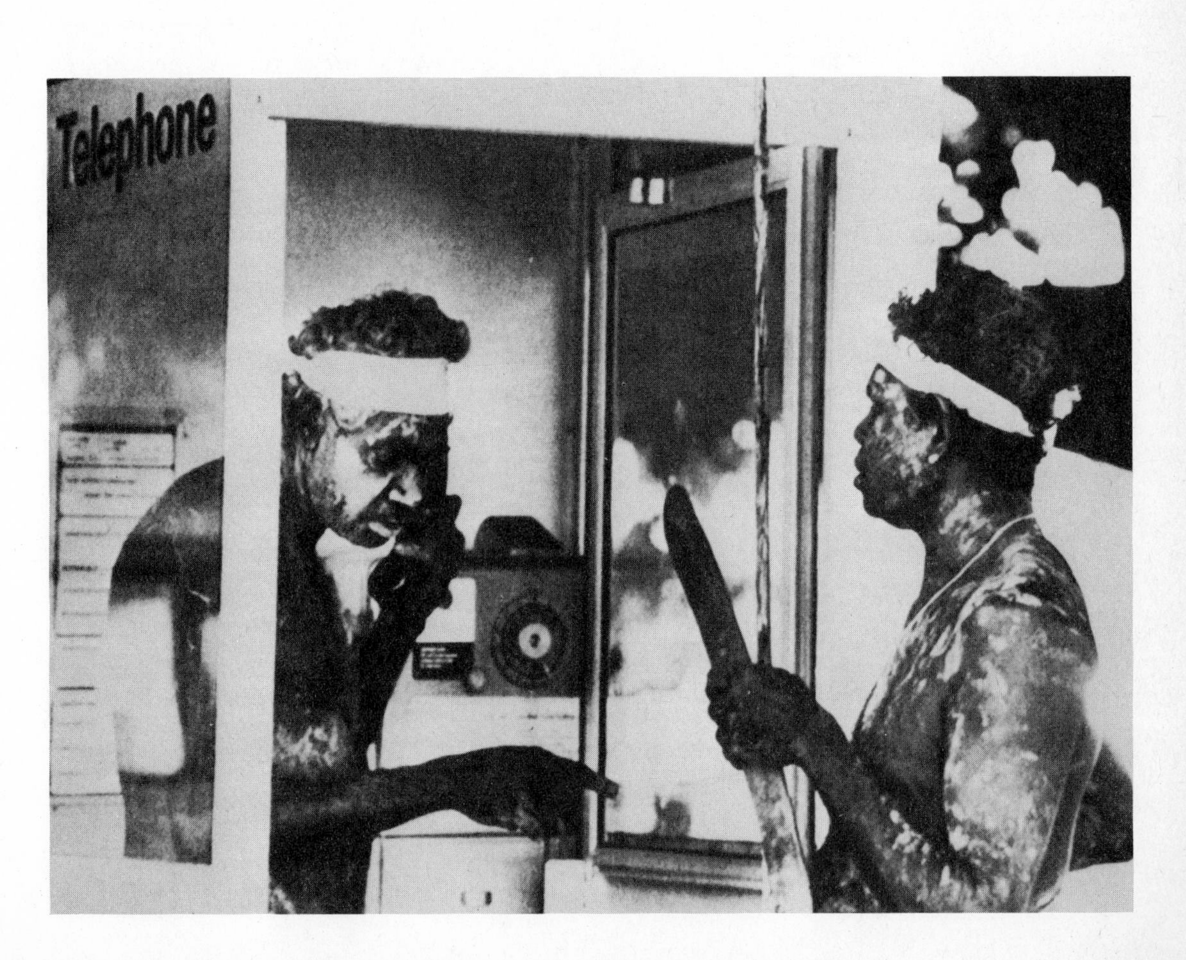

It can be easy to get the idea—from things like my ''filter'' diagram—that a cultural system is a static, unchanging set of complex relationships and that if any one thing changes, the whole system will fall apart. Of course, as you realize now, that's not the case. Cultures change all the time. To speak of culture as a ''system'' is to say that at any one point in time, all the facets must operate together. None can conflict with any other, and none can be inconsistent with the system as a whole or with the world view on which it is based. When something does change, other parts of the system must change to keep pace. As you can imagine, for most cultures this process of realignment and ''fine tuning'' is always going on. *Something* is always changing. And change is taking place these days at an ever-increasing rate.

It is important to understand just how cultures change and what sorts of processes are involved. In this way we can explain changes in the past. We can understand changes that are going on now. We can trace the cultural evolution that links past and present. And we can attempt to ''predict'' the effects of certain changes in the future.

THE PROCESSES OF CULTURE CHANGE

Every culture change—every new idea or new artifact—must start somewhere. Thus the bases of all culture change are the related processes of *invention* and *discovery*. Discovery is the realization of some natural ''law,'' be it about nature itself or about the nature of human behavior. Invention refers to the ''manufacture'' of an artifact, whether concrete or abstract, that puts that idea into action. For example, people had known about fires, which occur spontaneously in nature, for millions of years. But eventually someone discovered the nature of fire—its properties, how it starts, animals' reactions to it—and was able to invent ways to make it, maintain it, and use it. Similarly, someone may discover a new way of thinking about the interaction among human beings—for instance, the idea that each human possesses the right to life, liberty, and happiness.

That person may then proceed to invent a social system to implement the idea, to put it into action in the everyday, real world.

Of course, as I noted before, you can't expect every society to discover and invent everything. Thus the second process of culture change involves the spreading around of invented artifacts, the giving and taking of ideas and things among different societies. This is called *diffusion,* and as mentioned, it is responsible for some 90 percent of a society's cultural inventory. Though we are, by our very nature, an inventive, creative species, we nonetheless rely heavily on borrowed items for bringing about adaptive changes in our societies. And "forced borrowing" can bring about other sorts of changes, whether we like them or not.

This emphasis on diffusion is sometimes hard for us to grasp. This is because once an item has been borrowed, it is modified and adapted to our culture and thus becomes part of our cultural system. We don't think about, and may not realize, the fact that it did not originate here. The classic attempt to get this point across comes from anthropologist Ralph Linton in an article titled "One Hundred Percent American." Here are excerpts, just to give you an idea:

> Our solid American citizen awakens in a bed built on a pattern which originated in the Near East but which was modified in Northern Europe before it was transmitted to America. He throws back covers made from cotton, domesticated in India, or linen, domesticated in the Near East, or wool from sheep, also domesticated in the Near East, or silk, the use of which was discovered in China. . . . He takes off his pajamas, a garment invented in India, and washes with soap invented by the ancient Gauls. He then shaves, a masochistic rite which seems to have been derived from either Sumer or ancient Egypt. . . . On his way to breakfast he stops to buy a paper, paying for it with coins, an ancient Lydian invention. . . . As he absorbs the accounts of foreign troubles he will, if he is a good conservative citizen, thank a Hebrew deity in an Indo-European language that he is 100 percent American.

There are two other processes of culture change, sometimes listed separately, that I think are forms of the two basic processes just listed. The first is *acculturation.* This can be thought of as "rapid diffusion." It comes about when a society, under the influence of a more dominant society, quickly takes on aspects of the dominant society's cultural system. This can occur voluntarily or by force.

An example of voluntarily acculturation is the phenomenon known as *cargo cults*. Peoples on a number of South Pacific islands

Members of a cargo cult march with wooden rifles.

came into brief contact with industrialized technologies during World War II or even earlier. Generally liking what they saw, they wanted some of that technology, which they called—borrowing the English word—"cargo." Once the war was over, the islands were left pretty much as they were. To get the cargo back, peoples on these islands took on many of the trappings of Western culture as they remembered them.They began to use Western words like *cargo*. They started to dress like the soldiers they knew and to march around and carry rifles carved from wood. They worshiped sacred objects—old helmets, dog tags, and other military and personal items the soldiers left behind. And they created gods to whom they prayed for the return of the cargo. One of the most famous of these was named "John Frum."

Acculturation can also take place when one society is forced to take on the culture of a more dominant society as a result of conquest. Examples of this are, sad to say, numerous. One would be the acculturation of Native Americans. Another example is the slaves taken from their African societies and made to be a part of European and American cultures.

Another special form of change is *revolution*. This, in a way, is a form of "rapid invention," for it comes about as a result of changes from within a society. We usually think of the word in a violent context, and, indeed, many revolutions are violent—the American, French, and Russian revolutions come immediately to mind. But they can also be peaceful, a strong cultural statement by a portion of a population that in the end affects the whole society. The Anabaptist "revolution," although it led to violence against the Anabaptists, began as a peaceful attempt on the part of some persons to change certain aspects of their social system. The Protestant Reformation is a similar example. Even the social changes we saw in this country in the 1960s—the trends toward greater individual freedom of expression and more tolerance of varying lifestyles—were a result in part of a strong statement by America's young. The statement caught on and has affected our entire cultural system.

These processes, of course, should not be thought of as independent and separate. The "idea" for an invented change may have diffused from elsewhere. For example, it is said that the French Revolution was influenced in part by the ideals and success of the American Revolution. A Cherokee Indian named Sequoyah invented a writing system for the Cherokee language, stimulated by the fact that he had heard that the white men had a means for inscribing their language. And many symbols of the 1960s here—modes of dress, popular music, hairstyles, and slang expressions—were borrowed from English youth: the "fab" Beatles with their Carnaby Street fashions and "all you need is love" outlook on life.

These are the processes that bring about culture change. But there are other questions: In terms of the history of culture, can we perceive any overall trends? Any general rules for change? Any particular direction that culture change takes? Indeed, it was the search for answers to questions like these that characterized much of the early history of anthropology.

CULTURAL EVOLUTION

By the last third of the nineteenth century, largely as a result of the work of Charles Darwin, the idea was pretty well accepted that we had evolved from other creatures and that that evolution had taken place over millions of years. Furthermore, because of the extensive exploration that had been taking place for the previous 350 years, Europeans and Americans had a great deal of information about the vast cultural diversity that existed among the world's peoples.

It became only natural to attempt to explain this diversity in terms of the new evolutionary framework. In other words, if we had evolved biologically, we certainly had evolved culturally. As I discussed, there were attempts to account for "racial" variation in an evolutionary context. Why not account for cultural variation in a similar fashion, searching for general trends and directions?

One of the first schools of thought in this regard is generally associated with the English anthropologist Edward B. Tylor (1832–1917) and the American Lewis Henry Morgan (1818–1881). They have been called *classical evolutionists*. Their idea was that all societies pass through the same series of evolutionary stages. These stages they termed "savagery," "barbarism," and "civilization." The savage stage was characterized by a foraging subsistence pattern; barbarism by domestication, pottery, and the beginnings of metallurgy; and civilization by the invention of phonetic alphabets. Of course, each of these stages could be represented by existing societies, and thus the "obvious" explanation for the diversity of culture was simply that some societies had progressed farther than had others in the scheme of evolution.

You should be able to see some problems with this idea. First, it required that each society, as it evolved, independently invent the same innovations and artifacts. Second, it set up a predetermined scheme into which new data had sometimes to be forced. And it assumed that the goal of cultural evolution—the "highest" stage—was that exhibited by the society to which these men belonged. It was, in short, quite ethnocentric. In this regard it mirrored many of the studies of racial classification going on at the same time.

As if to answer that problem about independent invention, a second school arose, the *diffusionist* school. I have already mentioned the importance of diffusion to culture change. But this school, popular in the first decades of the present century, oversimplified the process. Its claim was that cultural innovation arose in a few centers of culture (or even just one), then spread (diffused) to the rest of the world. One English group, enamored of ancient Egypt, supposed that it had been the source of almost all culture except for the simplest of hunting tools. Everything we think of as cultural—from artifacts to social institutions—had been invented in ancient Egypt and had spread from there.

There were, however, less extreme forms of diffusionism. One, basically German, proposed a number of early cultural centers from which cultural traditions spread in ever-widening circles. This is called the *Kulturkreise* ("cultural circle") idea. It explains the modern presence of "less advanced" societies by saying that they failed to acquire the cultural innovations of the "circle" probably as a result of being pushed into out-of-the-way geographical regions by more advanced populations.

Again, you should see the problem here of a predetermined scheme—not derived from the data but set up beforehand—into which the data are fit. Moreover, we can see (although maybe they couldn't then) that culture shows far too much variation to be accounted for by having spread from just a few centers. And—the opposite of the previous problem—this idea doesn't give enough credit to independent invention. It assumes that most people are not capable of coming up with many new inventions.

An American school, associated with the famous Franz Boas (1858–1942) and called the *American historical school*, attempted to overcome some of the objections to the previous ideas. This school of thought rejected the concept of some overall evolutionary scheme, proposing instead that *both* independent invention and diffusion were important to culture change. And it added a new idea—that cultures are related adaptively to the environments in which they are found.

But the American school still oversimplified by attempting to describe a limited number of "culture areas" from which traditions spread steadily outward. It also simplified the relation of culture and environment, proposing that environment *determined* the nature of culture. Finally, it failed to include the idea that borrowed items are *selected* by the receiving society, which can accept them or reject them and which usually modifies them to fit its particular cultural system. (However, we shouldn't forget that it was Boas who first emphasized the necessity of fieldwork and the firsthand collection of data in anthropology.)

We have now gotten away from the search for some overall evolutionary scheme and from the idea that *either* invention *or* diffusion must play the key role. Culture change, as we've discussed, relies on both invention and diffusion, and the nature of a particular cultural system can be explained only by understanding how it is adaptively related to—but not determined by—the natural *and* cultural environments in which it exists.

In this context, culture change is analogous to biological evolution. Invention is like mutation—the origin of new variation. A mutation spreads through heredity, a new cultural innovation through diffusion. But the success of a mutation is dependent on its adaptive value: If it's useful, it's selected for; if not, it's selected against. The same holds true for cultural inventions: They are not just blindly accepted; they undergo selection with regard to their value and "fit" to a particular cultural system. The difference here—and it's an important one—lies in the fact that cultural innovations usually arise through conscious, purposeful thought, while biological mutations are random. That added dimension—human motivation—must not be ignored.

The foregoing does not mean we can't continue to look for regularities in culture change. Julian Steward (1902–1972), for example, sought to find cause-and-effect relations for cultural change, based on his assumption that similar environments and historical events produced similar types of cultures. The associations we discussed between subsistence pattern and other features of culture derive to a great extent from Steward's *cultural ecology* idea. At about the same time, Leslie White (1900–1975) proposed the idea for a trend in culture change that had cultural systems seeking to maximize, through technological innovation, the efficiency with which they used energy. He thus saw technology as determining the nature of a cultural system's social and ideological aspects. And more recently, Marvin Harris, in *Cannibals and Kings,* combines these other two approaches as he looks for similarities among societies resulting from cycles of production intensification, followed by the depletion of resources, followed by the invention of new, more efficient means of production.

CHANGE IN THE MODERN WORLD

Although culture change may be a "natural" phenomenon, it can present problems, especially during acculturation or when a society is trying to realign and maintain its system in the face of some change. Such situations are becoming increasingly frequent as the world in which we live becomes increasingly smaller. I saw an example of such a problem among the Hutterites.

In the summer of 1983, ten years after my first visit, I went back to some Hutterite colonies to collect more data and to get some photographs and videotape footage. This time I visited two American colonies, and the differences I perceived between the Canadian and U.S. Hutterites, and the difference of a decade, were striking.

First of all, it has been said (and it was my impression, though based on a small sample) that the U.S. Hutterites tend to be a little less open and a little more suspicious of outsiders than those in Canada. This may be because during World War I, many Hutterites who resisted the military draft on the grounds of their religion were jailed for their beliefs. In fact two Hutterites died in prison as a result of maltreatment. In addition, the Hutterites felt that the manner in which their colonies were being taxed in the United States was unfair. As a result, most Hutterites now live in Canada, where they are not drafted and where some tax arrangements have been made. Moreover, I sensed, although I can't document it, that there is more jealousy on the part of the non-Hutterites in the United States over the large and prosperous tracts of land that the Hutterites in the United States own and the large-scale farming operations they are able to maintain. This may be because land is somewhat more plentiful in Canada. At any rate, one of the two colonies I visited this last time was decidedly unwilling to let me do anything more than talk to one young man and take a few still photographs. This was in contrast to the Canadian colonies in 1973, who allowed me to get as "personal" as to take fingerprints and ask all sorts of questions about their families and individual histories.

Besides the differences of politics and location, the years have clearly brought other changes. It seems to me that the Hutterites are having a harder and harder time maintaining their way of life within the colony while at the same time participating in the modern Western economic system. The colonies are dependent on the income brought in from the sale of produce and, to a lesser extent, of handmade goods and of services such as farm equipment repair. Hutterites must be, and are, well versed in the ins and outs of the market system.

At the same time, as a result, they must try even harder to keep the outside out, to keep from having all these connections with society at large from influencing their young people and thus the continuation of their culture. This has become a serious problem. The young man I mentioned had, in fact, left the colony for a time to attend college. He had returned because he found himself unable to adapt to the kind of social existence found on the outside. He missed the security of the stable colony society. His sister, however, had left and had married a non-Hutterite. One of his brothers had also left, and a second brother I met—with styled hair, jeans instead of homespuns, and Nike running shoes—struck me as at least a potential candidate for leaving. Even the young man himself, though he had returned, was a little "different." He had an extensive library that reflected his continued interest in worldly matters normally outside the concerns of the colony. And he wore a wristwatch. This may seem rather inconsequential, but to the Hutterites, who gauge time more in terms of colony work than on some worldly scale, this was almost a sign of rebellion.

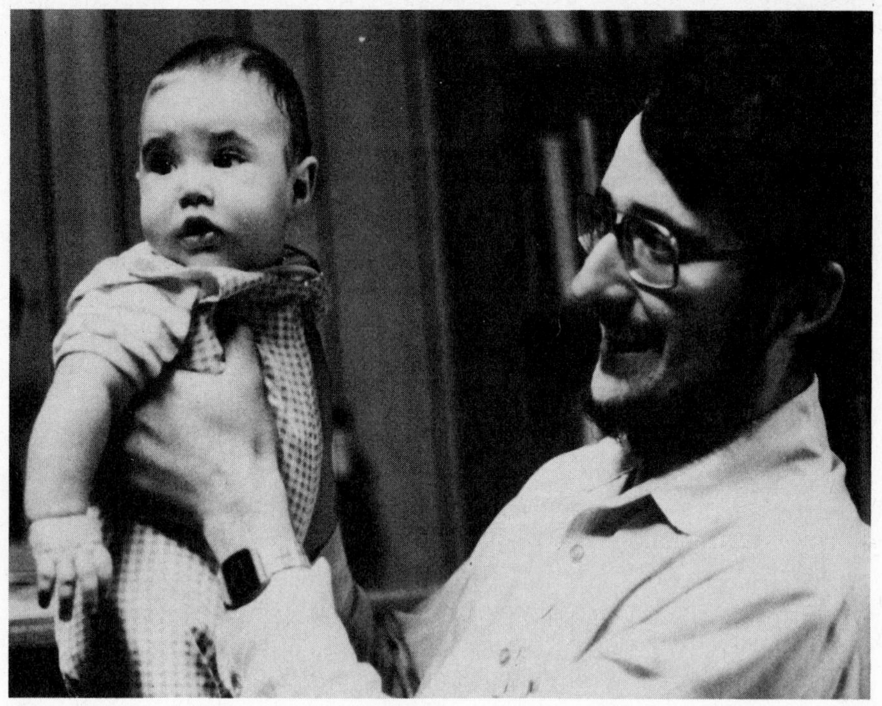

The next generation of Hutterites. Note the father's digital wristwatch.

Because keeping young people in the colony means literally the survival of the culture, the Hutterites were reluctant to talk about how many people left. I could get no hard data, but I have a distinct impression that the case of this one family is not unusual. After over 400 years of successfully maintaining their separation *from* the world while still being *in* it, they are now confronting a situation where that kind of separation seems impossible. On their solution to the problem rests the very future of their culture.

And as if to point out both the importance of the problem and a possible path out of it, we have the Society of Brothers. Founded in Germany in 1920, the Society leaders soon recognized their spiritual and social similarity to the descedants of the Anabaptists, especially the communal Hutterites. Over the next 50 years, the Society attempted to link up with the Hutterities but were denied a number of times. Finally, in 1974, certain differences were reconciled, and the Society officially became the Hutterian Society of Brothers. There are now four Society communities—in England, Pennsylvania, New York, and Connecticut.

Like the original Hutterites, the Society of Brothers lives communally, participating economically in, but socially and spiritually separate from, the outside. They farm, in an attempt to be as self-sufficient as possible, but their income stems from other things like book publishing and the manufacture of toys and devices for the handicapped. One of the differences that had caused the Hutterites not to accept them for so long is that young people in the Society attend public schools, and some go on to college. The reasons for this are twofold. First, again in an attempt at self-sufficiency, they are trying to staff their communities with their own physicians, dentists, teachers, and so on. This requires schooling and training best acquired on the outside.

But second, as I was told by a Society member, such freedoms given to young people tend to decrease the number of defectors. According to my Society informant, the Society loses far fewer people than do the ''Western Brethren,'' and this is one of the reasons. They feel, in fact, that if the Hutterites were less restrictive with their young people regarding contact with the outside, the young people would be less tempted to leave. Seeing how it is outside, they would choose colony life.

At the same time, though, I sense that even among the Society of Brothers, this can go too far. They are not without their defectors, and when a number of young people leave at the same time, or when a number from the same family leave, the parents are less willing to promote such free outside contact as attending college.

It is difficult to predict what will happen. In the meantime, with the Hutterites and the Brothers we have a ''living laboratory'' for culture change—right here within American society—and we can watch as these groups attempts to bring all aspects of their culture into line with the changes that are continually assaulting them and threatening the fabric of their lives.

As severe as these problems are for the Hutterites, however, not all societies even have the chance to exert some control over their culture change. In many cases change is forced upon a population by another, more powerful culture. One could get into all sorts of political and ideological arguments over whether some group is better or worse off after such a change. But from our cultural perspective and from what we've learned about cultural relativity, I think we can state that a people should at least have some say in the matter. This is not always the case.

We don't know, for example, what has become of the Dani. As I mentioned, the Indonesian government has closed off West Irian

Dani women with a government nurse.

to outsiders. But when last visited by Karl Heider in 1970, the Indonesians had brought a stop to warfare in the Grand Valley, and there was a government army and police post (inside which Dani were not permitted to carry their weapons), a first aid station, a landing field, a Catholic mission, a school, and lots of tourists. By then many Dani men were involved in building government roads in the Grand Valley, and many of the children were attending school and learning Indonesian. Many were also changing their religion. And, in a literal sense, the Dani were no longer of the Stone Age, as their wood and stone tools had been replaced with tools of steel. No matter what you think of the value of some of these changes, they were nonetheless imposed on the Dani from the outside, and, in the process, a culture has been lost.

We do know what's going on with the !Kung. In 1960 the !Kung of Namibia, a country controlled by the South African government, were settled in an area set aside for San peoples as part of South Africa's apartheid (racial separation) policy. There the people underwent what Richard Lee calls "directed social change." The men worked on road gangs and in workshops. The women spent their time with household chores, and the children went to school. Everyone was fed by the government. But this move to a sort of imposed welfare system has brought problems. In a society where everyone used to have something important to do, most men are now unemployed. Alcoholism and social violence are on the increase. And the !Kung are now involved in national and international politics.

Starting in 1966, the native peoples of Namibia began fighting for independence from South Africa under the South-West African People's Organization (SWAPO). To combat SWAPO, the South African government not only sent in its own troops but also recruited locals, and this included !Kung. Induced by good wages (up to $500 a month), the !Kung joined up in large numbers, for a war that few really understood and that involved the killing of the "enemy," who were some of their fellow native Namibians. Raids were even made over the border into neighboring Angola. Besides the obvious dangers of warfare and the problem of further divisions of native peoples, the pouring of large sums of money into the lives of the !Kung has led to an internal stratification (remember, these were once egalitarian people), with the consequent resentments and conflicts. Much of the money earned by the solidiers is spent on liquor, and fighting among soldiers on weekend passes has reached disturbing proportions. In a two-year period (1978–1980), Lee recorded seven homicides—a huge number for these "peaceful" people.

A !Kung man today.

This situation continues today, and predictions as to the future are risky at best. One interesting reaction on the part of the !Kung has been the movement of some families away from the government settlements and back into the traditional foraging areas, what Lee calls a "back to the bush movement." In independent Botswana, by the way, change for the !Kung there, though of course inevitable, is taking place more slowly, with far less influence from the government. And Botswana has to a great extent been able to stay out of the war in Namibia and Angola. But at any rate, the traditional !Kung way of life has been changed forever by changes imposed from the outside, with the risk of eradicating not only a culture but the people who practice it as well.

These, then, are the processes of culture change, some views on change in evolutionary perspective, and a look at some of the prospects and problems that change can pose. All these things must be understood as we attempt to solve some of the other problems that face us today as a species. For any solution will involve changes in cultures—changes that may have to be brought about rapidly and may be extensive. Let's end up with a brief look at some of these problems.

SUMMARY

Culture change takes place as the result of the interaction of invention and diffusion in their various forms. In this sense, culture change is like biological change, with its basis in the interaction of mutation and heredity. Moreover, as in natural selection, a new cultural item must undergo a selective process, its eventual inclusion into and role within a cultural system being determined by how well it serves that system and how well it fits into it. This analogy, of course, is not exact, in that people have a great deal of conscious control over the origin of new ideas, whereas mutations are random.

The simplistic search for overall trends and directions in culture change has been replaced by the recognition that culture and its changes are complicated affairs—complex cultural systems adapting a society to complex natural environments and to the cultural environment itself. Though we can continue to search for regularities—things like the connections between subsistence pattern, economic organization, kinship, and religion, or even broader things like Harris's ideas of production cycles—we must first understand individual situations. We must see how a particular culture interacts with its environments and how specific events affecting it have generated specific sorts of changes.

When changes occur—usually through the rapid forms of invention and diffusion—over which a society has little or no control, problems can arise. Change that is too rapid and extensive, especially if it is being controlled by some outside culture, cannot be gradually adpated to, and adopted into, a cultural system. All too often this leads to various degrees of human suffering. One current concern in anthropology is to try to aid people undergoing such rapid change—virtually inevitable in our world—and to advise societies that are in the position of having to bring about such change. We also advocate the rights of all people to have as much say as possible over the changes that will affect them.

NOTES, REFERENCES, AND READINGS

A number of good books are available on the general topic of culture change. One fairly short one that I recommend is Clyde M. Woods, *Culture Change* (Dubuque, Iowa: Brown, 1975). It covers the processes of change, outlines some of the important ideas about cultural evolution, and discusses the role of the anthropologist in advising about and even influencing the process of change in the modern world.

Ralph Linton's ''One Hundred Percent American'' first appeared in *The American Mercury* (1937). You can find it reprinted in many collections of anthropological readings.

The cargo cults are covered in the chapter by that name of Harris's *Cows, Pigs, Wars, and Witches,* referred to in earlier chapters. An article on the subject, ''Cargo Cults'' by Peter M. Worsley, appeared in the May 1959 *Scientific American*. And a book that covers the topic in the broad context of the place of South Pacific societies in the modern world is Edward Rice's *John Frum He Come* (Garden City, N.Y.: Doubleday, 1974).

The Society of Brothers is described in the Hostetler book on the Hutterites. An account of their history up to 1937, written by the wife of the group's founder, is *Torches Together* (Rifton, N.Y.: Plough Publishing House of the Woodcrest Service Committee, 1971), by Emmy Arnold.

Some discussion of recent changes imposed on the Dani can be found in Heider's *Grand Valley Dani,* cited earlier, and Richard Lee's

Dobe !Kung is the source for my description of that people's current situation.

Perhaps the most disturbing and moving account of what can happen to a people when outside change completely disrupts their lives is Colin Turnbull's *The Mountain People* (New York: Simon and Schuster, 1972). It is about the Ik of Uganda, whose culture and, according to Turnbull, ''humanity'' were utterly destroyed when they were forced to move from their homeland, where they were foragers, and to try to farm the steep slopes of some barren mountainsides.

chapter 15

State of the Species
The Edge of the Future

Any species, at any given moment, can be said to be living at the "edge" of its future. But for the human species, that image is, I think, particularly appropriate. Considering our current situation, we can see ourselves standing on the edge of a lush Eden of scientific, technological, medical, and social advances that can make all our lives longer and happier. Or we might be poised on the edge of a cliff, below us a deadly cauldron—a polluted, violent, nuclear nightmare.

Each of the prospects and problems facing us as we stand on the edge of our future is worthy of volumes, and volumes have been written on them. What I would like to do here is simply introduce some of these items and briefly discuss them within the theme and context we've been covering.

This is, of course, entirely appropriate in a book on anthropology, for two reasons. First, anything that deals with humans is relevant to this field. And these current problems, affecting as they do the entire species, are particularly relevant to a description of our modern state, what is often referred to as the "human condition."

Second, although no one would claim that anthropology could solve these problems, it is possible that the anthropological perspective might shed some new light on them, might expose some complex interrelationships not before apparent, might help articulate the causes of the problems, the understanding of which is a first step toward a solution.

But another word of caution: All the problems facing the human species today are so important, so current, and so pressing that they are being discussed not only in the scientific forum but in the forums of politics, religion, and philosophy as well. Thus it may be that striving for a totally objective opinion on them is an unattainable goal. Remember, under any circumstances, science is a part of culture.

So allow me to play it safe and offer what follows as a personal essay of sorts—by a scientist striving for objectivity and truth, but also by a person and, as such, a member of a culture, an "age set," a socioeconomic class, and a certain political-philosophical background. I therefore present this essay to stimulate discussion, to show how all human matters may be considered in the holistic anthropological perspective, and to suggest some ways in which this perspective might help in solving those problems.

At the center of any cultural system is world view. One word that might describe the world view of today's dominant cultures is *scientific*. Whether engaged in "hard" science, one of the "soft" sciences, or just the processes of rational thinking, all are based on the use of the scientific method in one form or another. And that affects the view of the people of those cultures in terms of their relations with the world and their potential control over it.

A symbol of scientific knowledge and control in our modern world is Albert Einstein's famous formula, $E = mc^2$. Most people are familiar with the formula. Few know what it means. And fewer still fully comprehend it. I guess I fall into the middle group. What the formula means is that in a given amount of matter, there is potential energy, equal in number of units to the speed of light squared. The speed of light is 186,000 miles per second, so we're talking about a lot of energy!

Recently, that formula has taken on new implications, for we often see it, on magazine covers and other illustrations, superimposed over a picture of a mushroom-shaped cloud or an orange fireball. But it's not the formula itself, of course, or what it means that is the problem. Nor is it the fact that we have learned how to get that energy out. The problem is one of the things we've learned to do with all that energy. And, mercifully, we've only done it twice—though, given the context, "only" here is pretty meaningless.

I refer, of course, to the atomic bombs used in 1945 on Hiroshima and Nagasaki. The bomb used on Hiroshima exploded with the power equivalent to 12,500 tons of TNT. In an instant, that bomb virtually destroyed an entire city and killed 100,000 people. Since then the arsenals of nuclear weapons, possessed by a half dozen countries, have grown and now total the equivalent of *20 billion tons* of TNT, about 1.6 million times the Hiroshima weapon.

We have long appreciated what such weapons can do in terms of their initial effects—the explosion, the fireball, and the blast wave—as well as longer-ranging effects from the radiation produced by a nuclear detonation. But when we apply our knowledge of ecological principles and interrelationships—the kind we discussed earlier—we now see two other results of nuclear warfare, results that in the long run are even more serious and terrifying than those we know so well from the bombings of Japan.

First, it has recently been hypothesized that the huge fires caused by the use of nuclear weapons would create enormous amounts of dense smoke. This smoke, full of particles, would rise into the Earth's atmosphere and block out the sun. The result would be what has been termed a "nuclear winter," a severe drop in the Earth's temperature leading, obviously, to the demise of any organism not adapted to cold conditions or to the year-round cold that such an event would cause.

There is evidence to support such an idea. In 1815 the Indonesian volcano of Tambora erupted with a gigantic explosion that shot tons of dust and ash into the Earth's atmosphere. This stuff was caught in the jet stream and by the summer of 1816 was spread throughout the skies of most of the Northern Hemisphere. It blocked out enough sunlight to cause unseasonable cold, which destroyed crops throughout Canada, Europe, and the United States. There was a blizzard in New England on June 6, for example, and many summer days there had highs of only 50 degrees Fahrenheit. It has been called "the summer that never was." The effect of even a "limited" nuclear war is hypothesized to be far greater than this.

Moreover, besides the purely biological effects, imagine, based on what we've discussed, what the cultural results would be. We've discussed throughout this book the intimate relationships between cultural systems and their natural and cultural environments. Such a sudden disruption of the natural environment, coming at the same time as a severe disruption of the world's social situation due to the war itself, could not be coped with culturally. There would be no time to adapt, nor any resources with which to adapt. Given the nature of our species as part of a social and economic "global community," the deleterious results of a nuclear winter would themselves be global in extent.

Of course, many organisms, and those humans who, for whatever reason, possessed the needed technology, might well survive not only the initial effects of a nuclear war but also the nuclear winter, which would eventually warm up once the dust settled. But there's another problem. A chemical reaction caused by nuclear explosions destroys ozone (a molecule of three oxygen atoms; the stuff we breathe has two). Life on Earth relies on a layer of ozone in the atmosphere to block out a large proportion of the sun's ultraviolet radiation—the rays that in small doses cause sunburn but in large doses are lethal. If the ozone layer were even partially depleted, life here might be impossible. Living creatures, including humans, would be severely burned and blinded. Plants would be destroyed, thus taking away food sources and oxygen producers. Life would be extinguished except maybe for a few very hardy creatures and those that live in caves, underground, or in the deep oceans. And even these might perish as a result of the severe disruption of the world ecosystem.

So we are now faced with a huge stockpile of these weapons of war, which not only destroy their specific targets (what everyone first thought was all they did) but also have the potential of destroying 3.5 billion years of evolution. This, of course, is assuming that these hypotheses are correct. There's only one way to find out however, only one experiment that could be conducted.

These awesome weapons, with their great numbers and terrible powers, seem to have taken on a life of their own. We simply don't know for sure just what they will do. (This has been the case all along, by the way. When the first atomic bomb was tested, some of the scientists involved were not certain that the atomic chain reaction that makes the whole thing work would *ever* stop!) But why these weapons were invented and manufactured in the first place and whether or not they will ever be used again are matters of another anthropological topic: the age-old problem of human violence.

We can, as we discussed, discount right away any notion that we are innately violent. We have no genes for rape, murder, and war. If anything, the evidence points to our being innately cooperative. Social creatures living in family units have to be. Too much violence against members of one's own species never got any species anywhere. We are, to be sure, aggressive, as is any living organism. This just means that we can act in the interests of our own survival—procuring food and protecting ourselves from danger. This can have an element of violence in it, as when a cheetah kills an antelope for food, but it is certainly a different phenomenon from the kind of intraspecific violence we're concerned with.

The problem for us is that we have given this aggressive potential cultural "triggers" and cultural "targets." We can commit violent acts—such as dropping bombs—against an enemy who is defined as such not because he overtly threatens our survival but because we are told he differs from us in some ideological matter. Or we commit rape not necessarily because of some uncontrolled action of our innate sexuality but because of the social and psychological statement such an action makes.

The violence that threatens our domestic, national, and international welfare has its origins in culture. Thus understanding culture and cultural differences is a key to understanding and solving these problems. Although it would be illogical to try to narrow down the cause of all human violence to one factor, we can, I think, make a generalization and say that to an extent the problem of human violence against other humans stems from the fact that we have fulfilled only one of the two criteria for a successful species.

Species success is gauged by (1) reproductive success and (2) longevity, which means having maintained a mutually beneficial relationship with the environment for a long period of time. We certainly are reproductively successful; there are 4.8 billion of us. But after a mere 5 million years on Earth, we are not doing too well in terms of our relationship with the environment.

First, we have clearly caused problems with the ''natural'' environment. I'll come back to that. But we have also caused problems in our cultural environment, and those are a result of our numbers. There are, in this context, too many of us for the kind of cultural structure we have.

An important adaptation for any species is some mechanism for limiting population size so as not to place too much strain on the parts of the environment—like food sources—that are vital to a species' survival. This is especially important for humans. For whereas natural selection takes care of any imbalance, like overpopulation, in the natural world, we can override nature with culture. Even foraging populations, who seem to us to live in such close contact with nature, are so culturally successful at manipulating and exploiting nature that they have to create means to limit their population growth. They do this, when times are normal, by nursing their young for extended periods of time. Milk production in the mothers stops ovulation and so acts as a natural contraceptive. But when resources are scarce, they may have to resort to infanticide and the voluntary suicides of the elderly.

With the invention of farming, with its assured food source and need for a larger labor force, we were ''allowed'' to have unrestrained population growth. This growth has continued and has indeed accelerated to the point that our world population may nearly double by the end of this century. In this regard we may be straining our environment to the breaking point.

One can argue that there are enough resources, like food, to go around. It has even been stated that, given our resources and technology, the United States could feed the world. But the fact is, under present conditions, that couldn't work even if it were theoretically true. For the human species is divided into thousands of subunits—our culturally defined societies and politically defined nations—and most of these subunits are further subdivided, by such things as ethnic origin, religion, socioeconomic class, and race. Such divisions make for unequal access to and distribution of basic resources. Access to resources is so uneven that thousands of people in the world starve to death every single day, while others of us grind up perfectly good food in our garbage disposals. So to say that there are too many of us does not necessarily refer to our absolute numbers, but it certainly does refer to the relative numbers of us as we are distributed in our various cultural population units. The species as a whole is a giant class-caste system.

It is this unequal access that I think is behind much human violence. Recall the idea that the origin of war—that is, large-scale, organized violence—coincides with the coming of farming, which placed in the hands of some far more material wealth than was possessed by those who had not yet invented or acquired this adaptation. The have-nots tried to get wealth away from the haves, who tried to protect themselves.

I suspect that behind most of our wars, though in a very complex way, is just such a phenomenon: the attempt to acquire or protect resources. The immediate motivation for fighting may be more abstract, as in the religious conflicts in Northern Ireland and India. But such ideological differences alone aren't reason enough to kill one's fellow human beings—especially when the religions in question specifically prohibit such an act! Rather, under the surface are some sort of real or perceived inequalities between groups of people who happen to be defined and identified in terms of the religion they practice. Religion becomes the motivation for fighting, but is not the real reason for it. This is certainly the case in Northern Ireland, where the conflict is over rule by, and ties with, predominantly Protestant England and related landholding and other economic matters.

The same can be said for domestic and social violence. Except in cases where those people committing the violent acts have a real psychobiological abnormality, most such violence is caused by some sort of inequality: racial or sexual discrimination and their economic ramifications; the economic problems that are said to be behind most marital conflicts; the jealousies created by socioeconomic stratification and the poverty and hunger that result when that stratification becomes too pronounced.

The solution to such problems as war and social violence are, of course, exceedingly complex. We understand that without even knowing what the solutions are. For although we can say that, generally, economic inequality is behind it all, each individual situation must be dealt with individually, in its own particular cultural context. Some sort of culture change is necessary in any and all cases, and we've seen how involved that is. But at least a first step is the understanding that these *are* cultural problems and that only by understanding how cultures operate can we hope even to begin searching for solutions.

The other problem I alluded to, which is also a result of our large numbers, is the problem of our negative impact on the natural environment. In our attempt to feed, clothe, house, and transport ourselves, we have put all sorts of substances into the water, the air, and living organisms that don't belong there—or we have done it so fast that nature has had no time to adjust. We have polluted water supplies. The air around industrial regions is often on the verge of being unbreathable. Rain in many parts of the world has become so acidic, as a result of industrial pollutants, that it is killing off the plant life it should be nourishing. And a further result of all this has been the extinction of dozens of plant and animals species each year.

Ecological relationships being what they are—namely, amazingly complex—we can't tell for sure just what all the results of these rapid environmental changes will be. Certainly an ecosystem can adjust to the loss of a species or two. But we should keep in mind that individual ecosystems interrelate with one another in an increasingly larger and complicated system, until the whole planet can be seen as an ecosystem itself. A change here can bring about some other change there. Any alteration of the environment involves taking a chance.

For example, when the Egyptian government built the Aswan High Dam up the Nile (''up'' the Nile is south), they did so in order to use the river for hydroelectric power. But the dam ended up adversely affecting the fishing industry in the Mediterranean around the mouth of the Nile. Why? Because the dam impeded the flow of nutrients carried downstream by the river. These nutritents were important food sources for small organisms in the sea, and these small organisms in turn were food sources for the fish. In addition, the dam decreased the size of the annual Nile floods, upon which farmers along the river had relied to replenish nutrients in the soil. Indeed, as someone once said of tampering with the environment, ''you can't do just one thing.''

We are now in a position where it is almost impossible to reverse the harm that has been done to our air, water, and other living creatures. You certainly can't bring back a species that has become extinct, nor can you just undo the effects of some industrial pollutant. Whatever we do to stop the further fouling of our world will itself bring about changes. You can clearly see the need to understand ecological relationships and evolutionary principles in order to grasp what has happened and to predict what may happen.

Moreover, whatever we do will involve changes in our cultural lives. We may at the very least have to give up a certain energy source or find alternative means of transportation. Understanding the place of such things within a culture is vital for predicting what will happen if and when we have to do without them and for perhaps aiding us through such a cultural transition.

One theme that is common to the consideration of and potential solution to all these problems is that of access to knowledge. Without that, we are truly at the mercy of the environment, with no control over our destinies. And it's a sad fact that there are those who would deny us access to certain spheres of knowledge or who would pervert our ability to pass on knowledge of certain types to the future generations for whom it will be so vital.

There are, as you're aware, a number of censorship movements, aimed in general at limiting access to literature and other art forms that express ideas unpopular with particular special-interest groups. But one movement is of special concern to us in the context of our overall topic: the movement known as "scientific creationism."

Creationism in general refers to any belief that a divine being created the universe, the world, and all the world's living inhabitants. There are numerous versions of this, including one that incorporates evolution by simply proposing that the creator created the evolutionary processes. But "scientific creationism," in its current form, holds the following ideas:

1. The universe, the Earth, and living creatures were the results of simultaneous, direct divine creation.
2. The creation took place about 10,000 years ago.
3. The only changes that have taken place have been minor alterations within general "kinds" of organisms.
4. The geological and fossil records are the results of a worldwide catastrophic flood.

You can see that these ideas are in direct opposition to all the scientific conclusions we've been discussing here:

1. The universe, the Earth, and living creatures arose as a result of knowable natural processes.
2. The universe began at least 12.0 billion years ago; the Earth was formed 4.5 billion years ago; life originated 3.5 billion years ago.
3. Species change through time, giving rise to new species.
4. The geological and fossil records are the results of billions of years of alterations in the face of the Earth and in the Earth's living creatures.

The new twist of "scientific creationism" is the claim that its ideas are supported by scientific evidence and that other evidence points to a refutation of the evolution model. Proponents of this idea say the fact that the creationism model coincides with one interpretation of the book of Genesis merely shows the literal accuracy of the Bible. Furthermore, then, since they see these two models as both "scientific," they feel both should be taught in science classes as viable alternative explanations for the origin and diversity of living things.

This argument is persuasive, especially in a society such as ours, concerned with religious freedoms and with our American sense of "fair play" and "equal time." But it is, very frankly, a clever ploy to promote a particular religious point of view. There is, as of right now, not one shred of scientific evidence in support of the creation model, while there are thousands of pieces of corroborative evidence in support of the evolution model. That is why, in this science book, I related to you only the evolution model. It is the consensus of modern mainstream science, based on the use of the scientific method.

To teach "scientific creationism" alongside evolution as viable scientific alternatives would be to violate the religious freedoms of people whose religion or personal beliefs do not prescribe a creationist interpretation. In addition, it would badly confuse students trying to learn how science operates and what conclusions science has arrived at. It would also confuse the distinction I noted between science and nonscience, the harmonious interrelationship of which is vital for the working of any culture.

Our future depends on the continual progress of our scientific knowledge, mediated by the nonscience of our value systems. Upon free access to, and sharing of, all knowledge rests our very survival. The problem is not the knowledge itself but what we do with it.

In 1922, when archaeologist Howard Carter first peered into the tomb of the Pharaoh Tutankhamen ("King Tut"), he was asked if he could see anything. "Yes," he replied, "wonderful things." In fact, all our species' accomplishments should fill us with wonder, from the civilization of ancient Egypt to the first pebble tools of our ancestors, from the modern computer to the reaping knife.

It would be sad indeed if our hypothetical astronaut anthropologists, returning home from our ruined planet, their ship loaded with remains of our wonderful things, were to shake their heads (or whatever) and wonder what happened to us.

In a modest but real way, all you've just learned about the human species is a first step toward trying to see that that doesn't occur.

NOTES, REFERENCES, AND READINGS

Thousands of books are available on the topics covered here, from every conceivable point of view and, certainly, of varying quality. I would like to recommend a few that I particularly like and find thought-provoking.

To my mind, *the* book on the issue of nuclear war is Jonathan Schell's *The Fate of the Earth* (New York: Knopf, 1982). It covers the basic facts about nuclear weapons and war, advances some ideas about the biological and cultural results of a nuclear war, discusses some of the cultural and psychological effects of living under the threat of such a war, and proposes some solutions to the problem. The only aspect not covered is nuclear winter. This is described in several technical works, but you can get the gist by reading Carl Sagan's article "The Nuclear Winter" in *Parade* (October 30, 1983).

The basic facts about the nature and growth of the human population and about the ecological relationships involved are in Paul R. Ehrlich and Anne H. Ehrlich, *Population, Resources, Environment* San Francisco: Freeman, 1970). For more on the population control devices practiced by human groups, see the chapter titled "Murders in Eden" in Harris's *Cannibals and Kings*. By now I hope you should be intrigued enough to want to read Harris's popular books, both of which I heartily recommend.

The best short work giving the essentials of the creatinism–evolution debate is *The Monkey Business: A Scientist Looks at Creationism* (New York: Washington Square Press, 1982) by paleontologist Niles Eldredge. Despite its "cutesy" title, it's complete, concise, and well written. And for some superb essays on the topic, try those in the section called "Science and Politics" of Stephen Jay Gould's *Hens' Teeth and Horses' Toes: Further Reflections in Natural History* (New York: Norton, 1983). One more time, let me say that I urge you to read anything and everything by Gould. His works are science—and the art of writing—at its best.

Glossary

absolute dating A technique for determining the specific age, in years ago, of an archaeological, paleontological, or geological feature.

acculturation The rapid diffusion of cultural items from one society to another, either by choice of the receiving society or by force from a more dominant society.

adaptation The ability of an organism or a society to thrive under particular environmental circumstances; made possible by the characteristics of that organism or society.

age-set A social unit made up of persons of approximately the same age.

agriculture Farming using intensive techniques such as plows, draft animals, and irrigation.

allele A variation of a gene.

altruism An act performed for the benefit of others with no regard for the welfare of the performer.

arboreal Adapted to life in the trees.

artifact Something which is artificially, rather than naturally, manufactured. Usually refers to human-made objects and institutions.

artificial selection Selection for reproductive success in plants or animals which is directed by humans. Also called "selective breeding."

balanced polymorphism Where the heterozygous form of a trait is the most reproductively successful, thus resulting in the maintenance of both alleles and the variable traits they produce.

balanced reciprocity Giving with the express expectation of the return of something of equivalent value.

band Political organization, typical of foragers, characterized by small, flexible populations with no social stratification.

bilateral Kinship system where the individual is a member of both the mother's and father's sides of the family.

biological determinism Outdated idea which said that human behavior is largely determined by the genes, with culture playing only a minimal role.

bipedal Standing upright, literally "two footed."

blade tool A sharp, small flake tool, usually worked over its entire surface, and made from a prepared core.

brachiation Form of locomotion using arm-over-arm swinging. Typical of gibbons.

carbon 14 Also called "radiocarbon." Absolute dating technique using the rate of decay of a radioactive isotope of carbon. Used for organic remains up to 50,000 years old.

cargo cult Generally refers to certain western Pacific societies whose ritual life centers on the attempt to bring back the remembered trappings of Western culture, the "cargo."

caste system A system of socio-economic stratification where the strata are stable, a person not being able to move out of the caste into which he or she was born. One's caste membership also determines such things as occupation and marriage partner.

cerebellum The part of the brain concerned with coordinating muscle movement.

cerebrum The part of the brain concerned with sensory interpretation, memory, and thought.

chiefdom Political organization with no central authority, but made up of a number of interacting subunits each with a leader, or "chief."

chromosomes The long strands in the nuclei of cells, made up of the genetic material.

civilization Literally "city making." A large, agriculturally-based, stratified population where most political, ritual, and economic activities take place in a central location, the "city."

class system A system of socio-economic stratification where the strata are open, that is, a person may move into higher (or lower) layers.

closed communication system A system with a finite number of signals, each with a specific meaning. The communication system of all organisms except humans.

co-dominant Alleles that are both expressed when in the heterozygous state.

continental drift The well-established theory that the Earth's continents move as the plates of which they are a part "float" on the liquid interior of the planet.

convergent evolution When two or more separate, unrelated species evolve similar adaptations in response to similar environments.

core tool A stone tool which is made by chipping away the unwanted portions of a rock; the remaining "core" is the tool.

cross cousins The children of your mother's brother and your father's sister.

cultural determinism The idea, discounted in its extreme form, that learned cultural ideas entirely explain any human behavior, biology playing virtually no part.

cultural ecology The study of the cultural adaptive relationships between a society and the environment in which it resides.

cultural materialism The idea, often associated with Marvin Harris, that cultural behaviors have a practical, usually economic, explanation.

cultural relativity Viewing the culture of another people from their perspective, not from that of one's own cultural background.

cultural universal Features which are found in all human societies. Marriage and the incest taboo are two examples.

culture Behaviors based on abstract concepts which are learned through extra-genetic transmission and are facilitated through the use of artifacts. A cultural system is an integrated collection of such behaviors practiced by a specific group of people, a society.

culture area A largely outmoded idea that the world could be divided into a limited number of geographical regions, each defined by a certain set of cultural features shared by the societies within it.

dermatoglyphics The study of the ridge-and-furrow patterns on the fingers, palms, soles, and toes.

descent line A string of nuclear families through time.

descent with modification The idea that organisms change over time and are related to one another as on a giant "family tree."

descriptive linguistics The study of the structure of human language in general and of the specific variations among languages.

differential reproduction The idea that some organisms reproduce more successfully than others. The measure of "fitness" within natural selection.

diffusion The movement of cultural ideas and items among societies. Cultural borrowing.

diffusionism The now outmoded belief that major cultural systems arose in one society (e.g. ancient Egypt) and spread to all others.

directional selection Natural selection for new adaptations in response to changing environmental conditions.

discovery The recognition and understanding of some natural process or "law."

displacement The characteristic of human language which enables us to talk about things and ideas which are not immediately occurring, but are "displaced" in time.

diurnal Describes organisms which are active during the day.

DNA Deoxribonucleic acid. The chemical which makes up the genetic code.

dominance hierarchy Social organization, such as in baboons, based on recognized status differences in power and influence.

dominant An allele which, when in the heterozygous state, "overrides" the other member of the gene pair and so is expressed in the phenotype.

duality Refers to the fact that human language is made up of many separate sound and meaning units which express ideas by being put together in different combinations.

ecology The study of the relationships among organisms within an environment and between organisms and the features of their environments.

ecosystem A type of environment. Limits and sizes vary depending upon the features and organisms of concern.

egalitarian Describes a society which lacks recognized differences in status and wealth.

ego The person from whose point of view a kinship system is analyzed.

endocast A cast made of the inside of something. Usually refers to the cast made of the inside of a skull so as to determine the size and shape of the brain.

estrus The period during which a female mammal has produced an egg which can be fertilized. It is characterized by the production of sight and/or scent signals which cause sexual stimulation of males.

ethnocentrism Making value judgments about another culture from the perspective of one's own cultural system.

ethnographic analogy Interpreting archaeological data, generally material artifacts, through the observation of similar items in use in existing societies.

ethnographic present Speaking of a society in the present tense regardless of the actual time period involved. A standard convention for anthropological writing.

ethnosemantics The study of the meanings and categories of words within a cultural system. Literally "cultural meaning."

ethology The study of behavior as a biological adaptive phenomenon.

evolution In biology, the idea that organisms change through time and are related to one another. Synonymous with "descent with modification."

experimental archaeology The process of trying to understand ancient skills and technologies by reproducing them.

extended family A string of nuclear families at a given time.

fixity of species The old, now disproved, idea that Earth's organisms were unchanging in both appearance and number.

flake tool A stone tool made from a flake taken off a core. At first these were the result of the manufacture of a core tool, but were later made independently. They are usually reworked to give them a specific shape.

folk taxonomy Cultural categories. The way people linguistically, and therefore conceptually, organize important things in their world.

foraging Relying on natural plant and animal food sources. Also called "hunting and gathering."

foramen magnum The hole in the base of the skull through which the spinal chord travels.

fossil Any remains of a life form from the past.

founder effect Evolutionary change resulting from the splitting of a population and the resultant "founding" of genetically new populations.

gametes Sex cells. In animals, the sperm and eggs.

gene flow Evolutionary change produced by genes entering a population via immigrants.

gene frequency The percentage of the various alleles of a gene in a given population.

gene pool The collection of all the genes in a population.

general reciprocity Giving with no expectation of specific return.

genes The basic units of the hereditary code. Made up of DNA.

genetic drift Evolutionary change due to statistical sampling of genes in the process of reproduction.

genetic markers Physical and chemical traits which can be observed and analyzed in order to determine the genetic identity of a population and genetic differences between populations.

genotype The actual combination of gene variants (alleles) possessed by an organism.

grid system A system of squares laid out over an archaeological site to control the horizontal dimension.

ground stone tool A tool made of hard stone which is shaped by grinding it with sand or some other abrasive material.

hand ax A stone tool, usually associated with *Homo erectus,* shaped generally like an ax head, and used for a number of heavy-duty tasks.

heterozygous When a pair of genes is made up of two different alleles.

historic archaeology The archaeology of a site from a period which had writing.

holistic In science, refers to a study which assumes an interrelationship among all its parts.

hominid Any human past or present. A member of family Hominidae.

homozygous When a pair of genes is made up of identical alleles.

horticulture Farming using using less intensive techniques such as human labor, digging sticks, and hoes.

hunting/gathering Relying on natural plant and animal food sources. Also called "foraging."

hypothesis A scientific "guess" to explain some set of observations.

incest Sexual relations with a person to whom you are closely related biologically, or culturally defined as being closely related.

industrialism Subsistence system based on mechanical rather than biological power.

inheritance of acquired characteristics Disproved idea that adaptive traits could be "willed" by an organism and then passed on to its offspring.

intensive foraging Hunting and gathering in environments which provide a great variety of food sources. Usually used with reference to areas opened up by the last recession of the glaciers.

invention Manufacture of an artifact—either concrete or abstract—which enables people to utilize a discovered natural principle.

kin selection Promoting the passing on of one's genes by aiding the survival or reproduction of one's kin.

kinship Your membership in a family and your relationship to other members of that family.

Lamarckism Synonym for "inheritance of acquired characteristics." Named for J.B. Lamarck, early proponent of the idea.

legal system A set of secular rules governing the behavior of individuals in a society.

limbic system The part of the brain, shared by all mammals, concerned with strong emotions like fear, anger, and care of young, and with sexual functions and the sense of smell.

lineage Line of descent. A family line.

lithic Referring to stone, especially with regard to artifacts.

macromutation A mutation involving many genes, or a few very important genes.

magic Ritual acts where people exercise control over the supernatural, rather than the other way around.

mammal The group of vertebrates characterized by constant body temperature, hair, live-born young, mammary glands, and complex brains.

mana A supernatural force possessed by an object or a person.

market system A system of trading goods and services using symbolic representations of wealth (money).

marriage A set of cultural rules for bringing male and female together to create the nuclear family and for defining their behavior toward one another, their children, and society.

matrilineal Kinship system where lineage membership is passed on through females.

medulla The part of the brain concerned with involuntary processes such as respiration and heartbeat.

men's association A social unit made up of the men in a society. Common in New Guinea.

microlith A small stone blade, usually attached to a handle or shaft to make sickles and similar tools.

mimicry In biology, when one species has evolved to resemble another for adaptive purposes.
money Symbolic representation of the value of a product or service.
monogamy Marriage system with only one of each spouse.
monogenic A trait controlled by a single gene.
monotheistic Religious system which recognizes a single supernatural being.
morpheme The smallest unit of meaning in a language.
multi-disciplinary A study which utilizes facts and methods from several fields.
mutagen Some environmental factor, such as a chemical, which causes genetic mutations.
mutation A sudden change in the material of heredity.
natural selection The process of evolution which operates through the differential reproduction of the better adapted members of a species.
neocortex The portion of the brain concerned with conscious thought.
niche The specific environment in which a species lives. The set of environmental circumstances with which members of a species come in direct contact.
non-science Knowledge based on faith which is not open to proof or disproof through scientific testing.
nuclear family The basic family unit, made up of parents and their children.
olfactory Having to do with the sense of smell.
omnivorous Adapted to a mixed vegetable and meat diet.
open communication system A system with basic units which may be combined in a virtually limitless number of ways to convey a virtually limitless number of meanings. The human communication system.
opposability The ability to touch, or "oppose" the thumb to the tips of the other fingers.
ovulation When a female mammal has produced an egg which can be fertilized.
pair-bonding The bringing together of male and female animals to form a permanent pair.
paleoanthropology The focus of anthropology which studies the human biological past.
parallel cousins The children of your mother's sister and father's brother.
participant-observation The technique of anthropological fieldwork where the anthropologist not only observes a society as an outsider but also tries, as much as possible, to act as a participating member of that society.
pastoralism The subsistence pattern which emphasizes herding of animals.
patrilineal Kinship system where lineage membership is passed on through males.
pebble tool Earliest stone tool. Made by taking a few flakes off one surface of a smooth stone, or pebble.

phenotype The result of the genetic code. A measurable, observable trait.
phoneme A unit of sound in a language.
pleiotropy When a set of genes influences more than one phenotypic trait.
Pleistocene The period of the most recent glaciations, or Ice Ages. Approximately the last 2 million years.
politics The secular, non-kinship means of organizing the interactions within a society and between that society and other groups.
polyandry Marriage system where a woman may have more than one husband.
polygamy Any marriage system which allows multiple spouses.
polygenic A trait controlled by more than one gene.
polygyny Marriage system where a man may have more than one wife.
polymorphism A trait which exhibits variation within a species.
polytheistic Religious system which recognizes more than one supernatural being.
potassium-argon Absolute dating technique which measures the decay of radioactive potassium into argon. Used on rocks of volcanic origin and good to the beginnings of Earth history.
pre-adaptation When traits, either neutral or originally adapted to one particular environmental niche, happen by chance to be adaptively valuable in a new niche.
prehensile Grasping. Usually refers to hands and feet.
prepared core A technique for stone tool manufacture involving the preparation of a core so as to be able to flake off numerous, similarly-shaped blade tools.
pressure-flaking Using a tool of bone, wood, or antler to "push" flakes off a stone core.
priest Anthropologically, a full-time, trained, paid religious specialist.
productivity The feature of human language referring to its ability to generate an almost infinite number of meanings. See "open communication system" and "duality."
prosimian Members of the primate suborder *Prosimii*. The oldest, most primitive primates.
quadrupedal Walking on all fours, literally, "four footed."
R-complex "Reptilian complex." The oldest part of our "thinking" brain, concerned with basic survival behaviors such as aggression, territoriality, and social hierarchies.
race A folk-taxonomic division of humankind based on a combination of biological and cultural traits.
rank society A society which strives for equal distribution of goods and services, but which achieves this through an organization based on recognized status differences.
recessive An allele which, in the heterozygous state, is "overridden" by a dominant allele and so is not expressed.
recombination In genetics, the process where gene pairs are broken up in

the production of sex cells, and are then put together in new and different combinations at fertilization.

redistribution Where surplus goods are collected centrally and then given out to those persons in need of them. An attempt to balance economic inequalities. See "rank society."

relative dating Dating technique which indicates whether an item is older or younger than another, and, sometimes, a general idea as to how much older or younger.

religion System of ideals and rule for behavior based on supernatural explanations for natural phenomena.

revolution Rapid cultural change generated from within a society. Can be violent or peaceful.

savanna Open grasslands, generally used in reference to Africa.

scientific creationism Actually a pseudo-science which claims to provide scientific evidence for a belief in divine creation of the universe and its inhabitants.

sexual dimorphism The characteristics which physically differ between the sexes of a particular species.

shaman A part-time, supernaturally "chosen," unpaid religious specialist.

sibling species Two species which are nearly identical, having diverged evolutionarily only in the recent past.

sibship A group of brothers and sisters.

site Any area containing human artifacts. Usually refers to areas of past human habitation.

social stratification When a society is "layered" according to differences in power and/or wealth.

society The group of people practicing a particular cultural system.

sociobiology The science which seeks biological bases and adaptive explanations for the behavior of organisms, including humans.

sorcery Activities which control the supernatural for evil purposes. See "magic."

specialization In biology, when a species relies on and is adapted to a limited set of resources. In anthropology, when members of a society have different and specified occupations and tasks.

speciation The evolutionary processes giving rise to new species.

species A genetically isolated, interbreeding group of organisms.

stabilizing selection Natural selection which maintains a species' adaptation to a particular set of environmental circumstances.

state system A political system with a central authority which governs all the individual units.

stereoscopic Vision which has true depth perception; 3-D vision.

stratigraphy Literally, the "description of layers." Refers to the relationships among the layers of rock and soil in the Earth's crust.

subsistence pattern The way in which a group of people find, acquire, and distribute necessary resources, especially food.

supernatural Anything beyond natural explanation.

symbol Something which represents something else without necessarily resembling it.

syntax Rules of word order in a language.

taboo A negative rule; tells people *not* to do something.

taxonomy Scheme for naming and classifying items so as to indicate their relative similarities and differences.

test pit A hole dug to determine the presence of artifacts and thus of an archaeological site.

theory A basic scientific idea. An hypothesis which has been tested and supported with no refuting evidence.

tool kit The set of tools characteristic of a particular group of humans. Usually refers to the artifacts of a certain stage of human evolution.

transitional form An organism showing characteristics of two evolutionary branches.

transmutation of species What was called "organic evolution" before and during Darwin's time.

tribe Political organization with no central or individual leaders, but where the subunits make collective decisions regarding the entire group, or "tribe."

triune brain The idea that the "thinking" part of our brain is made up of three interacting levels, reflecting the behavioral stages of vertebrate evolution.

unilineal Kinship system which traces descent through only one line, either the male's or the female's.

visual cortex The part of the brain which receives and interprets signals from the eyes.

war Large scale, organized violence between populations.

world view A society's set of assumptions about the nature of their world, and the values derived from them.

Bibliography

Abell, George O., and Barry Singer. *Science and the Paranormal: Probing the Existence of the Supernatural*. New York: Scribner, 1981.

Appleman, Philip, ed. *Darwin*. New York: Norton Critical Edition, 1970.

Ardrey, Robert. *African Genesis: A Personal Investigation into the Animal Origins and Nature of Man*. New York: Atheneum, 1961.

Arnold, Emmy. *Torches Together*. Rifton, NY: Plough Publishing House of the Woodcrest Service Committee.

Attenborough, David. *Life on Earth*. Boston: Little, Brown, 1979.

Balikci, Asen. *The Netsilik Eskimo*. New York: Natural History Press, 1970.

Barash, David P. *Sociobiology and Behavior*. 2d ed. New York: Elsevier, 1982.

Bleier, Ruth. *Science and Gender: A Critique of Biology and Its Theories on Women*. Elmsford, New York: Pergamon Press 1984.

Bohannon, Paul, ed. *Law and Warfare: Studies in the Anthropology of Conflict*. Austin: University of Texas Press, 1967.

Bordaz, Jacques. *Tools of the Old and New Stone Age*. New York: Natural History Press, 1970.

Bowen, Elenore Smith (Laura Bohannon). *Return to Laughter*. New York: Natural History Press, Anchor Books, 1964.

Bronowski, Jacob. *Ascent of Man*. Boston: Little, Brown, 1974.

Calder, Nigel. *Timescale: An Atlas of the Fourth Dimension*. New York: Viking Press, 1983.

Caplan, Arthur L., ed. *The Sociobiology Debate*. New York: Harper & Row, 1978.

Cartmill, Matt. "Rethinking Primate Origins." *Science*, 26 April 1974.

Cavalli-Sforza, L. L. *Elements of Human Genetics*. 2d ed. Menlo Park, CA: Benjamin, 1977.

Chagnon, Napoleon A. *Studying the Yąnomamö*. New York: Holt, Rinehart and Winston, 1974.

Davies, David. *The Last of the Tasmanians*. New York: Barnes & Noble Books, 1974.

Deetz, James, and Edwin S. Dethlefsen. "Death's Head, Cherub, Urn and Willow." *Nature History,* March 1967.

Douglas, Mary. *Purity and Danger: An Analysis of Concepts of Pollution and Taboo*. Baltimore: Penguin Books, 1966.

———. *Natural Symbols: Explorations in Cosmology*. New York: Vintage, 1973.

Durden-Smith, Jo, and Diane DeSimone. *Sex and the Brain*. New York: Arbor House, 1983.

Eimerl, Sarel, and Irven DeVore. *The Primates*. New York: Time-Life, 1974.

Eiseley, Loren. *Charles Darwin and the Mysterious Mr. X*. New York: Dutton, 1979.

Eldredge, Niles. *The Monkey Business: A Scientist Looks at Creationism*. New York: Washington Square Press, 1982.

Ehrlich, Paul R., and Anne H. Ehrlich. *Population, Resources, Environment*. San Francisco: Freeman, 1970.

Ember, Melvin, and Carol R. Ember. *Anthropology*. 3d ed. Englewood Cliffs, NJ: Prentice-Hall, 1981.

Fisher, Helen E. *The Sex Contract*. New York: William Morrow, 1982.

Forbes, Harriette Merrifield. *Gravestones of Early New England and the Men Who Made Them*. Princeton: Pyne Press, 1955.

Friedl, Ernestine. *Woman and Men: An Anthropologist's View*. New York: Holt, Rinehart and Winston, 1975.

Goodenough, Ward H. *Culture, Language, and Society*. 2d ed. Menlo Park, CA: Benjamin/Cummings, 1981.

Gould, Stephen Jay. *Ever Since Darwin: Reflections in Natural History*. New York: Norton, 1977.

———. *The Panda's Thumb: More Reflections in Natural History*. New York: Norton, 1980.

———. *The Mismeasure of Man*. New York: Norton, 1981.

———. *Hen's Teeth and Horse's Toes: Further Reflections in Natural History*. New York: Norton, 1983.

Greene, John C. *The Death of Adam*. New York: Mentor Books, 1959.

Hampel, Carl G. *Philosophy of Natural Science*. Englewood Cliffs, NJ: Prentice-Hall, 1966.

Hanson, Earl D. *Understanding Evolution*. New York: Oxford University Press, 1981.

Harris, C. Leon. *Evolution: Genesis and Revelations*. Albany: State University of New York Press, 1981.

Harris, Marvin. *Cows, Pigs, Wars and Witches: The Riddles of Culture*. New York: Random House, 1974.

———. *Cannibals and Kings: The Origins of Cultures*. New York: Random House, 1977.

———. *Cultural Materialism: The Struggle for a Science of Culture*. New York: Random House, 1979.

Heider, Karl. *Grand Valley Dani: Peaceful Warriors*. New York: Holt, Rinehard and Winston, 1979.

Hockett, C. F., and R. Ascher. "The Human Revolution." *Current Anthropology* 5(1964):135–168.

Hölldobler, Bert. "The Wonderfully Diverse Ways of the Ant." *National Geographic,* June 1984.

Hostetler, John A. *Hutterite Society.* Baltimore: Johns Hopkins University Press, 1974.

Hutter, Jakob. *Brotherly Faithfulness: Epistles from a Time of Persecution.* Hutterian Society of Brothers, Norfolk, CT: Deer Spring Press, 1979.

Jensen, Arthur R. "How Much Can We Boost IQ and Scholastic Achievement?" *Harvard Educational Review,* Winter 1969.

Johanson, Donald, and Maitland Edey. *Lucy: The Beginnings of Humankind.* New York: Simon & Schuster, 1981.

Jolly, Alison. *The Evolution of Primate Behavior.* New York: Macmillan, 1972.

Keesing, Roger, M. *Kin Groups and Social Structure.* New York: Holt, Rinehart and Winston, 1975.

Kennedy, Kenneth A. R. *Human Variation in Space and Time.* Dubuque, IA: Brown, 1976.

Kephart, William M. *Extraordinary Groups: The Sociology of Unconventional Life-Styles.* 2d ed. New York: St. Martin's Press, 1982.

Kummer, Hans. *Primate Societies: Group Techniques of Ecological Adaptation.* Chicago: Aldine, 1971.

LaBarre, Weston. *They Shall Take Up Serpents.* Minneapolis: University of Minnesota Press, 1962.

Lancaster, Jane. *Primate Behavior and the Emergence of Human Culture.* New York: Holt, Rinehart and Winston, 1975.

Laitman, Jeffrey T. "The Anatomy of Human Speech." *Natural History,* October 1978.

Lawick-Goodall, Jane van. *In the Shadow of Man.* New York: Houghton Mifflin, 1971.

Lee, Richard. *The Dobe !Kung.* New York: Holt, Rinehart and Winston, 1984.

Lee, Richard B., and Irven DeVore, eds. *Man the Hunter.* Chicago: Aldine, 1968.

Lessa, William A., and Evon Z. Vogt, eds. *Reader in Comparative Religion: An Anthropological Approach.* 3d. New York: Harper & Row, 1972.

Lieberman, Philip. *On the Origins of Language: An Introduction to the Evolution of Human Speech.* New York: Macmillan, 1975.

Linden, Eugene. *Apes, Men, and Language.* New York: Penguin Books, 1974.

Lindenbaum, Shirley. *Kuru Sorcery: Disease and Danger in the New Guinea Highlands.* Palo Alto, CA: Mayfield, 1979.

Linton, Ralph. "One Hundred Per Cent American." *The American Mercury* vol. 40, 1937.

Lustig-Arecco, Vera. *Technology: Strategies for Survival.* New York: Holt, Rinehart and Winston, 1975.

Manning, Aubrey. "The Work of Being a Bee." In *The Marvels of Animal Behavior.* Washington, D.C.: National Geographic Society, 1972.

McKusick, Victor A. *Human Genetics.* 2d ed. Englewood Cliffs, NJ: Prentice-Hall, 1969.

Mendel, Gregor. "Experiments in Plant Hybridization." In *Genetics: Readings from Scientific American,* edited by Cedric I. Davern. San Francisco: Freeman, 1981.

Miller, Jonathan, and Borin van Loon. *Darwin for Beginners*. New York: Pantheon Books, 1982.

Molnar. Stephen. *Races, Types, and Ethnic Groups*. Englewood Cliffs, NJ: Prentice-Hall, 1975.

Montagu, Ashley, ed. *The Concept of Race*. New York: Macmillan, 1964.

———. *The Natural Superiority of Women*. New York: Macmillan, 1974.

Montague, Susan P., and W. Arens, eds. *The American Dimension: Cultural Myths and Social Realities*. 2d ed. Sherman Oaks, CA: Alfred, 1981.

Morris, Desmond. *The Naked Ape*. New York: McGraw-Hill, 1967.

Nance, John. *The Gentle Tasaday: A Stone Age People in the Philippine Rain Forest*. New York: Harcourt Brace Jovanovich, 1975.

Napier, John, and P. H. Napier. *A Handbook of Living Primates*. New York: Academic Press, 1967.

National Geographic Society. *The Marvels of Animal Behavior*. Washington, DC, 1972.

Norbeck, Edward. *Religion in Human Life: Anthropological Views*. New York: Holt, Rinehart and Winston, 1974.

O'Brien, Eileen M. "What Was The Acheulean Hand Ax?" *Natural History,* July 1984.

Passingham, Richard. *The Human Primate*. New York: Freeman, 1982.

Patterson, Francine. "Conversations with a Gorilla." *National Geographic,* October 1978.

Pfeiffer, John E. *The Creative Explosion: An Inquiry into the Origins of Art and Religion*. New York: Harper & Row, 1982.

———. *The Emergence of Humankind*. 4th ed. New York: Harper & Row, 1985.

Pilbean, David. "The Descent of the Hominoids and Hominids." *Scientific American,* March 1984.

Rice, Edward. *John Frum He Come*. Garden City, NY: Doubleday, 1974.

Robert, D. F. *Climate and Human Variability*. 2d ed. Menlo Park, CA: Cummings, 1978.

Sagan, Carl. *The Dragons of Eden: Speculations on the Evolution of Human Intelligence*. New York: Random House, 1977.

——. *Broca's Brain: Reflections on the Romance of Science*. New York: Random House, 1979.

———. *Cosmos*. New York: Random House, 1980.

———. "The Nuclear Winter." *Parade,* 30 October 1983.

Salus, Peter H. *Linguistics*. Indianapolis: Bobbs-Merrill, 1969.

Schell, Jonathan. *The Fate of the Earth*. New York: Knopf, 1982.

Service, Elman R. *Profiles in Ethnology*. 3d ed. New York: Harper & Row, 1978.

Shepher, Joseph. "Mate Selection Among Second-Generation Kibbutz Adolescents and Adults: Incest Avoidance and Negative Imprinting." *Archives of Sexual Behavior* Vol. 27, 1971.

Smith, John Maynard. "Science and Myth." *Natural History,* November 1984.

Spradley, James P., and Michael A. Rynkiewich, eds. *The Nacirema: Readings on American Culture*. Boston: Little, Brown, 1975.

Stebbins, G. Ledyard. *Darwin to DNA: Molecules to Humanity*. San Francisco: Freeman, 1982.

Stross, Brian. "The Nature of Language." In *Language, Culture and Cognition:*

Anthropological Perspectives, edited by Ronald W. Casson. New York: Macmillan, 1981.

Thomas, Lewis. *The Lives of a Cell: Notes of a Biology Watcher.* New York: Viking Press, 1974.

———. *The Medusa and the Snail: More Notes of a Biology Watcher.* New York: Viking Press, 1979.

———. *Late Night Thoughts on Listening to Mahler's Ninth Symphony.* New York: Viking Press, 1983.

Turnbull, Colin. *The Mountain People.* New York: Simon & Schuster, 1972.

Vivelo, Frank Robert. *Cultural Anthropology Handbook: A Basic Introduction.* New York: McGraw-Hill, 1978.

Wenke, Robert J. *Pattern in Prehistory: Mankind's First Three Million Years.* New York: Oxford University Press, 1980.

Wheeler, Mortimer. *Maiden Castle.* Society of Antiquaries of London, 1943.

Wickler, Wolfgang. *Mimicry in Plants and Animals.* New York: McGraw-Hill, 1968.

Williams, Terry Tempest, and Ted Major. *The Secret Language of Snow.* San Francisco: Sierra Club/Pantheon, 1984.

Wilmsen, Edwin N. *Lindenmeier: A Pleistocene Hunting Society.* New York: Harper & Row, 1974.

Wilson, Edward O. *Sociobiology: The New Synthesis.* Cambridge, MA: Harvard, 1975.

Wilson, J. Tuzo, ed. *Continents Adrift and Continents Aground: Readings from Scientific American.* San Francisco: Freeman, 1976.

Woods, Clyde M. *Culture Change.* Dubuque, IA: Brown, 1975.

Worsley, Peter M. "Cargo Cults." *Scientific American,* May 1959.

Index